THE AMERICAN CIVIL WAR

We work with leading authors to develop the
strongest educational materials in history,
bringing cutting-edge thinking and best learning
practice to a global market.

Under a range of well-known imprints, including
Longman, we craft high quality print and
electronic publications which help
readers to understand and apply their content,
whether studying or at work.

To find out more about the complete range of our
publishing please visit us on the World Wide Web at:
www.pearsoneduc.com

THE AMERICAN CIVIL WAR

EXPLORATIONS AND RECONSIDERATIONS

Edited by

SUSAN-MARY GRANT AND
BRIAN HOLDEN REID

with an introduction by
JAMES M. McPHERSON

An imprint of **Pearson Education**

Harlow, England · London · New York · Reading, Massachusetts · San Francisco
Toronto · Don Mills, Ontario · Sydney · Tokyo · Singapore · Hong Kong · Seoul
Taipei · Cape Town · Madrid · Mexico City · Amsterdam · Munich · Paris · Milan

Pearson Education Limited
Edinburgh Gate
Harlow
Essex CM20 2JE
England

and Associated Companies throughout the world

Visit us on the World Wide Web at:
http://www.pearsoneduc.com

———————————————

First published 2000

ISBN 0 582 31835 1
ISBN 0 582 31838 6

British Library Cataloguing-in-Publication Data
A catalogue record for this book is available from the British Library

Library of Congress Cataloging-in-Publication Data
A catalog record for this book is available from the Library of Congress

10 9 8 7 6 5 4 3 2 1
04 03 02 01 00

Typeset by 35 in 11/13.5 pt Columbus
Produced by Pearson Education Asia Pte Ltd
Printed in Singapore

A TRIBUTE TO
PETER J. PARISH

CONTENTS

CONTENTS

NOTES ON CONTRIBUTORS

John Ashworth is the G.F. Grant Professor of American History at the University of Hull. He is the author of *'Agrarians and Aristocrats': Party Political Ideology in the United States, 1837–1846* (1983) and *Slavery, Capitalism and Politics in the Antebellum Republic*, a two-volume project of which the first, *Commerce and Compromise, 1820–1850*, was published in 1996.

Richard Carwardine is Professor of History at the University of Sheffield. He teaches and writes on American religion, politics and society in the nineteenth century, and is the author of *Transatlantic Revivalism: Popular Evangelicalism in Britain and America, 1790–1865* (1978) and *Evangelicals and Politics in Antebellum America* (1993).

Bruce Collins is Dean of Humanities at Ripon and York (an affiliated College of the University of Leeds). He was formerly Dean and Deputy Principal of University College, Scarborough, and Professor of International History at the University of Buckingham. Educated at Cambridge, he held a Harkness Fellowship in 1972–4, and taught at Middlesex Polytechnic and the University of Glasgow. He has written *The Origins of America's Civil War* (1981) and *White Society in Antebellum America* (1985), as well as numerous articles and essays on the 1850s in, for example, *Civil War History, Georgia Historical Quarterly, Historical Journal, History Today*, the *Journal of American Studies, Ohio History* and the *Pennsylvania Magazine of History and Biography*.

Robert Cook is a lecturer in American History at the University of Sheffield. He is the author of *Baptism of Fire: The Republican Party in Iowa, 1838–1878* (1994) and *Sweet Land of Liberty?: The African-American Struggle for Civil Rights in the Twentieth Century* (1998). He is currently writing a history of the United States in the Civil War era for Pearson Education.

[x]   **Martin Crawford** is a Reader in American History at Keele University. His main teaching and research interests are in Civil War, Appalachian, and Southern. His publications include *The Anglo-American Crisis of the Mid-Nineteenth Century* (1987); (editor) *William Howard Russell's Civil War: Private Diary and Letters, 1861–1862* (1992); and editor, with Alan J. Rice, of *Liberating Sojourn: Frederick Douglass and Transatlantic Reform* (1999). He is currently completing a study of a Southern mountain community during the Civil War period. He is editor of *American Nineteenth Century History.*

Joseph G. Dawson III is Professor of History and Director of the Military Studies Institute at Texas A&M University, College Station, Texas. He has published widely on American military history, in books, articles and contributions to edited works, most notably *Army Generals and Reconstruction* (Louisiana State University Press, 1982) and *Doniphan's Epic March: The 1st Missouri Volunteer Regiment in the Mexican War* (University Press of Kansas, 1999).

Susan-Mary Grant is lecturer in United States History at the University of Newcastle-upon-Tyne and Secretary of the Society of British American Nineteenth Century Historians. Her publications include *North Over South: Northern Nationalism and American Identity in the Antebellum Era* (2000) as well as a wide range of articles on antebellum America and on the development of American nationalism in the Civil War era in *Nations and Nationalism* and the *Journal of American Studies.*

Andrew R. Haughton studied at Glasgow University and at King's College London, where he completed a PhD in War Studies in 1998. Dr Haughton is presently working for the *Financial Times* in London. His study of tactics and combat in the American Civil War, *Training and Leadership in the Confederate Army of Tennessee*, will be published by Frank Cass in 2000.

Bruce Levine, Professor of History at the University of California, Santa Cruz, was educated at the University of Michigan and the University of Rochester. He has previously taught at Wayne State University, the University of Cincinnati, and Columbia University. His books include: *The Spirit of 1848: German Immigrants, Labor Conflict, and the Origins of the Civil War* (1992); and *Half Slave and Half Free: The Roots of the Civil War* (1992). He was also a principal author of the two-volume work, *Who Built America?: Working People in the Nation's Economy, Politics, Culture and Society* (1990 and 1992).

Patricia Lucie, MA, PhD, was the Director of the William J. Brennan Project, University of Glasgow from 1973 to 1998. Her publications include: *Freedom*

and Federalism, Congress and Courts, 1861–66 (1984), 'Discrimination Against [xi]
Males in the USA', in S. McLean and N. Burrows (eds), *The Legal Relevance of
Gender* (1988), together with a range of articles in the *Judicial Review*, the
Syracuse Law Review and the *Denning Law Journal.*

James M. McPherson is the George Henry Davis '86 Professor of American
History at Princeton University, where he has taught since 1962. He is the
author of a dozen books on the era of the American Civil War and Recon-
struction, and the editor of numerous additional works. In 1989 he won the
Pulitzer Prize in History for his book *Battle Cry of Freedom: The Civil War Era*
and in 1998 he won the Lincoln Prize for his book *For Cause and Comrades:
Why Men Fought in the Civil War*. In 1982 he was the Commonwealth Fund
Lecturer at University College London.

Donald Ratcliffe teaches American history at the University of Durham. He
has published many articles on the antebellum United States, notably in the
Journal of American History and the *Journal of the Early Republic*. He is the author
of two books focusing on national partisanship and popular experience in
the state of Ohio, *Party Spirit in a Frontier Republic, 1793–1821* (1998) and *The
Politics of Long Division, 1818–1828* (2000), published by Ohio State University Press.

Brian Holden Reid is Senior Lecturer in War Studies, King's College
London, and from 1987 to 1997 was Resident Historian at the British Army
Staff College, Camberley (of which he is a graduate). From 1984 to 1987
Dr Holden Reid was Editor of the *RUSI Journal*. Since 1993 he has been a
member of the Council of the Society for Army Historical Research, and in
1998 was elected Chairman. He is a Fellow of the Royal Historical Society,
Royal Geographical Society and the Royal United Services Institute. His
books include *J.F.C. Fuller: Military Thinker* (1987, 1990), *The Origins of the
American Civil War* (1996), *Studies in British Military Thought* (1998) and *The
American Civil War and the Wars of the Industrial Revolution* (1999).

David Turley is Director of the Centre for American Studies and a Senior
Lecturer in the School of History at the University of Kent at Canterbury.
He is the author of *The Culture of English Antislavery, 1780–1860* (1991) and
the editor of *American Religion* (1998). His longer-term research project is on
'Social Science and the Rise of an African-American Intelligentsia, c. 1890–
1930'.

PREFACE

The present volume was initially conceived as a collection of essays in honour of Peter J. Parish, currently the Mellon Senior Research Fellow in American History at the University of Cambridge and Professor Emeritus of American History, University of London. As well as being well-known for his work on the American Civil War, Peter Parish is an outstanding teacher, who has devoted a very large part of his long career in American History to the encouragement and guidance of his students, both undergraduate and postgraduate. He has also done a great deal to establish American History as an active and stimulating field of study. Parish served as Chairman of both the British Association for American Studies (BAAS) and, more recently, the British American Nineteenth Century Historians organization (BrANCH), which he co-founded. In his capacity as Director of the Institute of United States Studies, University of London, Parish nurtured the Institute as an active centre for research in American History, and as a place where American historians, from the UK and from abroad, would find both a warm welcome and a supportive environment for their research. Parish also served on the Marshall Aid Commemoration Commission and on the British-American-Canadian-Associates Committee, and was active in the English-Speaking Union during the 1980s and 1990s. Much of his working life was spent in Scotland – first at the University of Glasgow and then at the University of Dundee – and he served as Secretary and Vice-President of the Glasgow and West of Scotland branch and as President of the Dundee branch of the Historical Association. In 1987, Parish was the historical consultant on the Channel 4 series, *The Divided Union: The Story of the Civil War*, an impressive and popular series which introduced the subject of the Civil War to a British audience.

Since taking up his first post in American History at the University of Glasgow in 1958, Parish has published and lectured on a wide variety of topics, including articles on Abraham Lincoln and on Daniel Webster, on the American Constitution and on American federalism more generally, on American slavery and race relations, on the Civil War – both broadly and focused on specific battles – and, most recently, on American nationalism. His books over the years include *The American Civil War* (1975), which remains among the clearest and most accessible account of this fascinating but difficult period in American History, *Slavery: The Many Faces of a Southern Institution* (1979 and 1996), and *Slavery: History and Historians* (1989), and he has edited *Abraham Lincoln: Letters and Speeches* (1993) and the *Reader's Guide to American History* (1997).

In light of this, both the editors and the publisher felt that a simple collection of essays by his former students would hardly reflect the range of Parish's accomplishments, nor would it do justice to the extent of his influence on the subject of American History and its practitioners, both in Britain and in the United States. A collection of essays by Parish's former students and his colleagues would, it was felt, better reflect his standing academically. Above all, however, the editors wished the present volume to be one that would be both accessible to a broader market and which would offer genuinely new assessments on the area of Parish's major interest – the American Civil War. The focus on the Civil War was decided upon not just because it reflects his central preoccupation over many years, but because a single volume of this kind could serve both as a *vade mecum* for students and as a teaching text. The editors hope that, though many of the contributions raise new issues, each chapter will serve as a stimulating introduction to its subject, especially for undergraduates or those simply wanting to read more about a particular topic.

With this in mind, the editors have deliberately not attempted to impose any one perspective on the Civil War era, but have encouraged each contributor to produce an essay reflecting his or her particular interpretation of the subject. For example, in Chapter 1, Dr Ratcliffe emphasizes the durability of the bonds of Union before 1860, while in Chapter 3 Professor Carwardine argues that in certain respects these bonds were 'chronically weak'. Here is an instance of a clash of interpretation among historians, and in the course of their studies undergraduates need to grapple with such complexity, and discover that the cliché 'History will say . . .' is meaningless. Similarly, several of the chapters in this volume, particularly those which look at the experiences of African-Americans during the Civil War, cover the same ground, but from different angles. Here, too, the editors have chosen not to intervene. Alternative conclusions – even those based on the same or similar evidence

– are in no sense contradictory, but complementary. Only from the elaboration of debates between historians, and from an understanding of the wide range of interpretations that similar evidence can produce, can a fuller sense of the complexities of the period be achieved. For this reason the editors have sought to avoid imposing any kind of uniform approach to this complex subject. Consequently, this volume reflects, and adds to, the continuing debate on this central era in American history. Thus the design of the book serves to underline Parish's achievements, both as a teacher and an historian.

This volume has endeavoured to focus on those areas of the Civil War that Parish himself has concentrated on in the course of his career: the origins of the war, and the state of the American Union in 1861; the nature of leadership in the Union and the Confederacy respectively; the actual process of fighting the war, but placed in the context of the society in which the war was fought and taking full account of the wider issues which the war threw up; the centrality of the subject of slavery and emancipation, both to the Union and, in rather different ways, to the Confederate war effort; and, finally, the longer-term impact of the war on American society, on the American Constitution, and on American nationalism. The title of the concluding essay in this volume, indeed, is quite blatantly taken from the course 'From Union to Nation', that Parish taught at the Institute of United States Studies for many years. The contributors to this volume, both Parish's former students and his colleagues, have all benefited in numerous ways from his work as an historian. The editors, in particular, have benefited not just from his example as an historian, but from his wisdom as a teacher and mentor. This volume is both an acknowledgement of Peter Parish's achievements and a token of thanks for his continuing support over the years. Perhaps most fittingly, the willingness of so many friends and colleagues to contribute to this volume is testimony to the fact that the American Civil War remains – and will continue to be – a vibrant and rewarding area of study.

Brian Holden Reid
King's College London

Susan-Mary Grant
University of Newcastle-upon-Tyne

INTRODUCTION

This volume is truly a transatlantic tribute to Peter Parish. The authors of most of the essays are British scholars of United States history; some are Americans who have benefited from a transatlantic perspective. Nothing could be more fitting, for Peter Parish has taught many of the authors and influenced all of them. His own writings have greatly enriched our understanding of the American Civil War, of slavery and emancipation, and of British–American relations in the nineteenth century. His magisterial account of *The American Civil War* remains one of the best studies of that conflict a quarter century after its original publication. That book offered incisive insights about the issues that are further explored by the essays in the present volume: the roots of sectional conflict and secession; the ideological and military mobilization of North and South; the leadership of Abraham Lincoln and Jefferson Davis; the will to fight; command and strategy; slavery and emancipation as war issues; the role of blacks in both the Confederacy and Union; the economic impact of the war; the Constitution and civil liberties; and the nature of Union and Confederate nationalism.

Most important of all, perhaps, *The American Civil War* placed the conflict in its international setting. Parish's chapter on 'The War and the World' is the most lucid and concise treatment of that theme in print. That chapter and the next, 'Oceans, Rivers and Diplomatic Channels,' narrate the largely futile Confederate efforts for diplomatic recognition and intervention by European powers, and the largely successful countermeasures of Union foreign policy.

But 'The War and the World' goes beyond traditional diplomatic history. 'The issues at stake' in the Civil War, wrote Parish, 'found echoes in Britain and France, Spain and Russia, Canada and Brazil, and many other lands.' These 'great issues' included nothing less than 'slavery and freedom, democracy and privilege, self-determination and imperial ambition, majority rule and minority rights'. The United States was one of the few republics in the world in 1861, and by far the largest and most important one. Most republics through history had collapsed into tyranny or anarchy, or had been overthrown from without. France and the republics of Latin America provided a pointed contemporary object lesson. Would 'the great American experiment' of republican government and democracy also collapse? Those in the Old World, wrote Parish, 'who hated and feared the United States as the home of the demon democracy, and therefore as a dangerous example and incitement, welcomed what they took to be the total collapse of its political system' in 1861.[1]

That is why Abraham Lincoln insisted that 'the central idea pervading this struggle is the necessity . . . of proving that popular government is not an absurdity. We must settle this question now, whether in a free government the minority have the right to break up the government whenever they choose. If we fail it will go far to prove the incapability of the people to govern themselves.' Nor was this merely an American question, Lincoln said in his first message to Congress. It 'embraces more than the fate of these United States. It presents to the whole family of man, the question whether a constitutional republic, or a democracy . . . can, or cannot, maintain its territorial integrity.'[2] If the Union dissolved, the forces of conservatism in Europe would smile in satisfaction that the upstart republic of Yankee braggarts had gotten its comeuppance at last. Thus, as Parish noted, 'the president of the United States never doubted . . . that the conflict mattered for the whole world'.[3]

Given the centrality in Parish's book of the theme that 'America's trial by battle was a test of what liberty, democracy, and power meant at different levels and in many different places,' this introduction to *The American Civil War: Explorations and Reconsiderations* explores that theme. The framework for this exploration is Lincoln's belief in the Union as 'the last best hope of earth' that 'government of the people, by the people, for the people, shall not perish from the earth'.[4]

The American sense of mission blossomed with the earliest settlements in New England. 'We shall be as a City upon a hill,' said John Winthrop to his fellow Puritans as their ship approached Massachusetts Bay in 1630. 'The eyes of all people are upon us.' Four score years before Lincoln became president, George Washington declared that the impact of the American Revolution would not be confined 'to the present age alone, for with our fate will the destiny of unborn Millions be involved'.[5]

During the Civil War itself, ideologically motivated Union soldiers echoed Lincoln's statements that the fate of democratic government depended on Union victory. 'I do feel that the liberty of the world is placed in our hands to defend,' wrote a Massachusetts private to his wife in 1862. 'If we are overcome then farewell to freedom.' On the second anniversary of his enlistment, an Ohio private wrote in 1863 that he had not expected the war to last so long, but no matter how much longer it took, it must be carried on 'for the great principles of liberty and self government at stake, for should we fail, the onward march of Liberty in the Old World will be retarded at least a century, and Monarchs, Kings, and Aristocrats will be more powerful against their subjects than ever.'[6] Some former subjects of those kings who had emigrated to America expressed similar convictions. In 1864, a forty year-old Ohio corporal who had immigrated from England as a yound man wrote to his wife explaining why he had decided to reenlist for a second three-year hitch in the Union army. 'If I do get hurt I want you to remember that it will be not only for my Country and my Children but for Liberty all over the World that I risked my life, for if Liberty should be crushed here, what hope would there be for the cause of Human Progress anywhere else?'[7] Five months later he was dead before Atlanta.

Americans had never been reticent about proclaiming their God-given mission to carry the torch of liberty and democracy for all the world. But did peoples of other lands acknowledge that mission? Some certainly did. During the first century of its history as a nation, the United States was a model for European and Latin American liberals and radicals who sought to reform or overthrow the *anciens régimes* in their own countries. During the debate that produced the British Reform Act of 1832, the London Working Men's Association pronounced 'the Republic of America' to be a 'beacon of freedom' for all mankind. In the 1840s, English Chartists praised 'the bright luminary of the western hemisphere whose radiance will . . . light the whole world to freedom'. In the preface to the twelfth edition of Democracy in America, written during the 1848 uprisings in Europe, Alexis de Tocqueville urged leaders of France's newly created Second Republic to study American institutions as a guide to 'the approaching irresistible and universal spread of democracy throughout the world'.[8]

A British radical newspaper may have overstated the case when it declared in 1856 that the American democratic example was 'a constant terror, and an everlasting menace' to 'the oppressors of Europe, especially those of England . . . who maintain that without kings and aristocrats, civilised communities cannot exist'.[9] Nevertheless, a good many members of the British Establishment expressed delight, at least in private, as the 'immortal smash' of the dis-United States in 1861, which demonstrated 'the failure of republican institutions in time of pressure'. When Sir John Ramsden, a Tory member of the House of

Commons, expressed satisfaction that 'the great republican bubble had burst', cheers broke forth from the back benches.[10] The Earl of Shrewsbury looked upon this 'trial of Democracy and its failure' and proclaimed that 'the dissolution of the Union is inevitable, and . . . men before me will live to see an aristocracy established in America.' The *Times* of London, whose unconcealed anti-Americanism led it to sympathize with the Confederacy, considered the downfall of 'the American colossus' a good 'riddance of a nightmare . . . Excepting a few gentlement of republican tendencies, we all expect, we nearly all wish, success to the Confederate cause.'[11]

Peter Parish has wisely counselled us against overgeneralizing the class basis of British attitudes towards the American Civil War. Not all members of the aristocracy and gentry sympathized with the Confederacy; not all workers and middle-class liberals supported the Union. For the latter, the slavery issue was a particular sticking point. Because of constitutional restraints, and because of his need to keep the support of Democrats and border-state Unionists for the war effort, Lincoln made abundantly clear in 1861 that the Northern war aim was Union, not emancipation. Since 'the North does not proclaim abolition and never pretended to fight for anti-slavery,' asked an English journalist in September 1861, how 'can we be fairly called upon to sympathise so warmly with the Federal cause?'[12]

A good question, and one that Lincoln had wrestled with for a long time. As far back as 1854, in his famous Peoria speech, he acknowledged that 'the monstrous injustice of slavery deprives our republican example of its just influence in the world – enables the enemies of free institutions, with plausibility, to taunt us as hypocrites.' In September 1862 Lincoln agreed with a delegation of antislavery clergymen that 'emancipation would help us in Europe, and convince them that we are incited by something more than ambition.'[13] When he said this, the military and political equation had shifted to a point that now favoured emancipation, and a proclamation to that effect rested in a White House drawer, awaiting a military victory to give it force.

The battle of Antietam gave Lincoln his opportunity. But the preliminary Emancipation Proclamation he issued on 22 September 1862, to go into effect one hundred days later in all states still in rebellion, did not immediately sway British opinion. Many regarded it as a Yankee trick to encourage a slave insurrection, undertaken not from moral conviction but as a desperate measure to destroy the Confederacy from within because Union armies could not defeat it from without. Foreign Secretary Lord John Russell branded the Proclamation a vile encouragement to 'acts of plunder, of incendiarism, and of revenge'. Because the Proclamation was grounded on the executive's power, as commander-in-chief, to seize enemy property being used to wage war against the United States, it applied only to slaves in *Confederate* states, not in the loyal slave states. Choosing not to understand why, under the Constitution, Lincoln had to make this distinction, the London *Spectator* gibed that 'the principle asserted is not that a human being cannot own another, but that he cannot own him unless he is loyal to the United States.'[14]

But when the first day of 1863 arrived and Lincoln, contrary to the predictions of European cynics, actually issued the Proclamation, justifying it not only as a military necessity but also as an 'act of justice', and enjoining slaves to refrain from violence, a powerful pro-Union tidal wave swept liberal and radical circles in Britain. Young Henry Adams, secretary to his father Charles Francis Adams, the American minister to Britain, reported that 'the Emancipation Proclamation has done more for us here than all our former victories and all our diplomacy. It has created an almost convulsive reaction in our favor.' Huge mass meetings took place in England and Scotland where real workingmen, as well as those who professed to speak for them, roared their approval of pro-Union resolutions. One of Britain's staunchest supporters of the Northern cause, Richard Cobden, wrote that the largest of these meetings, at Exeter Hall in London, 'has had a powerful effect on our newspapers and politicians. It has closed the mouths of those who have been advocating the side of the South. Recognition of the South, by England, whilst it bases itself on Negro slavery, is an impossibility.'[15]

Cobden was not entirely correct. Not all mouths remained closed. Many Britons could never quite bring themselves to admire the United States or to favour Union victory – which was not necessarily the same thing as supporting the South. Nevertheless, when that Northern victory finally came at Appomattox, a Tory MP remarked sourly to an American acquaintance that he considered Union success a misfortune. 'I had indulged the hope that your country might break up into two or perhaps more fragments,' he said. 'I regard the United States as a menace to the whole civilised world.' Another Tory spelled out the menace as 'the beginning of an Americanising process in England. The new Democratic ideas are gradually to find embodiment.'[16]

The British public paid more attention to the American Civil War than did the people of any other European country. We know less about conservative attitudes toward the Civil War in other countries. What we do know, however, is that royalists in the early years of the war expressed satisfaction with the apparent failure of democracy. In 1862, the Spanish journal *Pensamiento Español* did not find it surprising that Americans were butchering each other, for that nation 'was populated by the dregs of all the nations of the world . . . Such is the real history of the one and only state in the world which has succeeded in constituting itself according to the flaming theories of democracy. The example is too horrible to stir any desire for emulation.' In France the policy of Napoleon III leaned toward the Confederacy. The French republican Edgar Quinet exaggerated only slightly when he wrote from exile in Switzerland in 1862 that Napoleon's purpose was 'to weaken or destroy Democracy in the United States . . . because in order for Napoleonic ideas to succeed, it is absolutely indispensable that this vast republic disappear from the face of the earth.'[17]

Whether or not Napoleon thought he could destroy republicanism in the United States, he did try to do so in Mexico. That country experienced its own civil war in the 1860s between a reactionary alliance of the church with large landowners and followers of the republican Benito Juárez. Under the pretext of collecting debts owed to the French citizens, Napoleon sent an army of 35,000 men to Mexico to overthrow Juárez. Napoleon collaborated with his fellow emperor Franz Joseph of Austria to establish Franz Joseph's younger brother Ferdinand Maximilian as emperor of Mexico, thereby reclaiming at least part of the vast Spanish domain once ruled by the Hapsburgs. King Leopold of Belgium, Maximilian's father-in-law, had an additional purpose in mind. Describing the Lincoln administration as characterized by 'the most rank Radicalism', Leopold feared that if the North won the war, 'America, in collaboration with Europe's revolutionaries, might undermine the very basis of the traditional social order of Europe.' Therefore he backed the installation of Maximilian on the throne of Mexico in 1864 'to raise a barrier against the United States and provide a support for the monarchical-aristocratic principle in the Southern states'.[18]

In contrast to these emperors in central and western Europe, Czar Alexander, the most absolutist of all, proved to be the Union's steadfast friend. This strange-bedfellow relationship was one of pragmatic self-interest: the Russian interest in a strong United States as a counterweight to Britain, and American dependence on Russia as a counterweight to British and French flirtation with recognition of the Confederacy in 1862. The following year the Russian fleet visited American ports, staying for months, ostensibly as a goodwill gesture but in reality to escape being bottled up in their home ports by the Royal Navy during a period of tension over Russian suppression of an uprising in Poland.

Although Russian policy supported the Union, the Czar's minister to the United States, Edouard de Stoeckl, privately believed the Northern cause hopeless. Stoeckl considered himself an aristocrat and like to be addressed

as 'Baron' though he had no title of nobility. He disliked democracy and regarded the Civil War as proof of its failure. In his dispatches to the Russian
foreign minister, Prince Alexander Gorchakov, Stoeckl wrote with apparent
satisfaction that 'the republican form of government, so much talked about
by the Europeans and so much praised by the Americans, is breaking down.
What can be expected from a country where men of humble origin are elevated to the highest positions?' He meant Lincoln, whom Stoeckl held in
low regard. 'This is democracy in practice, the democracy that European
theorists rave about,' he continued. 'If they could only see it at work they
would cease their agitation and thank God for the government which they
are enjoying.'[19]

Those theorists whom Stoeckl sneered at – European liberals and radicals
– experienced many moments of doubt and discouragement during the war,
moments when it seemed that Union defeat 'may well bring about the failure
of a society' had, in the words of a French republican, held up as 'defenders of
right and humanity'. When the Union finally triumphed, they breathed a sigh
of relief, even of exultation. The Italian republican Guiseppe Mazzini blessed
the Northern people, who 'have done more for us in four years than fifty
years of teaching, preaching and writing from all your European brothers
have been able to do.' None other than Karl Marx, who had followed the
American war with great attention, declared that 'as in the eighteenth century the American war of Independence sounded the tocsin for the European
middle class, so in the nineteenth century, the American Civil War sounded it
for the working class.'[20]

Even 'Baron' Edouard de Stoeckl experienced a conversion of sorts. Democracy was still not to his taste, but he ate humble pie and paid a handsome
tribute to the nation whose victory he had doubted until the fall of Richmond. By 'an irresistible strength of the nation at large', he wrote to Prince
Gorchakov, 'this exceptional people has given the lie to all predictions and
calculations', including his own. 'They have passed through one of the greatest revolutions of a century . . . and they have come out of it with their resources unexhausted, their energy renewed . . . and the prestige of their power
greater than ever.'[21]

This triumph encouraged reformers in Britain who wanted to expand
voting rights there. For almost four years, said Edward Beesly, a liberal professor of political economy at University College London, they had endured
the taunts of Tories who gloated about the 'immortal smash' of American
democracy. 'They insisted on our watching what they called its breakdown.
They told us that it was for ever discredited in England. Well, we accepted

the challenge. We staked our hopes boldly on the result . . . Under a strain such as no aristocracy, no monarchy, no empire could have supported, Republican institutions have stood firm. It is we, now, who call upon the privileged classes to mark the result . . . A vast impetus has been given to Republican sentiments in England.'[22]

Queen Victoria was in no danger of being toppled from her throne because of the outcome of the American Civil War. But a two-year debate in Parliament, in which the American example figured prominently, led to enactment of the Reform Bill of 1867, which nearly doubled the eligible electorate and enfranchised a large part of the British working class for the first time. This expansion of the suffrage would undoubtedly have come sooner or later in any case, but perhaps later rather than sooner if the North had lost the war, thereby confirming Tory opinions of democracy.

If progress toward democracy in Britain was, perhaps, an indirect consequence of the American Civil War, the triumph of Benito Juárez and republicanism in Mexico was in considerable part a direct result. The United States sent 50,000 veteran soldiers to Texas after Appomattox. None too subtly, Secretary of State Seward pressed the French to pull their troops out of Mexico. Napoleon did so in 1866, whereupon the republican forces under Juárez regained control of the country, captured Maximilian, and executed him in 1867. Three years later Napoleon himself lost his throne – an event attributed by the historian of the French republican opposition in part to the example of triumphant republicanism in the United States five years earlier.[23]

This is pushing things too far; France's third republic was born of French defeat in the Franco-Prussian War, not Union victory in the American Civil War. But perhaps it was more than coincidence that within five years of that Union victory, the forces of change had expanded the suffrage in Britain and toppled emperors in Mexico and France. It was also more than coincidence that after the abolition of slavery in the United States, the abolitionist forces in the two remaining slave societies in the Western Hemisphere, Brazil and Cuba, stepped up their campaigns for emancipation, which culminated in success two decades later. In 1871, referring to Brazil's commitment to the first steps toward abolition, an emancipationist in that country rejoiced 'to see Brazil receive so quickly the moral of the Civil War in the United States'.[24]

Lincoln would have been pleased if he had lived to witness the impact abroad of Union victory. Although he was not a vindictive man – quite the contrary – he would have enjoyed quiet pleasure in knowing that the outcome, in the words of Peter Parish, came as 'a considerable surprise to those who had seen in secession final proof of the fatal weakness of American federalism and democracy'. Lincoln, noted Parish, 'showed a truly remarkable

understanding of the cosmic significance' of the Civil War. But even he might
not have anticipated Parish's conclusion that 'if the war had ended in the
achievement of Southern independence, and a permanent division of the once
United States, the balance of world power and the shape of world politics in
the twentieth century would obviously have been completely different'.[25]
Perhaps we would today all be speaking German.

Notes

1. Peter J. Parish, *The American Civil War* (New York 1975) pp. 382–4.

2. Michael Burlingame and John R. Turner (eds), *Inside Lincoln's White House: The Complete Civil War Diary of John Hay* (Carbondale, Ill., 1997) p. 20; Roy B. Basler (ed.), *The Collected Works of Abraham Lincoln*, 9 vols (New Brunswick, NJ, 1953–5), IV, p. 426.

3. Parish, *American Civil War*, p. 383.

4. Ibid.; Basler (ed.), *Collected Works of Lincoln*, V, p. 537, VII, p. 23.

5. Quoted in Richard N. Current, 'Lincoln, the Civil War, and the American Mission', in Cullom Davis *et al.* (eds), *The Public and Private Lincoln: Contemporary Perspectives* (Carbondale, Ill., 1979) pp. 140, 141.

6. Josiah Perry to Phebe Perry, 3 October 1862, Josiah Perry Papers, Illinois State Historical Library, Springfield; Robert T. McMahan Diary, entry of 3 September 1863, State Historical Society of Missouri, Columbia.

7. George H. Cadman to Esther Cadman, 6 March 1864, Cadman Papers, Southern Historical Collection, University of North Carolina, Chapel Hill.

8. G.D. Lillibridge, *Beacon of Freedom: The Impact of American Democracy upon Great Britain 1830–1870* (Philadelphia, Pa, 1955) pp. 5, 40; Alexis de Tocqueville, *Democracy in America*, 12th edn, new English translation by George Lawrence, ed. J.P. Mayer (New York, 1969) p. xiii.

9. Lillibridge, *Beacon of Freedom*, p. 80.

10. William H. Russell to John Biglow, 14 April 1861, in John Biglow, *Retrospections of an Active Life*, 2 vols, (New York, 1909) I, p. 347; Ramsden quoted in Jay Monaghan, *Diplomat in Carpet Slippers: Abraham Lincoln Deals with Foreign Affairs* (Indianapolis, Ia, 1945) p. 116.

11. Earl of Shrewsbury quoted in Ephriam D. Adams, *Great Britain and the American Civil War*, 2 vol, (New York, 1925) II, p. 282; *Times* quoted in Frank L. Owsley,

King Cotton Diplomacy: Foreign Relations of the Confederate States of America, 2nd edn, revised by Harriet C. Owsley (Chicago, Ill., 1959) p. 186.

12. *Economist,* September 1861, quoted in Karl Marx and Friedrich Engels, *The Civil War in the United States,* ed. Richard Enmale (New York, 1937) p. 12.

13. Basler (ed.) *Collected Works of Lincoln* II, p. 255, V, p. 423.

14. Russell quoted in Howard Jones, *Union in Peril: The Crisis over British Intervention in the Civil War* (Chapel Hill, NC, 1992), p. 187; *Spectator,* 11 October 1862, quoted in Brian Jenkins, *Britain and the War for the Union,* 2 vols, (Montreal, 1974–1980) II, p. 153.

15. Cobden to Charles Sumner, 13 February 1863, in Belle Becker Sideman and Lillian Friedman (eds), *Europe Looks at the Civil War* (New York, 1960) p. 222.

16. Sir Edward Bulwer-Lytton to John Biglow [n.d.] April 1865, quoted in Sideman and Friedman (eds), *Europe Looks at the Civil War* p. 282; Harold M. Hyman (ed.), *Heard Around the World: The Impact Abroad of the Civil War* (New York, 1969) p. xi.

17. *Pensamiento Español,* September 1862, quoted in Sideman and Friedman (eds), *Europe Looks at the Civil War,* pp. 173–4; Quinet quoted in Serge Gavronsky, *The French Liberal Opposition and the American Civil War* (New York, 1968) p. 167.

18. Leopold quoted in Sideman and Friedman (eds), *Europe Looks at the Civil War* p. 98 and in A.R. Tyrner-Tyrnauer, *Lincoln and the Emperors* (New York, 1962) pp. 69, 109.

19. Albert A. Woldman, *Lincoln and the Russians* (Cleveland, Ohio, 1952) pp. 216–17.

20. *Revue des Deux Mondes,* 15 August 1861 and Mazzini quoted in Sideman and Friedman (eds), *Europe Looks at the Civil War* pp. 81, 282. Marx quoted in R. Laurence Moore, *European Socialists and the American Promised Land* (New York, 1970) p. 7.

21. Stoeckl to Gorchakov, 14 April 1865, quoted in Woldman, *Lincoln and The Russians* pp. 256–9.

22. Quoted in Harold C. Allen, 'Civil War, Reconstruction, and Great Britain', in Hyman (ed.), *Heard Around the World* p. 73.

23. Gavronsky, *The French Liberal Opposition* p. 13.

24. Harry Bernstein, 'The Civil War and Latin America', in Hyman (ed.), *Heard Around the World* p. 323.

25. Parish, *American Civil War* pp. 630, 647, 650.

PART ONE

THE POLITICAL FRONT

CHAPTER ONE

THE STATE OF THE UNION, 1776–1860

DONALD RATCLIFFE

H istorians of the American Civil War are often tempted to exaggerate the weakness of the Union before 1860. If the ties holding the various states together were fragile, it is easier to explain why the Union broke apart in the secession winter of 1860–1. Accordingly, historians often argue that state loyalties had always been stronger than national loyalties, that long-established differences between the states made a powerful central authority inappropriate and impossible, and that therefore the federal government had always been weak and inactive in the antebellum years. The story can then emphasize how the success of federal forces in the Civil War finally established the principle that the Union was sacrosanct and perpetual, while the undoubted expansion of federal power during the conflict created central institutions such as the Union had never previously possessed. Thus an American nation, based on a true American nationalism, developed only after 1860, largely as a consequence of four years of bloody internecine strife between North and South. In this respect, at least, many modern civil war historians would agree with the epic film-maker D.W. Griffith: for them too, the events of the 1860s marked 'The Birth of a Nation'.[1]

This view is, however, fundamentally misleading. In the first place, it underestimates the strength of the Union between the 1770s and the 1820s. Powerful nationalizing forces in the late eighteenth century created the United States as a coherent – if highly variegated and decentralized – republic that was bound together by a widely-felt sense of shared political identity. In this respect America was typical of the many European and European-settled nations that developed an exclusive self-awareness between 1765 and 1815 in response to either increasingly restrictive colonial rule or foreign conquest. Secondly, the system of federal government adopted in the United States in 1787–8 incorporated a central government with more real power than historians of the mid-nineteenth century often concede. Those powers were

[4]   deliberately used in the decades following 1789, enabling the federal government to make a decisive contribution to the survival, development and
further integration of the United States. Thus a proper appreciation of the
true strength of the antebellum Union, and the forces underlying it, requires
careful consideration of the period before the Missouri crisis.

Even after that sudden revelation of deep sectional differences over
slavery in 1819–20, the internal political dynamic of the Union served to
mitigate the sense of state and regional distinctiveness. American political
conflicts after 1828 operated within a national party system that had the
effect of easing, and at times directly counteracting, sectional differences. Thus
tendencies towards the creation of regional nationalisms were repeatedly overwhelmed by internal partisan divisions that led minorities to look for allies
in other states and regions. The dominance of national parties devoted to
maintaining a nationwide partisan consensus made possible the successful
engineering of sectional compromises, which after 1828 increasingly meant
reducing the scale of action of the federal government. In effect, the South's
growing concern for its own peculiar minority interests severely limited
the exercise of federal power in the immediate antebellum decades, which
explains why historians have sometimes exaggerated the inherent weakness
of the Union before the Civil War. The strengthening of national power in
the 1860s reflected, in part, the restoration of the political situation that had
existed before the South began to impose its deadening hand on the Union in
the thirty years before the war.

Foundations of the Union

The American Union, and the spirit of American nationality that underlay
it, were the creation of the eighteenth century. Originally, of course, each
of the Thirteen Colonies was a separate foundation, and developed its
own character, peculiarities and special interests; each colony had a direct
relationship with the Crown and, officially, none with its neighbours. Yet
colonial historians have detected a slowly growing sense of common American identity in the decades before 1740, though only afterwards did the
various colonies begin to share common experiences. Elites, religious and
political, cooperated on a continental basis, and often came together in dealing with their associates in Britain. Practical realities like intercolonial trade
and the postal service were reinforced by the needs of war against the French

and Indians and – above all – by the religious excitements of the Great Awakening.[2] Yet these developments did not mean that the colonies were growing away from Britain; on the contrary, if anything, they shared in the growing sense of Britishness that Linda Colley has discerned in Britain in the eighteenth century, and they took pride in their place in the triumphant British Empire. The menace of Indians and the presence of African slaves encouraged even non-British settlers to identify with their English-speaking neighbours, and racial and cultural affinity provided a common bond for all white, Protestant colonists.[3]

This shared political outlook was fully revealed after 1763 as the colonies came into conflict with the British government. Though each colony had its own grievances, the underlying rationale was the same and the common ideology gained clear expression in the resistance to the Stamp Act of 1765: Americans in all the colonies that possessed provincial legislatures found themselves struggling to preserve what they saw as basic protections of their rights and liberties as British citizens. The continuing argument quickly transposed this sense of a common British citizenship into an exclusive American self-identification, as the colonists concluded by 1774 that the failure of people in Britain to prevent the repeated threats to colonial liberties meant that the people there were corrupt and no longer capable of defending liberty. Thus the degeneration of the home country made America the last hope for the preservation of civil freedoms. In these circumstances, colonial newspapers, notably in the South, increasingly used the word 'American' as the common descriptor of the colonies and by 1773 were expressing a clear sense of continental identity. Even before fighting began, recent historians have detected the existence of 'a distinct American political community'.[4]

The very character of the Revolution assisted the social construction of this national feeling. The transfer of power to the former colonies was justified on the principle of the sovereignty of the people, but that principle was necessarily based on the assumption – clearly expressed in the Declaration of Independence of 1776 – that Americans constituted a single, coherent 'people'. Aware of the need for outward expressions of this identity, Americans everywhere adapted traditional British street celebrations into rituals that legitimized the new order; the toasts – initially always thirteen in number – offered at public festivals expressed national rather than provincial pride. Most importantly, the reports of the scattered events of the Revolution and of local celebrations then circulated through the press, giving them a national import and helping to create what Benedict Anderson has called an 'imagined political community'. Indeed, we might argue that the sense of American

[6]   nationality gained deep roots so quickly because the binding thread of a common 'print-language', so essential for creating an awareness of sharing a communal identity, was not restricted to an upper class, since literacy was already widespread and newspapers extraordinarily numerous. Hence the evidence of recent cultural historians increasingly suggests, in David Wald-streicher's words, that 'Americans practiced nationalism before they had a fully developed national state.'[5]

In practice, a Union government was established even before the separate states had a legal existence. Faced by British military and naval power, the colonies had no choice (as Franklin said) but to hang together. The Continental Congress, called in 1774, swiftly began to act in the collective interest of the colonies, authorizing a Continental Association to embargo trade with Britain, raising a Continental Army, issuing a Continental currency, and negotiating with foreign powers, long before its constitutional powers were defined. As the Virginia House of Burgesses insisted in 1776, it was inappropriate for a single colony to declare its independence and so the House pressed its representatives in Philadelphia to persuade Congress to take the critical step on behalf of the whole American people. It may have been difficult – in John Adams's famous phrase – to make thirteen clocks strike as one, but the United States took its stand as an integral political entity on the world scene long before any state asserted its sovereignty. When foreign powers recognized Congress as the legitimate and authoritative exponent of the Union's will, in both the French alliance of 1778 and the peace treaty of 1783, they in effect recognized the priority of the sovereignty of the United States.[6]

Popular commitment to the new republic gained deep emotional roots as a result of the War for Independence. Just as the French and Indian wars had a unifying effect on sentiment before 1763, so Americans sanctified their cause by the spilling of blood together in resisting the British effort to conquer them. Some recent historians have argued that the fighting between 1775 and 1781 had probably a greater impact on proportionately more of the American population than the Civil War four score and ten years later, as ordinary people all over the country bullied neighbours, fought skirmishes, had property impounded, and suffered harassment, injury and tragic loss. In the South, the last eighteen months of the struggle degenerated into a guerrilla, even terrorist, war between Patriot and Loyalist neighbours. The memory of the war subsequently became the touchstone of national feeling, just as the Civil War did for the late nineteenth century. Strikingly, the Congress agreed in the early 1780s that, since the war had been a common effort, those states

such as South Carolina that had paid out proportionately more than average [7]
for the war effort should be recompensed by the states that had paid less. A
congressional settlement commission promptly began to audit state accounts
in order to apportion the cost of the war among the states on a *per capita* basis,
though this commitment to back patriotic sentiment with hard cash remained
unfulfilled in the 1780s because of postwar financial difficulties and Congress's lack of authority.[7]

The weakness of Congress after the war reflects the reality that the new
republic was made up of thirteen very different and widely separated states,
each proudly asserting the provincial autonomy that it believed Britain
had threatened. Moreover, the ideology of the Revolution emphasized the
principle of self-determination and insisted that the states came together in
voluntary association. As a consequence, the Articles of Confederation (drafted
in 1776–7 but not ratified until 1781) expressed the conviction of the states
that Congress must not become an overpowerful central government that
might threaten the pluralistic and decentralized nature of the Union. But faced
after 1783 by the republic's ineffectiveness in dealing with hostile foreign
powers and imperial neighbours, and experiencing the disruptive social
and political consequences of the postwar financial and economic crisis,
politically aware Americans faced up to the need for constitutional revision
remarkably quickly. The new Constitution of 1787 was produced by a
nationally conscious political elite that welded together an overwhelming
coalition of merchants and urban artisans, young men and old patriots,
slaveholders and capitalists, major ports and financially overstrained states,
exposed frontier areas and metropolitan interests. The eleven state conventions that approved the Constitution before 1789 did so, overall, by a
2:1 margin.[8]

This decision has often been seen – like the initial act of union in 1776 –
as a forced response to the critical situation in which the newly independent
states found themselves. Thus, it is argued, continental institutions were
necessarily created before a true sense of nationhood existed. Since, according to John Murrin, 'American national identity was . . . an unexpected, impromptu, artificial, and therefore extremely fragile creation of the Revolution,'
the Founding Fathers were doomed to erect over their heads a national roof
that was not supported by the walls of popular nationalism. Of course, American national identity was ill-defined and the process of defining its meanings
would take many decades, lasting long beyond the Civil War, but many
indications confirmed that a basic sense of American political community did
already exist. For example, when Alexander Hamilton, James Madison and

[8] John Jay wrote a series of newspapers articles in 1788 to help secure the ratification of the Constitution in New York – the famous Federalist Papers – they necessarily emphasized the pragmatic utility of the Union and the merits of the new constitutional scheme, but their argument constantly assumed, and without expectation of disagreement, that a single 'American people' existed that rightly belonged together in some sort of political relationship.[9]

Indeed, the decision to create a 'more perfect Union' in 1787–8 cannot be satisfactorily explained without the prior existence of some sense of nationality. After all, those who opposed ratification of the Constitution – the 'Antifederalists' – controlled at least six of the ratifying conventions when they first met, but proved unwilling to vote the new scheme down. In the New Hampshire convention, a number of Antifederalists who had been instructed to vote against the Constitution voted for an adjournment instead; and the four-month interim was then successfully used to persuade their constituents that their fears of the proposed system were groundless. The truth was that the Antifederalists were not hostile to the Union: they wanted to preserve the existing 'Articles of Confederation and *Perpetual Union*' (my italics), but with a few necessary amendments that experience had already shown could not pass the amendment process laid down in the Articles, which required the agreement of all the states. Lacking a viable alternative of their own, enough Antifederalists were persuaded by the merits of the proposed scheme – and encouraged by the promise of a Bill of Rights – to produce the necessary majorities; and by the time of the first federal elections in the fall of 1788, even the most recalcitrant of their fellows had accepted the new framework and promptly worked within it. Their ideas persisted, but in future the former Antifederalists of 1787–8 would argue over the meaning of the Constitution, not its legitimacy.[10]

On any interpretation, the system of government established in 1787–8 was no mere token of national unity, but gave a remarkable range of power to the central authority. If the states retained sovereignty in important areas, the new federal government gained absolute control in many others. Just compare the powers undoubtedly conceded to the American Union in 1787–8 with those that some European countries nowadays are reluctant to concede to the European Union. The American people in their various states not only agreed to create a single market, with no internal barriers to the free movement of peoples and goods, but also established a central government worthy of the name – controlling a single defence policy, a single foreign policy, a single immigration policy, and even a single currency. Laws exercising these powers were to be determined by unqualified majority voting, and their application could not be limited by opt-out clauses for any particularist state. [9] Indeed, the Constitution required the people of a state to accept the operation, within their state, of an outside jurisdiction, possibly controlled by a rival interest; and that meant accepting not just externally-appointed executive officers but an external system of justice operating at the local level. Given the lack of a comparable sense of European nationality, can one imagine any country in present-day Europe submitting to the collection of direct taxes by officeholders appointed by outsiders? In practice, of course, the United States government would usually appoint residents of the state concerned as federal officers, but there was no guarantee that this would always happen, as many Southerners appreciated in 1860–1.[11] But the sense of American community among the politically active – and that was a lot of people – was strong enough in 1787 for the majority of their representatives to be persuaded that such a sacrifice could be made with safety.

Challenges defeated, 1789–1815

The new system had to confront great perils and challenges that underlined the weaknesses of the Union. Separatist movements, especially on the ill-defined margins of the country, toyed with ideas of secession and even of joining the Spanish or British empires. External menaces became ever more serious with the outbreak of war between France and Britain in 1793, and serious internal disagreements broke out over American policy. Major political parties appeared that fought bitterly, each unwilling to trust the other's loyalty to the federal republic. In the 1790s the ruling Federalists under President Washington believed that their Democratic Republican opponents threatened the Union with their powerful regional support in the Southern states. When the Democratic Republicans came to power under Thomas Jefferson after 1800, they in turn feared that the Federalists were plotting the secession of New England. Yet the failure of all these challenges demonstrated that the United States also possessed some inherent bonds of adhesive strength, not least a widespread feeling that Americans ought to stick together.[12]

Certainly the separatist movements were never quite as serious as they seemed. In the 1780s malcontent frontier areas sought autonomy from their parent state rather than from the Union, and flirted with Britain and Spain mainly because they feared that Congress would not satisfy their interests.

[10] Conspiracies in Vermont, Tennessee and Kentucky largely ceased once these states had been admitted to the Union in 1791 and 1792, and Western separatism disappeared entirely once the Northwestern Indians had been defeated in 1794 and the Mississippi fully opened to Americans in 1795. The Whiskey rebels of 1794 in western Pennsylvania – like the Shays rebels of 1786 in Massachusetts – wanted the repeal of unpopular taxes and a more responsive government, not separation from the United States, whatever seaboard interests may have feared. The Burr conspiracy of 1806–7 – which supposedly threatened the secession of the West – lacked popular support, and locally elected authorities were taking necessary steps to suppress it even before President Jefferson issued his admonitory proclamation.[13]

Similarly, the party contest that appeared in the 1790s acted to restrain sectional illwill as much as to express it. In practice, the hostility between the South and New England was mitigated by the divisions within the Middle Atlantic states which gave the South the opportunity to find allies in the North. When, in the war crisis with France in 1798–9, the Federalists passed measures that the Democratic Republicans thought unconstitutional, the legislatures of Kentucky and Virginia adopted condemnatory resolutions secretly drafted by Jefferson and Madison. Jefferson initially included in his draft the claim that a state government could nullify the operation of unconstitutional laws within its limits and so obstruct the operation of federal government, but he was persuaded to drop this assertion partly because it would lose the Democratic Republicans support in Pennsylvania and New York. Thus the hope of national victory through coalition with allies in distant states prevented the Virginia leaders from retreating into merely regional resistance to the federal government. Furthermore, having won power after 1800, Southern Republicans grew confident in their place in the Union and became far more sympathetic to the use of federal power to achieve national ends.[14]

By contrast, in New England the defeated Federalists developed a strong sense of regional distinctiveness after 1800, and in 1804 and 1808 some of the party's leaders floated plans for a separate New England confederacy. However, their doubts about the future of the Union arose mainly from fears about the damaging consequences of westward expansion and, for the most part, they remained loyal to the Union of the original Thirteen. The hardships of the War of 1812 roused some popular disunionism in the region, but the notorious Hartford Convention of December 1814 was always under moderate control and, as one participant later said, 'the vast majority of the members of the Convention were totally opposed to any measures tending to dissolve or impair the union of these states.'[15]

In any case the Federalist leadership appreciated that the example of Democratic Republican electoral success in 1800 showed the importance of
maintaining support outside New England. They may have lapsed into sulky
obstructionism after 1801, but they survived as a national party and underwent a significant popular revival in two-thirds of the states after 1807. In
the process they developed interstate connections that reached out to minorities in such unlikely places as South Carolina and Virginia, and in 1808 and
1812 held interstate meetings that have been seen as embryonic national
nominating conventions. Because the New England Federalist leaders now
had good reason to hope for success nationally, they deliberately diverted
and stifled secessionist talk at home. In any case, the Democratic Republican
party had begun to win considerable support in New England since 1801,
and this large persisting body of local voters loyal to the federal administration ensured that no attempt could seriously be made to lead the region into
secession even during the War of 1812.[16]

Thus the Union actually benefited from the development of two-party
conflict. Though men grieved that party passion threatened the future of the
Union, in practice each side accepted the principles and rules laid down
in the Constitution. Democratic Republican success in 1800–1 legitimized
opposition and demonstrated that governments could be changed peacefully.
Moreover, the new constitutional system had created a centre of executive
power and patronage that was both worth winning and visible to ordinary
people. Politics for a generation would be focused on winning control of that
centre, with both competing parties taking their names and identities from
national issues. Federal elections became the most important focus of popular
political involvement: though between 1804 and 1820 relatively few men
voted in presidential elections because the result was a foregone conclusion,
the largest turnouts seem to have come in congressional rather than in state
elections. Moreover, between 1807 and 1814, even state politics operated
according to national party lines in two-thirds of the states. The intense
rivalry between the parties down to 1815 concentrated awareness of the
Union, with federal elections serving as a reinforcing ritual of national
consciousness.[17]

Current social and economic developments also helped the Union to
survive these difficult years. For 40 years immigration from Europe had been
at an all-time low and during that period the use of the English language
extended considerably among the relatively few non-British Europeans in
the United States, furthering their cultural and political assimilation. Over
the same period the Second Great Awakening gave many thousands of

Americans a new religious awareness and drew them into local churches, mainly Methodist, that were associated together in national organizations; not only did these religious affiliations create formal organizational ties crossing state and regional lines, but evangelism provided 'a common world of experience' that most Americans shared.[18] Equally, the economic boom stimulated by high European wartime demand between 1795 and 1807 furthered the economic integration of the seaboard areas. Northern shipping interests increasingly depended on the carrying trade in Southern produce; Northerners in the seaports began to provide financial, insurance and marketing services for – and lend money to – customers in the South and West; and parts of New England became dependent on food supplies from the middle and western states. After 1807 embargo, non-intercourse and war encouraged the growth of manufacturing, notably in southern New England, and its prosperity depended on free access to markets in the middle states. And as the national debt began to increase after 1807, the number of people who had a vested interest in the federal government expanded, just as Alexander Hamilton had foreseen when he restructured the debt on a sound footing in 1790.[19]

Behind the Union sentiment that so persisted between 1775 and 1815 lay the sense of outside menace. The fear of competing and intruding neighbours, ruled by hostile European empires, provided a major motivation behind the strengthening of federal government in 1787–8, and the outbreak in 1793 of a world war involving those empires created a situation menacing to American security that lasted until 1815. Only after that date did the threat of outside enemies pass away and Americans begin to enjoy 'an excess of isolation' that perhaps served to weaken the bonds of Union.[20] If we add to the foreign threat before 1815 a common language, a broad-based print culture, a sense of racial unity and religious consonance, one-and-a-half centuries of colonial history, and the heroic national past of the Revolution, then the historic roots of American nationalism seem much more akin to those of European nations than is sometimes acknowledged.[21]

Using federal power, 1789–1848

Success in surmounting the challenges to the republic's survival also owed much to the efforts of those who commanded the federal government after 1789. Throughout the 1790s the Federalists used its new-found powers to create national institutions and establish the authority of central institutions.

Alexander Hamilton, as Secretary of the Treasury, deliberately endeavoured [13]
to exercise every power he thought could be deduced from the new Constitution – establishing not just direct taxes and excises, but a semi-independent
quasi-central bank. He demonstrated that the federal government was able to
exploit its new command of tariff revenues in a way individual states had not
been: in 1790 he solved the financial problems not only of the old Confederation but also of various states, by assuming their debts within the new
national debt and fulfilling the old Congress's promise to compensate those
states that had borne the main burden in the War of Independence. Then in
1794 President Washington led an army of 12,950 nationalized militiamen
– about the size of his old Continental army – to suppress the whiskey-tax
disorder in western Pennsylvania. The policy of asserting federal supremacy
finally came to a head in 1798–9 in response to the war crisis with France:
besides taking powers to control immigrants and restrain the expression of
political opinion through the Alien and Sedition Acts, the Federalists also
imposed a federal graduated property tax, levied on land, houses and slaves,
and collected directly by federally-appointed assessors and collectors. The
tax roused remarkably little serious resistance, with opponents objecting to
the tax as inequitable rather than illegitimate.[22]

The Democratic Republicans opposed the nationalist thrust of Federalist
policy, insisting that the Union was intended to be a decentralized confederation based on the principles of states rights. When they took power in
1801, they changed the tax policy and repealed the legislation of 1798–9,
but they also asserted federal power whenever necessity required. The basic
institutions – the bank (until its charter expired in 1811), the national debt,
the army and navy – were all preserved, if in more modest form. Though a
strict constructionist, President Jefferson proved perfectly willing, in national
emergencies, to exercise powers beyond the strict letter of the Constitution –
as over the Louisiana Purchase, the naval campaign against the Barbary
corsairs, and the Burr conspiracy. The embargo of 1808–9 required more
extensive measures of enforcement than even the whiskey excise had in the
previous decade; and Jefferson became the only president in American history to use federal troops for routine law enforcement in peacetime, in areas
where there was no insurrection or domestic violence or breakdown in
normal civil procedures.[23]

In effect, the diplomatic, maritime and economic difficulties that the United
States faced during the Napoleonic wars in Europe were converting many
Democratic Republicans to a more nationalistic outlook. The War Hawks
who appeared in Congress after 1810 demanded stronger federal military

[14] and naval preparations, militant defiance of European superpowers, and measures to promote greater economic independence. Involvement in the second
war against Britain, 1812–15, forced the parsimonious majority in Congress
to adopt some energetic policies, and war expenditure had to be met by
direct federal taxes imposed between 1813 and 1817. Despite its apparently
glorious end at the Battle of New Orleans, most Democratic Republicans
recognized that the war had almost proved disastrous because of the republic's inadequate infrastructure; in effect, the conflict had starkly demonstrated
how continuing economic underdevelopment created major obstacles to
national survival and integration. Thus the difficulty of defending the country
against Britain while remaining dependent on Britain for manufactured goods
prompted a shift in favour of tariff protection for American industry; the
obstacles to transporting men and supplies around the country encouraged
support for federal sponsorship of roads and canals; and the lack of an effective means of transferring funds and credits during the latter stages of the war
demonstrated the value of the earlier national bank. As a consequence, in 1815
President Madison advocated strong federal policies to remove these persisting obstacles to greater national strength, and Congress in 1816 duly adopted
the first openly protectionist tariff and chartered a second national bank.

In this postwar afterglow, American patriotism seemed rampant: delighted
that the republic had survived the trials of separatism and invasion, nationalist spokesmen became more fulsome, more optimistic, more rhetorically
extravagant, though still concerned to define the true character of the republic and uncertain of its moral integrity in the face of rapid material development.[24] The exercise of power on an interstate scale now seemed appropriate
not just to Congress, but also for the voluntary associations such as the American Colonization Society and many evangelical organizations that began to
operate on a national basis. Even the Federalists, embarrassed by their record
of obstruction during the war, ceased to function as an opposition party,
applauding the adoption by the Democratic Republicans of policies once considered Federalist. During this Era of Good Feelings, the creed of 'national
republicanism' became part of a virtually nationwide consensus and resulted
in the formulation of the 'American System', a programme that advocated
advancing economic independence by means of enhanced tariff protection
and promoting internal integration through a grand scheme of federally
financed internal improvements. Furthermore, the Supreme Court under John
Marshall sustained this broad extension of federal authority, by not only adopting Hamiltonian interpretations of the Constitution but insisting on its own
power to override decisions of the state courts.[25]

However, as the administrations of James Monroe and John Quincy Adams endeavoured to press the American System ever further in the 1820s, so resistance swelled. The South, initially part of the nationalist consensus in 1816, shifted its position after 1819: economic depression persuaded many Southerners to blame federal economic policy for their financial embarrassments, while the Missouri crisis taught them to fear federal interference in their relations with the South's racial minorities. Some Southerners – notably in South Carolina and Georgia – even began to calculate the value of the Union. They were joined by states-rights advocates and old Jeffersonians – in both North and South – who wished to return to the old landmarks of Democratic Republicanism, and reduce the powers that the Union had recently taken unto itself. With the assistance of malcontents of many kinds, this strict-constructionist coalition won power under Andrew Jackson in 1828 and proceeded to cut back the power of the central government.[26]

As a consequence, by the mid-1830s the acute French political observer and analyst, Alexis de Toqueville, could report that under Jackson the federal government was 'losing strength, retiring gradually from public affairs, and narrowing its circle of action.'[27] The 1828 Tariff of Abominations – the highest tariff of the antebellum years – was cut back considerably in 1832 and 1833. Jackson's Maysville veto of 1830 ended schemes for a great federal programme of internal improvements. His Bank veto of 1832 and subsequent war on the national bank destroyed that possible instrument of central management. Opposition to this decentralizing programme gained expression through the Whig party of the 1830s and 1840s, which continued to argue that the federal government represented a potentially effective instrument for promoting the general welfare and strengthening the Union. The Whigs won the political argument in the severely depressed conditions of 1840, when they promised a new burst of federal activity comparable with the 1790s and the 1820s, but the early death of President William Henry Harrison in 1841 brought to power a proponent of states rights, Vice-President John Tyler, who prevented them from reversing the cutbacks of the 1830s. After 1845 the Democratic President James K. Polk self-consciously renewed the Jacksonian policy of limiting federal power in domestic affairs, and never again would the Whigs secure the full control of Congress that they needed in order to implement positive national policies.

The process of retraction by the federal government during the 1830s shifted responsibility for economic development on to the state governments, and revealed that the Jacksonian Democrats believed that the Union could be kept together best by a process of devolution. As Jackson himself conceived,

[16] a self-denying federal government that limited itself to a 'few and simple, yet important, objects' would be most likely to hold together a Union made up of increasingly dissimilar parts. Thus states-rights policies were quite compatible with devotion to the Union, as Jackson demonstrated by his stout defence of federal authority when South Carolina obstructed the collection of tariff duties within her limits in the Nullification crisis of 1832–3. In the process Jackson redefined the nature of the Union. Whereas the Federalist tradition saw the Union as a corporate entity expressing the oneness of the American people – which presumably would always exist – the dominant Democratic Republican ideology traditionally emphasized the voluntary nature of the Union, which tacitly implied that states could choose to leave if they wished. Since 1815, however, the growth of 'national republicanism' had seen many Democratic Republicans supporting active federal policies that presumed a continuing future for the common interest of the Union. President Jackson offered a resolution of this ambiguity when, in the face of South Carolina's challenge to federal authority, he made it clear that the reduction of central government was not meant to cast doubt on the Union's perpetuity. In his Nullification Proclamation of December 1832 he asserted its permanence in a way no previous president had felt necessary, and so established the principle of states-rights Unionism that would enable many Northern Democrats to support the Union in the Civil War.[28]

The centrality of federal government

State governments exercised considerable power, especially in the last decades before the Civil War, and had direct influence on the everyday lives of their citizens. They managed day-to-day economic life, regulated manners and maintained law and order, in ways prohibited to the federal government. Yet that government, far from being insignificant or inactive, always determined the main directions of national development, even after the cutbacks that began in the 1830s. The federal government may have been, in John Murrin's oft-quoted phrase, 'a midget institution in a giant land', but it helped to ensure that the midget citizenry in the seaboard states would by 1848 win command of an ocean-to-ocean empire.[29]

The primary responsibility of the federal government remained national defence. Longstanding hostility to a standing army ensured that, except in moments of unusual crisis, the United States would have only a small regular establishment and that stationed mainly on the frontiers. However, Jefferson,

as an ostensibly anti-military president, recognized the potential influence of
the regular establishment in national life, and founded West Point to imbue
the future officer corps with Democratic Republican values. Even a small military establishment generated a demand for supplies and cultivated valued skills:
US Engineers, for example, prepared the way for grand internal-improvement
schemes – especially during the operation of the General Survey Act between
1824 and 1838 – and federal armouries made an important contribution
before the Civil War in developing techniques of mass production.[30] The wars
of 1775–83, 1812–15 and 1846–8 generated important political forces,
especially in developing an *esprit de corps* among officers that transcended state
loyalties. Thus former officers played an important role in the 1780s in
bringing about the Constitution, while veterans and their widows subsequently
besieged the federal government with claims for compensation and pensions.
These were normally granted by private legislation, though after 1816 general legislation provided pensions for Revolutionary veterans. The Mexican
War of 1846–8 would raise divisive political issues, yet it too generated a
national pride in combined military triumph much as the War of 1812 had,
as the nomination of military leaders for the presidency in 1848 and 1852
demonstrated. Inevitably US Army officers from the South faced an agoniz-
ing choice in 1861 when they found themselves having to break with comrades they had previously served alongside.

Before the Civil War, the federal government employed more people in
delivering the mails than in any other civilian activity. Yet this statistic was
not a mark of its inconsequence as a government, but of the centrality of the
Post Office in national life. Since the days of Benjamin Franklin the mail
system had provided an important bond for literate people in the coastal
areas. Then the Post Office Act of 1792 started a communications revolution
which brought all parts of the country into regular touch with each other.
The Post Office developed systematic contacts across the republic, organizing collection, conveyance and delivery, and its subsidies created the nation's
stage-coach system, at least until Congress withdrew the subsidies in 1845.
Indeed, public transport would scarcely have existed in many parts of the
South and West had it not been for the 'mail stages'. Most importantly,
after 1792 newspapers were carried free of charge and so the Post Office
generated – and subsidized – a system of news interchange that made possible the extension of print culture throughout the republic. Down to the 1850s
the mails carried more newspapers than letters, and reading a newspaper
became a great collective ritual that confirmed the participation of the citizenry
in the republic's affairs.[31]

The federal government also retained control over some key elements of the economy. Though it did not exploit its power over interstate commerce as it would after the Civil War, it retained an undisputed command over external commerce at a time when the United States remained essentially an exporter of agricultural surplus and an importer of manufactured goods. No one, not even in South Carolina, questioned the federal government's exclusive right to impose tariffs on imports, though many came to doubt whether it could use that power to foster economic growth. In practice from 1816 to 1857 the tariff always retained a protective element: the compromise tariff of 1833 guaranteed a reasonable (if decreasing) level of protection until 1842, when it was replaced by a frankly protectionist Whig tariff; and even the free-trade Walker tariff of 1846 imposed higher rates on imports that might compete with American manufacturers. The antebellum norm was to impose tariffs primarily for revenue purposes but with some 'moderated protection' for key industries.[32]

Thanks to its command of import duties, the federal government could generate revenue to a degree the states could not rival. Federal assumption of state debts solved their financial problems in 1790, and thereafter until the War of 1812 the states raised relatively little revenue through taxation. A large part of their expenditure – including the costs of maintaining and using the militia – was paid for them by the federal government, at least down to the 1820s. In the next decade, the paying-off of the national debt in 1833 raised the possibility of further federal largesse. Since large-scale internal-improvement schemes were now out of the question, Congress distributed the federal surplus among the states in 1836–7 for them to use as they saw fit, in the face of objections from those who thought such a measure would make the states dangerously dependent on the central government. The Panic of 1837 demonstrated that many states did not have the resources to finance the loans they had taken out since 1830 to finance public works, and in 1840 the Whigs proposed a new assumption of state debts to restore American credit. Although blocked by states-rights supporters, this and other Whig proposals demonstrated the continuing financial superiority of the federal government.[33]

Equally significant was the federal government's control over the currency. In 1787 the Founding Fathers carefully prohibited the state governments from issuing paper money and gave the federal government the exclusive right to issue gold and silver coin, which alone, they believed, constituted real money. However, the supply of gold and silver was limited and, after the turn of the century, state-chartered commercial banks increasingly met demand by issuing paper money. The two Banks of the United States (1791–1811 and 1816–

36) were not designed to act as central banks but both began to develop techniques that compelled the local banks to restrict their note issues to an appropriate proportion of their specie base. Around 1830 some Southern and Western parts of the country were almost totally dependent on the services of the national bank, while state banks themselves on balance appreciated the stability that the national bank brought to paper issues. Most state bankers therefore disapproved of Jackson's veto in 1832 of the bill rechartering the national bank. Destroying the monster bank did not, however, end federal monetary control, since the Treasury had in any case been the main agent of quasi-central-banking supervision, and the federal Independent Treasury system functioned reasonably well from 1846 to the Civil War.[34]

Beyond that, the federal government remained responsible for the conquest of the continent. That meant not only preserving national security and resisting the claims of neighbouring European empires, but controlling the aboriginal population and persuading them to sell their lands to the federal government, which then supervised the process of settlement. The military threat of Indians east of the Appalachians had been defeated during the Revolution, but the Indians of the Mississippi Valley remained a formidable obstacle. Federal troops were essential in defeating the Indians of the Old Northwest in 1794–5, and in smashing their attempted military revival before and during the War of 1812. Only the federal government could mobilize enough power to persuade Indians to move west, as Georgia recognized in 1802. During Jefferson's presidency alone the Indians relinquished legal title to what later became southern Indiana, Illinois, Missouri and northern Arkansas, while between 1815 and 1820 General Jackson acquired by treaty from the Indians a fifth of Georgia, half of Mississippi, and most of Alabama. When the remaining Five Civilized Tribes refused to remove across the Mississippi in the 1820s, Southerners threatened to take matters into their own hands in defiance of federal authority, but they preferred to elect the leading Southern Indian fighter to the White House, where he could do the job so much more efficiently for them. Under President Jackson the federal government spent $60 million on buying 100 million acres east of the Mississippi, and thereby, among other things, opened up the future Black Belt of Alabama and Mississippi to cotton and slaves. This process, largely accomplished by 1840, provided a powerful reason for Southern loyalty through the sectional tensions of the 1830s.[35]

If relations with the Indians remained a federal responsibility, so did the provision of government in the newly opened Western territories. Under the Northwest Ordinance of 1787, each Western territory remained directly

[20] under central control, with a governor and three judges-cum-legislators appointed by and directly reponsible to the federal government. On attaining a population of 5,000 free adult males the territory could elect a legislature to make laws, but subject to the same externally appointed governor. This was a system reminiscent of British control of its American colonies, except that the territorial governors were paid from the metropolis and not by the colonists. On attaining 60,000 inhabitants the territory could apply for statehood on the same terms as the original states. Thus Congress not only retained direct command of the colonies on behalf of the whole Union, but could create new states – and so all states in future would either be created by Congress or be the equals of its creations.[36]

Moreover, the federal government not only commanded governmental jurisdiction but possessed the title of most lands in the West outside Kentucky and Tennessee. As anticipated in the late 1770s, the Union gained huge strength when, between 1781 and 1802, it acquired the claims to Western lands possessed by seven of the states. Not only did this transfer remove a potential source of future conflict, it gave the federal government a vast inheritance, held in common on behalf of all the states. Initially seen as primarily a source of revenue for the whole republic, the Western lands provided a powerful bond for the Union, and before 1830 statesmen like John Quincy Adams and Henry Clay saw the public domain as a patrimony to be used for improving and developing the quality of national life. From at least 1803, the federal government gave to the new Western states tracts of land which were then sold or rented to assist education and internal improvement. The Eastern states never directly benefited from this treasure trove to the extent that some had hoped, though the proceeds of land sales were distributed among all the states according to population in the early 1840s. In practice the primary purpose of federal land policy, since at least 1800, had been to promote settlement as much as to raise revenue. Thus by its generous policies the federal government carried through perhaps the greatest act of privatization in history, distributing millions of acres to thousands of private individuals, even before the Homestead Act of 1861.[37]

Though this policy reduced the government's own resources, it also ensured that large numbers of people in the public-land states remained beholden to the federal government even after statehood had been attained. Government officers determined the process of survey and sale, and local development in new areas focused around the business of the land office. Moreover, the system of selling federal land on credit between 1800 and 1820 meant that about half the farmers north-west of the Ohio River fell into debt to the federal government, which in 1821 granted them substantial relief to ensure they did not lose their lands following the Panic of 1819. The federal government remained a major landowner in the new states, much to the annoyance of Illinois and Missouri, which demanded that public lands within their limits be ceded to them. In 1832 President Jackson advocated cession, but the vested interests of the seaboard states prevented the dispersal of the public domain, despite the adoption of a permanent preemption law in 1841. The same act granted all new states half a million acres each to help finance state internal improvements and in 1854 Congress agreed to progressively cheapen unsold lands, but federal control of the public domain remained an awkward limitation on the autonomy of new states. As late as 1852, Southeastern and Northeastern congressmen voted together to preserve the public lands as a resource for the whole Union rather than give them away to homesteaders.[38]

Similarly, internal improvements remained an important sphere of federal activity. After 1789 the federal government sought to develop interstate communications, and even President Jefferson recognized that the states needed federal help to develop roads and canals which were essential to their development but beyond their means, though he wanted an explicit constitutional amendment to give the federal government this power. After 1819 federal and state governments, including states-rights Virginia, cooperated in joint-stock companies that undertook to build major roads and canals – and even the first long-distance railroad anywhere, the Baltimore and Ohio. These schemes of the 1820s proceeded on the assumption that the necessary power could be deduced by broad construction of the Constitution, but the Maysville Veto of 1830 laid down clear criteria limiting federal authority. While that decision stopped great national schemes of internal improvement and subsequently federal spending on new projects fell considerably, some expensive projects were maintained, notably those already underway as well as river and harbour improvements. In particular, Congress continued to build the National (or Cumberland) Road across Ohio, Indiana and Illinois, but gradually ceded the road to the various states through which it ran and voted its last appropriation in 1838. Despite all efforts to reduce federal responsibilities for internal improvements, Congress still made generous land grants to the states for such projects, since even states-rights advocates accepted that the federal government was not restricted by the Constitution in its exercise of its rights as a landowner. Moreover, newly-opening areas persistently requested financial assistance from Congress – and often received it, at least until the Panic of 1857 embarrassed federal finances.[39]

[22]   The operations of the federal government in critical areas of the nation's life ensured that it would attract all those who sought public office and distinction. The most prestigious offices, both elective and appointive, were federal rather than state, including those that operated within the states. Federal judges had a prestige and security that made them renowned among lawyers. Customs collectors in the major ports handled money in undreamed-of amounts. Land offices brought business to a town and those in charge enjoyed great political influence and considerable local patronage, especially as surveyors enjoyed unusual opportunities for locating the best lands for themselves and their friends. Even postmasters gained great advantages since (until 1847 or even 1855) recipients always paid the postage and so had to collect their letters from the local post office, which, outside the great commercial centres, were usually set up in the postmaster's private business premises.[40] All who wished to gain eminence, to establish a career of distinction, to gain respect as a leading man, looked to federal even more than state office as the route to advancement – and so ensured that national politics would remain central to public life.

Patterns of political conflict, 1816–52

The extent of federal power and influence inevitably aroused contest and opposition that might prove fatal to the continuance of the Union. Such conflicts at times expressed regional tensions which, as President Washington had feared, could threaten the territorial integrity and unity of the republic. Yet, ironically, the party system that dominated American politics between 1827 and 1853 operated, like that of 1796–1816, to reduce sectional antagonisms and further national integration. Like the major churches, the parties created among a mass electorate loyalties and commitments that transcended state boundaries and provincial loyalties.

     When party hostilities between Federalist and Democratic Republican faded after 1815 amid the postwar glow of nationalist consensus, the national partisan allegiances that had undercut particularism in the previous twenty years weakened and made the onset of heightened sectional feeling in 1819–20 difficult to overcome. Certainly Martin Van Buren believed that the alarming crisis over the admission of Missouri arose because of the weakening of national party differences in the preceding years. As a consequence he determined to revive the old party of Jefferson, putting together a coalition of 'the planters of the South and the plain republicans of the North' that would mitigate the strong sectional antagonisms deriving from the crisis of the early 1820s. He was able to do so largely because, as in the 1790s, the ethnic and social divisions within the Middle states produced political allies and gave hope to the Southern minority. Thus in his first administration (1829–33) Andrew Jackson was able to lead a national coalition that brought Northern support for measures which were essentially designed to appease the South, and so ensured that South Carolina's challenge to the Union over the protective tariff in 1832–3 would receive little support in the rest of the South.[41]

Between 1827 and 1833 Jackson's Democrats and their National Republican opponents embraced strong regional feelings at their core, and it is questionable how far such a sectionally-based system of national partisanship would be able to construct effective compromises of sectional issues. After 1833, however, the pattern of party conflict changed significantly. As in the early 1800s, the Southern-centred party extended its support into New England, exploiting old political allegiances and new industrial grievances. More significantly, the South – for the first time in its history – divided within itself in federal politics. An opposition party appeared that by 1836 had created powerful bases in Georgia, Louisiana, North Carolina and Tennessee, and by 1839 had joined hands with the anti-Jacksonians in the North to form the new Whig party. As a consequence through the 1840s this so-called 'Second Party System' contradicted sectionalism: Southern politicians and voters preferred to cooperate with their party colleagues in other sections and struggled against party opponents in their own states and regions. Even state politics reflected national party divisons, and voting in Congress demonstrated that on all issues except those relating to slavery, national issues found supporters and opponents in all sections of the Union.[42]

Party politics ceased to reflect sectional tensions by the late 1830s because sectional differences were being overwhelmed by the common experience of economic change. Many groups in both North and South were benefiting from the growing commercialization of American life that the Whig party wished to sponsor further. Not just Northern businessmen but Southern planters recognized the role that banks were playing in making possible the extension of commercial agriculture and the servicing of internal and transatlantic trade. Farmers who saw canals and roads under construction that could take their produce to distant markets, allowing them to concentrate on growing cash crops and relieving their families of the manifold labours and deprivations of self-sufficiency, favoured the use of taxpayers' money to make such improvements possible. Others, in both North and South, perceived the

[24]   consequences of this so-called 'market revolution' as unacceptable, and preferred the cautious and restraining approach of the Democratic party. Artisans who found their economic autonomy undermined and their skills devalued
objected to the growth and competition of larger-scale industrial activity.
Labourers who were paid in rapidly depreciating bank notes complained of
cheating capitalists. Farmers who suffered from the competition of newly
opening areas or who were distant from the benefits of the extending market
system became strongly aware of the harmful social and moral effects of other
people's material progress. And the residual conservatism of isolated small
farmers was as powerful in Northern hills and Western prairies as in the piney
woods of the South.[43]

Underlying the party division therefore lay the simple fact that economic
change gave the various regions common experiences and made them more
interdependent. The Northwest became a food exporter and supplied the cities of the East as well as those parts of the South that were not self-sufficient
in food. The extension of cotton cultivation may have extended the peculiar
world of the slave plantation across the Deep South, but it also created commercial needs that were serviced by Northerners. As a result, leading Northern
businessmen endeavoured to prevent political conflict over slavery, recognizing the extent to which their business interests were involved in the provision of financial and marketing services to the cotton South. In return, the
larger planters appreciated that the extension of cotton manufacturing in New
England would extend the market for their ever-expanding staple production, and Southern Whigs in Congress in 1846 accordingly opposed the
reduction of tariff protection for manufacturers in 1846. Equally, Northern
Whigs appreciated the interest many Southerners, especially in Appalachian
areas, had in the distribution of the proceeds of federal land sales to help
finance state internal-improvement projects.[44]

Even as the sectional crisis rose to its crisis in the 1850s, economic developments served to underwrite the Union. In the Northeast industry grew without significant tariff protection, and the textile industry became well enough
established to have little need for protection against foreign manufactures
and, in the case of woollens, more concerned for keeping duties on their
imported raw materials as low as possible. The extension of commercial
agriculture in the West gave the Old Northwest the same outlook as most of
the Southern states – an interest in encouraging transatlantic trade and keeping trade barriers as low as possible. Heightening regional specialization
created mutual bonds that served to promote compromise as the crisis between North and South reached its height.[45]

The challenge of slavery, 1819–50

One sign of the strength of this Union was the effectiveness with which the main threat to its survival was handled. The house divided against itself did stand; a Union that was half slave, half free, did survive for seventy years. Between 1776 and 1804 Northerners abolished slavery in their own midst because the institution was immoral, had harmful effects on white society, and contradicted the principles upon which the republic was based. Many leading Southerners agreed, but recognized that the section's economic dependence on slavery and widespread fears of the consequences of releasing hordes of 'Africans' made emancipation impossible there. These severe differences over the future of slavery could be accommodated in 1787 by a federal structure that allowed states to determine the nature of their own internal institutions. As long as slavery could be regarded as a local and not a national problem, the federal government could ignore the question of its existence and instead simply focus on the practical consequences of slavery. Such issues as federal apportionment, the importation of slaves, and the return of fugitives were settled in 1787 and the arrangements made then duly honored in the following decades. Behind this sectional agreement lay not just a desire to create a republic for white men, but also the fact that many Northerners combined their antipathy for slavery with a conviction that Negroes were an inferior and dangerous people who must be restrained from polluting white society.[46]

The one issue that could not be handled with comparative ease was the question of slavery expansion. If slavery was an inherited, necessary evil, then its continuation where it already had some existence could be accepted, as in the Old Southwest in 1790 and the new state of Louisiana in 1812. In new areas where the republic could engrave its own features – as in the Old Northwest – most Northerners (and, initially, antislavery Southerners) assumed that freedom would reign. But when, in the case of Missouri in 1819, Northerners took this principle to mean that Congress could prevent a new state from choosing slavery for itself, Southerners recognized that this claim implicitly challenged the very constitutional right upon which the Southern states depended for their freedom from federal interference over slavery. The South's representatives successfully defended this point in 1820, but had to accept in return that slavery could not expand into the Louisiana Purchase north of 36° 30'. Thereafter Southerners were always conscious that, during the Missouri crisis, a Northern majority had clearly demonstrated its fundamental dislike of the institution of slavery.[47]

[26]   This new watchfulness accounts for the rapid shift of most Southerners to a states-rights outlook in the 1820s. Whereas the majority of Southern politicians had become increasingly nationalistic since 1801 and shared in the postwar consensus, they now adopted the standpoint of the Old-Republican strict constructionists, essentially as a weapon of sectional defence. They turned against the American System as much because it enhanced the power of the federal government as because of its economic effects, which in any case benefited some parts of the South. As some Old Republicans warned, the government that could dig a canal could also free a slave. Though the direct threat to slavery may seem minimal in the 1820s, the widespread dislike of slavery in the North was obvious and, as William Freehling has observed, the more sensitive of Southerners saw menaces where none was intended. Thereafter the South needed constant reassurance – and secured it after 1828 through the election of Jackson and the Democrats' commitment to giving the South every possible satisfaction.[48]

Ironically, the very strength of the Union brought on a greater crisis in the 1830s. The most committed antislavery men in the North began to argue that the existence of slavery anywhere in the nation stained the consciences of all truly Christian Americans, and therefore action must be taken immediately to end the sinful institution. Thus even Garrisonian abolitionists, who would later conspicuously place conscience before Union, conceived of North and South as being part of the same moral and political community. Moreover, improvements in the means of daily contact between the sections allowed these 'modern abolitionists' to bring their message home to the South by the circulation of antislavery materials through the mails. This challenge united the whole South against external interference, but a series of minor sectional compromises between 1835 and 1838 – one, for example, tacitly allowed local postmasters to censor the mails – gave the South every reassurance that the federal government would not allow any Northern interference in the South's peculiar institution. The federal compromise over slavery could be reaffirmed in this way because many antislavery Northerners were unwilling to embrace an extremist crusade that not only risked driving the South out of the Union, but also threatened to introduce racial equality and a horde of northward-moving freed blacks.[49]

As a result, even in the 1830s and early 1840s politicians and voters behaved as though they belonged to a national political community. The willingness of the North to reject the abolitionists made possible the internal division of the South and the operation of the nationally focused Second Party System. When Texas won its independence from Mexico in 1836, the primary concern of presidents and Congress was to prevent its request for annexation from disrupting national (and party) unity. When President Tyler in 1843 decided to pitch his campaign for reelection on an expansionist platform, he appealed to pent-up Southern frustration over Texas and anxiety about apparent abolitionist successes in the courts and churches. Finding their Southern support attracted to Tyler's campaign, the Democratic party took up the cause of Manifest Destiny, but handled the Texas issue as essentially a matter of national security, with Democrats all over the Union seeing expansion as an American rather than a purely Southern cause.[50]

The subsequent war with Mexico and the acquisition of a new empire in the south-west in 1848 raised once more the very issues that had been so threatening in the Missouri crisis. The South remained as concerned as ever to preserve its system of racial control and labour exploitation, while even antiabolitionist Northerners opposed the extension of slavery into areas where slavery had been banned before American acquisition. On this question no lasting compromise could be found, yet in 1850 national sentiment proved strong enough to find one on the basis of leaving the issue to the people who actually settled each of the newly acquired territories. Thus many Northerners conceded the possibility of slavery expansion, on two spurious assumptions: firstly, that the South wanted only the nominal right to expand slavery rather than its actual expansion, and, secondly, that slavery could not in fact expand into a climate hostile to staple production. North and South had found another compromise over slavery, but the long, bitter argument over slavery expansion in the late 1840s had driven the two sections apart and forced them to take up hostile positions in which each section began to define its own essence and virtue in contradistinction to the other.[51]

Sectional nationalisms

The development of sectional nationalisms had proved extraordinarily difficult before 1846. The Missouri crisis had heightened the historic sense of New England distinctiveness and moral superiority, and commentators in the 1820s began to speak of the 'universal Yankee nation' that was spreading from the north-east westwards into New York and Ohio. But most other Northerners, including religious dissenters of New England origin, could not accept Yankee cultural hegemony and there was little evidence of a distinctive Northern nationalism before the 1850s.[52] Similarly, the parallel

[28] sense of Southern nationalism gained its first formal articulations in the South Carolina upcountry in the 1830s, but it did not reflect the reality of Southern sentiment, for the South continued to share many loyalties – partisan, religious, associational, commercial and familial – with residents of the free states. Moreover, the South was culturally and economically less distinct from the North than Southern nationalists claimed. Indeed, their abortive attempts late in the antebellum period to create a separate Southern culture, Southern economic independence, a Southern literature, were all tacit acknowledgements that in reality Southerners – like New Englanders – continued to be part of the rich tapestry of American national life.[53]

Though some sense of Southern distinctiveness existed from before the Revolution, for most Southerners allegiance to the South did not contradict allegiance to the Union – any more than the sense of American distinctiveness had contradicted loyalty to Britain before 1763. Even in independent Texas, between 1836 and 1845, the Fourth of July had been celebrated along with the anniversary of San Jacinto, since the sense of Texan nationality never excluded affection for the American Union.[54] Before Southerners could think of creating a separate nation they had to go through a process akin to that of 1763–76: their commitment to Southernism *and* Americanism had to be transformed into the sense that non-Southerners were twisting Americanism into something that contradicted traditional shared values. Undeniably, that sense of revulsion accelerated in the crisis of the late 1840s, as Virginia demonstrated in 1849 when it repealed the oath of loyalty to the United States customarily required of state office holders. Yet most Southerners hesitated and continued to cling to the Union in 1850, despite all the warnings of Southern nationalists and proslavery radicals.

Through the 1850s many Southerners continued to work within the federal system to achieve their ends. As the Democratic party became the main vehicle through which the majority of Southerners expressed their political aspirations after 1850, so they were able to command the party that automatically became the majority party nationally. Secure in their influence over presidents Franklin Pierce and James Buchanan, they were able to ensure that federal power was used only in ways that were acceptable to the South. They pressed for foreign policies that might gain more slave territory and so maintain the number of slave states in the Union. They actually opened to slavery territories like Kansas that had long been guaranteed free soil, and prevented the exercise in the territories of federal powers that had been commonplace in the Union's Western empire of 1787–1848. The only positive uses of federal power most Southerners now favoured concerned the protection of slavery, as they insisted on the execution of the arbitrary Fugitive Slave Act of 1850 and finally, in 1860, demanded that Congress impose a slave code on the territories.[55]

The South's ability to dictate federal policy derived from the usual divisions within Northern society and politics. Indeed, in a real sense, the North had never existed: the various distinctive regions north of the Mason-Dixon line and the Ohio River were united by little beyond their economic interconnections, their partisan ties, and their common commitment to the Union. The term, 'the North', had been imprecise and was often used – even as late as 1844 – simply for New England.[56] But when Southerners ripped up the Missouri compromise in 1854 and seemed determined to impose proslavery policies on the Union, they prompted the creation and electoral growth of a purely Northern political party – the Republicans – that reflected not the tradition of sectional compromise but the defence of non-Southern interests. In the process, Northerners began to create an ideology that projected a clear idea of what a nation uncorrupted by the 'Slave Power' should be and should do.[57]

The Republicans were able to become the official spokesmen for a Northern version of American nationalism because Southern leaders in Washington rejected policies that had won the Democratic party support in the North in the past. Thus Southerners enabled the Republican party to broaden its policy stance from its original single issue – the exclusion of slavery from the Far West by congressional law – and embrace the idea that the federal government must be freed from the denying hand of Southern negativity. In particular, Southern politicians were preventing the federal government from taking practical steps to alleviate the North's economic difficulties following the Panic of 1857. The Secretary of the Treasury, Howell Cobb of Georgia, refused to ease the financial situation by using the monetary instruments that his predecessors had developed. The recession hit the iron and coal industries in Pennsylvania, New Jersey and southern Ohio especially hard, largely, it was claimed, because Congress had reduced the tariff to its lowest levels early in 1857, but the Southern Democrats refused to restore even the modest level of incidental protection available between 1846 and 1857. Southerners also persuaded the president, in 1859 and 1860, to veto measures that might speed up the settlement of the territories, even though until recently many Southerners had been willing to support federal financing of internal improvements or the granting of western lands to actual settlers on generous terms. Similarly, the proposal that federal aid for higher education should be granted to all states in the form of land grants was vetoed by President Buchanan after

[30]   it passed Congress. Hence the Republican party could begin to demand that
the federal government, once freed of corrupting influences, should take positive action to assist economic recovery and progress; in the process it shifted
the focus of Northern politics from the future of slavery to the preservation of
free labour, and so broadened its appeal to ordinary Northern farmers and
working men. As a result, the Republicans achieved in 1860 what had hitherto been impossible – a landslide in the Northern states alone, sufficient to
win them federal power.[58]

The war would demonstrate that the rebels' emerging spirit of Confeder-
Almost inevitably, therefore, the accession to power by the Republicans
was bound to see an assertion of federal power, a return to active government, such as the national Whig party had demanded before 1854 and the
South had prevented since. It was this threatened restoration of federal
authority by men they could no longer trust – and who owed nothing to
Southern votes – that persuaded the South to carry out what James McPherson
has called a 'preemptive counter-revolution'; hysterical with fear that Northern meddling with slavery might upset their system of racial control, they
determined to secede from a Union that the 'Black' Republicans were about
to command. The creation of the Confederacy in 1861 showed not that a
sense of Southern nationhood already existed, but that many Southerners
desired independence from external threats. Unlike their fathers in 1776,
the various states seceded individually, not as part of a consciously nascent
nation, and piecemeal raked together their Confederacy as an aftermath. The
best they could do was to copy, with extra protection for slavery, the only
Union they had known and revered.[59]

The war would demonstrate that the rebels' emerging spirit of Confederate nationalism lacked the long-established emotional roots that held the Union
side together. In the course of the struggle the sense of exclusive Southern
nationality would grow, forced on by the experience and necessities of the
war, and yet Southerners would accept forced reunification with remarkable
ease after 1865. As Kenneth Stampp has commented, Reconstruction would
show that most Southerners could accept the restoration of the Union but
not federal intrusion in its internal race relations.[60] However, in seceding, the
Confederacy had deprived itself of the constitutional and political protections that slaveholders enjoyed within the old Union, and the war had seen
the Union strengthened – at least temporarily – in ways they could not have
foreseen in their worst nightmares. The victorious North now insistently re-
created the American nation according to the image it had evolved of a Union
without slavery in the years immediately before the war, while the revolutionary experience of the war transformed American nationalism: it now

developed – at least for the time being – the sense of a unitary nation, directed   [31]
by a central democratic government that would turn national ideals into
conscious reality.[61]

The antebellum Union had survived so long because of the immense
emotional and practical investment that Americans had made in it. Each year
they reenacted the Declaration of Independence and revered the founders of
the republic. They constantly debated the meaning of the Union, its character and its limits; and while they disagreed, they nearly always assumed the
desirability of its continuance. A tradition of constitutional Unionism developed that made compromise a good in itself, an expression of the highest values
of the nation.[62] And when the price of adhering to that Union became too
great for the majority of Southerners in 1860–1, Americans elsewhere – and
many Southerners – believed that they had no choice but to fight for the
preservation of the Union and the flag that symbolized it. Their persistence
and self-sacrifice in the face of disaster, death and destruction proved once
more how truly and profoundly attached and committed Americans were to
the national (if decentralized) existence they had come to prize long before
the Civil War.

Notes

1. This chapter has been stimulated by years of discussion with Peter Parish,
    whose lectures and writings on American nationalism and the antebellum
    Union I have learned much from, and yet I still find myself stubbornly in dis-
    agreement with him. I am grateful both to him and to the editors for their help-
    ful comments on (and continuing dissent from) my argument. May the debate
    continue! See especially Peter J. Parish, 'An exception to most of the rules: what
    made American nationalism different in the mid-nineteenth century?' *Prologue*
    27 (1995), pp. 219–30; 'A talent for survival: federalism in the age of the civil
    war', *Historical Research* 62 (1989), pp. 178–92; and (with rather less disagree-
    ment on my part) 'American nationalism and the nineteenth-century con-
    stitution' in Joseph Smith (ed.), *The American Constitution: The First Two Hundred
    Years* (Exeter, 1988), pp. 63–82; Brian Holden Reid, *The Origins of the American
    Civil War* (London, 1996), esp. pp. 35–42; Susan-Mary Grant, 'Nationalism'
    in Peter J. Parish (ed.), *Reader's Guide to American History* (Chicago, 1997),
    pp. 478–81.

    The weakness of the Union before 1860 is emphasized by, among others,
    James Stirling Young, *The Washington Community, 1800–1828* (New York,

1966); Robert H. Wiebe, *The Opening of American Society: From the Adoption of the Constitution to the Eve of Disunion* (New York, 1984); Richard P. McCormick, 'The Jacksonian strategy', *Journal of the Early Republic* 10 (1990), pp. 1–17, esp. 2–5. Liah Greenfeld, *Nationalism: Five Roads to Modernity* (Cambridge, Mass., 1992), pp. 399–484, assumes the weakness of the Union while providing evidence to the contrary.

The war's impact is emphasized in Allan Nevins, *The War for the Union*, 4 vols (New York, 1959–71); James M. McPherson, *Battle Cry of Freedom: The Civil War Era* (New York and Oxford, 1988); Richard Franklin Bensel, *Yankee Leviathan: The Origins of Central State Authority in America, 1859–1877* (Cambridge and New York, 1990). For a judicious discussion of the war's impact on the state of the Union, see Peter J. Parish, *The American Civil War* (London, 1975), esp. pp. 378–80, 630, 637–42.

2. Carl Bridenbaugh, *The Spirit of 1776: The Growth of American Patriotism Before Independence, 1607–1776* (New York and Oxford, 1975); Richard L. Merritt, *Symbols of American Community, 1735–1775* (New Haven, Conn., 1966).

3. Linda Colley, *Britons: Forging the Nation, 1707–1837* (New Haven, Conn., 1992); Winthrop D. Jordan, *White Over Black: American Attitudes toward the Negro, 1550–1812* (Chapel Hill, NC, 1968). On the Anglicization of the colonies, see Jack P. Greene and J.R. Pole (eds), *Colonial British America: Essays in the New History of the Early Modern Era* (Baltimore, Md, 1984).

4. Merritt, *Symbols of American Community*, p. 182. See also Pauline Maier, *From Resistance to Revolution: Colonial Radicals and the Development of American Opposition to Britain, 1763–1776* (London, 1973); Ann Fairfax Withington, *Toward a More Perfect Union: Virtue and the Formation of American Republics* (New York and Oxford, 1991), esp. pp. 18–19, and Greenfeld, *Nationalism*, pp. 399–422.

5. Edmund S. Morgan, *Inventing the People: The Rise of Popular Sovereignty in England and America* (New York, 1988); David Waldstreicher, *In the Midst of Perpetual Fetes: The Making of American Nationalism, 1776–1820* (Chapel Hill, NC, 1997), quotation p. 112. Benedict Anderson's influential *Imagined Communities: Reflections on the Origin and Spread of Nationalism* (London, 1983) does not directly discuss the United States, but before 1820 it fits very closely his category of 'popular linguistic-nationalisms'.

6. Merrill Jensen, *The Founding of a Nation: A History of the American Revolution, 1763–1776* (New York and Oxford, 1963), pp. 679–81; Richard B. Morris, *The Forging of the Union, 1781–1789* (New York, 1987), pp. 55–76.

7. John Shy, *A People Numerous and Armed: Reflections on the Military Struggle for American Independence* (New York and Oxford, 1976); Charles Royster, 'Founding a nation in blood: military conflict and American nationality' in Ronald

Hoffman and Peter J. Albert (eds), *Arms and Independence: The Military Character* [33]
of the American Revolution (Charlottesville, Va, 1984), pp. 25–49; Edwin
J. Perkins, *American Public Finance and Financial Services, 1700–1815* (Columbus,
O, 1994), pp. 213–15.

8. Leonard W. Levy (ed.), *Essays on the Making of the Constitution* (1969; 2nd edn,
Oxford, 1987), p. 108. See also Robert A. Rutland, *Ordeal of the Constitution:
the Antifederalists and the Ratification Struggle of 1787–1788* (Norman, Oa,
1966).

9. John M. Murrin, 'A roof without walls: the dilemma of American national iden-
tity' in Richard Beeman, Stephen Botein, and Edward C. Carter II (eds), *Beyond
Confederation: Origins of the Constitution and American National Identity* (Chapel
Hill, NC, 1987), pp. 333–48 (quotation, p. 344). Incidentally, why 'artificial'?
And why, if unexpected and impromptu, '*therefore* extremely fragile'? *The
Federalist Papers* are available in Penguin Classics, edited by Isaac Kramnick
(Harmondsworth, 1987).

10. Patrick T. Conley and John P. Kaminski (eds), *The Constitution and the States: The
Role of the Original Thirteen in the Framing and Adoption of the Federal Constitution*
(Madison, Wisc., 1988), pp. 186–98; Steven R. Boyd, *The Politics of Opposition:
Antifederalists and the Acceptance of the Constitution* (Millwood, NY, 1979);
Richard Ellis, 'The persistence of Antifederalism after 1789' in Beeman, Botein
and Carter (eds), *Beyond Confederation*, pp. 295–314.

11. Holden Reid, *Origins of American Civil War*, pp. 199, 234, 305.

12. The sectional basis of the parties is emphasized in James Roger Sharp, *American
Politics in the Early Republic: the New Nation in Crisis* (New Haven, Conn., 1993).

13. Thomas P. Slaughter, *The Whiskey Rebellion: Frontier Epilogue to the American
Revolution* (Oxford, 1986); Francis Philbrick, *The Rise of the West, 1754–1830*
(New York, 1965), esp. pp. 234–52.

14. Adrienne Koch, *Jefferson and Madison: The Great Collaboration* (New York and
Oxford, 1950), pp. 174–260; William N. Chambers, *Political Parties in a New
Nation: The American Experience, 1776–1809* (New York, 1963).

15. James M. Banner, Jr., *To the Hartford Convention: The Federalists and the Origins of
Party Politics, 1789–1815* (New York, 1970), pp. 84–121, 294–350 (quotation, p. 333).

16. David Hackett Fischer, *The Revolution of American Conservatism: The Federalist
Party in the Era of Jeffersonian Democracy* (New York, 1965); Banner, *To the
Hartford Convention*, pp. 294–350; W.A. Robinson, *Jeffersonian Democracy in
New England* (New Haven, Conn., 1916).

[34] 17. Waldstreicher, *Perpetual Fetes*, pp. 177–245. Integrative effects of political parties are discussed in William N. Chambers, 'Parties and nation-building in America' in Joseph G. LaPalombara and Myron Weiner (eds), *Political Parties and Political Development* (Princeton, NJ, 1969), pp. 79–106. For the national focus of politics, the reality of mass parties, and the extent of popular participation in this period, see Donald J. Ratcliffe, *Party Spirit in a Frontier Republic: Democratic Politics in Ohio, 1793–1821* (Columbus, Oh, 1998).

18. Maldwyn A. Jones, *American Immigration* (Chicago, 1960), pp. 75–9; Donald G. Mathews, 'The Second Great Awakening as an organizing process, 1780–1830', *American Quarterly* 21 (1969), pp. 23–43.

19. Robert A. East, 'Economic development and New England Federalism, 1803–14', *New England Quarterly* 10 (1937), pp. 430–46. See also Curtis P. Nettels, *The Emergence of a National Economy, 1775–1815* (New York, 1962).

20. Frederick Marks, *Independence on Trial: Foreign Affairs and the Making of the Constitution* (Wilmington, Del., 1986); A.E. Campbell, 'An excess of isolation: isolation and the American civil war', *Journal of Southern History* 29 (1963), pp. 161–74.

21. This view comports with that of older historians, for example, Merle Curti, *The Roots of American Loyalty* (New York, 1946).

22. Stanley M. Elkins and Eric L. McKitrick, *The Age of Federalism, 1789–1801* (New York and Oxford, 1993); Slaughter, *Whiskey Rebellion*, pp. 190–221; Dall W. Forsythe, *Taxation and Political Change in the New Nation, 1781–1833* (New York, 1977), pp. 51–7.

23. Leonard W. Levy, *Jefferson and Civil Liberties: The Darker Side* (Cambridge, Mass., 1963), pp. 114–20, 137–40.

24. Fred Somkin, *Unquiet Eagle: Memory and Desire in the Idea of American Freedom, 1815–1860* (Ithaca, NY, 1967); Paul C. Nagel, *One Nation Indivisible: The Union in American Thought, 1776–1861* (New York and Oxford, 1964) and *This Sacred Trust: American Nationality, 1798–1898* (New York and Oxford, 1971).

25. George Dangerfield, *The Era of Good Feelings* (New York, 1952) and *The Awakening of American Nationalism, 1815–1828* (New York, 1965).

26. Ibid.; Charles S. Sydnor, *Development of Southern Sectionalism, 1819–1848* (Baton Rouge, La, 1948); William W. Freehling, *Prelude to Civil War: The Nullification Movement in South Carolina, 1816–1836* (New York, 1966); Norman K. Risjord, *The Old Republicans: Southern Conservatism in the Age of Jefferson* (New York, 1965).

27. Alexis de Tocqueville, *Democracy in America* (1835, 1840), edited by Phillips Bradley (New York, 1945), vol. 1, p. 432. Though Tocqueville was pessimistic

about the future of the Union, he acknowledged its strengths and recognized
that the Americans 'still constitute a single people . . . united by . . . common
opinions.' Ibid., pp. 398–433 (quotation, pp. 409–10).

28. McCormick, 'The Jacksonian strategy' esp. pp. 9–12; Kenneth M. Stampp,
'The concept of a perpetual Union' in Stampp, *The Imperiled Union: Essays on the
Background of the Civil War* (Oxford, 1980), pp. 3–36. The idea that the Union
was indissoluble had been implicit long before 1832, as, for example, in the
outlook of Northern Democratic Republicans during the Missouri crisis;
see Major L. Wilson, *Space, Time, and Freedom: The Quest for Nationality and the
Irrepressible Conflict, 1815–1861* (Westport, Conn., 1974), pp. 46–7. For the
continuing constitutional strength of the Union, even with a Supreme Court
that was dominated after 1837 by Jackson's states-rights appointees, see
Harold M. Hyman and William W. Wiecek, *Equal Justice Under the Law: Constitutional Development, 1835–1875* (New York, 1982), pp. 8–19, 55–85.

29. John Murrin, 'The great inversion, or Court versus Country: a comparison of
the Revolution settlements in England (1688–1721) and America (1776–
1816)' in J.G.A. Pocock (ed.), *Three English Revolutions, 1641, 1688, 1776*
(Princeton, NJ, 1980), p. 425. Parish, 'A Talent for Survival', pp. 179–84,
exaggerates the inactivity of the antebellum federal government.

30. Richard H. Kohn, *The Eagle and the Sword: The Federalists and the Creation of
the Military Establishment in America, 1783–1802* (New York, 1975); Theodore
J. Crackel, *Mr Jefferson's Army: Political and Social Reform of the Military Establishment, 1801–1809* (New York, 1987); Daniel J. Elazar, *The American Partnership:
Intergovernmental Co-operation in the Nineteenth-Century United States* (Chicago,
1962); and Merritt Roe Smith, *Harpers Ferry Armory and the New Technology*
(Ithaca, NY, 1977).

31. Richard R. John, *Spreading the News: The American Postal System from Franklin to
Morse* (Cambridge, Mass., 1995).

32. F.W. Taussig, *The Tariff History of the United States* (New York, 1905), pp. 68–154.

33. Elazar, *American Partnership*, pp. 31–2, 71–3, 88, 100–9, 200–9; Paul
Studenski and Herman E. Kroos, *Financial History of the United States* (1952; 2nd
edn, New York, 1963), pp. 56–9, 99–102; Reginald C. McGrane, *Foreign
Bondholders and American State Debts* (New York, 1935).

34. Bray Hammond, *Banks and Politics in America, from the Revolution to the Civil War*
(Princeton, NJ, 1957); Jean Wilburn, *Biddle's Bank: The Crucial Years* (New York,
1967); John M. McFaul, *The Politics of Jacksonian Finance* (Ithaca, NY, 1972);
Richard H. Timberlake, *The Origins of Central Banking in the United States* (Cambridge, Mass., 1978).

[36]   35. Anthony F.C. Wallace, *The Long, Bitter Trail: Andrew Jackson and the Indians* (New York, 1993), p. 4.; Ronald N. Satz, *American Indian Policy in the Jacksonian Era* (Lincoln, Neb., 1975).

36. Jack F. Eblen, *The First and Second United States Empires: Governors and Territorial Government, 1784–1912* (Pittsburgh, 1968).

37. Benjamin H. Hibbard, *A History of the Public Land Policies* (New York, 1939); Elazar, *American Partnership*, esp. pp. 131–9, 207–22.

38. Malcolm J. Rohrbough, *The Land Office Business: The Settlement and Administration of American Public Lands, 1789–1837* (Oxford, 1968); Daniel Feller, *The Public Lands in Jacksonian Politics* (Madison, Wisc., 1984); Hibbard, *Public Land Policies*, esp. pp. 181–96; Kenneth C. Martis, *The Historical Atlas of United States Congressional Districts, 1789–1983* (New York, 1982), p. 23.

39. Carter Goodrich, *Government Promotion of American Canals and Railroads, 1800–1890* (New York, 1960); Philip D. Jordan, *The National Road* (Indianapolis, 1948); Elazar, *American Partnership*, pp. 1–69, 131–43, 265–9.

40. Rohrbough, *Land Office Business*; John, *Spreading the News*; Satz, *Jacksonian Indian Policy*.

41. Richard H. Brown, 'The Missouri crisis, slavery, and the politics of Jacksonianism', *South Atlantic Quarterly* 65 (1966), pp. 55–72.

42. Charles G. Sellers, 'Who were the Southern Whigs?' *American Historical Review* 59 (1954), pp. 335–46; Richard P. McCormick, *The Second American Party System: Party Formation in the Jacksonian Era* (Chapel Hill, NC, 1966); Joel H. Silbey, *The Shrine of Party: Congressional Voting Behavior, 1841–1852* (Pittsburgh, Pa, 1967) and *The Partisan Imperative: The Dynamics of American Politics Before the Civil War* (New York and Oxford, 1985); Michael F. Holt, *The Political Crisis of the 1850s* (New York, 1978), esp. pp. 17–38.

43. Harry L. Watson, *Liberty and Power: The Politics of Jacksonian America* (New York, 1990); Charles Sellers, *The Market Revolution: Jacksonian America, 1815–1846* (New York, 1991); Donald J. Ratcliffe, 'The crisis of commercialization: national political alignments and the market revolution, 1819–1844' in Melvyn Stokes and Stephen Conway (eds), *The 'Market Revolution' in America: Politics, Religion, and Society, 1800–1880* (Charlottesville, Va, 1996), pp. 177–201.

44. Douglass C. North, *Economic Growth of the United States, 1790–1860* (New York, 1961); Silbey, *Shrine of Party*.

45. Stanley Coben, 'Northeastern business and Radical Reconstruction: a re-examination', *Mississippi Valley Historical Review*, 46 (1959), 67–90; Philip S. Foner,

Business and Slavery: New York Merchants and the Irrepressible Conflict (Chapel Hill,
NC, 1941); James L. Huston, *The Panic of 1857 and the Coming of the Civil War*
(Baton Rouge, La, 1987).

46. Donald L. Robinson, *Slavery in the Structure of American Politics, 1765–1820*
(New York, 1971); Jordan, *White Over Black*.

47. Robinson, *Slavery in the Structure of American Politics*; Glover Moore, *The Missouri
Controversy* (Lexington, Ky, 1953). Too many historians, including Moore,
underestimate the power of Northern antislavery sentiment – conservative and
racist as it was – before 1830; see Ratcliffe, *Party Spirit*, pp. 47, 69–71, 231–4.

48. Risjord, *Old Republicans*, esp. p. 242; Brown, 'Missouri crisis, slavery, and
politics of Jacksonianism'; Freehling, *Prelude to Civil War*.

49. John, *Spreading the News*, pp. 257–80; Lorman Ratner, *Powder Keg: Northern
Opposition to the Antislavery Movement, 1831–1840* (New York, 1968).

50. James C.N. Paul, *Rift in the Democracy* (Philadelphia, 1951); Holt, *Political Crisis*,
pp. 39–66.

51. David M. Potter, *The Impending Crisis, 1848–1861* (New York, 1976).

52. Shaw Livermore, *The Twilight of Federalism, 1815–1830* (Princeton, NJ, 1967),
pp. 95–7. The term 'yankee' properly referred to people from New England.

53. John McCardell, *The Idea of a Southern Nation: Southern Nationalists and Southern
Nationalism* (New York, 1979); David M. Potter, 'The historian's use of nation-
alism, and vice versa' in Potter, *The South and the Sectional Conflict* (Baton Rouge,
La, 1968), esp. pp. 60–83.

54. Mark E. Nackman, *The Rise of Texas Nationalism: A Nation Within a Nation* (Port
Washington, NY, 1975), esp. p. 149, n. 26.

55. Holden Reid, *Origins of American Civil War*, pp. 158–65, 180–1, 192–3, 203–
14, 228–31, and references therein.

56. Robert V. Remini, *Daniel Webster: The Man and His Times* (New York, 1998),
pp. 596–7.

57. Ibid., pp. 131–47, 157–70, 175, 179–87; Susan-Mary Grant, 'Representat-
ive Mann: Horace Mann, the Republican experiment and the South', *Journal of
American Studies* 32 (1998), pp. 105–23. See also Eric Foner, *Free Soil, Free Labor,
Free Men: The Ideology of the Republican Party Before the Civil War* (New York and
Oxford, 1970); Susan-Mary Grant, 'When is a nation not a nation? The crisis of
American nationality in the mid-nineteenth century', *Nations and Nationalism* 2
(1996), pp. 105–29.

[38]   58. Holden Reid, *Origins of American Civil War*, pp. 170–4, 214–20, 238–9, and the references therein. See also Timberlake, *Origins of Central Banking*, p. 82; Elazar, *American Partnership*, pp. 221–2.

59. McPherson, *Battle Cry of Freedom*, p. 245; Holden Reid, *Origins of American Civil War*, pp. 234, 240–4, 267–78, 297–9, 310–11, 348–63; Peter J. Parish, 'The road not quite taken: The constitution of the Confederate States of America' in Thomas J. Barron, Owen Dudley Edwards and Patricia J. Storey (eds), *Constitutions and National Identity* (Edinburgh, 1993), pp. 11–25.

60. Emory M. Thomas, *The Confederate Nation: 1861–1865* (New York, 1979); Kenneth M. Stampp, 'The Southern road to Appomattox' in Stampp, *Imperiled Union*, pp. 246–69.

61. Susan-Mary Grant, 'The charter of its birthright': the Civil War and American nationalism', *Nations and Nationalism* 4 (1998), pp. 163–85, and references therein.

62. Nagel, *One Nation Indivisible*; Peter Knupfer, *The Union As It Is: Constitutional Unionism and Sectional Compromise* (Chapel Hill, NC, 1991).

CHAPTER TWO

SOUTHERN SECESSION IN 1860–1

BRUCE COLLINS

P eter Parish once recalled having given a lecture offering an analysis, nuanced and sophisticated as one would expect, of four major inter-pretations of a particular historical event. At the end of the lecture a student asked, 'But which one is the right one?' This has always been the dilemma for scholars of the coming of the Civil War and more precisely of its main pre-cipitating event, the coming of secession in the South during the winter of 1860–1. It is sometimes easier to say where interpretations are wrong than where a particular interpretation is wholly right. The historian is classically engaged in the perennial dilemma of trying to reconcile long-term historical developments with precise political decisions. Some of the most recent general interpretations of the period continue to highlight this fundamental dilemma. John Ashworth, in a monumental work of which the first volume has so far appeared, provides an excellent example of the highly structured workings of long-term economic and social factors in his analysis of the com-ing of confrontation between the two sections.[1] On the other side James McPherson, in his trenchant and highly successful re-assessment of the mid-nineteenth century and the Civil War in particular, argues repeatedly for the importance of contingency.[2] In this chapter I would like to examine a particular theme central to an understanding of secession and consider how recent works have illuminated and clouded it.

Nearly one hundred years ago the Southern white historian Ulrich B. Phillips wrote of Georgia's experience of secession, 'It is not easy to deter-mine whether the policy of secession was radical or conservative. Its advo-cates as well as its opponents claim the quality of conservatism for their respective causes, and each party had some ground to their contention.'[3] In considering the nature of secession we have to distinguish between the political actions adopted during the winter of 1860–1 and the longer-term social and cultural values which those who took those political actions

[40] embraced. One initial interpretative dilemma is how far we assume that those involved in Southern political decision-making (as legislators, party leaders, or voters) understood, and agreed in their understanding, Lincoln's analysis of the long-term future of the United States as being ultimately wholly free or wholly slave and viewed the Republican party as representing a policy and inclination which would put slavery on the road to ultimate extinction. If there was widespread understanding of these Republican positions, then those espousing secession would have been social conservatives and those opposing secession would have in effect been endorsing a potentially radical change in the structure of the existing slave-based Southern society. While this chapter will return to this particular theme, its initial focus will be on the narrower question of whether politicians were conservative or radical in the immediate political context of 1860–1.

Conservatives or radicals?

In the last few decades the view that secession was a conservative act by establishment politicians has been most clearly put by Michael P. Johnson in a case study of Georgia. He argues that a new state constitution drawn up by the secessionist convention in March 1861 revealed the ultimate intentions of those who had embraced secession. Various specific acts taken to revise the constitution of Georgia showed, in his analysis, that the leading secessionist politicians sought to entrench the slaveholders' political power within the state. Secession and subsequent constitutional change amounted to an intentional 'double revolution'. As Johnson emphasizes, 'without the second half of the revolution, the first had little meaning as some conservatives had long understood and some enthusiastic secessionists were beginning to recognize.' The concern which lay behind this desire on the part of the slaveholding elite to entrench their political power following their departure from the Union arose from a widespread fear among slaveholders that non-slaveholders would increasingly oppose slavery once an administration took office in Washington which was itself against slavery extension and highly critical of the institution.[4] To sustain this analysis that secession was a reactionary conservative movement clearly requires evidence to show that this fear was widespread among the slaveholding political elite and that there was indeed a substantial threat from non-slaveholders dissatisfied with or even opposed to the continued existing of the institution of slavery. A great

deal of work has been done by historians to substantiate these claims. The
argument that there was indeed widespread anxiety and dissatisfaction
with slavery from the 1830s – which in itself galvanized a small minority of
dedicated proslavery politicians and publicists to stifle such growing sentiments – is the theme of William Freehling's emerging magnum opus, of
which the first volume has appeared.[5]

A second and wholly different view of the coming of secession derives
from an analysis of the dynamics of what recently historians have called the
politics of slavery. Since any political system is a highly competitive one in
which the pursuit of prominence, position and place provides a powerful,
and sometimes overwhelming, motive force, much of what happened in 1860–1
is explained through the dynamics of political competition. In any political
environment, those who are out of office seek to pursue office for its own
sake. This is done both through formal opposition parties and through the
competition for leadership and influence within a party in power. Given the
relative weakness of formal opposition parties in the deep South, which led
secession in 1860–1, much of the cutting edge of driving political ambition
came from within the ruling Democratic party. As national slavery issues
had dominated political rhetoric and debate in the Southern states during the
1850s, it followed that the quest for office would hinge on playing up themes
and rivalries which revolved around the defence of slavery in the national
political arena. Once national sectional rivalries over slavery extension
exploded into prominence after 1854, competition within the Southern Democratic party concentrated essentially on where individual politicians and their
supporters placed themselves on the spectrum of arguments and assertions
concerning the appropriate defence of the institution of slavery within the
United States. It has long been argued, as for example by Horace Montgomery
in 1950 in analysing the secession convention in Georgia, that the secessionist political process 'was from its inception in the control of the extremists'.[6]
This is, of course, a highly convenient argument for more restrained Southerners to put concerning their own past; the unpleasant initiative in driving
the South to the most extreme defence of slavery is conveniently attributed to
Southerners of the least politically or emotionally admirable character. Clement
Eaton in 1961 portrayed the planters as moulding their lives on the model of
the English gentry but failing to engage in debate about the South's political
and social future in a sufficiently open-minded manner. A Whiggish belief
in 'orderly progress' and scorn for pro-slavery extremists, as well as abolitionists, had become 'overwhelmed during the emotional crisis that preceded
the Civil War'.[7] Michael Holt described the period after November 1860 as

[42] one in which the 'radicals orchestrated a powerful campaign of propaganda and pressure'. They flourished because of the particular state of public opinion which gripped the lower South during 1860. Allan Nevins had argued that much of the lower South experienced a 'frenzy of excitement', with South Carolina being 'like a bed of charcoal suddenly leaping into flames'. Holt describes 'the frenzy that characterized the deep South after Lincoln's election' while David Potter and Don E. Fehrenbacher remarked that 'all of the States were acting in an atmosphere of excitement approaching hysteria'. In these circumstances, William J. Cooper has seen the operation of secession as the work of the more youthful radical politicians with the well established leaders of the lower South relegated to the back seat.[8]

The main thrust of both these approaches to understanding secession derives from an emphasis on the political reaction to the debates over slavery which had racked America during the 1850s. A third approach to an understanding of secession flows from an attempt to unravel the role played in those political events by longer-term structural economic changes that were affecting both North and South during the 1840s and 1850s. While no one nowadays subscribes to the view that somehow an industrial North confronted an agricultural South, there is widespread agreement that extensive industrialization and urbanization affecting the whole country in the mid-nineteenth century had profound implications for politics across all sections. Yet the precise workings of that impact, and the relationship between political developments and the spread of an industrializing economy have, predictably, been subject to widely differing interpretations.

One view, most elaborately advanced by J. Mills Thornton, holds that secession was enacted by radical politicians who sought to preserve the radical tradition associated with the purest form of Jacksonian Democracy. The social model advanced by the Jacksonians portrayed an ideal America as a society of independent farm owners and small-scale producers whose existence was hardly touched by government interference and whose earnings and livelihood were not sapped and exploited by unregulated banks or ruthless and corrupt business corporations. This radical ideal, which in many parts of the South during the 1840s seemed indeed to fit reality, no longer squared with the increasing pressures of commercialization during the 1850s. As a consequence younger radical politicians exploited the national debate over slavery extension to advance the cause of secession as a means of freeing the South from the main engine of industrial and commercial growth which was located in the North. But the crisis of modernization existed within the Southern states. The radicals' dynamic energy arose therefore partly in antithesis to

the political order of the Southern states individually, since the political
establishment condoned increasing commercial development in the 1850s.[9]
This argument thus combines an appreciation of the major economic changes
which affected America in the mid-nineteenth century with an analysis of
politics which is located in the individual Southern states. That analysis is
predicated upon the notion of intense internal competition for power rack-
ing a Democratic party which both embodied the radical Jacksonian tradition and yet formed the political establishment throughout the 1850s. If at
one level, this argument describes secession as being intended to conserve
the Southern way of life, at another level it depicts the force which divided
Southern politics in 1860 as a radical quest for the preservation of a past
golden age rather than a conservative accommodation to the South as it
existed.

The more deep-rooted variant on the assessment of the impact of economic
changes derives from the Marxian tradition. This claims that there were deep
sectional antagonisms flowing from wholly different economies, with the one
based on a system of slavery and the other based on a system of free labour.
Ultimately, for those writing in the Marxian tradition it was the slaveholding
class acting as a class which swept all before it in a decision, setting aside all
local and sub-regional differences, that strictly followed class interests.[10] The
most recent elaboration of this view argues that the Southern system, although
compatible with merchant capitalism, became increasingly incompatible with
the industrial capitalism of the North that emerged in the 1850s, and that
the slaveholding class, given the strength of their hegemonic power over the
non-slaveholding Southern whites, ensured the break-up of the Union.[11] In
one sense, therefore, the impact of economic developments has given rise
to one interpretation which portrays secession as a politically radical act. A
further interpretation is derived from Marx's contemporary writings which
depict secession as a conservative resistance to the dynamic changes brought
about through both the industrialization of the North and its agricultural
expansion into the mid-West.[12]

Underpinning much of this debate is a fundamental disagreement over the
nature of the political process and its relationship to the underlying structure
of white society in the mid-nineteenth century. One view has long been that
politics did not empower ordinary, poorer non-slaveowning whites to express
their true interests and sentiments. J. Morgan Kousser has emphasized,
'Repeated outbreaks of nonslaveowner and yeoman dissent from the 1830s
through the 1890s undermined the view that all white Southerners agreed
that the protection of slavery and white supremacy ought to be the constant

theme of politics.' Stephen Ash in a recent study has argued that during the war itself the arrival of the Union armies in central Tennessee unblocked 'the surging tide of militancy among poorer whites'; yet this tide rapidly receded owing to 'inertial forces among the poor whites themselves'.[13] Such inter-pretations have become increasingly powerful and important in the last forty years because they open lines of enquiry to a Southern past which is not bigoted, dominated by the values of a slaveholding elite, and racist in its defence of slavery and segregation. It is also important because it flows from the most powerful assumptions about the relationship between popular rule and war.

Americans have long adopted the ideas promulgated by Tom Paine – the great publicist of American rights in 1776 – in his later work, *The Rights of Man*. One of his central arguments was that monarchical governments made war not peoples. One reason for this was that monarchs and their courts did not bear the financial costs of wars and conquering expeditions, but instead loaded them on to their subjects, most recently, in the eighteenth century, through borrowings made possible by national debts. Paine argued that if those who paid for wars made the decisions concerning martial adventures then wars would cease to be an option. Countries with truly representative systems of government would never go to war with each other.[14] This pow-erful contention, so central to the making of the earlier American revolution against British rule, has remained a shaping consideration in American thinking and indeed democratic thinking ever since. If it remains axiomatic that demo-cratic peoples do not go to war with each other, it therefore follows that the secession crisis had to be produced by the actions of an anti-democratic elite. This was part of the dilemma raised by the coming of the Civil War in 1861. Lincoln, in July 1861, resolved the dilemma by underscoring the probability that in no state of the South did a majority of the qualified electorate seek secession, with the possible exception of South Carolina itself.[15] It became convenient for conservative-minded apologists for the old South to assert that secession was the handiwork of extremist radicals. And it has become important for those promoting racial integration and harmony in the last fifty years to argue that the political order of the 1850s was not founded upon genuinely widespread white consent. Yet the truth behind such a claim is extremely difficult to sustain given the facts that Southern states' voters tended to vote overwhelmingly in favour of Demo-cratic candidates and that Southern Democrats by 1860 had come to pro-mote secession.

Models of secession

Let us now turn to examine the three different models of secession as a conservative or radical revolution in turn.

First, the extent to which the Republican acquisition of power in Washington was seen as the precursor for the establishment of a Republican movement within the South itself has been exaggerated. The conservative reformers in Georgia, described by Michael P. Johnson, produced a new constitution for their state which cut the size of the state senate and made the judiciary appointive rather than elective. This was certainly a procedure which tended to the protection of slavery and other property rights. But, having made a case for the importance and sweeping nature of the constitutional changes produced in early 1861, Johnson then has a problem explaining how it was that the democratic electorate supported this new constitution which apparently went so flagrantly against their interests. Johnson's contention that the campaign mounted by the conservatives was a brilliant exercise in popular patriotism suggests if anything that the mass electorate were indifferent to the issue or incapable of understanding where their own best political interests lay.[16]

In fact, a more general point can be made that the issue of proto-Republicanism was very infrequently raised in the deep South in 1860-1. The fear may have been cited by secessionists, but it came low down the lists of secessionists' grievances and anxieties. The clearest statement that the Republicans in power in Washington would create a free labour party throughout the South within four years comes in a letter from Senator Robert Toombs to his fellow-Georgia politician, Alexander H. Stephens.[17] The latter was notably reluctant to join the secessionist camp, and argued against immediate secession in the late 1850s. Toombs was self-evidently trying to put the strongest possible pressure on his prominent colleague; he had already concluded that the Union would have to end if the Republicans captured the White House in 1860. This argument followed his own decision for secession and did not contribute to that earlier decision. Moreover, a collection of speeches delivered from 12 to 19 November in Georgia – including addresses by Thomas R.R. Cobb and Robert Toombs, who were leading secessionists – makes no reference to a Republican threat to internal Southern politics; the danger postulated was from federal government interference.[18] Nor did the South's subsequent experience suggest much basis for any internal threat from potential Republicans.

[46]   During the war, poorer whites expressed resentment against major slave-owners and their pretensions, but few of them supported Unionism or populist political movements galvanized by Republicans. Despite internal class resentments, the Union army when it arrived in the upper South, was still identified as an invading force and the main source of the problems which ordinary whites faced. The Union armies' presence was not always unwelcome and indeed could be beneficial – in providing food and security against widespread banditry and disorder in the wake of local Confederate defeat – but the general good conduct of the Northern soldiers did not mean that they or the Republican Party were widely popular or acceptable. After the war, in state elections in 1867, the Republicans secured the support across the South of only about 15 per cent of eligible white voters.[19] Non-slaveholding white Southerners' reluctance to back the Republicans has been attributed to Confederate nationalism fostered by the war itself, and to the spirit of self-defence provoked by the intrusion of an invading army into ordinary Southerners' homelands.[20] But the logic of such hypothesizing could readily run in the opposite direction. Let us assume that the individual states' majorities for secession were obtained through the political will of the slaveholding elite, through trickery and often intimidation, and through a rushed timetable that denied secession's opponents a long enough period in which to organize their campaigning. Let us assume further that the war, with its privations, taxes, inflation and requirement that poor men fight to protect slaveholders' interests, confirmed many non-slaveholders' suspicions of and resentments against the planters and the political elite. Having been denied a proper say in the decision for secession and then having been squeezed by wartime impositions, surely these non-slaveholders, who never believed – we are told – the pre-war rhetoric about a separate South and the benefits of slavery, would have welcomed the Republicans even more warmly because of the way in which they had been treated in the late 1850s. In fact, little of this happened. Yet the explanation that this indifference resulted from the vibrancy, or at least viability, of wartime Confederate nationalism seems strained. If the decisions of 1860–1 ran as thoroughly and deeply against majority white opinion as has been claimed, it would surely be improbable that remembrance of so vast a betrayal at so devastating a cost would have disappeared by 1863–4. This failure of the Republican party, portraying itself as the poor whites' friend after a conflict in which poorer whites had fought and suffered for the slaveholders' interests, shows how very little real prospect there had been for the development of a proto-Republican crusade in the antebellum South.

Nor was this at all surprising. The Democratic party itself articulated values which were perfectly consistent with the non-slaveholders' aspirations. The political and financial impositions thrust by Southern state governments upon ordinary citizens were extraordinarily weak. The legal system was loose; punishments were light; the restrictions on personal movement and access to subsistence resources were negligible. Legislative petitions submitted to state legislatures show very little articulation of class grievances in the 1850s, when the most significant issue raised in such petitions concerned temperance reform in the middle of the decade. Militia duties fell far short of being oppressive. Taxes remained incredibly low. For example, 48 of 132 Georgia counties in 1860 either made no returns on local school taxes or reported none having been raised.[21] Peter Wallenstein has noted that the non-payment of poll tax disqualified voters and speculated that the rich might well have paid the taxes of poorer voters in order to secure their votes; yet the annual poll tax in Georgia in the 1850s was 25 cents per white male aged 21 to 60 years, at a time when a labourer in that state could easily earn 50 cents in a day.[22] The physical environment of the antebellum South was scarcely idyllic; but it offered extraordinary amounts of physical and psychological space for poorer and middling whites. Through most of Mississippi, Alabama, up-state Georgia and even much of South Carolina in the 1850s, there were scarcely any towns and no politically mobilized channels of discontent against the prevailing order.[23] It is scarcely credible that a Republican ideology founded upon quite complex notions of wage labour, highly commercial agriculture, thriving market towns, high levels of education, moral concerns about enslavement, and a commitment to a dynamic mixed economy galvanized by a more elaborate banking system and tied together by more diverse forms of transport corporation, should have commanded more than a very limited appeal in the rural pre-war South.

The second interpretation seems equally untenable. It is easy to see why secession was portrayed as a radical strategy pushed forward by the younger generation of politicians out of office within the South. Naturally, the election campaign of November 1860 and the subsequent elections for state conventions were accompanied by much excitement, propaganda, even sometimes physical violence. Among Democrats, a good deal of the work in the counties of the Southern states and in the delegate conventions was indeed the responsibility of younger politicians and younger lawyers on the make.[24] But this phenomenon may be partly explained by the fact that, among the Democrats, the older men were already office holders and therefore in positions which required some circumspection during a crisis which would lead to a

[48] constitutionally dangerous conclusion. The secession movement in that sense created a separate track of political activity from that in which the party leadership already engaged. Younger party activists were clearly far better suited to opening up that parallel track, but this did not mean that the established politicians objected to this activity or were reluctant to engage themselves in the process of secession. There were also advantages to be had in bringing fresh faces into the movement. Senator James H. Hammond of South Carolina was delighted at the speed of secession and emphasized that 'it was a movement of the *People* of the South' and not a 'bullying movement of the politicians'. And to set against the accounts of secession which portray it as accompanied by violence and intense propaganda, we have other observations. The Reverend C.C. Jones of Savannah, Georgia, noted of a large crowded meeting in the city which supported secession: 'The meeting was remarkably peaceful and orderly and elevated, with an entire absence of folly and rowdysim.' More generally for the South Carolina low country, it has been noted that the arguments for secession were strongly and widely pressed throughout the years 1858–60 and that by 1860 almost all the prominent clergymen in the coastal and interior low country supported disunion. In Texas F.B. Sexton, chairman of the state Democratic convention of 1860, wrote of a secession meeting: 'The sober, reflecting, sterling men of the country were present and no division of feeling existed.'[25]

The more important fact is that the political leadership of the South created the crisis which led to secession. The insistence, articulated first in the mid-1840s and then redoubled from 1854 onwards, that slavery had to be introduced into new territories acquired in the west formed the main argument of the Democratic party leadership. By September 1858 Senator Albert G. Brown of Mississippi told a party meeting in his state, 'you must give up the Union or give up slavery'. He explained:

> The sentiment of hostility to the South and its institutions is widening and deepening at the North every day. Those who tell you otherwise are deceived or they wilfully deceive you. Twenty years ago this sentiment was confined to a few fanatics; now it pervades all classes, ages and sexes of society. It is madness to suppose that this tide is ever to roll back. . . . I was raised in awe, in almost superstitious reverence of the Union. But if the Union is to be converted into a masked battery for assailing my property and my domestic peace, I will destroy it if I can, and if this cannot be done by direct assault, I would resort to sapping and mining. . . . Now, as in 1850, I do not fear the consequences of disunion. I do not court it, but I do not dread it.[26]

The only remaining guarantor of the Union was the Democratic party. Yet Brown dismissed the doctrine of popular sovereignty – which Northern Democrats saw as vital to their electoral chances within their section – as 'a wicked cheat or a mischievous humbug'. The attempt represented by that doctrine to compromise the constitutional and political issues created by the drive for slavery's extension into the western territories was further torpedoed by Brown and his fellow senator from Mississippi, Jefferson Davis, in February 1859. They introduced senate resolutions insisting upon federal government protection for slaveholders in all the federal territories. This demand for a so-called federal slave code destroyed the extraordinary efforts by which Northern Democrats had tried to paper over the increasingly broad cracks in their own national party's political edifice.

During the summer of 1859 Democratic state conventions in, for example, Mississippi and Louisiana, made absolutely no concessions on national policy to their northern Democratic colleagues. The only forward-looking policy that they demanded was the annexation of Cuba from Spain. Such a measure had been formally recommended to the Senate by its Committee on Foreign Relations in January 1859, with the extraordinary assertion that acquisition had long been a strategic goal of the United States and that popular support for that measure commanded 'a unanimity unsurpassed on any question of national policy that has heretofore engaged the public mind.' Of course, the aim was to add 581,000 slaves (out of 1,586,000 people on the island) to America's population.[27] The Mississippi Democratic state convention of July 1859 declared openly that a Republican victory in the presidential election of 1860 would lead to Mississippi's preparations, singly as a state or in cooperation with other states, to secede.[28] In December 1859 Vice-President John C. Breckinridge addressed the legislature of his home state of Kentucky. He portrayed the Democrats as the guarantors of the Constitution and tried to moderate Southern opinion by saying that he hoped there would never be a need for a federal slave code, preferring instead that Southerners rely for the protection of slavery within the territories upon the executive branch of the federal government. But he had no doubts that the Republican party posed a dreadful threat to Southern rights and the South's future, stressing 'we will have no peace until the Republican Party is destroyed, which can only be done by producing a reaction upon the public mind of the North.'[29] Yet when Breckinridge became the Southern Democrats' presidential candidate in 1860 he offered nothing to the Northern Democrats to enable them to beat the Republicans upon their home ground. The last months of 1859

[50] had spread despondency among many in the Southern political elite. John Brown's raid upon Virginia, with clear evidence that some Republicans had supported this highly dangerous direct action, and the easy victory of the Republican party in New York state elections, prefiguring a strong Republican performance in the North in the following year's presidential contest, decisively fuelled that sense of gloom. Senator Robert Toombs of Georgia wrote to a close confidant on 4 December 1859 that, if the Republicans won the election of November 1860,

> I see no safety for us, our property and our firesides except in breaking up the concern. I do not think it wise for the South to suffer a party to get possession of the government whose principles and whose leaders are so openly hostile not only to her equality but to her safety in the Union, and . . . if such a calamity should come, we should prefer to defend ourselves at the doorsill rather than await the attack at our hearthstone. I think it madness to wait for what some people call 'an overt act'.[30]

In the same month, Governor M.S. Perry of Florida indicated in his annual message to the state legislature that he favoured 'an eternal separation from those whose wickedness and fanaticism forbid us longer to live with them in peace and safety'. Governor Joseph E. Brown of Georgia at the same time told his state legislature that the arguments were over and that the state now needed to look to its armaments for protection in the future. In February 1860 the Alabama state legislature followed the Democratic state convention's resolutions by calling for elections to a state convention if a Republican won the presidency. This motion was passed by a virtually unanimous majority. By early April the political elite in Texas was preparing itself for the strong possibility of secession.[31]

The record of the Southern Democratic leadership from the introduction by Brown and Davis of their federal slave code resolutions in February 1859 to the presidential election of November 1860 demonstrates unambiguously its total lack of interest in, let alone commitment to, defeating the Republican movement in the North. The only concern which the Democratic leadership of the Southern states displayed in this period was to ensure that the national Democratic party maintained a firm commitment to the constitutional principle of permitting slavery in the western territories of the United States. Given this extraordinary preoccupation with legalism and constitutionalism and the potentially explosive consequences of allowing that preoccupation to open the way to a Republican victory in the presidential election of 1860, it is difficult to see how Avery Craven could have concluded, 'As the summer of

1859 wore on, it became increasingly apparent that conservative men and attitudes dominated the South.'[32] The conservative position, of insisting on the complete defence of slavery, played into the radicals' hands and of course sat very ill with the normal requirements of conservative statesmanship, namely to manage necessary changes in ways which minimize the subsequent disturbance to the prevailing order.

The fact that the political establishment did nothing to avert a crisis leading to secession weakens the third interpretation being considered here. This claims that the radical younger politicians in the Democratic party sought to purify their party by removing the political elite, through constant pressure for more radical national policies to protect slavery. If the elite was actually doing all it could to protect slavery in the national political arena, then this particular way of outflanking the elite would appear to have been a somewhat unpromising approach.

Southern modernization?

But it is still worth considering the extent to which there was a modernization crisis in the lower South during the 1850s. The argument for a modernization crisis contends (simply summarized) that the incumbent Democratic establishment came under increasing suspicion as having sold out to essentially Whig ideas, and therefore provoked a drive by radical younger politicians to return the South to Jacksonian verities of rampant individualism, closely controlled banks and business corporations, and more widely celebrated agrarian virtue. The purification of the Democratic party therefore meant opposition to banking and to state financial assistance to railroads as well as the promotion of secession. Although the outcome of that process might have proved to be politically and ideologically complex, the basic premise remains that modernization reshaped the political order.[33] Yet the case for widespread modernization can be gravely overstated. Southerners did indeed build up their railroad system in the 1850s but the railroads themselves were instruments of changing commercialization rather than vehicles for economic revolution. There were after all only railroads. They were very useful in speeding up access to the market, but most of the Southern effort put into the building of railroads in the 1850s took the form of lumber, for constructing the tracks and rolling stock, as well as for providing fuel.[34] Southern railroad systems had very little manufacturing impact on the slave

[52]   states in the mid-nineteenth century; moreover, there were relatively few new towns arising as railway junctions. Atlanta did indeed flourish in this role but it was still a very modest-sized town by 1860. So, too, in banking the deep South maintained almost exactly the same share of US bank liabilities of circulation and deposits by 1860 as it had in 1850, and it remained a section of the country with relatively primitive banking facilities. In the case of Alabama, where the modernization crisis has been described by Thornton, the number of banks did indeed multiply during the decade, but only from two in 1850–1 to eight in 1860. This hardly became the 'rather extensive banking system' described by Thornton.[35]

To illustrate more fully the difficulties of establishing a close relationship between secessionism and a modernization crisis let us turn to the example of Georgia.[36] There a new governor, Joseph E. Brown, was elected in 1857 as a young ambitious politician who was to become a keen secessionist in 1859–61 and who represented the hill country of the state, which was economically deprived by comparison with the seaboard and the middle section. Georgia faced intense disputes over banking and railroads in the late 1850s and this would fit in with the general notion of public concern about the impact of economic change on social and political values. Following the years 1850–6 when numerous new banks were chartered in the state, the banking system suspended specie payments in October 1857 in the midst of a national banking crash. Under a law of 1840 any bank suspending payments lost its charter; so there was clearly a demand immediately from the banks for special legislative permission for such suspension. The state House of Representatives passed a bill permitting suspension by 64 votes to 50 in December 1857. But among the members whose party affiliation has been identified, a small majority of Democrats (37 to 40) failed to support this major piece of legislation.

Governor Brown decided to veto the suspension legislation measure amidst a burst of pure Jacksonian anti-banking rhetoric. This veto was itself overturned by a two-thirds majority, with more Democrats now favouring the banks than opposing them. Such a legislative reversal led Brown to engage in a public campaign during 1858 against the banks and their behaviour during the financial crash. Many politicians commented that Brown planned to make bank reform and the establishment of a state sub-treasury system a key plank in his own re-election campaign in 1859 and newspaper rhetoric began to depict Brown as a new Jacksonian hero waging a populist crusade against vested economic interests. This image would fit the model of a secessionist Jacksonian crusader opposed to the political establishment and to economically privileged institutions. But in fact the issue emerged only as a result of the panic of 1857, and not as a structural issue before that crash, and the issue receded from public consciousness and debate during 1859 and 1860 when the financial panic's consequences ebbed for the South. Cotton prices remained buoyant and cotton exports boomed at the end of the decade, so acting counter-cyclically to the remainder of the American economy.

The other area in which state policy intersected with major economic institutions concerned railroad development. Georgia had provided sub-stantial state financial aid for railroads before 1853, with the state debt burgeoning during the years 1851–3. The state's finances then stabilised from 1855 to 1860 when the state enjoyed one of the most stable periods in its fiscal history to that date. Although one might have assumed that the Demo-crats' opponents, political descendants of the Whigs, would have favoured state support for the extension of the state's transport infrastructure, in fact the opposition pressed before 1857 for the sale of the state-owned Western and Atlantic Railroad. In response, Democrats in 1857–8 put up proposals for further state aid to four railroads, although these schemes were defeated in the state legislature in both 1857 and 1858. While small majorities of Demo-crats favoured further aid, the opposition members overwhelmingly opposed extension. Given this record, little pressure remained by 1859 for big new financial schemes to aid the state's railroads. Yet some of the keenest support for additional state aid to the railroads came from northern Georgia, the moun-tain region from which the governor himself came, and which wanted extra support for railroads to overcome the area's remoteness and economic back-wardness. This area, which on the whole was anti-banking in sentiment, was at the same time favourable to railroad development in 1857–8.

The most thorough-going enemies to further modernization in the later 1850s were not the Jacksonian radicals. The so-called promotional, Whiggish opposition party's lack of enthusiasm for further state aid was both partisan (since they wished that the ruling Democrats should get no further jobs or patronage) and related to the fact that the opposition was strongest in estab-lished urban centres which already had adequate transport services. The dynamics of political competition, and the regional and sub-regional balance of economic self-interest had far more to do with the way in which economic issues were handled than did an ideological crusade to restore Georgia to Jacksonian simplicities. But Democrats who opposed corporate power were not necessarily frustrated political 'outs'. In the midst of the row over railroad development, the Secretary of the Treasury, Howell Cobb, urged Governor Brown not to involve their home state in aiding railroads: 'Guard our good

[54]   old state I pray you, from this quicksand, which has foundered so many of our sister states.'[37]

The experience of Georgia was in some ways replicated in Mississippi. There, however, no banking expansion occurred during the 1850s to provoke a need for radical reform. Efforts to loosen some of the very tight regulations governing the issue of small denomination banknotes were defeated by anti-bank or anti-paper currency Democrats in 1857–8. The Democrats' leading state newspaper at Jackson, the state capital, hammered away against any moves to bring about the wider issuance of paper currency, denouncing banks as 'vampires' and 'soulless corporations'. It welcomed hints in late 1857 that a national debate over paper currency might lead to the 'resuscitation of this old Jackson Democratic issue'.[38] Although the state governor, William McWillie, in 1857–9 urged state aid to the development of railroads, the Democratic majority in the state legislature resisted any such recommendations. Interestingly enough, the argument for such promotion of the railroad network derived strength in the governor's mind from the need to bolster Mississippi's independence as a state.[39] Even this argument cut no ice with the legislators, many of whom were reminded (if they did not themselves recollect) that the state had got into considerable debt in the late 1830s and 1840s through the over-ambitious provision of financial assistance to railroad companies. The more general point from Mississippi stands out starkly. No process of state-backed modernization swept the state during the 1850s to provide a target for disaffected purists to criticize or reject.

More generally, while important economic and commercial changes affected the South in the 1850s, and no doubt created anxieties for many old Jacksonians, it is impossible to link these anxieties to programmes of modernization in particular states. Moreover it is difficult to link them to secessionism, especially since many ideological secessionists argued for diversification and at least some degree of industrial development in order to strengthen the South's chances of securing an independent economic existence in the future. Moreover, while it is easy to see that a Jacksonian model existed for a producerist economy, the practice of politics by the Democratic party in the 1850s meant that the ideological model was often ignored or severely qualified by Democratic state parties. The strongest potential example for a politician trying to launch a Jacksonian-style crusade in the late 1850s was Governor Brown of Georgia and he did not subscribe to anti-modernization ideas on the state's role in assisting railroad development. Nor did economic circumstances encourage him to persist with anti-banking themes after 1858.

Nature of the secession crisis [55]

The secession crisis from Lincoln's election and to the establishment of the Confederacy in February 1861 had long been forecast. As Don E. Fehrenbacher has written,

> All the passion of the sectional conflict became concentrated, like the sun's rays by a magnifying glass, on one moment of decision that could come only once in history – that is, the *first* election of a Republican president. If secessionists had not seized the moment but instead had somehow been persuaded to let it pass, such a clear signal for action might never again have sounded.[40]

The Southern political establishment led that process.

As Jefferson Davis wrote on 17 January 1861, 'The Election was not the Cause it was but the last feather which you know breaks the Camel's back.' Senator Davis had played a full role in arguing for the most complete form of possible federal protection for the institution of slavery during early 1859. By January 1860, he was satisfied that 'there has been a great advance in public opinion towards the Southern rights creed. We are now all-powerful at the South, but are still in a minority at the North.' In May 1860, in a long Senate speech, he repeatedly stressed that the government of the United States consisted of a 'compact' between sovereign members. That compact depended upon vital principles of equality between the states and respect for and adherence to 'community independence'. While he argued that he hoped the Democrats would re-unite as a national conservative party, he would accept no compromise by acceding to the Northern Democrats' ideas concerning popular sovereignty in the territories. At the same time he argued that agitation which had started as a quest for sectional power had now developed into a full-blown Northern attack on slave society. From 21 September 1860 to the presidential election Davis toured quite extensively in his native state of Mississippi. Immediately after the election his own preference was to try to move cautiously to try to ensure that eight to ten states acted together. But, interestingly enough, he advised Robert Barnwell Rhett of South Carolina that if his state seceded and the federal government tried to coerce it back into the Union, then the whole South would unite to defend South Carolina's actions; at the same time, he advised that South Carolina need not wait for Abraham Lincoln to enter the White House before seceding. Within Mississippi, Davis, together with the state's other senator and congressmen, met the governor in early November for a two-day session. Although Davis argued for delay and for secession only by a number of states working together, the group decided by a four to three majority to call a special session of the state legislature to discuss the situation. On 30 November Davis contacted Eli Whitney concerning the shipment of arms to Mississippi. In early December he was speaking in the Senate of impending war and the secession of his own state, and on 14 December he added his name to a declaration that the Union could not work and that a Southern confederacy had to be organized speedily. On 5 January 1861 Davis joined a caucus of senators from Georgia, Florida, Alabama, Louisiana, Texas, Arkansas and Mississippi which resolved that those states should secede immediately and that a convention should meet at Montgomery, Alabama, on or before 15 February to form a new government. When he delivered his own personal farewell address to the United States Senate on 21 January 1861, Davis asserted that he had conferred with the people of Mississippi before the decision to secede had been taken and that for many years he had maintained that the right of secession was 'an essential attribute of State sovereignty'.[41]

While Davis did not, immediately on Lincoln's election, publicly call for secession and confrontation, he had every reason to proceed with caution. He knew the risks of taking such a step from his experience of the struggle in Mississippi in 1850–1 over the acceptance of the compromise of 1850. At that time he had adopted a strong state's rights approach and had found himself in advance of political opinion within Mississippi, defeated in his effort to ensure the rejection of the compromise measures.[42] The experience of 1851, when state political opinion had accepted a political accommodation which he wished to reject, would naturally have made him cautious in the crisis of 1860. Such a reaction was reinforced by the fact that Davis himself wanted to see a concerted response by the Southern states to the challenge of Lincoln's election. Southern leaders discussed at enormous length from November 1860 to February 1861 the various tactical considerations which influenced secession. Some Southerners wished to wait until Lincoln occupied the White House and to see whether there was an overt act against slavery or the South which would then become the occasion for a grand reaction right across the whole section. Within the deep South, probably a majority of political leaders came to the view that secession should occur before Lincoln did in fact take up power in the first week of March 1861. But there were many different arguments as to how far the intending secessionist states should wait to co-operate together or simply follow their own individual paths out of the Union. While many of the younger hot-heads may have sought immediate action, the more experienced political leaders, the vast majority of

whom were trained lawyers, naturally sought to consider some of the legal,
constitutional and, ultimately, military consequences of individual states' acts
of secession.

But to conclude from the public enthusiasm for secession of some of the
younger activists, and the reluctance among many of the political establishment to declare immediately and explicitly for secession, that the leading
Democrats of the deep South were fiercely divided over secession exaggerates those essentially tactical differences. Disagreements over procedure and
precise tactics were only to be expected in a situation which was potentially
highly complex and, to put it mildly, fraught with explosive and dangerous
consequences. The fact remains that even moderate Democrats had been closely
involved since the summer of 1860 in tactical cooperation with those who
were known to be committed to secessionism. The Southern Democratic
candidate for the presidency, John C. Breckinridge, had never himself pressed
for a federal slave code or commented on the right of secession, but he had
not dissociated himself from out and out dis-Unionists such as William Yancey
of Alabama. One Southern newspaper pointed out, 'Mr Breckinridge claims
that he isn't a dis-Unionist. An animal not willing to pass for a pig shouldn't
stay in the stye.'[43]

By 1860 all the Democratic party organizations of the seven deep South
states, and indeed many of those of the upper South as well, had placed their
own preoccupations with the future guarantee of the position of slavery within
the Union at the heart of all political debate. In setting national political agendas
by 1860, Southern Democratic party organizations made no concessions
whatsoever to Northern political opinion. Every so often Southern Democratic leaders pointed out the advantages of their own view of the Union as
a compact between the States and America as a pluralistic society in which
different religious and civil preferences would be allowed to flourish through
the operation of state sovereignty. But the political programme they offered
to the nation was an essentially passive one, of adhering to an agreed structure which permitted states to get on with the ordering of their own internal
affairs. Where the Federal government was concerned they insisted increasingly on full federal protection for slaveowners to move into federal territories with their property rights in slaves guaranteed. They also supported
occasionally an assertive foreign policy, including the possible acquisition
of Cuba, with its slaves, from Spain. But, significantly, accompanying this
vision of a limited government in America as a whole, an increasing number
of Southerners became ideological secessionists. They believed that the
safety for their section lay ultimately outside the Union since Northern public

opinion was becoming increasingly critical of, if not actually hostile to, slavery and all its ramifications.

It has been suggested that a longer period of reflection after November 1860 might have prevented the decision to secede. This makes sense if it is assumed either that the politicians did not represent the interests or opinions of the Southern electorates, or that the arguments for secession were novel or fresh. In fact, the defence of Southern constitutional rights and the case against Northern antislavery and the Republican party had been repeated in election after election throughout the 1850s. Even in South Carolina, the least democratic state of the South, the issues which dominated the secession crisis had been debated fully, publicly and repeatedly in 1851–2 and in 1858–60.[44] Nothing new emerged in 1860 except an explicit assessment of the timing of secession, and even that factor had been aired from 1857 and, in some quarters, earlier.[45] Moreover, no basis existed for reconciling Southern claims with the Republicans' firmly held positions, other than through one side's capitulation to the other.[46]

The extent of Southerners' commitment to the pro-slavery cause is well illustrated by the limited assistance offered by Southerners from the upper slaves states to the process of political compromise in the early months of 1861. Much serious discussion focused on resolving the dispute between the seceded deep South states and the federal Union. From various schemes put forward, most notably the so-called Crittenden compromise, named after a prominent Kentucky senator, it is easy to demonstrate how far even moderate political leaders of the upper South went in their adherence to slavery. All the various compromise schemes endorsed by politicians from the upper South stipulated that slavery would be protected by constitutional amendment in states where it already existed. So, too, a constitutional amendment would prohibit Congress from interfering with slavery in existing territories in America south of the line 36°30', the old Missouri compromise line of 1820. The proposed Crittenden compromise went even further and stated that any territory acquired in future by the United States which lay south of the line of latitude 36°30' would be open to slavery; this claim was rejected by virtually all Republicans since it gave every encouragement to Southern politicians to press for the acquisition of territories in the Carribbean or from Mexico. But even without that particular additional protection, all the various compromise schemes entrenched slavery where it already existed and offered some prospect for the future extension of slavery into territories which could conceivably become additional slave states.[47] This latter concession was anathema to Republicans. Once Republican politicians decided to reject these particular constitutional proposals, then the compromise movement in the upper South had nothing to build upon.

As events transpired, of course, Lincoln's decision to coerce the South Carolinians after they fired upon Fort Sumter wrecked any hopes for a compromise peace among politicians from the upper South. The resort to force was wholly unacceptable to them. Both on constitutional grounds and in terms of the political limits upon the use of force which the upper South required, those political leaders of the upper South who were often referred to as the reluctant dis-Unionists were actually also reluctant Unionists.[48] Public reactions to the secession crisis well illustrate the rapid decline in Unionists' support in the wake of secession and particularly in the aftermath of the firing upon Fort Sumter. A study of Lawrence County, Alabama, which was the county most opposed to secession in that state, shows that by February 1861 opposition to secession had fallen, with most public leaders in northern Alabama moving to support separate state secession. Once the war began, concerted efforts were made to organize the county for military action and to hold county society together during the war. When in 1862 there was a direct federal military presence in the county, men were stimulated in large numbers to join together in defending their homeland. In Tennessee there was a dramatic shift in opinion. On 9 February 1861 all four major geographical divisions of the state voted heavily for pro-Union delegates to a convention. After Fort Sumter, however, political opinion in the state shifted dramatically and a referendum on 8 June 1861 resulted in majorities of 68 per cent, 80 per cent and 89 per cent of voters favouring secession in three of the state's divisions, with only Eastern Tennessee voting by 69 per cent to 31 per cent against separation. That eastern division of the state had only 9 per cent of its population enslaved in 1860.[49] Lincoln's claim, that the secessionist majorities, even in Virginia and Tennessee, resulted from coercion or the implicit threat of coercion, has not been substantiated other than by reference to specific instances which may or may not have been representative.[50] Historians' desire to see secession as an undemocratic, even deliberately anti-democratic, act can affect the weight given to such evidence. There is plentiful contrary evidence that a sense of gloomy inevitability influenced the Upper South once fighting began. For example, a leading North Carolinian Unionist, Zebulon B. Vance, noted that when news of Fort Sumter arrived, his hand fell 'slowly and sadly by the side of a Secessionist'.[51]

Most Southern Unionists believed that the Union should make concessions on the extension of slavery which the Republicans, who had secured the presidency through wholly constitutional and legitimate means, rejected as a policy. They also required that the Union should restrict its ability to act as a government by avoiding the legitimate use of force in the defence of its territories and its fortifications. The leading Upper South politicians there-fore assumed that the Federal government was indeed a compact between the states and that the presidential election of 1860 lacked legitimacy. These views were scarcely compatible with Unionism in 1861. Lincoln rejected the doc-trine of state sovereignty and its corollary, the right of peaceful secession. He claimed that a small group had systematically developed and propagated that 'sophism': 'With rebellion thus sugarcoated, they have been drugging the public mind of their section for more than thirty years.' He therefore also rejected the Southern challenge to the whole concept of 'a constitutional republic, or a democracy – a government of the people, by the people' having the right to defend 'its territorial integrity, against its own domestic foes'.[52] Instead, Southern Unionists reacted as if the new administration in Washing-ton was simply there as a deal-maker rather than as a political movement which had won the presidential election in every state of the North, in a section which incorporated the majority of the people of the nation. This persistent refusal to abide by the majoritarian decision showed the extent to which even the Upper South endorsed the ideological secessionists' state rights views and their insistence on the fullest possible constitutional defence of the institution of slavery.[53]

The discussion in this chapter began by asking how far secession was a conservative or radical act. Some historians have tended to portray secession as the action of radical hot-heads throwing aside the restraints and conven-tions of the political system. If this political radicalism served the self-evidently conservative objective of preserving slavery, it was also inspired, in some accounts, by a desire to entrench a radical, Jacksonian economic and social order. Against this dynamic, politically radical model of Southern secession may be set various interpretations which insist that the crisis of 1860 was the handiwork of the slaveowning elite. Some such interpretations set the break-down of the Union as an almost inevitable structural crisis that had to erupt if the South continued in its determination to adhere to slavery. Republican free labour ideology reflected the changing Northern mode of production and articulated the contradictions which could only increase between an industrializing and commercial system and a slave-based economy still set in the stage of merchant capitalism. Other interpretations argue that secession was brought on by a political elite. In one view, the slaveowning class feared the future emergence of a Southern Republican movement among

the non-slaveowners, and used secession as a means of introducing constitutional changes to constrain the rights, powers and opportunities of non-
slaveowning citizens. In another view, the elite had choked off popular
antislavery dissent for decades and wished to create a new republic in which
their dominance could be preserved. These various interpretations all raise
difficulties when confronted with the events of the 1850s.

The qualifications offered in this chapter point the way to examining
secession with two controversial considerations firmly in mind. The first
acknowledges that the South was, mainly, a viable and indeed lively democracy by the standards which prevailed in the 'western world' before 1918.
While there were defects and lapses in this polity, the Southern system was
(for whites) far more open and democratic than any other in the mid-nineteenth
century world, except for the North's. Voter participation far exceeded, for
those enjoying the vote, the level of white male participation today. That
white democracy, offering plentiful scope for ambitious political opportun-
ists to enter and manipulate, spawned no significant antislavery political movement in the 1850s. Indeed, after the war the record of Southern white support
for the Republicans or for reform in race relations proved to be pathetic. George
M. Fredrickson's argument for the existence of a Herrenvolk democracy in
the South provides a convincing explanation of this phenomenon, even though
his interpretation disappoints those who would like to believe that ordinary
non-slaveholding whites only supported the slave system because they were
duped by the hegemonic power of the slaveocracy's ideology.[54]

A second fundamental contention needs to be linked to this notion of a
viable Southern democracy. Despite all their personal rivalries, animosities
and jockeyings for place and power, Southern politicians agreed that their
section faced a major political crisis in the 1850s. That crisis may have been,
in important respects, intensified by the politicians themselves or by Southern
fire-eaters promoting an array of arguments in favour of separation. But the
debate over slavery was not controlled by Southern politicians and propa-
gandists. Northern antislavery and abolitionist sentiment grew enormously
from the 1830s and it permeated Northern religious as well as political life.[55]
The pro-slavery apologists' claim that Northern opinion became increasingly
critical of slavery during the 1850s flowed from neither fantasy nor political
gamesmanship. Congressional debates may have become exasperatingly
legalistic, but they translated into legislative and constitutional terms those
far wider concerns over the South's peculiar institution. It was no wonder
that Southern politicians became almost entirely preoccupied with the defence

[62] of slavery and the South from 1854 onwards. Although they had the leeway to contain and channel that debate – choosing instead on occasions to intensify it – they could never control the national controversy over slavery.

The ideological secessionists' position was formulated in the 1830s and widely promoted from the late 1840s. The turbulent debates of the mid-1850s over the fate of slavery and the newly opened territories of Kansas and Nebraska simply served to strengthen and propagate the views of those who had seen that Northern antislavery opinion would inevitably increase. In July 1851 Jefferson Davis, while campaigning in Mississippi, had declared, 'If secession presented the only alternative to social and political degradation, he believed Mississippi would adopt the alternative, even had her citizens to leave their widows and orphans alone to weep upon her fields.'[56] Later in the decade Davis did nothing to prevent the drift to secession; indeed his political actions accelerated that movement. And when the secessionist crisis came he involved himself deeply in the management of the process towards secession, in the realization that secession was likely to lead also to war. The arguments which came to a head in 1860 had been debated exhaustively, in election after election and in state after state, during the 1850s. They concerned the very future of the South in the Union. No political movement of any significance arose in the South after 1854 to proclaim the importance of other issues or to dismiss the politics of slavery as merely projecting the concerns and interests of an elite. Southern politicians put the vital question of the future of the section's political and social order repeatedly and passionately to their white electorates throughout the decade. The overwhelming response was that slavery and slaveholding rights should be defended with the utmost vigilance and vigour. Given the white electorates' repeated endorsements of this agenda, the secessionists acted logically in 1860. The probability remains – however unpalatable to us – that there was far more consistency between the decision to secede and the beliefs held by white electorates than recent interpretations of these events have allowed. Jefferson Davis's declarations offer a salutary reminder that politicians often do what they say they will do.

Notes

1. John Ashworth, *Slavery, Capitalism, and Politics in the Antebellum Republic*, vol. I: *Commerce and Compromise, 1820–1850* (Cambridge, 1995), pp. 13–15, 493–8. Excellent discussions of the social and ideological gulf between the sections

may be found in, for example: Eric Foner, *Politics and Ideology in the Age of the Civil War* (Oxford, 1980), ch. 3; Bruce Levine, *Half Slave and Half Free. The Roots of the Civil War* (New York, 1992).

2. James McPherson, *Battle Cry of Freedom. The Civil War Era* (New York, 1988), pp. ix–x. There is an excellent analysis in Brian Holden Reid, *The Origins of the American Civil War* (London, 1996), pp. 260–79.

3. Ulrich B. Phillips, *Georgia and State Rights* (Yellow Springs, Ga, 1968 reprint of 1902 edn), pp. 207–8.

4. Michael P. Johnson, *Toward a Patriarchal Republic: The Secession of Georgia* (Baton Rouge, La, 1977), pp. 106, 123.

5. William W. Freehling, *The Road to Disunion*, vol. I: *Secessionists at Bay, 1776–1854* (New York, 1990), pp. 185–210, 289–307, 459–74.

6. Horace Montgomery, *Cracker Parties* (Baton Rouge, La, 1950), pp. 248–51.

7. Clement Eaton, *The Growth of Southern Civilization, 1790–860* (New York, 1961), pp. 1–2, 297, 313, 323–4. An important work on Southern critics of slavery links some of those dissenters with the Whigs. Carl N. Degler, *The Other South. Southern Dissenters in the Nineteenth Century* (New York, 1974), pp. 79–96, 166–9.

8. Michael F. Holt, *The Political Crisis of the 1850s* (New York, 1978), pp. 219, 221, 224, 240; Allan Nevins, *The Emergence of Lincoln*, vol. II: *Prologue to Civil War 1859–1861* (New York, 1950), p. 318; David M. Potter (completed and edited by Don. E. Fehrenbacher), *The Impending Crisis 1848–1861* (New York, 1976), p. 500; William J. Cooper, Jr, *Liberty and Slavery. Southern Politics to 1860* (New York, 1983), pp. 268–76.

9. J.Mills Thornton III, *Politics and Power in a Slave Society: Alabama, 1800–1860* (Baton Rouge, La, 1978), pp. xviii–xix, 268–76.

10. Karl Marx and Frederick Engels, *The Civil War in the United States* (New York, 1961 edn), p. 81.

11. Ashworth, *Slavery, Capitalism, and Politics in the Antebellum Republic*, pp. 345–50, 361–5. Elizabeth Fox-Genovese and Eugene D. Genovese, *Fruits of Merchant Capital: Slavery and Bourgeois Property in the Rise and Expansion of Capitalism* (Oxford, 1983), pp. 3–25.

12. Marx and Engels, *The Civil War*, pp. 66–70.

13. J. Morgan Kousser, review in *Journal of American History*, vol. 73, no. 1 (June, 1986), p. 189; Stephen V. Ash, *When the Yankees Came: Conflict and Chaos in the Occupied South, 1861–186* (Chapel Hill, NC, 1995), p. 194.

[64]

14. Thomas Paine, *Rights of Man* (Harmondsworth, Middx, 1984 edn.), pp. 8–9, 260–4, 268.

15. Roy P. Basler (ed.), *The Collected Works of Abraham Lincoln*, vol. 4 (New Brunswick, NJ, 1953), p. 437.

16. Johnson, *Toward a Patriarchal Republic*, passim.

17. Robert Toombs to Alexander H. Stephens, 10 Feb. 1860, in Ulrich B. Phillips (ed.), *The Correspondence of Robert Toombs, Alexander H. Stephens, and Howell Cobb*, in American Historical Association, *Annual Report*, 1911, II (Washington, DC, 1913), p. 462; see also p. 450.

18. William W. Freehling and Craig M. Simpson (eds), *Secession Debated: Georgia's Showdown in 1860* (New York, 1992), pp. 5–50, 116–44. On the danger of federal interference, see pp. 27, 29, 47.

19. Ash, *When the Yankees Came*, pp. 218, 220; Richard H. Abbott, *The Republican Party and the South, 1855–1877: The First Southern Strategy* (Chapel Hill, NC, 1986), pp. 38–40, 72–3, 136–8.

20. Drew G. Faust, *The Creation of Confederate Nationalism: Ideology and Identity in the Civil War South* (Baton Rouge, La, 1988), pp. 14–16, 21, 81, 84 effectively analyses the articulation of a Confederate nationalism while arguing that it was designed to serve the slaveholders' interests.

21. Bruce Collins, *White Society in the Antebellum South* (London, 1985), pp. 8, 101–4, 117–18.

22. Peter Wallenstein, *From Slave South to New South: Public Policy in Nineteenth-Century Georgia* (Chapel Hill, NC,1987), pp. 41, 44–5.

23. Collins, *White Society*, pp. 28–9, 84–9, 118–19.

24. William L. Barney, *The Secessionist Impulse: Alabama and Mississippi in 1860* (Princeton, NJ, 1974), pp. 62–3, 80, 92–4.

25. Drew G. Faust, *James Henry Hammond and the Old South: A Design for Mastery* (Baton Rouge, La, 1982), p. 360; Robert M. Myers (ed.), *The Children of Pride: A True Story of Georgia and the Civil War* (New Haven, 1972), p. 634; Stephanie McCurry, *Masters of Small Worlds: Yeoman Householders, Gender Relations, and the Political Culture of the Antebellum South Carolina Low Country* (New York, 1995), p. 289; William L. Buenger, *Secession and the Union in Texas* (Austin, Tx., 1984), p. 127.

26. Natchez, *Mississippi Free Trader*, 27 Sept. 1858.

27. *Appendix to the Congressional Globe*, 35th Congress, 2nd Session (Washington, DC, 1859), pp. 90–4. The proposal offered a tactical opportunity to expose

Southern moderates such as John C. Crittenden as insufficiently 'Southern'. Crittenden opposed the measure on the expedient grounds that its timing was inappropriate; Spain would not sell and American could not afford to buy. Idem., pp. 158–9.

28. William C. Davis, *Jefferson Davis. The Man and His Hour* (New York, 1991), p. 273.

29. *A Political Text-Book for 1860* (New York, 1860), pp. 153–4.

30. Phillips (ed.), *The Correspondence of Robert Toombs, Alexander H. Stephens and Howell Cobb*, pp. 448, 450.

31. Ollinger Crenshaw, *The Slave States in the Presidential Election of 1860* (Baltimore, Md, 1945), pp. 228, 242, 247; Buenger, *Secession and the Union in Texas*, pp. 48–9.

32. Avery Craven, *The Coming of the Civil War*, 2nd edn (Chicago, 1957), p. 406.

33. Thornton, *Politics and Power*, pp. 268–80, 291–312, esp. 302, 305–6, 436.

34. Albert Fishlow, *American Railroads and the Transformation of the Ante-Bellum Economy* (Cambridge, Mass., 1965), pp. 118–32, 157. Railroads' demands for iron and machinery were considerable, but they did not stimulate much industry in the South. Idem., pp. 144–5, 149–50, 156.

35. Thornton, *Politics and Power*, pp. 282–7; quotation at 285.

36. For the following two paragraphs, see: Bruce W. Collins, 'Governor Joseph E. Brown, economic issues, and Georgia's road to Secession, 1857–1859', *Georgia Historical Quarterly*, 71, (1987), 189–225.

37. Idem., p. 219.

38. Jackson, Miss., *Mississippian and State Gazette*, 23 Dec. 1857, 3 Feb. 1858; see also 16 Dec. 1857, 13, 20 Jan., 17 Feb., 15 Sept., 10 Nov., 1, 8 Dec., 1858.

39. *Journal of the House of Representatives of the State of Mississippi for 1858* (Jackson, Miss., 1858), pp. 13–21.

40. Don E. Fehrenbacher, *The South and Three Sectional Crises* (Baton Rouge, La, 1980), p. 63.

41. Lynda L. Crist and Mary S. Dix (eds), *The Papers of Jefferson Davis*, vol. 7, 1861 (Baton Rouge, La, 1992), p. 14; Lynda L. Crist and Mary S. Dix (eds), *The Papers of Jefferson Davis*, vol. 6, 1856–1860 (Baton Rouge, La, 1989), pp. 254, 257–64, 271, 276; Davis, *Jefferson Davis*, pp. 284, 286–8, 291; *The Papers of Jefferson Davis*, vol. 7, p. 19. The future president of the Confederacy has been depicted as a highly reluctant secessionist in Barney, *Secessionist Impulse*, pp. 195–6; Cooper, *Liberty and Slavery*, pp. 273–4.

[66]   42. Clement Eaton, *Jefferson Davis* (New York, 1977), pp. 77–9.

43. William C. Davis, *Breckinridge. Statesman. Soldier. Symbol* (Baton Rouge, La, 1974), pp. 231–2, 237–9.

44. William E. Gienapp, 'The crisis of American democracy', in Gabor S. Boritt (ed.), *Why the Civil War Came* (New York, 1996), p. 122; John Barnwell, *Love of Order: South Carolina's First Secession Crisis* (Chapel Hill, NC,1982), pp. 166–90; McCurry, *Masters of Small Worlds*, pp. 278–9.

45. Long and considered discussions of future options may be found in leading Democratic newspapers in the Deep South, e.g., Milledgeville, Ga, *The Federal Union*, 21 July 1857, 23 March 1858; Natchez, *Mississippi Free Trader*, 9, 16 Aug., 25 Oct. 1858.

46. Gienapp, 'The Crisis of American democracy', p. 123.

47. Daniel W. Crofts, *Reluctant Confederates: Upper South Unionists in the Secession Crisis* (Chapel Hill, NC, 1989), pp. 196–209, 308–33.

48. This explains a response recently emphasized: 'Conservative politicians suddenly manifested a strange passivity, a debilitating lassitude that allowed the secessionists to seize the initiative.' George C. Rable, *The Confederate Republic: A Revolution against Politics* (Chapel Hill, NC, 1994), p. 35. Rable stresses the similarity of fears and rhetoric among secessionists and cooperationists. What he describes as a revolution against politics could be seen as a widespread recognition that the defence of slavery in 1860–1 was a decision that genuinely transcended normal party political debate. Idem., pp. 11, 18, 20, 22, 32.

49. Paul Horton, 'Submitting to the 'Shadow of Slavery': the Secession crisis and Civil War in Alabama's Lawrence County', *Civil War History*, LXIV (1998), pp. 111–36; Jonathan M. Atkins, *Parties, Politics and the Sectional Conflict in Tennesee, 1832–1861* (Knoxville, Tenn., 1997), pp. 241, 244–50.

50. Basler (ed.), *Collected Works*, IV, 437; John Niven, *The Coming of the Civil War 1837–1861* (Arlington Heights, Ill., 1990), p. 131.

51. Paul D. Escott, *Many Excellent People: Power and Privilege in North Carolina, 1850–1900* (Chapel Hill, NC,1985), p. 35.

52. Basler (ed.), *Collected Works*, IV, 433, 426.

53. This point has also been made by Richard H. Sewell, *A House Divided: Sectioinalism and Civil War, 1848–1865* (Baltimore, Md, 1988), p. 80. See also, Potter, *The Impending Crisis*, p. 484; McPherson, *Battle Cry of Freedom*, p. 239.

54. George M. Fredrickson, *White Supremacy: A Comparative Study in American and South African History* (Oxford, 1981), pp. 154–5.

55. Richard J. Carwardine, *Evangelicals and Politics in Antebellum America* (New Haven, Conn., 1993) has brought out the significance of religious issues to antebellum politics.

56. Lynda L. Crist (ed.), *The Papers of Jefferson Davis*, vol. 4, *1849–1852* (Baton Rouge, La, 1983), p. 213.

CHAPTER THREE

ABRAHAM LINCOLN, THE PRESIDENCY, AND THE MOBILIZATION OF UNION SENTIMENT

RICHARD CARWARDINE

To experience war is to experience force, and Americans of the Civil War era knew that raw truth better than any other generation in their nation's history. If the Confederacy was subject to the greater devastation of its physical landscape, and the greater proportionate loss of life, the Union suffered its own grievous human agonies. Victory, the Lincoln administration gradually learned, would come only as the North's superiority in manpower and material resources expressed itself in the force of bullet, bayonet and shell, and in the physical destruction of the enemy – and that would mean unprecedented bloodshed on both sides.[1]

Military coercion of the Confederacy demanded political coercion on the Union home front. Few aspects of Abraham Lincoln's presidency have attracted more discussion than his use of emergency executive powers. Responding swiftly to the Confederates' attack on Fort Sumter in April 1861, he called up the militia, proclaimed a blockade, and ordered the use of Treasury funds for war supplies, all before he called Congress into special session in July. He subsequently suspended the writ of habeas corpus and sanctioned arbitrary arrests throughout the country, abolished slavery by presidential proclamation, and began his own programme of national reconstruction. Here was an agenda sufficient to elicit cries of dictatorship both from Confederates and from Northern political foes. Whatever the justice of that charge – and recent scholarship has not wholly exonerated the sixteenth president[2] – there is universal agreement that the nation's unprecedented crisis spurred Lincoln and the executive branch into forceful, interventionist and even coercive leadership. Earlier generations had expressed fears for the future of republicanism – whether from the executive 'usurpation' of Federalists in the 1790s or from the tyranny of 'King Andrew' Jackson four decades later – but no previous administration had deployed political and military power as energetically as did the Union government during the Civil

War. Moreover, the earnestness with which the civilian and military agents of the administration set about their task suggests how far they believed Union success depended upon coercion. These included government control of the telegraph, suppressing newspapers careless with confidential military information, seizing presses, arresting deserters, detaining those who encouraged opposition to the draft, prosecuting and banishing pro-Confederate editors, and deploying provost-marshals and troops to police the polls or intimidate opponents. Maryland and other contested border areas were transformed into armed camps, while Peace Democrat ('Copperhead') strongholds in the Northwest and Middle Atlantic states felt the firm hand of Union commanders behind the lines.

But for all that, what is remarkable about Lincoln's success in sustaining support for the Union's formidable four-year war effort is just how little it depended on executive coercion, repression and the long arm of the War Department. The main task facing the Union administration was not how to coerce or dragoon an unwilling population into an unwanted conflict; rather it was how best to encourage, nurture and sustain a potent Union patriotism. The North's superiority over the Confederacy in manpower and matériel gave hope of eventual victory, but this would only count if the enthusiasm for war that immediately followed the bombardment of Fort Sumter were consolidated into a longer-term appetite for the fight. Given that Lincoln secured a handsome reelection in 1864 and that Union voluntary enlistments remained extraordinarily high throughout the conflict, it might seem that a resilient popular Unionism needed little nurturing from above. But without a clear articulation of the war's purpose by the Union leadership in general, and the president in particular, it is doubtful whether the people of the North would have retained their collective will to continue so gruelling and expensive a conflict. Neither James Madison in the War of 1812 nor James K. Polk in the conflict with Mexico had been entirely successful in harmonizing national sentiments behind their leadership, and by definition these had been less divisive struggles than an internecine civil war. The burden of what follows is that one of Lincoln's greatest achievements was his articulation of a rationale for the war and its sacrifices; that its formulation and reformulation were shaped in terms which, from his shrewd reading of public opinion, he judged would resonate with mainstream Unionists and cement the war coalition; that for its dissemination he and his administration imaginatively exploited a formidable network of governmental and voluntary agencies; and that the keynote of his presidential leadership of the Union was persuasion, not coercion.

Lincoln and the Union

There are a number of strands in the rope which bound Lincoln resolutely to the Union, 'this favored land', as he described it in his First Inaugural Address.[3] These included his profound faith in the nation's material potential: by temperament an 'improver', he watched with pleasure the Union's galloping economic progress, to which his political career in the 1830s and 1840s had been chiefly devoted.[4] More commonly, however, Lincoln addressed the moral and political purposes of the Union. Central to his faith were the Revolution's remarkable legacies, and the Republic's cornerstones: the Declaration of Independence, with its philosophical celebration of equality, and the Federal Constitution, the guarantor of freedom. Thanks to the founding fathers, the United States enjoyed a unique and unprecedented liberty, whose distinctive features included self-government, or government by the consent of the governed, a bill of rights which guaranteed a variety of religious and civil freedoms, and a commitment to meritocracy.[5]

Lincoln shared in the widespread sense of American exceptionalism, or uniqueness. 'Most governments have been based, practically, on the denial of equal rights of men . . . ; ours began, by *affirming* those rights.' The American Union had a special role in world history, a duty to act as a beacon of liberty to all. When the South Carolinians turned their guns on Fort Sumter they pressed an issue which had cosmic not just local meaning: 'It presents to the whole family of man, the question, whether a constitutional republic, or a democracy – a government of the people, by the same people – can, or cannot, maintain its territorial integrity, against its own domestic foes. . . . It forces us to ask: . . . "Must a government, of necessity, be too strong for the liberties of its own people, or too weak to maintain its own existence?"'[6]

In his first inaugural address and his special message of July 1861 Lincoln played the political philosopher, the historian and the pragmatist to show why the Union had to be perpetual. The political philosopher declared that 'no government proper, ever had a provision in its organic law for its own termination.' Acquiescence in secession was acquiescence in anarchy, the acceptance of minority rule, an invitation to repeated secessions that would Balkanize North America. Lincoln the historian insisted that the Union was 'much older than the Constitution' of 1787, having been formed even before the Declaration of 1776. The object of the Federal Constitution had been '*to form a more perfect union*'. And then there were the practical constraints of geography: 'Physically speaking, we cannot separate. . . . A husband and wife may be divorced, and go . . . beyond the reach of each other; but the different parts of our country cannot do this.'[7] Ultimately, though, Lincoln's vision of the Union drew less on a calculation of practicalities, than on a romantic, even spiritual, feeling. Alexander H. Stephens, Lincoln's Whig associate from Georgia, and the vice-president of the Confederacy, later reflected that Lincoln's Unionism assumed the character of religious mysticism.

The pre-war Lincoln celebrated the Union as a matchless instrument of liberty even though it simultaneously tightened the shackles and manacles of the slave. As the war progressed he came to see that, to preserve the freedoms honoured by the Declaration of Independence and the Constitution, he had to embrace emancipation. But he moved cautiously. He made no mention of slavery when he defined the administration's purpose in his message to Congress early in the conflict. During the first twelve months or so of the war he overturned the military emancipations of Generals John C. Frémont and David Hunter; he sacked his Secretary of War, Simon Cameron, for publicly proposing the arming of black soldiers; he continued to cherish cautious schemes of compensated emancipation and the colonizing of free blacks in overseas settlements. He was unenthusiastic about the two Confiscation Acts passed by Congress. When Horace Greeley of the New York *Tribune* published his 'Prayer of Twenty Million', calling on the president to grasp the nettle of emancipation, Lincoln's reply appeared only to confirm his cautious pragmatism. The Emancipation Proclamation, when finally issued on New Year's Day 1863, freed only those slaves over whom the proclamation could have no immediate influence.

Over the next two years, however, Lincoln followed through the logic of that Proclamation, by arming black troops, refusing to renege on the promise to emancipate, invoking 'a new birth of freedom' in the majesty of the Gettysburg Address, incorporating in the Republican party's platform in 1864 the promise to secure a constitutional amendment ending slavery, and using presidential patronage after his reelection to ensure that Congress voted for that very amendment. On the eve of his death, Lincoln was even proposing that certain categories of freedmen be given the vote. The circumstances of war had allowed Lincoln legitimately to redefine the purpose of the Union so as to give freer rein to his own natural antislavery instincts.[8]

Lincoln refused to compromise that vision of the Union. For as long as he was president, and while the nation remained sundered, he would continue the fight. The photographic portraits of Lincoln, aged and fatigued, in the final months of the war are a measure of the personal cost of that resolve. There is no clearer statement of his determination than his words in the summer of 1864, as the Union armies under Grant suffered battlefield slaughter on an unprecedented scale. 'We accepted this war for . . . a worthy object, and the war will end when that object is attained. . . . [It] has taken three years; it was begun or accepted upon the line of restoring the national authority over the whole national domain. . . . I say we are going through on this line if it takes three years more.'[9]

Reading the public

Lincoln openly acknowledged that the steps by which he redefined the war for the Union as a war against slavery were guided by his reading of public opinion, and that he feared too early an embrace of emancipation would shatter the Union consensus. This sensitivity to popular mood was entirely in keeping with the conviction of the pre-war Lincoln that 'public sentiment is everything. With public sentiment, nothing can fail; without it nothing can succeed.' By this he did not mean pandering to popular prejudice, nor brazen demagoguery, nor compromising his fundamental principles, but rather moulding public opinion for the better within the inevitable constraints that 'a universal public feeling' necessarily imposed.[10] This respect for the people was entirely understandable in a politician whose first years in public life coincided with the advent of mass democracy and whose natural environment was the small, face-to-face communities of the West, where individual citizens felt close to those who governed them. Growing up amongst the farmers of Kentucky and Indiana, Lincoln had an empathy for common folk that ensured a continued rapport with the rural and small-town electorate of Illinois, and kept him alert to nuances in public sentiment, even as his success as a lawyer and officeholder put social distance between him and them: only once in his career, and that early on, did he lose a popular election.

The influential newspaperman, John W. Forney, came deeply to admire Lincoln's feel for what the public would tolerate. 'Lincoln is the most truly progressive man of the age', he judged, 'because he always moves in conjunction with propitious circumstances, not waiting to be dragged by the force of events or wasting strength in premature struggles with them.'[11] Specifically, Lincoln's wartime concern not to push mainstream Union sentiment towards emancipation faster than it wanted to go meant turning a deaf ear to the impatient appeals of antislavery radicals, while simultaneously nudging border-state conservatives towards a more realistic appraisal of events. But the question arises: how could he be sure what that mainstream opinion was?

As a state politician, the Illinois circuit lawyer and aspiring politician had enjoyed a face-to-face relationship with his constituents, but the nation's president and commander-in-chief was mostly restricted to the executive mansion. Remote from his roots, surrounded by officeholders, ever more exhausted by the unremitting burden of directing the war, bombarded by conflicting advice, and rarely straying from the nation's capital, how could he know and track the turbulent thoughts of ordinary Americans?

Election returns offered a series of snapshots of political opinion. On average a significant congressional or state election occurred in the North every other month during the four years of war. Lincoln, whose grasp of electoral topography and arithmetic was second to none, spent many an hour in the telegraph office (located in the War Department, just a short walk from the White House) awaiting and analyzing outcomes. Broadly speaking, election results allowed the administration to plot the course and strength of Union opinion throughout the war. Thus, the Republicans' success in New England in spring 1861 appeared to endorse the new administration's policy of coercion of the Confederacy. Winning various state contests outside New England later that year only with the support of War Democrats seemed to vindicate its conciliatory approach towards border-state conservatives. In the congressional and state contests in the fall of 1862, the most serious electoral test of the war to date, Lincoln's administration suffered a serious popular rebuff, especially in the mid-West and the lower North, though the extent to which this represented the electorate's hostility to the policy of emancipation and the assault on the South's social system, as opposed to a critical commentary on the Union army's lack of energy and success, was not so easy to gauge.[12] Using voting figures as a commentary on matters of national policy could be like reading braille with a gloved hand.

Dealings with political leaders at national and state level held out for Lincoln opportunities for more nuanced analyses of popular mood. From his deliberately broad-based and inclusive cabinet he heard often dissonant voices advancing a range of views which ran the gamut of Unionist opinion – disharmony, in this case at least, acting as a source of presidential strength not weakness. More sensitive still to public feeling were those in elective office, notably state governors and United States Congressmen, whom Lincoln considered his eyes and ears in each constituency. From Andrew G. Curtin of Pennsylvania, Richard Yates of Illinois, Oliver P. Morton of Indiana, John A. Andrew of Massachusetts, and other loyal governors, the president received commentaries on the general management of the war, on electoral prospects, and on the public's view of particular administration policies across a range of salient issues: confiscation, colonization, emancipation, black troops, the draft, reconstruction. But, as Lincoln discovered to his cost, though they were closer than he to the grass-roots, their judgments were not infallible. Thus, taking William Dennison's advice in the spring of 1861 to heed popular will and convert the 90–day militiamen into three-year volunteers, Lincoln was forced into retracting his approval in the face of the men's anger and threat of mutiny.[13] Governors and other state politicians had their own axes to grind, of course, and Lincoln had always to remain on the lookout for self-interested pleading disguised as objective testimony. His grasp on the slippery confusion of events in Missouri, for instance, was undoubtedly weakened by the ambiguities and defectiveness of his information. Unsurprisingly, he sent his own White House secretaries, John G. Nicolay and John Hay, on a variety of missions to establish the state of local political feeling.

Newspapers, the lifeblood of the American political system, provided Lincoln with another means of keeping his finger on the pulse of opinion. In his days as an aspiring Illinois politician he had been an insatiable reader of the party political press, but the rigours of office gave the harassed president far less time to indulge this appetite. Francis Carpenter, the portrait painter who observed his daily routine over a six-month period, recalled only one instance when he saw Lincoln casually browsing through a newspaper. Actually, papers abounded in the White House. In addition to the three Washington dailies (the *Morning Chronicle, National Republican* and *Star*) which were laid out on Lincoln's study table, a variety of the Union's leading papers provided his secretaries with the materials from which they could mine the interesting editorial matter and items of political importance they judged they should bring to the president's attention. When for a brief interlude early in the war events conspired to interrupt the daily flow of papers, a sense of isolation and even desperation seized the occupants of the executive mansion. Lincoln had a healthily sceptical attitude to press criticism, which rarely moved him to anger and which he commonly dismissed as 'noise' and 'gas', generated by ignorance and editorial self-importance. Still, he could not afford to ignore editors as conduits of opinion. When, in the dark days of the summer of 1864, those whom he trusted anxiously brought him reports of opinion hardening against the administration, he came as close as he ever did to abandoning the high ground of antislavery Unionism.[14]

Loyal editors also bombarded the president with unsolicited advice in hundreds of private letters. These represented only a small fraction of the mail that at times threatened to submerge the White House secretariat. Nicolay handled Lincoln's huge correspondence before his inauguration; subsequently the responsibility fell on Hay's young shoulders. As the volume rose, to reach a peak of two mailbags (some 500 letters) daily during the mid-point of Lincoln's reelection year, an additional secretary was required. Much of the correspondence comprised requests for civil jobs and military commissions. There were diatribes and hate mail, too, from which Lincoln was generally shielded. But many letters came from those whom one secretary described as 'good and true men', often unlettered and humble, pouring out their 'deepest heart sorrows' and offering their advice on the conduct of affairs. Of course, Lincoln had time to handle only a fraction of what arrived, perhaps a dozen or so letters a day; according to Hay, the president personally read no more than one letter in fifty. But those he did review, together with the summaries and annotations provided by his secretaries, gave him a chance literally to read public opinion. Each phase of the conflict prompted earnest suggestions about the best policies and strategy for victory.[15]

Many wrote to the president as an alternative to paying the personal call that the constraints of geography, time and expense prevented. Yet the most remarkable feature of Lincoln's tenure of office were the throngs of ordinary citizens who came to the capital to pour through the White House doors, intent on a private interview on one of the president's regular public days. Lincoln never lost his determination to remain accessible – to be 'the attorney of the people, not their ruler'. William H. Seward remarked that 'there never was a man so accessible to all sorts of proper and improper persons'; the president himself described his office hours as 'the Beggars' Opera'. He never lost his keen sense of his own ordinariness and his kinship with common folk. He cherished republican simplicity, shunned the imperial style, and protested strongly when the general-in-chief, Henry W. Halleck, detailed a cavalry detachment, clattering along with sabres and spurs, to guard the presidential carriage.[16]

In consequence of what Henry J. Raymond called Lincoln's 'utter unconsciousness of his position', ordinary men and women regarded him more as a neighbour to be dropped in upon than as a remote head of state. 'Mr Lincoln is *always* approachable and this is greatly in his favor,' explained the Washington correspondent of the New York *Independent*. 'The people can get at him and impress upon him their views without difficulty.' Though his visitors included, in the words of one observer, 'loiterers, contract-hunters, garrulous parents on paltry errands, toadies without measure, and talkers without conscience', Lincoln was adamantly opposed to restricting access. 'I feel – though the tax on my time is heavy – that no hours of my day are better employed than those which bring me again within the direct contact and

[76] atmosphere of the average of our whole people.' Each meeting, he maintained, served 'to renew in me a clearer and more vivid image of that great popular assemblage out of which I sprung. . . . I call these receptions my "*public-opinion baths*;" for I have but little time to read the papers and gather public opinion that way.' Sometimes he felt himself bombarded and besieged but, even so, these encounters with ordinary folk worked to invigorate his 'perceptions of responsibility and duty'.[17] Probably more than any other single agency, they provided the down-to-earth oxygen lacking in the rarefied political air of wartime Washington.

Reaching the public: the power of language

Listening was only one part of the business of leadership. Communicating the aims and rationale of war was just as essential to Union victory. Lincoln's authority as a democratic politician in antebellum America derived very largely from his campaign oratory. Though physically awkward, he was a natural and fluent speaker, with a clear, pleasing, penetrative tenor voice, and his speeches combined clarity, logic, moral force, substance, spontaneity, wit and good humour. Yet after his nomination for the presidency in May 1860 he never took to the stump again and, once in the White House, he made only very limited use of a weapon that had done so much to win him the high regard of Republicans nationally. As president, he spoke in public nearly one hundred times. Mostly these were not full-blown speeches but modest remarks, often unscripted; they included short addresses to troops passing through Washington, impromptu responses to musical serenaders, and statements to visiting delegations – of clergymen, border-state representatives, free blacks and others. Almost all were made in the capital. His two inaugural addresses and his speech at Gettysburg were rare, set-piece exceptions to this general picture.[18]

We may wonder about Lincoln's reluctance to speak in public, given his proven rhetorical abilities, his confidence in the power of language, and his reiterated certainty that Americans responded well to the truth, when logically and clearly presented. The explanation lies partly in his conventional attitude that it was not quite proper for a president to make speeches at all, and certainly not during election campaigns, when stump-speaking would smack of partisanship not statesmanship. No less influential was the pressure of presidential business, whose schedule gave Lincoln little of the time he felt he required to prepare an effective speech. Almost all his great addresses, as at Springfield in June 1858 and at the New York Cooper Union in February 1860, followed careful deliberation, even sustained research. His First Inaugural was the product of protracted thought, meticulous preparation and several drafts. Once the war began, the competing demands on the president and commander-in-chief left little time for speech-writing, or for travelling outside Washington. Since, unlike modern presidents, he used no ghostwriter (though the Secretary of State wrote the words that Lincoln spoke when foreign ministers were presented) and since he feared he might be led into careless, off-hand remarks (which explains why he fretted at the approach of musical serenaders, who always expected a few words), we should not be surprised that he spoke so little in public and that the two most celebrated speeches of his presidency, the Gettysburg address and the Second Inaugural, were as short as they were sweet.

Some have considered Lincoln's reticence a probable mistake, a damaging and self-inflicted wound, to be contrasted with Jefferson Davis's recourse to speaking tours to bolster Confederate morale.[19] But this judgment should be qualified, not least because of Lincoln's alternative and sometimes brilliant use of the written word to communicate the purposes of the administration. The most formal of the president's documents, his annual and special messages to Congress (which were forwarded from the White House, to be read out by a clerk in the legislative branch, and were subsequently published in the press), naturally consumed much of his time and blended routine information, analysis of events, explanation of the administration's course, and occasionally soaring rhetoric. Then there were the published accounts of many of Lincoln's interviews with White House visitors, including his scripted responses. Probably most effective of all were his carefully crafted public letters to particular individuals, designed to rally Northern opinion or prepare it for imminent changes in policy, and each addressing issues crucial to the conduct and outcome of the war: notably, emancipation and racial issues in his letters to Horace Greeley (August 1862), James C. Conkling (August 1863) and Albert Hodges (April 1864); conscription policy, to New York Governor Horatio Seymour (August 1863); and treason, military arrests and the suspension of habeas corpus, to Erastus Corning (June 1863).

Lincoln perhaps regretted being unable to give voice to his own words: he was keenly alert to matters of intonation and emphasis (evident in his private recitation of Shakespearean soliloquies and in his canny advice to an actor playing Falstaff on how to get the best out of a line); significantly, he accompanied his letter to Conkling, designed to be read out at a Union rally, with guidance on how it should be delivered.[20] His enforced near-silence made him all the more attentive to the quality of his prose, which he sought to imbue with colour, life and energy. When, in his intended message to the special session of Congress in July 1861, Lincoln described the rebellion as 'sugar-coated', the government printer objected to what was then judged an un-dignified expression. Lincoln was unimpressed by the distinction his critic drew between the racy language appropriate for a mass-meeting in Illinois and the prose of an historic, formal document: 'that word expresses precisely my idea, and I am not going to change it. The time will never come in this country when the people won't know exactly what *sugar-coated* means!'[21] Some-times Lincoln's lively metaphors got the better of him: even the adoring Hay judged the letter to Conkling, with its allusion to the navy as 'Uncle Sam's web-feet', to be scarred by 'hideously bad rhetoric . . . [and] indecorums that are infamous'.[22] But in the main the president's prose was arresting, lucid and strikingly economical.

Reaching the public: the agency of party

In practice, it made no great difference whether Lincoln spoke or wrote. What really counted was that his words and opinions reached and moved the widest possible audience. Lincoln's personal exertions in defining the administration's objectives were only part of the overall strategy by which the federal government harnessed Union sentiment. In seeking out the most potent agencies to mobilize that opinion, the Government had to look beyond its official mechanisms, for governmental institutions in the early republic had been chronically weak. The most powerful and extensive networks in the nation were voluntary associations. Preeminently these were twofold: the political parties – their voluntarism supplemented and com-promised by the rewards of government patronage – and the churches, with their associated philanthropic agencies. Through these networks, energetic-ally exploited, a president tied to the White House was able project himself and his cause into the heartland of the Union and beyond. The historian David Donald has emphasized Lincoln's essential passivity in the face of events, but there is little evidence of this in the president's efforts to mobilize opinion behind the war effort.[23]

Lincoln needed no lessons in how the power of party might promote a cause.[24] His presidential victory in 1860 had depended far less on his

personal appeal than on the skill with which Republican organizers had projected him as the embodiment of the party's philosophy and platform; despite limited funds and a still developing organization, they yet managed to
sustain a stunningly effective 'hurrah' campaign, marked by swarms of speakers,
enthusiastic meetings, 'Wide-Awake' marching clubs, high expectations,
and crusading energy. But Lincoln's election to the presidency and nominal
leadership of the party did not mean that the organization, whatever its
potential for war mobilization, would effortlessly fall into line behind him.
The Republicans were a fragile, decentralized coalition with no experience
in national office. There were few established Lincoln loyalists in Congress.
Organizationally the party was in practice little more than an agglomeration
of local and state bodies. Philosophically, too, it was divided, as internal conflicts over emancipation, the conduct of the war, and reconstruction would
show. Many of the president's most querulous and vociferous critics throughout
the war were Republicans. Lincoln's essential task, if it were to become a truly
effective rallying force for the adminstration, was to bind it together and
impose his authority on it.

For these purposes he had at hand a potent weapon: presidential patronage. There was nothing new in a president fusing his roles as party leader
and chief executive by distributing government jobs to the party faithful. But
Lincoln had the added bonus of controlling appointments to the thousands
of new offices occasioned by the wartime expansion of the army and government departments. An experienced and skilful party manager, who possessed
a potent combination of tenacity, patience and command of detail, he devoted
an enormous slice of his time to disposing of these posts. It was a wearisome
and even draining exercise, as he sought to avoid gratuitously upsetting the
competitors for office while yet remaining even-handed towards the various
party factions, including his critics. But his attentiveness and refusal to be
bullied undoubtedly paid off. He built up a bank of congressional indebted-
ness, by meeting the patronage requests of interceding Congressmen, and
created such highly effective cadres of supporters at state level that he easily
outmanoeuvred those who had hoped to prevent his running for a second
term. Lincoln's complete mastery of the party's nominating convention at
Baltimore in June 1864 was a measure of the skill and diligence with which
he had attended to the minutiae of internal party affairs.[25]

The spontaneous demonstrations of Union patriotism that immediately
followed hostilities at Fort Sumter meant Lincoln's call to arms scarcely needed
re-echoing by grass-roots Republicans, though in fact local party leaders leapt
to beat the martial drum, and mobilize men and resources, in unyielding

response to secessionist defiance.[26] However, as the early enthusiasm gave way first to frustration and then to war-weariness, it grew increasingly urgent to remind people of the Union's meaning. Lincoln looked to his Congressmen, governors and local leaders to spread within their constituencies the themes of his formal addresses, and to sell each new development of policy as it was defined: the Emancipation Proclamation, the use of black troops, the unacceptability of peace on the terms of 'the Union as it was'. It was an expectation by no means realized in every case, as Republican conservatives jibbed at emancipation, while radicals, criticizing Lincoln's caution, articulated more ambitious objectives in less emollient language. But an influential core of party loyalists, notably amongst the Republican governors, persistently proved their worth to Lincoln as interpreters of the administration's purpose.

All Northern governors in 1861 were loyal party men. They owed their office to the party; they had been energetic and essential agents of national victory in 1860. As the war progressed they encouraged the president to take more power into federal hands, and became themselves increasingly dependent on Washington: without War Department funds Governor Morton of Indiana would have had to recall a Democratic legislature which, bitterly opposed to an emancipationist war, had refused appropriations; in the critical state elections of 1863, especially in Connecticut, Ohio, and Pennsylvania, Lincoln's interventionism included dispensing patronage, getting troops furloughed home to vote, and ensuring that government clerks were given leave (and free railroad passes) to reach the polls. Thus the demands and protectiveness of party increasingly bound state and national governments together, and their mutual dependence had huge implications for Washington's communication of the Union's purpose. For one thing, it made possible political stage-management in cultivating public confidence. After McClellan's retreat from Richmond in the summer of 1862, Lincoln feared that a call for a further 100,000 men, though badly needed, would provoke 'a general panic and stampede . . . so hard it is to have a thing understood as it really is.' Instead, in a scheme involving Seward, Thurlow Weed, and Republican governors Edwin Morgan of New York and Curtin of Pennsylvania, Lincoln got the loyal governors to sign a memorial ostensibly emanating from them but in reality drawn up by the administration.[27]

The interdependence of state and national administrations, as Eric McKitrick has shrewdly argued, became even more salient after the mid-term electoral setbacks of 1862: Democratic gains led state Republican organizations into energetic defence of national policy – notably in justifying emancipation as essential and consistent with the original purpose of the war – and into lambasting their opponents, now encouraged to bolder calls for peace, as traitors. In this context, Republicans read their victories in the state elections of 1863 not simply as local successes but as a triumph for Lincoln's administration. Candidates for even the lowest local offices, in asking people to vote Republican, were urging an endorsement of the war, its purposes, and its leaders. Wartime elections provided the arena, and the Republican party the means, for 'continual affirmation and reaffirmation of [national] purpose'.[28]

One of the most powerful ligaments of party and its most ubiquitous instrument of political persuasion was the newspaper press. Lincoln's experience in Illinois had taught him its value in developing amongst subscribers a common understanding and intent. He had written occasional articles, provided financial subsidies, and indeed bought one paper – the Illinois *Staats-Anzeiger* – to promote Republicanism within the German immigrant community. Those editors and correspondents who helped him into the presidency in 1860 soon found themselves the beneficiaries of a clutch of lucrative foreign appointments, postmasterships, customs-house posts and other jobs in his gift. At about the same time, the ridicule that a hostile press heaped on him for arriving for his Washington inaugural secretly, in disguise and by night, was a salutary reminder of the power of the press to shape opinion for the worse as well as the better.[29]

Cultivating a sympathetic press became a wartime priority. Persuasion, not constraint, was the watchword. Lincoln was generally hesitant about gagging hostile papers, urging military forbearance in response to the irritations offered by the Chicago *Times* and other 'Peace Democrat' sheets; he bore no direct responsibility for the War Department's censoring of military information. Systematic news management and the modern press conference were, of course, developments of the future, and even a loyal press was not necessarily biddable: Lincoln was apparently furious when his letter to Conkling, despite restrictions, appeared word for word in the trusted New York *Evening Post* two days before it was due to be first read at a Union meeting in Springfield, Illinois. Still, the president – and his White House secretaries – had available a variety of means to reward loyalty and broadcast the administration's unbending Unionism. Lincoln allocated lucrative government printing contracts to selected Republican papers; composed a few articles specifically for newspaper circulation; and carefully placed his public letters to Greeley, Hodges and others in the most appropriate journals, from where they were later copied by others across the Union. Unsurprisingly, loyal correspondents made up the presidential trainload to Gettysburg in November 1863, their place on the platform assured; hundreds of local papers subsequently printed and celebrated Lincoln's speech, in repudiation of Democratic ridicule of a 'silly, flat and dish-watery utterance'. Probably most important of all, Lincoln, though not dependably accessible to reporters, made sure his office door was open when the issue demanded it. Editors in whom he trusted, including the young Noah Brooks of the Sacramento *Daily Union* and Simon P. Hanscom of the Washington *National Republican*, were quite frequent visitors. A number were rewarded with government posts at home and abroad.[30]

No editor was more loyal to the administration than John W. Forney, a Philadelphia ex-Democrat whose admiration for what he termed Lincoln's 'unconscious greatness' was no doubt underscored by the president's part in getting him elected as secretary of the Senate and in securing commissions for his sons. The undeviating Unionism of his Philadelphia *Press* gave it every appearance of a White House organ. It not only defended the president against the charge of violating civil liberties, but in July 1862 made a remarkable volte-face to support emancipation (the same month that Lincoln first raised a change of policy with his cabinet) – a shift which, in hindsight, suggests Lincoln's blessing. We can also see Lincoln's handiwork in Forney's establishing a new daily paper in Washington towards the end of 1862. With the editorial stance of the influential, mass-circulation New York *Tribune* increasingly uncertain, as Horace Greeley oscillated nervously between support for the administration and alarmed defeatism, the president had suggested to Forney that he turn his *Sunday Morning Chronicle* into a daily. Supported by government funds (in payment for printing federal notices and advertising) and given easy access to the White House, Forney developed a newspaper which carried a message of uncompromising Unionism daily to thousands of troops in the Army of the Potomac. His papers would set the tone for the pro-administration press in 1864 by being the first to endorse Lincoln's renomination, when many other Republican editors doubted his ability to win. The president's opponents called Forney 'Lincoln's dog'.[31]

Cheap newspapers provided Lincoln with one vehicle for propagandizing the Union, cheap pamphlets another. Civil War Americans witnessed an unprecedented torrent of polemical and exhortatory pamphlet literature. At first many titles were individually financed and produced, but from the early months of 1863 pamphlet and broadside publishing achieved extraordinary levels of coordination and activity under the direction of several new publication societies. These bodies grew naturally out of existing Union Leagues and Loyal Leagues, those extra-party associations set up to rally Union morale in the bleak winter days of 1862–3. Their models included the most impressive of all pre-war publishing and distribution agencies, the American

Tract Society. In New York, Boston and Philadelphia distinguished professionals and intellectuals like Francis Lieber joined with representatives of the business classes to raise huge sums for the free distribution of Union propaganda, with the intention of combating defeatism amongst troops and civilians, and countering the 'disloyal' effusions of Democratic presses. The Philadelphia Union League's Board of Publications, the largest and most efficient of these societies, raised tens of thousands of dollars towards the wartime production of well over a hundred different pamphlets and broadsheets, and distributed over a million items of literature in army camps and on the home front.[32]

Naturally enough, Lincoln's own words formed part of this loyalist torrent. But he was more directly involved, too. A measure of his attention to the Union's propaganda machinery lies in how he responded to Democratic criticisms of the suspension of habeas corpus. His public letter of June 1863 to Erastus Corning in defence of 'strong measures . . . indispensable to the public Safety' was not merely reproduced in friendly newspapers. Lincoln had it printed and sent to Republicans across the country on the frank of his private secretary. As Mark Neely has noted, this kept the chief executive personally immune to charges of squalid electioneering but indicated the importance he attached to the letter's circulation. The recipients included Francis Lieber, who wrote to assure the president that the Loyal Publication Society of New York would run off ten thousand copies. Around half a million of what another New Yorker described as 'the best Campaign document we can have in this state' were produced for voters and for soldiers in the field.[33]

The role of the New York, Philadelphia and other publication societies in the autumn elections of 1863 (notably in securing Curtin's gubernatorial victory in Pennsylvania) leaves no doubt that at bottom they were adjuncts of the Republican party, and formidable ones at that. But their association with the Union Leagues also reflects Lincoln's and the Republicans' efforts to widen their coalition by incorporating as many Union Democrats as possible. Pertinent here was the anonymous article that Lincoln ('an Illinoisian') wrote for the *Daily Morning Chronicle* during the crisis over General Ambrose Burnside's suspension of the Chicago *Times* in the summer of 1863: the president was at pains to remove the slur that Forney had unfairly cast on the paper's previous editor, James Sheahan, a loyal Union Democrat and now editor of the Chicago *Post*. Lincoln's intervention revealed both his sure grasp of the newspaper scene, and his determination to do nothing to alienate actual and potential supporters on the middle ground of politics. Here was the key to many of the

[84]   developments of 1864: the renaming of the Republicans as 'the Union party'; the publication societies' carefully targeted distribution of unprecedented quantities of materials to wavering voters; and Lincoln's overtures to independent, Democrat-inclining editors like James Gordon Bennett of the New York *Herald*.[34]

Lincoln's reelection triumph in November 1864, as much as the Union victory sealed at Appomattox itself, was proof positive of how magnificently the Republicans' networks of speakers and publicists could mobilize opinion. Of course, there were also contingent elements at work in McClellan's defeat: notably, the Union commanders' roster of late-summer successes (Mobile Bay, Atlanta, the Shenandoah) and the Democrats' myopia in adopting a peace platform at their Chicago convention. But it was the Republican party itself which constituted Lincoln's most potent weapon. Controlling its patronage, enjoying the personal support of enough of its key editors, and living by his wits, Lincoln secured his renomination in June. Thereafter the party, despite political wobbles in July and August, cranked up a formidable campaigning machinery. Lincoln himself, according to Francis Carpenter, declared, 'I cannot run the political machine; I have enough on my hands without *that*. It is the *people's* business, – the election is in their hands.' This was technically correct, but the statement is silent over not only the president's deep desire for reelection (he liaised closely with Henry J. Raymond, chairman of the national committee), but also the unflagging efforts of party managers to show the people what their business actually was.[35]

Whatever the frictions between the powerful state committees and the Union Congressional Committee, between the localities and the centre of a mainly decentralized party, the organizers' passion for the Union generated literally millions of printed items and ensured an insistent chorus of political speakers – all in addition to the routine appearance of hundreds of daily papers. Lincoln had been by no means the unanimous choice of Republican editors and publicists earlier in the year. But from early September onwards the alternatives for the party's thousands of activists were clear enough. Better Lincoln, whatever his failings, than a Democrat whose platform effectively wrote off the sacrifices of war. Thanks to the cumulative efforts of the party's publicists during the president's first term, even Lincoln's Republican critics knew that the president – whatever they asserted about his errors in judgment, his lack of vigour in executive action, and his enfeebling kind-heartedness – was still a tenacious defender of the Union, honest and unbendable in purpose, lacking in airs and graces, and a man of unimpeachable integrity. He was also widely regarded as morally upright and God-respecting – characteristics which, as we are about to see, had important implications for engaging a second cluster of national networks in the cause of Union.

Reaching the public: churches and philanthropic organizations

The churches and the benevolent organizations they sustained can claim to have been the first truly effective national networks in the United States. More consistently than any other governmental or voluntary agency in the early republic they drew ordinary people into an arena extending beyond their locality and state. Being a member of a church usually meant being part of a denominational connection whose preachers and press gave members a taste of the world beyond, mobilizing them in pursuit of ambitious benevolent causes, national and international in scope. At the outbreak of civil war this network of churches and related philanthropic reform societies presented the North with a potent weapon. Recruiting their ministerial and lay leaders as active advocates of the Union cause would allow the administration to broadcast directly to the nation's largest complex of subcultures. In particular, it would harness the forces of evangelical Protestantism – the millions of Methodists, Baptists, Presbyterians, Congregationalists, and others, who formed the most formidable religious grouping in the country.

The American experiment of separating church and state had done little to blunt the political appetites of religious leaders or church members. In the antebellum years, despite a minority strain of political quietism, not only were most male church members deeply involved in politics, but Protestant ministers themselves were amongst the most active partisans. Whigs and Democrats annexed the support of different religious clusters, with the anti-Catholic, moral reforming, nativist elements of the former leading it to claim the title of 'the Christian party'. But it was the Republican coalition of anti-slavery Whigs and third-party remnants of Libertymen and Free Soilers that more properly deserved the name. The party that put Lincoln into power drew much of its moral energy from the distinctive 'Yankee' religious culture of New England and its diaspora. The Republicans' collective conscience was shaped by an optimistic millennialism, a modern or 'New School' Calvinism (chiefly located in Congregational, New School Presbyterian and some Baptist churches), and a strain of Methodist social activism influenced by Calvinist

[86] ideas of citizenship. Though many Northern evangelicals remained true to
the Democratic party in 1860, antislavery (and anti-Catholic) clergy and lay
leaders regimented their followers more effectively than ever before in the
Republican cause of barring the spread of slavery and emancipating free
white men from the tyranny of the slave power.[36]

Lincoln was fully alert to the value of the unprecedented fusing of religion
and politics in the campaign of 1860. He could equally have been in no doubt
about the subsequent rallying of the Northern churches to the cause of
Union. Bombarded throughout the war by resolutions from ecclesiastical
bodies, besieged by religious deputations, and in regular receipt of the New
York *Independent*, the most influential of all religious papers, Lincoln and his
White House secretaries were well equipped to gauge the shifts in religious
opinion. Northern clergy, divided before the war over slavery, now united
in defence of the Union. Much of their analysis, even their words, echoed
Lincoln's own. Secession constituted rebellion and treachery when urged, as
by Confederates, without good cause. It was an act of national suicide and
anarchy, for its underlying principle destroyed all government. To destroy
the American Union was to end a unique experiment in political and religious
freedom, one revolving around government by the people, 'the best form of
government on earth'. At issue was the question 'whether liberty, strength,
and permanency are incompatible conditions in the same body politic'. To
sustain republicanism was to fight 'for free government in our land and in all
the lands for all ages to come'.[37]

The Union was not just politically significant. It had a spiritual dimension,
too. Protestants prized the Union as the vehicle for God's unique role for
America within human history. What the historian James Moorhead has
described as the 'acute millennial consciousness' of North American Protestants, carried to the New World by the original Puritan settlers and successively passed down to each new generation, gave the new nation a powerful
sense of being God's instrument in the coming of His Kingdom. Its physical
geography and natural resources indicated the oneness that God had intended
for it. For the first seven decades of the republic's existence most Protestants
believed that the fusion of evangelical piety and republican government
would have such a powerful moral effect that the Kingdom of God would be
inaugurated by persuasion alone, without the need for arms. But Southern
secessionists, in an act of destruction that challenged God's providence,
had changed all that. And whereas in the antebellum generation, the call to
defend the Union had been the cry of Northern conservatives eager to find
common ground with Southern churches, it now became, in Moorhead's

words, a cry 'infused with a new moral significance. . . . The holy Union that Northerners defended was no longer the compromise-tainted object of earlier years; it was democratic civilization in collision with an alien way of life.'[38]

If the majority of Protestants accepted the government's initial definition of the war exclusively as a struggle to re-establish the Constitution and laws, there were those, like Thomas Eddy, who predicted from the start that the 'logic of events' would transform it into an assault on slavery. He was right. As fugitives and captured slaves began to fill the Union camps, the government became further complicit in slavery; as the hopes of early victory dissolved into embarrassing failure and cruel defeat, church leaders increasingly judged slavery the essential cause of the nation's difficulties and saw slaves themselves as a huge resource – 'the commissariat of the rebel army' – to be confiscated and freed. As the suffering persisted in defiance of evangelicals' appeals for Divine assistance, so they convinced themselves that the conflict was a punishment for the sin of oppression. Frémont's proclamation thus elicited a widespread chorus of delight, its revocation bitter disappointment. Through 1862 even previously cautious evangelicals warmed to emancipation and the use of black troops as the only means of restoring the Union. A growing consensus judged that slavery had to die, a conclusion commonly expressed in the language of the Apocalypse. American history, the culmination of world history, would resolve the battle between Antichrist and the Christian order; between Southern slavery, feudalism and the Cavalier mentality on one side, and freedom – Yankee and Puritan – on the other.[39] Lincoln's Emancipation Proclamation was an essential act of purification which would, in cleansing the nation, open the way to victory.

Lincoln worked hard to keep open two-way channels with the leaders of this influential constituency, and to deal sensitively and respectfully with them, aware not only of their power but also of the deep reservoir of goodwill on which he could draw. Here we should note that Lincoln never wore his religion on his sleeve; indeed, his personal beliefs remain an enigma to the historian. His Old School Presbyterian church-going in both Springfield and Washington gave him a context congenial to his Calvinist, even fatalist, temperament, but there is no evidence that he ever responded to the evangelical's demand for immediate repentance from sin. He may well have been drawn to sceptical writers in his youth, but now in later life the responsibilities of leadership, and the burdens imposed by public and personal tragedy, brought him face to face with questions of ultimate reality; the experience appears to have deepened his faith in a divinity from whom he sought inspiration and strength.[40] It is not clear how far Lincoln's cultivation of the company of

[88]   religious leaders, especially evangelicals, had to do with his own spiritual quest, but there is no doubt that those contacts provided him with a way of both reading and reaching potent opinion-formers.

The president's overtures to religious men and women took a variety of forms. His private conversations with informal visitors to the White House extended across the full gamut of denominational affiliation; Lincoln, with his lifelong aversion to sectarian narrowness, offered an inclusive welcome. Some came to lecture, some to deliver homilies, some to seek appointments, others merely to pay respects or renew acquaintance. They included the strategically placed, such as editors of mass-circulation papers, denominational leaders, and distinguished abolitionists. There were representatives of the chief wartime philanthropic agencies, particularly the United States Sanitary Commission, which bound thousands of local groups into a national soldiers' relief organization. At other times, Lincoln met more formally with delegations from particular denominations (Friends, Presbyterians, Baptists and others), from particular localities (notably the visit of leading Chicago clergy in September 1862), and from particular causes (including temperance advocates and the US Christian Commission). Lincoln clearly knew how to squeeze political benefit out of these occasions, commonly responding to their formal addresses with his own carefully crafted words.

Lincoln's use of a visiting deputation of Methodists in May 1864 provides a fine example. A committee of five leading members of the quadrennial General Conference of the Methodist Episcopal Church meeting in Philadelphia had been appointed to deliver an address to the president, to assure him of the denomination's continuing support for the Union and its war aims, including emancipation. One of the party, Granville Moody, knew the president quite well. His colleagues sent him ahead to arrange a meeting at the White House. Lincoln, with the Union party's nominating convention only weeks away, seized the chance to stage-manage the occasion. He asked Moody to leave a copy of the address and invited the committee for the next day. On admission the members were received 'with great courtesy' by the president and senior members of his cabinet. Lincoln stood 'straight as an arrow' as he listened to their address. He then took from his desk the brief response that he had prepared overnight. In five short sentences he thanked them, endorsed their sentiments, ensured that other churches would take no offence by his singling out Methodists for praise, and then flatteringly described them as 'the most important of all' denominations: 'It is no fault in others that the Methodist Church sends more soldiers to field, more nurses to the hospitals, and more prayers to heaven than any.' After a brief conversation the ministers withdrew, much impressed with Lincoln's generous, high-toned remarks. Returning to their conference the next morning, proudly clutching a signed copy of the president's words to show their colleagues, they were taken aback to discover that a full account of the meeting had already been published in the daily papers. The White House had telegraphed the news the previous day; the story had gone into type in Philadelphia even before the committee had left Washington.[41] Lincoln's reply was designed not just for his five visitors but for the other 7,000 ministers and nearly one million members of the largest, most influential denomination of the land. Nothing would be left to chance.

There were other ways of reaching out to the influential religious element, not least through presidential patronage, which offered a means of stroking the institutional egos of churches. But Lincoln's most powerful weapon was the spoken and written word. In speeches designed specifically for religio-philanthropic audiences, as with his addresses to Sanitary Fairs and denominational groups; in documents intended for a specifically religious purpose, as with his calls for national fasts and days of thanksgiving; and in his set-piece speeches, which might not be cast in expressly religious language but which were evidently rooted in a moral understanding of America's meaning and future (as at Gettysburg) and appealed to the better, deeper side of human nature – in all of these ways Lincoln used words, often biblical, which persuaded the public that the administration was under the guidance of a man who recognized his dependence on Divine favour. A perceptive commentator remarked that both president and people 'seem . . . to imagine that he is a sort of halfway clergyman'.[42] In fact, as Lincoln's remarkable Second Inaugural Address revealed, the president's understanding of the Almighty's role in Union affairs was far more subtle and tentative than that of many professional theologians.[43] It also showed a president capable of a meaningful engagement with the nation's Christian leaders.

The administration's efforts achieved their reward. Mainstream Protestants translated their full-blooded Unionism into a form of patriotic politics that encouraged even some previously apolitical clergy to become the arm of the Republican party. Silent prayers for the president were necessary but in themselves inadequate: vociferous support for the administration became a duty. Church meetings consciously yoked the sacred and the secular: congregations sang 'America' and the 'Star-Spangled Banner' and cheered the sanctified stars and stripes that fluttered over their buildings. A minority of dissident radical voices within evangelical Protestantism (including George B. Cheever, Charles G. Finney, Theodore Tilton, and – intermittently – Henry Ward

[90] Beecher) criticized the administration; at the other pole were hostile pockets of conservative, even Southern-oriented, churches mainly in the lower North. But the heartland of evangelicalism was aggressively and dependably loyal to Lincoln and his party. The most widely circulating Protestant newspapers in the Union, especially the cluster of regional *Christian Advocates* that gave Methodist editors such a commanding platform, remained staunch supporters of the government. A network of potent clerical speakers took to the rostrum and pulpit for the Republicans. Bishop Matthew Simpson, who criss-crossed the country as an 'evangelist of patriotism', was unsurpassed in his power to melt an audience to tears, or rouse it to the heights of passionate enthusiasm for the war-torn flag.[44] There was nothing coincidental about the president's engaging Simpson to substitute for him in opening the Philadelphia Sanitary Fair in June 1864.[45] Lincoln had no need to take the stump himself when he could rely on a ready-made army of speakers willing to act for him.

Collectively evangelicals worked to prepare the nation for sacrifice in an extended and gigantic war. Press and pulpit steeled women to the knowledge that victory would cost the lives of thousands of sons, brothers and husbands; reassured young men that there was a sweetness in dying for their country and its noble, millennial cause; and prepared all for a protracted war that would impose a massive financial burden. They speculated on God's likely purposes in allowing battlefield defeats. They boosted popular morale during the lowest ebb of Union fortunes, in 1862 and 1863. They echoed the government's calls for troops, endorsed the introduction of conscription, and became recruiting agents themselves. They defended the administration's suspension of habeas corpus, and welcomed strong-arm action against draft resisters and dissenters who overstepped the limits of legitimate opposition. Border evangelicals like Robert J. Breckinridge and William G. Brownlow stiffened the spines of middle-state Unionists. Chaplains and agents of the Sanitary and Christian Commissions ensured that the serving men of the Federal armies did not lose sight of the high purposes of the Union administration.[46]

The political engagement of evangelical Protestant networks was no more vividly demonstrated than in the presidential canvass of 1864. Even before Lincoln saw off his Republican critics and secured his renomination in June, all the evidence indicated that he enjoyed the support of the majority of the nation's active Christians. A minority of radicals looked hopefully at running Salmon P. Chase; but when that movement collapsed even fewer thought well of the Frémont boom and the gathering of his disparate supporters at Cleveland. Splitting the Union vote seemed at best a risky experiment. The widespread Protestant reading of the president as God's agent was only underscored by the Union party's platform, endorsing a constitutional amendment that would forever remove slavery from the republic; and by Lincoln's subsequent confirmation that acceptance of a slave-free Union was the only acceptable basis for peace negotiations. Throughout spring and summer various gatherings across the denominational spectrum cried out for the passage of the amendment, and declared (as a deputation of the Baptist Home Missionary Society told Lincoln) that 'God had raised up His Excellency for such a time as this'. The Union victories in early September seemed to confirm that at last the nation was truly moving in harmony with the Almighty's wishes. The Democrats' Chicago platform so alarmed the residual rump of radical critics of the administration that they hurried back into the Union party fold, angered by the threat of a compromise peace, and emphasizing cause before candidates, platforms before men. They joined mainstream evangelicals, Quakers and liberal Protestants to form a broad front of political activists.[47]

The final two months of the campaign witnessed the most complete fusing of religious crusade and political mobilization in America's electoral experience. Baptist and Congregational associations, Presbyterian synods, and Methodist conferences more or less explicitly told their members to vote the Union ticket. Hundreds of clergy took the stump and (after the fashion of Robert Breckinridge, who had chaired the Baltimore convention in June) became organizational activists. Henry Ward Beecher was employed as a speaker by the National Republican Committee. Religious tract society agents distributed literature. Religious newspapers called on churches to become Republican clubs. The election was in no sense an exercise in acclamatory politics, let alone the cult of personality. Yet Lincoln was presented as an Old Testament prophet and leader of his people. A common theme was the president's integrity. John Gulliver, the Congregational minister of Norwich, Connecticut, praised him for his antislavery resolve throughout the turns and twists of war: 'Slow, if you please, but *true*. Unimpassioned, if you please, but *true*. Jocose, trifling, if you please, but *true*. Reluctant to part with unworthy official advisers, but *true* himself – *true as steel!*' The campaign wrapped Lincoln, the Southern-born Westerner of unorthodox belief, in the mantle of high-principled New England Puritanism.[48]

Instrumental here was Lincoln's shrewd use of national fasts and days of thanksgiving throughout his presidency. Simply by calling them he won credit as a leader remorseful for the sins of the nation and alert to his and his people's dependence on God; it reinforced a view of the president as the Almighty's particular agent in the Union's struggle; it did him particular good amongst those who believed the nation's Constitution defective in not acknowledging the sovereignty of God. Equally important, the services themselves gave ministers a special opportunity to offer thanks for victories achieved, to identify the public sins that occasioned national humiliation, and to rally support for future struggle. They gave the millions who attended them a consciousness of belonging to a single community united in sacrifice and aspiration. We are mistaken if we see the meetings as emptily routine. By a short proclamation Lincoln could use one of his most supportive networks to secure a national charge of adrenalin. He chose his occasions with careful deliberation, as his political opponents understood. When he selected Sunday 10 September 1864 as a day of thanksgiving for recent victories he was effectively encouraging every minister to wave the Union-Republican flag in his pulpit. Opposition Democrats, sensing low political campaigning, cried foul when Union clergy used their pulpits to read out the proclamation and attribute the turn of events to God's intervention. Then, on 20 October, Lincoln issued a further Proclamation of Thanksgiving: with the election under three weeks away he pointedly wrote of the Union's hope, under 'our Heavenly Father', of 'an ultimate and happy deliverance' from the trials of war, and the triumph of 'the cause of Freedom and Humanity'.[49]

'There probably never was an election in all history into which the religious element entered so largely, and nearly all on one side.'[50] We lack hard statistical proof to sustain this judgment of the *Christian Advocate and Journal*, the chief Methodist newspaper, on the outcome of the 1864 campaign. But the impressionistic evidence is very powerful that the big evangelical denominations, and the small, radical antislavery churches, together with the Unitarians and other liberal Protestant groups, swung behind Lincoln in even greater proportions than they had in 1860. McClellan appears to have retained the Democrats' hold on Catholic voters. He may also have won a majority of Episcopalian and Old School Presbyterian voters. But the Protestant centre of gravity was firmly within a Republican/Union party that seems to have won over many Baptists and Methodists, and even Old School Presbyterians, who had previously been Democrat in loyalty.[51] In a celebratory editorial, written in the grey dawn after election day, Theodore Tilton attributed the Union victory to 'nothing less than an over-ruling Divine Hand outstretched to save the Republic'.[52] More prosaically we can see it as the result of an extraordinary mobilization of Union opinion by those who saw themselves as God's servants: the leaders of the Protestant churches.

Limitations of space preclude considering other networks of moral or non-coercive influence that contributed to this energizing of Unionism. They included (paradoxical as it may seem) the North's most potent physical force, the Union army. Federal troops constituted a mighty weapon whose informal operations on the home front were less easily measured than the battlefield impact of their bullets and bayonets but which in their own way worked to stiffen patriotism. Most troops were staunch Republicans, loyal, even devoted, to Lincoln, and remained convinced of the political and moral values symbolized by the flag under which they served; they generally voted the Union ticket at elections and exercised an unquantifiable but indisputable influence over their families and home communities. That influence reached its apogee in the election that brought an extraordinarily high proportion of voters to the polls, returned Lincoln to the White House, and opened the way to a reconstituted Union free from slavery.[53]

The Union leadership's chief means of mobilizing wartime opinion, however, were the Republican party and the Protestant churches. Lincoln used them concertedly to articulate the moral purposes that underpinned the material concerns of Northern Unionism. Constrained by popular racism and a persisting Democratic opposition, Lincoln could not ignore conservative, loyalist public sentiment. But there was more to the president than the shrewd manager who went only as fast as the ambitions of conservatives would allow. What kept the Union going, both on the home front and the battlefield, was a sense of purpose and republican vision that owed much to the more radical perspectives of New England and its cultural diaspora. Lincoln's fluctuating relations with the most radical in his party, those who sought to effect a social and racial revolution, were scarcely easy. But his steadfastness of purpose and his skill in handling the instruments of communication, allied to a firm moral perspective, made him the architect and anchor of an ethically-renewed Union.

Notes

1. Indispensable amongst the modern studies of Lincoln and the Civil War are Peter J. Parish, *The American Civil War* (London, 1975); James M. McPherson, *Battle Cry of Freedom: The Civil War Era* (New York, 1988); Philip Shaw Paludan, *The Presidency of Abraham Lincoln* (Lawrence, Ks, 1994); David Herbert Donald, *Lincoln* (London, 1995).

2. James G. Randall, *Constitutional Problems under Lincoln* (rev. edn, Urbana, Ill., 1951); Mark E. Neely, *The Fate of Liberty: Abraham Lincoln and Civil Liberties* (New York, 1991); Herman Belz, *Abraham Lincoln, Constitutionalism and Equal Rights in the Civil War Era* (New York, 1998), pp. 17–43.

[94]   3. Roy P. Basler (ed.), *The Collected Works of Abraham Lincoln* (9 vols, New Brunswick, NJ, 1953–5), vol. 4, pp. 270–1.

4. Gabor S. Boritt, *Lincoln and the Economics of the American Dream* (Memphis, Tenn., 1978).

5. Charles B. Strozier, *Lincoln's Quest for Union: Public and Private Meanings* (Urbana, Ill., 1987), Mark E. Neely, *The Last Best Hope of Earth: Abraham Lincoln and the Promise of America* (Cambridge, Mass., 1993), Garry Wills, *Lincoln at Gettysburg: The Words that Remade America* (New York, 1992), and Paludan, *Presidency of Abraham Lincoln* offer shrewd interpretations of Lincoln's Unionism.

6. Basler (ed.), *Collected Works of Abraham Lincoln*, vol. 2, p. 222; vol. 4, p. 426.

7. Basler (ed.), *Collected Works of Abraham Lincoln*, vol. 4, pp. 264–5, 269.

8. LaWanda Cox, *Lincoln and Black Freedom: A Study in Presidential Leadership* (Columbia, SC, 1981).

9. Basler (ed.), *Collected Works of Abraham Lincoln*, vol. 7, p. 395.

10. Basler (ed.), *Collected Works of Abraham Lincoln*, vol. 2, pp. 89, 255–6; John G. Nicolay and John Hay, *Abraham Lincoln: A History* (10 vols, New York, 1890), vol. 2, p. 149.

11. Tyler Dennett (ed.), *Lincoln and the Civil War in the Diaries and Letters of John Hay* (New York, 1939; repr. 1988), p. 146.

12. Mark E. Neely, 'The Civil War and the two-party system', in James M. McPherson (ed.), *'We Cannot Escape History': Lincoln and the Last Best Hope of Earth* (Urbana, Ill., 1995), pp. 88–92; David Homer Bates, *Lincoln in the Telegraph Office: Recollections of the United States Military Telegraph Corps during the Civil War* (New York, 1907); William B. Hesseltine, *Lincoln and the War Governors* (New York, 1955), pp. 141–3, 221–8, 265–9.

13. Hesseltine, *Lincoln and the War Governors*, p. 178.

14. F.B. Carpenter, *Six Months at the White House with Abraham Lincoln* (New York, 1866), pp. 230–1; Robert S. Harper, *Lincoln and the Press* (New York, 1951), pp. 96–7, 184–7, 308.

15. Harold Holzer (comp. and ed.), *Dear Mr. Lincoln: Letters to the President* (Reading, Mass., 1993), pp. 5–35; Dennett (ed.), *Diaries and Letters of John Hay*, pp. 19, 47.

16. Carpenter, *Six Months at the White House*, p. 245; Mark E. Neely, *The Abraham Lincoln Encyclopedia* (New York, 1982), p. 220; Dennett (ed.), *Diaries and Letters of John Hay*, p. 143.

17. Carpenter, *Six Months at the White House*, pp. 95–6, 281; *Independent*, 20 Oct. 1864; Holzer, *Dear Mr. Lincoln*, p. 12.

18. Waldo W. Braden, *Abraham Lincoln: Public Speaker* (Baton Rouge, La, 1988).

19. David Donald, *Lincoln Reconsidered: Essays on the Civil War Era* (2nd edn, New York, 1961), pp. 57–60; William E. Gienapp, 'Abraham Lincoln and presidential leadership', in James M. McPherson (ed.), *'We Cannot Escape History': Lincoln and the Last Best Hope of Earth* (Urbana, Ill., 1995), pp. 77–8.

20. Dennett (ed.), *Diaries and Letters of John Hay*, p. 139; Neely, *Abraham Lincoln Encyclopedia*, p. 68.

21. Carpenter, *Six Months at the White House*, pp. 126–7.

22. Dennett (ed.), *Diaries and Letters of John Hay*, p. 91.

23. Donald, *Lincoln*, pp. 14–15 and passim.

24. Eric L. McKitrick, 'Party politics and the Union and Confederate war efforts', in William Nisbet Chambers and Walter Dean Burnham, *The American Party Systems: Stages of Political Development* (New York, 1967), pp. 117–51, presents a powerful case for the value of party to the Union cause; Neely, 'The Civil War and the two-party system', pp. 86–104, offers a cautionary note.

25. Harry J. Carman and Reinhard H. Luthin, *Lincoln and the Patronage* (New York, 1943), pp. 228–60 and passim; Allan G. Bogue, *The Congressman's Civil War* (Cambridge, 1989), pp. 31–40, 51.

26. Robert J. Cook, *Baptism of Fire: The Republican Party in Iowa, 1838–1878* (Ames, Iowa, 1994), pp. 137, 142–3; Hesseltine, *Lincoln and the War Governors*, pp. 147–54; Bogue, *The Congressman's Civil War*, pp. 56–7.

27. Hesseltine, *Lincoln and the War Governors*, pp. 198–200, 314–15, 319–39.

28. McKitrick, 'Party politics and the Union and Confederate war efforts', pp. 148–9, 151.

29. Harper, *Lincoln and the Press*, pp. 76, 87–91; Neely, *Abraham Lincoln Encyclopedia*, pp. 223–4.

30. Michael Burlingame (ed.), *Lincoln Observed: Civil War Dispatches of Noah Brooks* (Baltimore, Md, 1998), pp. 1–11, 66; Dennett (ed.), *Diaries and Letters of John Hay*, pp. 26, 76, 138, 203; Harper, *Lincoln and the Press*, pp. 173–5, 221, 282–9.

31. Of the 30,000 copies of the *Morning Chronicle* printed daily, 10,000 went to the Army of the Potomac. Dennett (ed.), *Diaries and Letters of John Hay*, p. 146; Harper, *Lincoln and the Press*, pp. 109–12, 175, 179–84.

32. Frank Freidel (ed.), *Union Pamphlets of the Civil War* (2 vols, Cambridge, Mass., 1967), vol. 1, pp. 1–24.

33. Basler (ed.), *Collected Works of Abraham Lincoln*, vol. 6, p. 264; Neely, 'The Civil War and the two-party system', pp. 93–4.

34. Harper, *Lincoln and the Press*, pp. 263–4; Basler (ed.), *Collected Works of Abraham Lincoln*, vol. 6, pp. 251–2; Dennett (ed.), *Diaries and Letters of John Hay*, pp. 129, 215.

35. Carpenter, *Six Months at the White House*, p. 275; Carman and Luthin, *Lincoln and the Patronage*, pp. 261–99; David E. Long, The *Jewel of Liberty: Abraham Lincoln's Re-election and the End of Slavery* (Mechanicsburg, Pa, 1994), pp. 187–93, 235–7 and passim.

36. Richard J. Carwardine, *Evangelicals and Politics in Antebellum America* (New Haven, Conn., 1993), pp. 296–307.

37. *Northwestern Christian Advocate* (Methodist; Chicago), 13, 28 Aug., 16 Oct. 1861.

38. James H. Moorhead, *American Apocalypse: Yankee Protestants and the Civil War 1860–69* (New Haven, Conn., 1978), pp. x, 39.

39. *Northwestern Christian Advocate*, 12 June, 4 Sept. 1861; Victor B. Howard, *Religion and the Radical Republican Movement 1860–1870* (Lexington, Ky, 1990), pp. 11–67; Moorhead, *American Apocalypse*, p. 112.

40. William J. Wolf, *The Almost Chosen People: A Study of the Religion of Abraham Lincoln* (New York, 1959); Allen C. Guelzo, 'Abraham Lincoln and the doctrine of necessity', *Journal of the Abraham Lincoln Association* 18 (Winter, 1997), pp. 57–81.

41. Granville Moody, *A Life's Retrospect: Autobiography of Rev. Granville Moody, D.D.*, ed. Sylvester Weeks (Cincinnati, O, 1890), pp. 441–5; George Peck, *The Life and Times of Rev. George Peck* (New York, 1874), pp. 378–81.

42. Howard, *Religion and the Radical Republican Movement*, p. 71.

43. Mark A. Noll, '"Both pray to the same God": The singularity of Lincoln's faith in the era of the Civil War', *Journal of the Abraham Lincoln Association* 18 (Winter, 1997), pp. 1–26.

44. George R. Crooks, *The Life of Bishop Matthew Simpson of the Methodist Episcopal Church* (New York, 1890), pp. 377–86.

45. Robert D. Clark, *The Life of Matthew Simpson* (New York, 1956), pp. 238–40; J. Matthew Gallman, *Mastering Wartime: A Social History of Philadelphia during the Civil War* (Cambridge, 1990), pp. 148–51.

46. David B. Cheseborough (ed.), *God Ordained This War: Sermons on the Sectional Crisis, 1830–1865* (Columbia, SC, 1991), pp. 6–8, 83–122.

47. Howard, *Religion and the Radical Republican Movement*, pp. 68–89; John R. McKivigan, *The War against Proslavery Religion: Abolitionism and the Northern Churches* (Ithaca, NY, 1984), pp. 192–4; James M. McPherson, *The Struggle for Equality: Abolitionists and the Negro in the Civil War and Reconstruction* (Princeton, NJ, 1964), pp. 260–86.

48. New York *Independent*, 1 Sept., 27 Oct., 3 Nov. 1864.

49. Basler (ed.), *Collected Works of Abraham Lincoln*, vol. 8, pp. 55–6.

50. New York *Christian Advocate and Journal*, quoted in Moorhead, *American Apocalypse*, p. 156.

51. Howard, *Religion and the Radical Republican Movement*, pp. 88–9; Dale Baum, *The Civil War Party System: The Case of Massachusetts, 1848–1876* (Chapel Hill, NC, 1984), pp. 91, 95–100; Stephen L. Hansen, *The Making of the Third Party System: Voters and Parties in Illinois, 1850–1876* (Ann Arbor, Mi., 1978), pp. 142–3.

52. *Independent*, 10 Nov. 1864.

53. The ideological element in Union soldiers' motivation is emphasized in James M. McPherson, *For Cause and Comrades: Why Men Fought in the Civil War* (New York, 1997).

CHAPTER FOUR

JEFFERSON DAVIS AND THE CONFEDERACY

MARTIN CRAWFORD

Despite the publication in 1991 of a new biography and reports of others in preparation, Jefferson Davis's status in the Civil War pantheon shows little sign of improvement. Davis revisionists must surmount a number of serious obstacles, not the least of which is what the historian Clement Eaton – a confirmed supporter – called the Mississippian's 'self-defeating personality'.[1] Above all, the Confederate president's reputation continues to suffer by comparison with that of his Federal rival, Abraham Lincoln. This is the result not merely of Davis belonging to the wrong side, but also because of the uninspiring manner in which he characteristically expressed himself. Nothing that Davis said or wrote during his four years as Confederate leader resonates in the way of countless Lincoln utterances. As David Potter memorably concluded, Jefferson Davis 'seemed to think in abstractions and to speak in platitudes.'[2]

Yet Jefferson Davis was a pivotal actor in the political and constitutional drama of nineteenth-century America, a leader whose 'broad consistency of purpose', to borrow a phrase from Bruce Collins, establishes him as an indispensable guide to the practical and ideological vicissitudes of the movement for Southern independence that culminated in four years of civil war.[3] Whatever his individual failings, and those of the cause over which he presided, Davis was, we should never forget, the first and only elected leader of the putative Southern nation, the Confederate States of America. Like all American presidents, Davis combined the dual functions of chief executive and head of state, charged both with the efficient running of the government and with embodying and articulating the values and aspirations of the people who had elected him. He also served as the commander-in-chief of his new country's armed forces, a job which, as a West Point graduate and Mexican War veteran, he arguably approached with the greatest enthusiasm of all.

Davis and Confederate nationalism [99]

Between February 1861 and April 1865 the fate of Southern slaveholding nationalism ultimately rested on Jefferson Davis's pained shoulders. But how appropriate a choice was Davis as the Confederacy's leader? The question is usually answered by highlighting the formal qualifications that he brought to the presidential office. Undoubtedly, experience in both the executive and legislative branches combined with a distinguished military record should not be dismissed lightly. And indeed popular expectations of the new Confederate leader were extremely high in 1861. Touring the Southern states in the early summer of that year, the British journalist William Howard Russell was repeatedly bombarded with the same question: 'Have you seen our President, sir? don't you think him a very able man?' Russell interviewed Davis in Montgomery on 7 May and found him a somewhat unprepossessing figure. But, if sceptical of the secessionist ship of state Davis captained, Russell could not fail to be impressed by the universal admiration and confidence with which Southerners regarded their new leader; this the celebrated war correspondent felt might prove of 'incalculable value' in the troubled days ahead.[4]

Jefferson Davis of Mississippi had been elected the provisional president of the newly founded Confederate States of America on 9 February 1861. A former Senator, cabinet member, and soldier with an unimpeachable record as a defender of Southern rights, his election nonetheless represented a significant dilution of the radical political energies of the secession movement. Yet as Paul Escott has noted, Davis's reluctant conversion (or reconversion) to the secessionist cause made him a more representative Southerner than fire-eaters such as Albert Gallatin Brown, his Senate colleague and perennial political rival, who had recently opposed him.[5]

Like all leading nineteenth-century Southern politicians, Jefferson Davis paid regular homage at the altar of states rights. The doctrine of states rights, which was based upon the compact theory of the Constitution, derived its continuing authority from a combination of idealistic and pragmatic appeals to popular reason, and by the secession period it had become, in E. Merton Coulter's phrase, the Southerner's 'deepest political passion'.[6] After the death of John C. Calhoun in 1850 it was Jefferson Davis's responsibility, as the leading Southern Democrat, to maintain the fight for the political and constitutional integrity of the states over the issue of slavery's extension into the western territories. Yet by the end of the decade, during which his own political fortunes fluctuated considerably, Davis had shifted from his earlier states rights radicalism towards a more nationalist vision of how the South's interests could best be protected; in Escott's words, he became 'a man struggling to protect the South within the Union'.[7] Throughout the secessionist winter Davis stayed firmly in the 'cooperationist' camp, and it was with feelings of genuine sadness that he delivered his valedictory speech to the United States Senate on 21 January 1861. 'Had he been bending over his father, slain by his countrymen,' his wife later recalled, 'he could not have been more inconsolable.'[8]

Jefferson Davis's nationalism embodied a profound respect for the Union and the Constitution which transcended the specific circumstances within with the slave South found itself. 'If I have a superstition, sir, which governs my mind and holds it captive, it is a superstitious reverence for the Union,' he admitted in June 1850.[9] For Davis, therefore, as for Webster, Lincoln and other mid-nineteenth century political leaders who had been nourished upon the founding mythology of the Revolution and its aftermath, the Union had come to represent a powerful emotional commitment, the abandonment of which could only be contemplated under the most dire circumstances. It is surely no coincidence that Davis's hero, and the man who largely inspired his early political endeavours, was Andrew Jackson, whose uncompromising nationalist stance against the South Carolina nullifiers Davis had endorsed, even as he rejected the coercive means Jackson would have employed to bring the Palmetto state to heel. (According to his wife's memoir, Davis, as a serving officer, claimed he would have resigned his commission rather than be employed in military action against a sister Southern state.)[10]

There is a second, often unremarked aspect to Davis's antebellum nationalism. Throughout the 1840s and 1850s the Mississippian's strongest political enthusiasm next to defending Southern rights was undoubtedly the expansion and development of the American West. As a product of the westward movement himself – his family had moved from Kentucky to Mississippi in pursuit of new cotton lands – Davis consistently supported proposals to encourage western expansion both within and beyond the United States' existing territorial borders. Unlike his great mentor Calhoun, Davis apparently saw little to fear in the annexation of Mexican lands, even though he opposed the All-Mexico movement and, like the South Carolinian, warned against the mixing of the races that such expansion could encourage.[11] Indeed, so enthusiastic was Davis about the Mexican conflict that in 1846 he resigned his seat in Congress in order to pursue the issue at first hand as the colonel of the First Mississippi regiment of volunteers. The following decade, first as Secretary of War in the Pierce administration and subsequently in the Senate,

Davis fought passionately for the construction of a transcontinental railroad. He also played an instrumental role in the Gadsden Purchase Treaty of 1853, which added a further 45,000 square miles to the territory of the United States, and in the unsuccessful movement to acquire Cuba.[12]

Throughout the late antebellum period Davis's expansive nationalism did not come into conflict with the regional interests which, as a leading Southern politician, he was pledged to protect. In most instances the two commitments plainly complemented one another: in advocating the transcontinental railroad, for example, Davis clearly hoped that the preferred Southern route would help compensate for the slave states' increasing economic disadvantage within the Union; it would also encourage slaveholding migration to the West, thus further promoting the South's regional influence. For Jefferson Davis, as for the vast majority of his contemporaries, regional economic and political interests were best advanced within an expanding national Union in which the distinctive rights of all communities were recognized and protected. Speaking in Newark, New Jersey, in July 1853, Davis gave full rhetorical rein to this vision of a broadening union of compatible interests and liberties. Although there are many different states, the Mississippian argued, 'we have but one history, one pride, one destiny,' under which the Union can go on 'expanding wider and wider until its great temple reaches not only from sea to sea, but from pole to pole.'[13]

By the end of the 1850s, as John McCardell has described, the South's defence of its regional or sectional interests had metamorphosed into a movement for southern nationalism. The ideological and cultural underpinnings of this movement were clearly revealed during the nullification crisis of the early Jacksonian period, but it was not until after the secession of the slave states in the winter of 1860–1 that Southern nationalism achieved concrete realization in the establishment of the Confederacy. In one respect, therefore, white southerners' choice of Jefferson Davis as Confederate president would seem to have been an ideal one, in that he, perhaps unusually among his planter-statesman contemporaries, combined a traditional states rights commitment, with its implied protection of local interests, with a dynamic vision of national progress through which the South's economic and social resources could be harnessed for the common good. At the same time, it was not immediately clear how Davis's antebellum expansionism could be yoked to the cause of establishing a Southern national identity. The question remains: what distinctive national identity did Jefferson Davis envisage as he sought to persuade ordinary Southerners to abandon long-held loyalties in return for the uncertain benefits of Confederate citizenship?

In his Inaugural Address, delivered to a large and enthusiastic crowd in the provisional capital Montgomery on 18 February 1861, Jefferson Davis attempted to give tangible expression to the new Confederate nationality.[14] Davis's address, which was generally well received in the South, has invariably been overshadowed by that of his Northern counterpart, but it remains a highly significant speech, albeit a characteristically prosaic one. The speech followed the general pattern of nineteenth-century inaugurals which, as Jeffrey K. Tulis has observed, were more concerned with articulating the president's understanding of republican principle than with outlining specific policies or initiatives.[15] There was a familiar preoccupation with constitutional issues, again in conformity with prevailing practice, as well as the predictable invocations to the 'virtue and patriotism of the people' and to Davis's 'humble distrust' of his own abilities to perform the duties assigned to him.

No amount of rhetorical convention could disguise the critical situation faced by the new republic and its leader in February 1861. 'We are without machinery, without means, and threatened by a powerful opposition,' Davis wrote to his wife a few days after the Inaugural.[16] In his speech Davis was concerned to stress both the innate justice of the Confederate cause and the peaceful and responsible manner in which his government's domestic and international duties were to be discharged. At the same time he was determined that such sentiments would not be misunderstood as either a sign of weakness or, perhaps more likely, as an indication that the South might voluntarily re-enter the Union. Although recognizing that the provisional Constitution allowed for the admission of new states to the Confederacy, Davis nonetheless suggested that 'a reunion with the States from which we have separated is neither practicable nor desirable.'[17]

At the heart of Davis's dilemma was the problem of defining the true character of the Southern nation. In February 1861 the self-styled Confederate States of America consisted of a mere seven states: South Carolina, Mississippi, Alabama, Florida, Georgia, Louisiana, and most recently, Texas. The people of these states, through their secession conventions, had reclaimed the sovereign powers originally delegated to the Federal Union and voluntarily reorganized themselves into a new confederation. But what distinguished them from those states that remained in the old Union, and upon what common foundation would popular allegiance to the new constitution and government be established? Unless such questions could be answered, the future of the Confederate States as a separate and independent nation could hardly be guaranteed.

In his Inaugural Address, therefore, Jefferson Davis was forced to confront not only the practical (and frightening) implications of the new Confederate nationalism, but also, more fundamentally, to give texture and meaning to the founding process itself. The people of the Southern states, after all, were not merely being asked to support a new administration, but to transfer their loyalties from the old Union, which had nourished and protected them since 1789, to a new and untried confederation whose very existence was threatened by the Federal government's refusal to admit the legality of secession. As a reluctant secessionist himself, Davis was acutely aware of the fragile political foundations of the new nation. The vote for delegates to the secession conventions had revealed significant divisions in the deep South states, and only in Texas would secession be ratified through popular referendum. Moreover, in the upper South there were few positive signs in February 1861 that secession would ever be consummated, and without such politically and economically strategic states as Virginia and Tennessee, the Confederacy's independence was likely to be short-lived.[18]

Jefferson Davis's solution to the problem of defining the South's incipient nationalism involved two distinct themes. Firstly, he attempted to ease the transfer of national loyalties from the old Union to the new Confederacy by invoking the founding spirits of 1776 and, perhaps a little more surprisingly, of 1787. According to Davis's explanation, the secession movement had been based upon the same constitutional principle as that underpinning the colonial separation from the British empire nearly a century earlier. It illustrates, he said, in the highly familiar language of the revolutionary architect after whom he was named, 'the American idea that governments rest on the consent of the governed, and that it is the right of the people to alter or abolish them whenever they become destructive of the ends for which they were established.'[19] Southerners were after all exceedingly proud of their role in the Revolution, and Davis's invocation was a persuasive ideological and emotional appeal to the patriotic instincts of a conservative and tradition-minded people. But it was also an attempt to sustain a much needed social unity in the South by reminding white Southerners of all classes of their shared revolutionary heritage.

Similar motives also dictated an appeal to the wisdom of 1787, although here Davis's logic was necessarily more circumspect. After all, the Federal Union had not only overseen the South's political and material progress, but it was also the source of the region's greatest anxiety and the catalyst, through take-over by hostile political forces, of the secession crisis itself. The touchstone of Davis's argument was the new Confederate Constitution, the

[104]   provisional form of which had already been agreed prior to the inauguration. As Davis explained it, the new constitution was a faithful reflection of the original document, 'differing only from that of our fathers in so far as it is explanatory of their well-known intent'.[20] Here again, as with the appeal to the Southerner's revolutionary heritage, Davis was attempting to reassure his people that the extraordinary steps that were now being taken implied no radical discontinuity with prior experience. The new Confederate government was to be the pure constitutional and political expression of America's founding wisdom, cleansed of the destructive ambitions which had forced the break-up of the old Union.

Davis's second appeal was if anything even more ambitious than his first: it involved nothing less than an attempted fabrication of a Southern social identity. Although the new president admitted that the South's actions, like those of the American colonists, had been taken out of 'necessity' and not 'choice', he was adamant that the Confederate nation would be based, not upon some artifical division of sovereignty, but upon genuine social, economic and cultural differentiation between North and South. Unlike the manufacturing and navigating communities of the north-eastern United States, Davis claimed, Southerners were an 'agricultural people', whose long-term interests would best be served through the establishment of an independent, unified nation. 'To increase the power, develop the resources, and promote the happiness of the Confederacy, it is requisite that there should be so much of homogeneity that the welfare of every portion shall be the aim of the whole,' he insisted. [21]

As a piece of presidential exhortation at the founding of a new state, Davis's address had much to recommend it; as an accurate representation of Southern social reality, it left a good deal to be desired. Despite its undeniably agrarian character, the South by 1861 was a far more complex and diverse society than Davis was apparently willing to admit. Throughout the antebellum period, Southern capitalists had sought to liberate the region from its commercial dependency upon the North, and although the movement had largely failed – in great part because of the continuing success of cotton and the agrarian tenacity of the planter class – the initiatives did at least demonstrate that the forces of economic modernization had not completely bypassed the slave states.[22] A prominent member of the Southern planter establishment with strong trading links to urban centres such as New Orleans, Davis was undoubtedly sensitive to the changes that his society was already experiencing and that in the long term would reduce the cultural divide between North and South; but in his early presidential rhetoric he gave few signs of articulating a dynamic nationalist vision within which such evolution could be accommodated. Nor – crucially for the new republic's future – did Davis give any indication of how the communities of the upper South could successfully be incorporated into a Confederate nationalism whose cultural, economic and political wellsprings had derived so manifestly from the states of the lower South.

Yet Davis's vision was unmistakably nationalist. Despite his constitutional sermonizing on the origins of secession, there is little indication from the Inaugural Address at least that the new president was about to preside over a government in which the rights of the individual states would be paramount. As Paul Escott has noted, the reassuring degree of social homogeneity that Davis recognized within the South undoubtedly led him to believe that an effective central government would be highly appropriate, especially since the new Constitution, like its Federal counterpart, made the laws of the Confederate government the supreme authority.[23]

A strict constructionist with strong nationalist tendencies, Jefferson Davis undoubtedly felt that here was a real opportunity to forge a workable relationship between the states and the central government in which the legitimate needs of both would be adequately protected. As it turned out, this new federalism was only partially successful, and for four years an intense political rivalry developed between Davis and various of the state political leaders – notably governors Joseph E. Brown of Georgia and Zebulon Vance of North Carolina – which scholars such as Frank L. Owsley used to consider as *the* determining factor in the Confederacy's defeat. However, as historians now acknowledge, the states rights controversy, strictly defined, was less damaging to the South's war effort than formerly conceived, and on few, if any, occasions did state obstructionism prevent Davis actually implementing Confederate military or civil authority.[24]

But viewed in other, less narrowly legalistic ways, the relationship between the central government and the people of the various states was a far from creative one, and overall the Confederate leadership, and Jefferson Davis in particular, failed to articulate a credible national or federal vision, comparable to that of Abraham Lincoln in the North, through which the cause of Southern independence, with all its implied sacrifices, could effectively be sustained. This deficiency embraced all aspects of Confederate policy and activity. Historians have noted, for example, the impressive strides taken by Southern entrepreneurs to narrow the gap with the industrializing North. But as Mary A. DeCredico and others have shown, efforts to achieve greater national coordination met strong resistance from those who feared that government encroachment would erode their sovereign rights. It was not until February 1865, for example, that the Richmond government took steps to establish central authority over the Confederacy's railroads – vital to the republic's war effort – and by then it was too late.[25]

The political arguments also affected popular morale in the Confederacy. Already by the second year of the war, their resentment fuelled by the imposition of military conscription, many people in the South were beginning to regard Confederate nationalism as potentially destructive of the ends for which the conflict was being waged. After 1863 popular discontent increased throughout the Confederate States. Although such dissent rarely coalesced in any politically coherent form, the actions of men such as William W. Holden, the Raleigh editor who saw threats to liberty around every corner, undoubtedly contributed to the South's loss of confidence in the independence struggle. As one disillusioned (and hungry) North Carolina soldier observed from his mud-spattered winter quarters near Petersburg on New Year's Eve, 1864, 'we have trampled our own Liberties under our feet in attempting to establish a Nationality that was not intended for us.'[26] In an important recent study, Gary W. Gallagher has argued persuasively that by the midpoint of the war the principal agency for sustaining Confederate nationalism – and with it the military struggle – was not the Davis government but the Army of Northern Virginia. Gallagher concludes that as faith in Jefferson Davis and the political structure weakened, 'belief in Lee and his army grew, countering the divisive effects of politics, suffering and defeatism'.[27]

In the final analysis, Jefferson Davis's defensive nationalism was neither one thing nor the other: too powerful an instrument in the eyes of states rights Southerners, who were naturally fearful of a renewed onslaught on their freedom, it also proved inadequate to the task of resituating Southerners' larger patriotic instincts and obligations, with perhaps predictable consequences for the long-term establishment of Confederate independence. The root of Davis's difficulty, and of the society he had been elected to govern, was its conservatism. As we have seen, in his Inaugural Address the president attempted to justify the secession movement and to facilitate the transfer of Southern loyalties from the old to the new union, invoking, among other things, the founding spirit of 1776 and 1787. 'The right solemnly proclaimed at the birth of the United States, and which has been solemnly affirmed and reaffirmed in the Bill of Rights of the States subsequently admitted into the Union of 1789, undeniably recognizes in the people the power to resume the authority delegated for the purposes of government. Thus the sovereign States here represented have proceeded to form this Confederacy.' At this point, however,

Jefferson Davis appeared to undermine his own argument by specifically dis-associating the secession movement from the radical tradition from which its legitimacy ostensibly derived, concluding, 'it is by abuse of language that their act has been denominated a revolution.'[28]

Throughout his founding address Davis had been particularly concerned to locate the South's actions within the American revolutionary tradition, even to the point of appropriating the language of the Declaration of Independence itself. Yet within a few sentences he explicitly denies that a revolution was actually taking place. Such inverted logic, as Emory Thomas has noted, was probably disregarded by the mass of Davis's audience;[29] nevertheless, there can be no doubting the precise distinction that the president was seeking to enforce. By denying the revolutionary character of the new nation, the Confederate leader was attempting to ensure that the founding process was not accompanied by any alteration in the existing social, economic and political fabric. By 1861, the word 'revolution' had acquired dangerous insurrectionary overtones for conservatives in both Europe and America, and Davis was bound to be concerned lest the radical enthusiasms of the secession winter should metamorphose into a genuine movement for change within Southern society. The Confederate president took the rhetorical point further in February 1862 in his second Inaugural Address, observing that secession had been undertaken to 'save ourselves from a revolution which, in its silent but rapid progress, was about to place us under the despotism of numbers . . .'.[30]

Role of slavery

Jefferson Davis, it should be remembered, was not only the constitutional head of the Confederate States but also a wealthy Mississippi cotton planter and thus, in a more general sense, the elected guardian of the dominant economic and political interests within Southern society. For the conservative planter class, the secession movement had promised both liberation from Northern tyranny and also the less welcoming prospect of unbridled popular challenges to the established order. In the event, radical control of the secession process had already been superseded, and by February 1861 it was the political moderates such as Davis himself who were firmly in charge. Yet the potentiality for domestic upheaval had by no means disappeared, particularly since the Confederacy quickly become embroiled in a disruptive and largely internal war for national survival. Adjourning the Confederate Congress in February 1862, another leading planter-statesman, Howell Cobb of Georgia, who had presided over the constitutional deliberations in Montgomery twelve months earlier, argued that the South's 'revolution' was unique in its conservatism. 'Usually revolutions are the result of the excited passions of the people whose patience is exhausted, and hence their popular tendencies have too frequently degraded them into anarchy and discord,' Cobb concluded.[31]

Jefferson Davis's instinctive fear of revolution not only embraced potential challenges to the political and economic power of the planter class from the white majority but was also based upon fears of a radical subversion of the Southern racial order. It is a telling fact that both in the Inaugural Address and in subsequent speeches during the war's first year, Jefferson Davis avoided any mention of black slavery, the one aspect of Southern society which fundamentally distinguished the region from the rest of the American union. On one level, Davis's aversion to discussing slavery can be said to reflect the continuing and widespread apprehensions over the possibility of slave rebellion; however, it also demonstrated the profound difficulty that the president faced in attempting to fashion a legitimate national identity, based upon the existing realities of Southern life. Slaveholders formed only a minority of Southerners, and Davis was surely aware of the potential social fragmentation – and therefore the collapse of his vision of national 'homogeneity' – that would arise if substantial numbers of whites (not to mention their black neighbours, slave and free) sought to dissent from the region's dominant labour and caste system.

As scholars have now begun to insist, black slavery was the Confederacy's true Achilles heel. As he toured the deep South in the immediate aftermath of Fort Sumter, William Howard Russell found reassurances about the security of the slave system increasingly hard to swallow. 'There is something suspicious in the constant never-ending statement that "we are not afraid of our slaves,"' the British correspondent reported from Montgomery.[32] Fears of insurrection arguably played a key role in determining the Confederacy's destiny from the outset, and as the war bit deeper, the regime's waning control over its three and half million black slaves proved decisive to its outcome. Approximately 600,000 slaves abandoned their plantation and farm homes during the war and entered the Union lines; nearly a quarter of the fugitives enlisted in the Federal army.[33] Davis himself was not immune from slavery's erosions: in May 1862 a number of his slaves robbed the plantation house at Brierfield, Mississippi before running away; the same month his Richmond coachman, William Andrew Jackson, also escaped. (Jackson subsequently travelled to England where he took a leading part in arousing pro-Union opinion. Jefferson Davis's biographers omit all mention of his slave coach-man's exploits, despite the fact that the escape to Union lines at least was well publicized.)[34]

To argue that the antebellum South's most distinctive feature was black slavery is hardly novel, but it is important to acknowledge how fundament-ally committed this society – especially the cotton states of the deep South from where Jefferson Davis's legitimacy and authority primarily emanated – had become to maintaining the existing racial order. As the South's vital labour force, black slaves were subjected to a unique form of racial and class subordination. Yet we should also acknowledge how instrumental a role race played in maintaining the stability of white society. Although the social, economic and cultural bonds that linked the yeoman farmer to his wealthy planter neighbour were complex ones, it was race that in so many ways pro-vided the final and secure basis for class stability in the nineteenth-century South. In no other part of America did race play such a vital role in structur-ing relationships between the various social groups than in the uniquely biracial society of the Southern states.[35]

The planter class did not survive the war intact; new men came to govern in the South. But the redeemer leadership of the post-Reconstruction era continued to employ race as the most effective means of ensuring that neither the newly emancipated blacks nor the lower orders of white society would mount any serious political challenge to governing class authority. African-American political subordination in the rural South in the late nineteenth century was facilitated by new forms of economic dependency, while the majority of Southern whites continued to believe that their liberty could only be secured by resisting black progress in any meaningful form. When in the Populist revolt impoverished white farmers threatened to break out of the traditional patterns of class dependency and even to suggest a limited coop-eration with their black counterparts, the response from the southern Demo-cratic leadership was swift and brutally efficient. By the beginning of the twentieth century black, and to a lesser extent, lower-class white disenfran-chisement had helped reestablish the traditional relationship between race, class and power which the Populists and, by different means, the invading Yankees had threatened to subvert.

Jefferson Davis's conscious avoidance of the 'central theme' of Southern history, therefore, provides an important clue to the ultimate bankruptcy of Confederate nationalism.[36] Ironically, by failing to confront the issue of black

[110]   slavery in his founding rhetoric, Davis implicitly undermined his own argument for a distinctive Southern nationality. And as the conflict progressed, and Confederate military deficiencies were cruelly exposed at Gettyburg, Vicksburg and elsewhere, the president's ideological appeal to Southerners became founded on little more than resisting the barbaric Northern conduct of the war, now made more barbaric by what was seen as Lincoln's incitement to servile insurrection.[37] As the war took a dramatic new course following Lincoln's emancipation decree in January 1863, Jefferson Davis showed how few ideological resources he now had at his disposal. 'Every crime which could characterize the course of demons has marked the course of the invader,' the president told an impromptu crowd at the Confederate White House a few days after the decree came into effect. 'By showing themselves so utterly disgraced that if the question was proposed whether you would combine with hyenas or Yankees, I trust every Virginian would say, give me the hyenas.'[38]

Davis's conservatism

In order to win the war, Jefferson Davis not only had to commit the South to creating a more centralized state and to initiate a programme of rapid industrialization, both in defiance of the region's tradition (as he himself had articulated it), but also, the deepest irony of all, to consider abandoning slavery itself. In November 1864, faced with an acute manpower shortage reflective both of declining popular enthusiasm for the war and of the tremendous human losses suffered by the Confederacy's armies, President Davis called for 'a radical modification in the theory of the law' regarding black slavery and contemplated arming the South's servile population in order to resist the northern troops who were attempting to set them free.[39] This limited and ambiguous emancipation proposal, which was passionately resisted throughout the South, was the final admission of the inadequate and ultimately unsustainable character of Davis's nationalist vision, the defects of which had already been apparent in his founding address in Montgomery nearly four years earlier. The South may have been a distinctive society in 1861, as its new President had insisted, but the most vital element in its distinctiveness – the relationship between race, class and power – was also its greatest burden, and for Davis to have challenged it openly would have conceded the very argument the Confederacy had been founded to defend.

Confederate nationalism failed, therefore, because, as Drew Gilpin Faust has argued, it sought to prescribe change in the service of continuity, and then proved unable to contain or to explain the social, economic and political transformations generated by civil war.[40] The extent to which this deficiency could have been overcome through a more creative application of Confederate federalism remains open to question. Much has been written about the structure and style of Confederate politics, and especially about the failure to develop a party system through which, it is argued, principle and practicality could more effectively have combined. As George Rable has noted, however, the suggestion that the absence of parties in itself proved harmful to the Confederate war effort 'rests more on assumptions than evidence'.[41] Parties in some shape may conceivably have developed had the war lasted beyond the spring of 1865, but rebuilding a competitive party system in a region, the lower South, from whence they had disappeared a decade before, would have proved a Herculean task.

Yet by comparison with the Federal states, where Abraham Lincoln was able to deploy partisanship to crucial advantage, Confederate politics was a conspicuously disputatious art, a cacophony of voices ill-tuned to the harmonious needs of wartime nation-building. And here Jefferson Davis must share responsibility. Too much of Davis's energy during the war was dissipated in querulous argument, in warding off political enemies real or imagined, too little in shaping, articulating and promoting the policies needed to defeat the real foe. 'I am no stranger to the misrepresentation of which malignity is capable, nor to the generation of such feeling by the conscientious discharge of duty; and have been taught by a disagreeable experience how slowly the messenger of truth follows that of slander,' he characteristically complained in August 1863.[42] Similar behaviour obtained in his relations with his senior military commanders and advisers. As Frank E. Vandiver noted, before the war Davis had been a progressive, an innovator on military matters, but as president he found these same qualities unacceptable in his subordinates.[43] Fiercely loyal to his friends, equally intolerant of his enemies, Davis's temperamental rigidity contrasts sharply with Abraham Lincoln, the master pragmatist. As William J. Cooper has recently commented, Davis's absolute identification with the Confederacy led him to demand 'the same full measure of selfless devotion' in others. Those who questioned or disagreed with him became for Davis 'a challenge to the cause' itself.[44]

Finally, what other aspects of Jefferson Davis's character and beliefs proved inhibiting after 1861 and potentially helped to dilute his effectiveness as the South's leader? Several historians have analysed, for example, the religious

[112] component of Confederate nationalism; yet Davis himself, notwithstanding his regular calls for public fasting (nine times during the Confederacy) was not a particularly devout man and only joined a church after the Civil War had begun – and then only at the insistent urging of his wife Varina. Significantly, Davis became a member of the Southern Episcopal Church, whose conservative philosophy could only serve to distance him further from the daily concerns of his increasingly suffering citizenry.[45]

We might also wish to return to the issue of slavery, the 'cornerstone' of the Confederacy, in his vice-president's celebrated phrase. What were Davis's real feelings about the South's peculiar institution? Jefferson's elder brother, Joseph, ran one of the most benign plantation regimes in the South, and at Brierfield, the president's own slaves experienced a similar regime, including the establishment of a court system with slave jurors.[46] Moreover, in his first important Senate speech in July 1848, Davis had explicitly denied that slavery was a permanent condition for black southerners. At the same time he confirmed his belief in white supremacy and in the ultimate separation of black and white in any post-emancipation South, a position he would consistently uphold. As his most recent biographer has concluded, while few men of Davis's age and place held such enlightened views toward the treatment and condition of slaves, it was a largely abstract view, and 'he retained his fundamental distrust of the intellect, reliability, and "humanity" of the black man.'[47] In this matter, as in so many others, Davis was the representative Southern slaveholding patriarch, unwilling or unable to free himself from his region's racial and class prescriptions.

New research and fresh perspectives may shed more light on these and other issues, although the absence of a substantial corpus of private correspondence for the war years will limit revisionism. However, whether they will provoke greater sympathy for the man or, less likely, for the cause he represented, is unclear. Jefferson Davis came to Montgomery in 1861 better equipped than any of his planter-statesman contemporaries to head a new Southern slaveholding republic. Admittedly, the Confederate States of America was no ordinary experiment in nation-building. Barely had Davis assumed office when the fuse of war was ignited. Plagued by illness and personal tragedy – his young son Joseph fell to his death while at play in May 1864 – his tenure in office proved as demanding as that of any American chief executive before or since. Jefferson Davis was a determined and capable man, a man of principle, but his history tends to confirm the old adage that societies get the leaders they deserve. For all his qualities, Davis remained bound to the South's reactionary ideal, his values, and those of the class he represented, conspicuously at odds with the modern world.

Unlike his Federal rival, Jefferson Davis survived the violence of civil war
and for the rest of his long life – he died in New Orleans in 1889 at the age of
eighty-two – he could reflect on his role as Confederate leader. The New
South proved less than kind to the ex-president. After his release from Federal
prison in May 1867, Davis spent his remaining years in vain attempts to
repair his economic fortunes, and in preparing his memoir of the sectional
struggle, finally published in 1881 as *The Rise and Fall of the Confederate Government*. Accurately described by Robert Penn Warren as a work of 'legalistic
and constitutional apologetics' (Davis's latest biographer bluntly calls it a
'terrible book'),[48] there are precious few signs in its fifteen hundred pages
that the lessons of defeat had been learned. In the opening chapter Davis
insisted that the 'opinions and sympathies of the world' had been misled
by the antithetical use of the terms 'freedom' and 'slavery' but, in a revealing
moment, he accepted that the misunderstanding was natural, given that the
idea of freedom was 'captivating', that of slavery so 'repellent' to the moral
sense of mankind. 'Southern statesmen may perhaps have been too indifferent
to this consideration – in their ardent pursuit of principles, overlooking the
effects of phrases,' he concluded.[49] It was perhaps the closest Jefferson Davis
ever came to an admission of failure.

Notes

1. Clement Eaton, *Jefferson Davis* (New York, 1977), p. 273. The most recent
   biography is William C. Davis, *Jefferson Davis: The Man and His Hour* (New
   York, 1991). The most comprehensive of the earlier studies is Hudson Strode,
   Jefferson Davis, 3 vols (New York, 1955–64).

2. David M. Potter, 'Jefferson Davis and the political factors in Confederate
   defeat', in David Donald (ed.), *Why the North Won the Civil War* (paperback edn,
   New York, 1962), p. 103. Among the many comparisons made between
   Davis and Lincoln as war leaders, perhaps the most favourable to the former is
   provided by Rembert W. Patrick, who argues that Davis 'was able to get pro-
   portionately more from his people, resources of the South considered, than was
   Abraham Lincoln from his.' Patrick, *Jefferson Davis and His Cabinet* (Baton Rouge,
   La, 1944), p. 45.

3. Bruce Collins, 'The making of Jefferson Davis', *Journal of American Studies* 18
   (December 1984), p. 439.

4. William Howard Russell, *My Diary North and South* (2 vols, London, 1863),
   vol. 2, pp. 376–7. Russell's first impressions of Davis are revealed in Martin

[114]   Crawford (ed.), *William Howard Russell's Civil War: Private Diary and Letters, 1861–1862* (Athens, Ga, 1992), p. 52.

5. Paul D. Escott, *After Secession: Jefferson Davis and the Failure of Confederate Nationalism* (Baton Rouge, La, 1978), p. 18.

6. E. Merton Coulter, *The Confederate States of America, 1861–1865* (Baton Rouge, La, 1950), p. 401.

7. Escott, *After Secession*, p. 7.

8. Quoted in John McCardell, *The Idea of a Southern Nation: Southern Nationalists and Nationalism, 1830–1860* (New York, 1979), pp. 333–4.

9. Quoted in Paul C. Nagel, *One Nation Indivisible: The Union in American Thought* (New York, 1964), p. 101.

10. Eaton, *Jefferson Davis*, p. 17.

11. Eaton, *Jefferson Davis*, p. 65.

12. Davis, *Jefferson Davis*, pp. 129–254, provides the most authoritative account of the future president's antebellum career.

13. Dunbar Rowland (ed.), *Jefferson Davis, Constitutionalist, His Letters, Papers and Speeches* (10 vols, Jackson, Miss., 1923), vol. 2, p. 252.

14. For the text of Davis's Inaugural Address, see James D. Richardson (ed.), *Messages and Papers of the Confederacy* (2 vols, Nashville, 1906), I: pp. 32–6. The occasion is described in Davis, *Jefferson Davis*, pp. 306–10.

15. Jeffrey K. Tulis, *The Rhetorical Presidency* (Princeton, NJ, 1987), pp. 47–51.

16. Jefferson Davis to Varina Howell Davis, 20 February 1861, in Linda Lasswell Crist *et al.* (eds), *The Papers of Jefferson Davis*, 9 vols to date (Baton Rouge, La, 1971–), vol. 7, pp. 53–4.

17. Richardson, *Messages and Papers*, I, p. 33.

18. See David M. Potter, *The Impending Crisis* (New York, 1976), pp. 485–554.

19. Richardson, *Messages and Papers*, vol. 1, p. 32.

20. Richardson, *Messages and Papers*, vol. 1, 35. For the full text of the permanent Constitution, see ibid., I, pp. 37–54. See Charles R. Lee, Jr, *The Confederate Constitutions* (Chapel Hill, NC, 1963) for a detailed examination of origins and texts.

21. Richardson, *Messages and Papers*, vol. 1, pp. 34–5.

22. Among the studies that offer insight into the changes occurring in the late antebellum South, see J. Mills Thornton III, *Politics and Power in a Slave Society:*

Alabama, 1800–1860 (Baton Rouge, La, 1978); and Mary A. DeCredico, *Patriotism for Profit: Georgia's Urban Entrepreneurs and the Confederate War Effort* (Chapel Hill, NC, 1990), pp. 1–20.

23. Escott, *After Secession*, pp. 75 6.

24. The classic view of states rights was promulgated by Frank L. Owsley, *States Rights in the Confederacy* (Chicago, 1925). The modern critique began with David R. Scarboro, 'North Carolina and the Confederacy: the weakness of states rights during the Civil War', *North Carolina Historical Review* 56 (April 1979), pp. 133–49. Richard E. Beringer, Herman Hattaway, Archer Jones, William N. Still Jr, *Why the South Lost the Civil War* (Athens, Ga, 1986), pp. 203–25, examines the issue in detail.

25. DeCredico, *Patriotism for Profit*, pp. 72–104. The South's 'military-industrial revolution' during the war is examined in Emory M. Thomas, *The Confederate Nation, 1861–1865* (New York, 1979), pp. 206–14; and Thomas, *The Confederacy as a Revolutionary Experience* (Englewood Cliffs, NJ, 1971).

26. Alfred Blevins, quoted in Martin Crawford, *Passages of War: Ashe County, North Carolina from the 1850s to the 1870s* (Charlottesville, Va, forthcoming). On the causes and consequences of declining Southern morale, see in particular, Escott, *After Secession*, pp. 94–225.

27. Gary W. Gallagher, *The Confederate War* (Cambridge, Mass., 1997), p. 87.

28. Richardson, *Messages and Papers*, vol. 1, p. 33.

29. Thomas, *The Confederate Nation*, p. 62.

30. Richardson, *Messages and Papers*, vol. 1, p. 131. The idea of secession as 'counterrevolution' is strongly pursued in James M. McPherson, *Battle Cry of Freedom: The Civil War Era* (New York, 1988), pp. 234–75.

31. Howell Cobb, in Michael Perman (ed.), *Major Problems in the Civil War and Reconstruction* (Lexington, Mass., 1991), pp. 238–9.

32. Crawford, *William Howard Russell's Civil War*, p. xxxvi.

33. William W. Freehling, *The Reintegration of American History: Slavery and the Civil War* (New York, 1994), p. 237. For slavery's impact on early Confederate military capabilities, see Armistead Robinson, 'In the shadow of Old John Brown: Insurrection anxiety and Confederate mobilization, 1861–1863', *Journal of Negro History*, 65 (Fall 1980), pp. 279–97. Clarence Mohr, *On the Threshold of Freedom: Masters and Slaves in Civil War Georgia* (Athens, Ga, 1986), is an invaluable study.

[116]   34. The Brierfield episode is described in Davis, *Jefferson Davis*, p. 409. On William
             Jackson, see R.J.M. Blackett, 'Cracks in the antislavery wall: Frederick
             Douglass's second visit to England (1859–1860) and the coming of the Civil
             War', in Alan J. Rice and Martin Crawford (eds), *Liberating Sojourn: Frederick
             Douglass and Transatlantic Reform* (Athens, Ga, forthcoming). For accounts of
             Jackson's escape, see *The Liberator*, 25 May 1862; *Harper's Weekly*, 7 June 1862.
             I am greatly indebted to Richard Blackett for alerting me to Jackson's history.

        35. See Randolph B. Campbell, 'Planters and plain folks: the social structure of the
             antebellum South,' in John B. Boles and Evelyn Thomas Nolen (eds), *Interpret-
             ing Southern History: Historiographical Essays in Honor of Sanford W. Higginbotham*
             (Baton Rouge, La, 1987), pp. 48–77, for a useful overview.

        36. U.B. Phillips, 'The central theme of Southern history', *American Historical Re-
             view* 34 (October 1928), pp. 30–43, asserted that the essence of Southernism
             was the common resolve that the South should remain a white man's country.

        37. See Escott, *After Secession*, pp. 168–95.

        38. 'Speech at Richmond', in Crist, *Papers of Jefferson Davis*, vol. 9, pp. 12–13.

        39. See Robert F. Durden, *The Gray and the Black: The Confederate Debate on Eman-
             cipation* (Baton Rouge, La, 1972), pp. 101–6.

        40. Drew Gilpin Faust, *The Creation of Confederate Nationalism* (Baton Rouge, La,
             1988), p. 84.

        41. George C. Rable, *The Confederate Republic: A Revolution Against Politics* (Chapel
             Hill, NC, 1994), p. 210. The classic exposition of the argument concerning the
             comparative role of political parties in North and South is to be found in Eric
             L. McKitrick, 'Party politics and the Union and Confederate war efforts', in
             William Nisbet Chambers and Walter Dean Burnham (eds), *The American Party
             Systems: Stages of Political Development* (New York, 1967), pp. 117–51.

        42. Jefferson Davis to John C. Pemberton, 9 August 1863, in Crist, *Papers of
             Jefferson Davis*, vol. 9, p. 334.

        43. See Frank E. Vandiver, *Rebel Brass: The Confederate Command System* (Baton
             Rouge, La, 1956), pp. 40–3. The two most recent studies of Davis's relation-
             ship with his military commanders are Steven E. Woodworth, *Jefferson Davis
             and his Generals: the Failure of Confederate Command in the West* (Lawrence, Ks,
             1990); and Woodworth, *Davis and Lee at War* (Lawrence, Ks, 1995). Also valu-
             able is George Green Shackleford, *George Wythe Randolph and the Confederate
             Elite* (Athens, Ga, 1988). Randolph was Confederate Secretary of War from
             March until November 1862.

44. William J. Cooper, Jr, 'Jefferson Davis and the sudden disappearance of South- [117]
    ern politics', in Charles W. Eagles (ed.), *Is There a Southern Political Tradition?*
    (Jackson, Miss., 1996), pp. 27–42 (quotations on pp. 40–1).

45. Davis, *Jefferson Davis*, pp. 416–17. On the evangelical foundations of Confed-
    erate nationalism, see Faust, *Creation of Confederate Nationalism*, pp. 22–40.

46. Joseph Davis's antebellum 'experiment' in slave management is described in
    Janet Sharp Hermann, *The Pursuit of a Dream* (New York, 1981), pp. 3–34,
    which also discusses the regime at Brierfield. See also Eaton, *Jefferson Davis*,
    pp. 33–46.

47. Eaton, *Jefferson Davis*, pp. 68–70; Davis, *Jefferson Davis*, p. 690. Although
    Jefferson Davis accepted the management methods established by his older
    brother, their views on slavery differed sharply. See Hermann, *Pursuit of a
    Dream*, p. 32.

48. Robert Penn Warren, *Jefferson Davis Gets His Citizenship Back* (Lexington, Ky,
    1980), p. 90; Davis, *Jefferson Davis*, p. 676.

49. Jefferson Davis, *The Rise and Fall of the Confederate Government*, 2 vols (London,
    1881), vol. 1, p. 6.

PART TWO

THE MILITARY FRONT

CHAPTER FIVE

THE FIRST OF THE MODERN WARS?

JOSEPH G. DAWSON III

Writing fifteen years after General Robert E. Lee surrendered his army at Appomattox, Adam Badeau maintained that, 'It was not [only] victory that either side was playing for, but existence.' Badeau continued: 'If the rebels won, they destroyed a nation; if the [United States] government succeeded, it annihilated a rebellion.' As former military secretary and aide-de-camp to General Ulysses S. Grant, Badeau may offer insights into Grant's approach to waging war: 'But above all, he [Grant] understood that he was engaged in a people's war, and that the people as well as the armies of the South must be conquered, before the war could end. Slaves, supplies, crops, stock, as well as arms and ammunition – everything that was necessary in order to carry on the war was a weapon in the hands of the enemy; and of every weapon the enemy must be deprived. . . . It was indispensable to annihilate armies and resources; to place every rebel force where it had no alternative but destruction or submission.'[1]

Beginning in 1861, Americans fought over political objectives that could not be compromised. First, and foremost, the North sought complete reunion with all the states that had claimed to secede. After eighteen months of intensifying conflict, on 22 September 1862 President Abraham Lincoln announced his preliminary Emancipation Proclamation, adding the objective of destroying slavery to the goal of reunion. On the other hand, Southerners had created a slaveholders' republic, the Confederate States of America, where the institution of slavery would be protected and encouraged. During the first eighteen months of war, President Jefferson Davis, other national and state officials, and most Southern newspaper editors, showed no willingness to restore the Union or abolish slavery. Following the campaigns of autumn of 1862, the war became increasingly bitter and hard-fought, exceeding both the scale and destructiveness of anything that Americans could have predicted in 1861. Both sides called upon government to organize their resources, manufacture

[122] or import munitions and matériel, and field several armies, most of them larger than any armies raised in other American wars.[2] Federals and Confederates battled gallantly, but increasingly disregarded civility.[3] By the summer of 1864, after more than three years of fighting, many Americans decided that one side would have to completely give up its objectives. The war would not be resolved by trading a state or two, or compromised by simply adjusting boundaries here or there. Either the United States would be restored, or not; either the Confederacy would be independent, or not; either slavery would be abolished or perpetuated indefinitely.[4]

During the early months of conflict, President Lincoln and President Davis both hoped to fight a limited war, meaning that partial mobilization and commitment of limited forces might persuade their opponents to quit, thus winning their objectives.[5] Surprisingly, the recently-formed Confederacy demonstrated a remarkable national resiliency, despite the fact that the North held clear advantages in important war-making categories, including more than 2 to 1 in population, 2 to 1 in railroad mileage, and 5 to 1 in number of factories. But Northerners took much longer than expected to make their advantages felt.[6] Making a transition toward total war, Union leaders never uttered the phrase 'unconditional surrender', but that was what they practically demanded from the Confederacy by 1865.

Features of modern war

Historians offer differing evaluations of such phrases as *modern war* and *total war*, and thus there are differing views about placing the American Civil War in either category, or determining whether it was the first modern war.[7] In *Men in Arms*, Richard A. Preston, Alex Roland, and Sydney F. Wise, conclude that the Civil War 'was the first great war to be fought in the era of the Industrial Revolution' and that each side fought for a 'total' objective. The hallmarks of modern warfare include features such as governments raising mass national armies, having industrialized economies to supply them, and calling upon ideology to inspire soldiers. Although the American Civil War included all of these modern elements, the authors argue that the Napoleonic Wars (1800–15) marked the beginning of modern warfare.[8]

Certainly, warring Americans of the 1860s drew upon modern technology. Improved artillery, such as the Napoleon cannon, fired projectiles up to one mile and was especially devastating against attacking infantry inside 200 yards. Moreover, single-shot, muzzle-loading rifles, such as Springfields and Enfields, carried by infantrymen of both sides, more than doubled the killing zone over old smooth-bore muskets. Those rifles fired bullets accurately to 200 yards and could hit targets at twice that range. Select units, mostly cavalry on the Union side, carried breech-loading magazine rifles that permitted high volumes of fire. Soldiers could be taken under fire at longer ranges and those moving forward in the attack could suffer casualties for longer periods of time. Battlefields were wider and deeper than ever before.[9]

Both North and South raised large armies of citizen-soldiers expected to serve for up to three years. Some 2 million Northerners and more than 900,000 Southerners donned uniforms during the war. Most of these citizen-soldiers enlisted on their own accord; conscription acts passed by their respective congresses prompted others to enlist rather than suffer the perceived stigma of being drafted.[10]

Modern war-making involved greater use of railroads and telegraph. North and South established their own military telegraph offices, relaying messages quickly across expanses of territory. Railroads transported soldiers and supplies on both sides, and a few heavy cannons were mounted on railway cars. Bolstered by an act of Congress, in 1862 President Lincoln authorised the US Military Railroad, a network using a standardized gauge of 4 feet, 8.5 inches, giving logistical support to Federal forces moving into the South. Although he used powers of persuasion, Jefferson Davis found that Southern railway owners were less cooperative than he would have hoped; the president was reluctant to control railroad rates. Putting aside states rights, Davis and the Confederate congress designated national funds for building tracks to fill critical gaps in the South's lines, connecting Danville, Virginia, with Greensboro, North Carolina, and Selma, Alabama, with Meridian, Mississippi.[11]

Another modern aspect of the Civil War incorporated ideology to inspire both sides. For the North, the concept of 'the Union' took on virtually religious significance. Many Northerners believed that the United States exemplified democratic government, economic opportunity, and individual rights. They decided that not only America but the world would be worse off if the United States fell apart. By early 1863, Lincoln's controversial decision to emancipate the slaves played its part in motivating a large percentage of Northerners. For Southerners, fighting for national independence intertwined with states rights and property rights – owning slaves. Patriotism meant the freedom to maintain the 'Southern way of life' and protect 'Southern institutions'. Lincoln's announcement of a policy to free the slaves lent a moral overtone to the war. Abolishing slavery, no matter that it created new controversies over the status and rights of blacks, matched the long-standing American assertions of individual freedom and opportunity embodied in the Declaration of Independence of 1776.[12]

Another important feature of a modern war involved the use of naval power. Both navies commissioned new ironclad or armoured ships powered by steam engines, and the Union also manufactured warships with revolving turrets, a significant improvement in design. In April 1861 President Lincoln imposed a blockade on the Confederate coast from Virginia to Texas. Scorned by Southerners as a 'paper blockade', it was obviously weak during the war's early months. By the end of 1862, however, the Federal blockade grew stronger. Union warships presented an 'evident danger' to large ocean-going ships trying to enter or leave a Southern port, ending any chance for routine commercial relations between the Confederacy and other nations. During 1863 blockade runners shifted to small, fast steamers. By the end of the war more than 400 Federal vessels blockaded the Southern coast. Moreover, the blockade hindered routine diplomatic relations between the Confederacy and Europe. Therefore, the blockade's effectiveness can be calculated in ways other than the number of ships passing into and out of the Confederacy. The North also employed considerable naval power in riverine operations. Building new shallow-draft ironclads, the Union navy cooperated with the army in joint operations against Confederate forts and cities. Naval power thus contributed to the Federal government's efforts to reassert its authority over the seceded states.[13]

Delineating acceptable methods of warfare and calling for combatants to adhere to restrictions when dealing with non-combatants was also a modern feature of the American Civil War. Concerned that the war was longer and more ghastly than expected, in December 1862 Secretary of War Edwin M. Stanton called upon Professor Francis Lieber, of Columbia University, to draft a code for the conduct of war. A board of Federal officers edited Lieber's Code and published the result in April 1863 as General Orders No. 100, *Instructions for the Government of Armies of the United States in the Field*. General Orders No. 100 defined war between governments, set criteria for soldiers' conduct (especially with civilians), described functions of martial law and military courts, spelled out expectations of behaviour for persons in occupied areas, and classified actions of guerrillas. Lieber's Code provided both the model and language for Europeans at the international Hague Conventions of 1899 and 1907.[14]

Yet another modern aspect of the struggle came when the Union established military government in the former Confederate states after the war,

imposing Federal authority in ways inconceivable to America's Founders. The
area to be restored to the Union was large and no other US government agency
or agencies, such as the Treasury Department or the Justice Department, could
handle the process of reconstruction. Only the army was capable of both
constabulary and administrative duties leading to the country's reunification.
The army's myriad duties included supervising schools, banks, courts, railroads
and voter registration. During reconstruction, Southern state governments
were led by loyal civilian officeholders or, in some instances, army generals
appointed and influenced new officials who were expected to carry out the
laws of Congress until loyal state governments were elected by voters registered by the army. The US Congress held the authority to seat Southern
congressional representatives and senators, and thus was able to decide when
states had been reconstructed.[15]

Nature of total war

Several historians have concluded that the American War between the States
was a modern war and also a *total war*. Although few have agreed exactly how
to define total war, historian Daniel Sutherland summarized that its 'principal themes have always been the disruption of the enemy's logistical base
and the destruction of civilian morale'.[16] Others insist that total war means
wide-scale attacks on civilians themselves, not just finding ways to undercut
their morale or destroy the enemy nation's resources and industrial and
agricultural production.[17] Among the first to suggest that 'total war' could be
applied to the Civil War was J.F.C. Fuller, a British army officer and military
analyst. In his study of *The Generalship of Ulysses S. Grant*, Fuller asserted that
'the Confederacy was crushed physically, economically, and morally, [in
contrast to] the Central Powers [in the Great War, that] were never morally
defeated'. Furthermore, Fuller contended: 'The Northern problem of conquest meant not only defeating the enemy's armed forces and occupying his
capital, but subduing the will of an entire people and occupying the whole of
their country.' Fuller concluded: 'The political object of the war was so clear,
namely, union or disunion, that no other course could be adopted.'[18]

   The Second World War affected scholars' views about the Civil War. A
number of them elaborated upon Fuller's suggestions. In an essay, 'General
William T. Sherman and total war', and later in a book, *Merchant of Terror*,
John B. Walters asserted that at the outset Sherman's 'attitude toward the

[126] enemy was essentially that of the orthodox professional soldier of the period
– interested in the game itself as it was being played by the two armies rather
than in personalising the enemy'. After more than a year of war, however,
Sherman began to see things differently: 'When one nation is at war with
another all the people of the one are enemies of the other.' Even more em-
phatically, Sherman stated to his brother, US Senator John Sherman, that 'the
entire South, man, woman, and child are against us [the North], armed and
determined'. As the conflict intensified, Sherman decided that he must 'wage
war so terrible', reaching the lives and property of many Southern civilians
as well as the Confederate armies. Taking steps to destroy the Southerners'
economic base and transportation network, Sherman also aimed at their
morale and psychological outlook. Sherman's devastating campaign through
Georgia and the Carolinas were the culmination of his terrible approach to
waging war.[19]

Influenced by J.F.C. Fuller's writings, T. Harry Williams made one of
the strongest statements by an American historian. Williams flatly contended
that 'The Civil War was the first of the modern total wars.' In *Lincoln and his
Generals* (1952), Williams argued that President Lincoln became a masterful
commander in chief, marshalling the North's resources and military might to
subdue the South completely, creating a modern general staff in the process.
After further reflection, Williams qualified his views. Writing in 1981, he reiterated that 'there could be no compromise, no partial triumph for either
side. One or the other had to achieve a complete victory.' He concluded:
'The totality of these objectives led some historians to call the Civil War a
total war. The label is somewhat exaggerated, as neither side put forward
the absolute effort required of many nations in World War I or World War
II. . . . Still, the Civil War missed totality by only a narrow margin.'[20]

Numerous other historians joined the ranks of those describing a total
war. For instance, to Frank E. Vandiver, the conflict 'had become total. All
elements of the population were affected; all had some part in the whole
effort.' Along the same lines, Bruce Catton contended that Grant was 'fighting
. . . a total war, and in a total war the enemy's economy is to be undermined
in any way possible.' Russell F. Weigley argued that Northern political
and military leaders gradually came to believe that 'nothing less than total
victory' would result in the goal of national reunification and Northern military leadership agreed on using a 'strategy of annihilation'. Emory M. Thomas
concluded that 'by 1865, under the pressure of total war, the Confederate
South had surrendered most of its cherished way of life.' Phillip S. Paludan
postulated that 'Grant's war making has come to stand for the American
way of war. For one thing, that image is one of total war demanding uncon-

ditional surrender.' In influential books and essays, James M. McPherson maintained that the Union war effort blended military, diplomatic, economic, political, social and ideological threads to produce a total war. In *Battle Cry of Freedom*, McPherson pointed out that in 'Grant and Sherman the North acquired commanders with a concept of total war and the necessary determination to make it succeed'. Identifying Lincoln's ultimate goal in the most resounding way, McPherson emphasized the president's 'Strategy of Unconditional Surrender'.[21]

From the outset, North and South fought over a central issue – whether two nations would exist where only one had stood before. Although that issue could not be compromised, both sides expected that the war would be limited in certain ways. Few expected that the war would have great impact on civilians' lives or change society. Instead of lasting only a few months with a few battles fought in only a restricted geographical area, the war went on for fifty months; Union and Confederate armies fought battles in nineteen states and territories. In the East, opposing forces fought from Gettysburg, Pennsylvania, south to Olustee, Florida. Battles swept across the continent from the Atlantic Coast westward to Glorieta, near Santa Fe, New Mexico, and raged up and down the Mississippi River Valley. Altogether, the fighting covered an area approximately equal to that between the River Rhine to Moscow and from the Bosporus to the Baltic. Some Americans might have anticipated that the war could be fought out if each side fielded only two or three armies. Eventually, a dozen armies carried Union or Confederate banners, enrolling nearly 3 million men in blue and grey uniforms between 1861 and 1865.[22]

The longer the war lasted, the greater the geographical area it covered; the more men who served in uniform, the greater the involvement of both governments in order to provide the supplies necessary to support extraordinarily large armies and continue the war. Beyond what anyone would have expected in 1861, the Union and the Confederacy mobilized their economies and populations. In many ways, the demands of the wider war called for unusual cooperation between governments and businesses, especially railroads, and War Department contracts became vital to many industries. Ironically, in the Confederacy the marriage of government and business, and the growth of government agencies, had the greater impact. Another way to consider the war efforts of North and South was to postulate that, because of its greater strength and resources, the North conducted a modern war by less than total means, but the South eventually called upon nearly total effort from its people.

The Confederacy's leaders found after a year of warfare that their national government had to step into the economy in unforeseen ways. In order to wage a modern war, the Confederate government surpassed the old US government's number of employees, eventually hiring more than 70,000 persons in its several agencies, most in the War Department. During the 1850s, few Southerners were convinced that industrialization would benefit their region. In 1861, Confederates were unable to find enough private companies to supply all of their needs for the war effort, prompting them to establish government factories to produce gunpowder, uniforms, tents and firearms. Colonel Josiah Gorgas, Chief of the Confederate Ordnance Bureau, worked wonders in wartime production. Seeking greater access to overseas resources, the government commandeered one-third space on blockade-runners in 1863. Although its contracts provided the livelihood for almost every Southern rail line, the government refused to nationalize the railroads. The Confederate government gradually assumed a decisive place in the economic life of the struggling nation; Confederate contracts were vital for many businesses and industries.[23]

Looking to the North, historians have debated the impact and consequences of the Civil War on the US economy. The demands of war generated growth in some economic sectors, hurt some, and left others almost unaffected. War Department contracts spurred expansion in companies making gunpowder, firearms and ammunition, but also in production of all kinds of leather products, including shoes, boots and harnesses. The Union army demanded tremendous quantities of meat and other foodstuffs to feed its units. Coal-mining increased. Woollens production doubled to make up the loss of cotton. Workers produced new wagons by the score and the government purchased thousands of horses and mules to pull them. By the end of the war, the Federal government employed almost 200,000 civilian workers in all of its departments, nearly quintupling the civilian employees of 1861. Overall, Northern manufacturing was up in 1865, but it had not grown at the same rate as during the 1850s. The key features were the tremendous expansion in government employment and the signing of Federal contracts that sustained the war effort.[24]

Social dimension of war

Taking a truly revolutionary step, the Federal government enlisted African-Americans in great numbers into the army and navy, indicating how the expanding modern war disrupted the antebellum society. When the US War

Department held off on pushing for new units and enlistments began to decline during 1862, one solution to finding more soldiers was to enlist blacks. Lincoln opened the door for this possibility when he issued the preliminary Emancipation Proclamation on 22 September 1862, following the Union victory in the Antietam campaign. Earlier, Radical Republicans had called for black enlistment and a few radical generals had created black units prematurely, but Lincoln disbanded them. Beginning in 1863, the necessity for more soldiers to prosecute the war to victory realized the Radicals' dream of arming former slaves. Eventually, more than 180,000 African-Americans served in the Federal army, under the leadership of white officers; another 10,000 blacks wore Union navy uniforms. Thousands more contributed to the Northern war effort as teamsters and labourers. Some historians have argued that by comprising 10 per cent of the Northern soldiers and sailors, blacks provided the margin of victory for restoring the Union. Officially styled the 'US Colored Troops', African-Americans in the army radicalized the war by striking directly at the Southern social system based on slavery. Controversies erupted. Confederates shot black soldiers who surrendered, returned black prisoners to slavery, and mistreated white officers leading the 'Colored Troops'. In the last weeks of the war, ironically, the Confederate congress authorized the creation of experimental units of black soldiers to serve the South, but the war ended before many were enrolled.[25]

Other controversies flared over government restrictions or violations of civil liberties. Relying on his executive authority, President Lincoln ordered arrests of civilians under martial law and suspended the writ of habeas corpus. These actions took place especially in the border states of Maryland, Kentucky and Missouri, but also occurred in other states. Perhaps as many as 18,000 persons were arrested and held without trial during the course of the war – what seemed amazing violations of civil liberties to later generations. During 1861–5, however, President Lincoln and other Federal officials were worried about opposition to the Union by those they considered subversive. Individuals, such as former Democratic Congressman Clement Vallandigham, and secret groups, such as the Knights of the Golden Circle, were suspect. Because of public outcry against his actions, Lincoln signed the Habeas Corpus Act in March 1863, giving him legal authority to make other arrests. In retrospect, Northern critics' questioning the conscription policy or finding fault with Lincoln's leadership appeared less threatening than it did during the war. The president, however, suspected treason and believed that traitors had to be dealt with sternly. Authorized by an act passed by the Confederate Congress, Jefferson Davis also suspended habeas corpus, but not on so wide a scale as Lincoln. More than 4,000 southern political prisoners were arrested by Confederate authorities.[26] Although some historians have downplayed the significance of these arrests, those actions raised the spectre of tyrannical government action in wartime.

Furthermore, the two congresses enacted laws having other consequences for civilians. Confiscation Acts passed by the US Congress in August 1861 and July 1862 combined to empower the North to confiscate all real and movable property (including slaves) of anyone providing aid or service to the Confederacy. Thus, the institution of slavery started to unravel even before Lincoln's Emancipation Proclamation. In March 1863 the Confederate Congress passed, despite protests from state governments, an act authorizing the Southern government to impress any item necessary for use by the Rebel armies. Circumventing states rights, the Confederate government created new ways to touch its citizens.[27]

In both North and South the war affected women. In the South, the departure of so many men into the military called for women to take on new tasks. In addition to household chores, more women found jobs in schools, hospitals, businesses, government offices and factories. On the farms, especially in the South, women not only worked in the fields but also became supervisors and bookkeepers. Other women contributed to the war effort. In the North, the United States Sanitary Commission productively channelled efforts of volunteer workers, including many women. Southern women rolled bandages, baked foods and volunteered in numerous other ways. Historians debate how women's place in society changed due to the war, but the war required or offered opportunities for women to work in ways that were out of the ordinary for many of them, and can be interpreted to show a widening, modern war.[28]

Successful commanders grew to understand that the Civil War was a brutal contest of wills that demanded sledgehammer blows but General George B. McClellan was the personification of limited warfare. One of the most important Union commanders and modernist in his ability to master complicated logistics, McClellan also demonstrated remarkable talents to organize, train and inspire a national army. But he campaigned cautiously; after creating the marvellous Army of the Potomac, he was reluctant to send it into battle. He also opposed taking actions against slavery – that is, he was not out to upset the Southern social system. In a letter to a Virginian, for example, McClellan explained his outlook: 'I have done my best to secure protection to private property, but I confess that circumstances beyond my control have often defeated my purposes. I have not come here [to Virginia] to wage war upon the defenseless, upon non-combatants, upon private property, nor upon the domestic institutions of the land.' The general mistakenly believed that, whenever the war ended, the nation could only be restored on the basis of the Union as it stood in 1860.[29]

To some, Robert E. Lee appeared Napoleonic in his tactical offensive style, but he also could summon the rhetoric of total war. According to Lee's adjutant, Colonel Charles Marshall, Lee believed 'that every other consideration should be regarded as subordinate to the great end of the public safety, and that since the whole duty of the nation would be war until independence should be secured the whole nation should for the time [of war] be converted into an army, the producers to feed and the soldiers to fight.' But Lee seemed shocked about the war's destructiveness and the actions taken by Union forces. Even under the conditions of limited war that prevailed during 1861, Lee was astounded by what he considered the unwarranted conduct of Union troops, including 'pillaging', 'burning' and 'robbing'. Receiving news of raids along the Atlantic coast in 1862, Lee wrote his son: 'No civilized nation within my knowledge has ever carried on war as the United States government has against us.' Although historian T. Harry Williams called Lee 'the last of the great old-fashioned generals', there was no doubt that Lee was also aggressive and took great risks to win Confederate independence; he twice launched powerful offensives into the Union states.[30]

Departing from McClellan's traditionalism, Major General John Pope unleashed powerful rhetoric of war-making. Having won victories in the Mississippi Valley, Pope came east, levelling bombast in all directions and calling for the North to begin waging a harsher war against secessionists and slaveholders. Pope was unable to deliver on his own promises of a more destructive war. His defeat at Lee's hands in the Second Battle of Bull Run, Virginia, in August 1862, forced President Lincoln to seek more determined commanders to take the fight to the enemy.[31]

Widening destructive scope

One of these commanders was William T. Sherman. Southerners and some historians have pictured Sherman and his campaigns tilting the scales to total war. Maturing under Grant's tutelage and foreshadowing the shape of things to come, in 1862 and 1863 Sherman moved against the enemy's economic infrastructure in Mississippi, destroying railroads in Meridian and Jackson, the state capital. Worse lay ahead in Georgia, South Carolina and North Carolina. After taking the railroad centre of Atlanta, Georgia, on 1 September 1864, Sherman led an army of 60,000 veteran troops across the state. Marching in loose formations fifty miles wide, their eventual destination was the Atlantic port of Savannah, more than 200 miles away from Atlanta. Sherman's goals were those of modern war: to destroy everything of military value but also to ruin the South's will to prosecute the war – simultaneously destroying economic resources and morale. Sherman summarized his intent to Grant: '[I]t is a demonstration to the world, foreign and domestic, that we have a power which [Jefferson] Davis cannot resist. This may not be war, but rather statesmanship, nevertheless it is overwhelming to my mind that there are thousands of people abroad and in the South who will reason thus: If the North can march an army right through the south, it is proof positive that the North can prevail in this contest, leaving only open the question of its willingness to use that power.' No Confederate army blocked his path, and like a human hurricane, from 15 November to 22 December 1864 Sherman's catastrophic raid damaged or destroyed railroads, bridges and war supplies along with many civilian homes, businesses and much personal property. Moreover, thousands of slaves fled their owners, creating a terrible logistics burden for Sherman, but further undermining slavery throughout the South. In the Carolinas, Sherman's army further demonstrated the power-lessness of the Confederate government. From February to April 1865 Union troops pillaged across two states, burning two dozen towns, including much of Columbia, South Carolina's capital, ripping up railroads, laying waste crops, incinerating factories, and leaving a trail of unprecedented destruction in their wake.[32]

Major General Philip H. Sheridan's campaign in Virginia's Shenandoah Valley paralleled Sherman's destructiveness. During the summer of 1864 two armies sparred while moving up and down the Shenandoah Valley. Union soldiers damaged several towns and that damage so infuriated General Jubal Early that he retaliated by raiding northward and razing the town of Chambersburg, Pennsylvania. Although the strength of the two valley armies varied, Sheridan's 40,000 outnumbered Early's by about 2 to 1. A series of hard-fought engagements culminated in a Union victory at the Battle of Cedar Creek on 19 October. Obeying Grant's orders to leave 'the Shenandoah Valley . . . a barren waste' and taking a systematic approach, Sheridan set out to ruin the area known as 'the breadbasket of the Confed-eracy'; its bountiful farms had sustained Lee's army. Barns and crops, farms and fences, mills and shops all fell to the torch; Union soldiers hauled off food and livestock, leaving little of value to anyone. The Shenandoah Valley never fed Lee's army again.[33]

Mentor to Sherman and Sheridan, Ulysses S. Grant rose from obscurity in 1861 to the height of American military power in 1864.[34] Forging a modernistic cooperative relationship with Union naval officers, Grant became the temporary darling of Northern journalists in the early spring of 1862 after demanding the 'unconditional surrender' of Fort Donelson, Tennessee. However, the Battle of Shiloh, Tennessee, on 6–7 April produced horrific casualties. More than 20,000 Federals and Confederates were killed, wounded, and missing. Shiloh transformed Grant's outlook about what it would take to restore the Union. He recalled in his memoirs: 'I gave up all ideas of saving the Union except by complete conquest. Up to that time it had been the policy of our army, certainly of that portion commanded by me, to protect the property of the citizens whose territory was invaded, without regard to their sentiments, whether Union or Secession. After this [battle], however, I regarded it as humane to both sides to protect the persons of those found at their homes, but to consume everything that could be used to support and supply armies.'[35]

Grant never again discounted the Confederates' devotion to winning independence and, accordingly, came to understand the tremendous military force that would have to be marshalled and applied in order to smash the rebellion and produce national reunion. It proved impossible to destroy armies on the battlefield, but Grant trapped three Confederate armies during the war (at Fort Donelson, Vicksburg and Appomattox), and forced them to surrender, destroying their usefulness and also damaging Southern morale. Looking beyond the battlefield, Grant decided that destruction of enemy resources must be given high priority. Working with Sherman and Sheridan, Grant sought ways to undercut the Southern war effort by depriving the Confederacy of whatever it needed to fuel its war machine.[36]

As Union armies ground their way into the Confederacy, they targeted cities – places with industrial capacity. In May 1862 the Union navy delivered a 10,000–man Federal army to capture New Orleans, the South's largest city, biggest port, and a major banking centre as well as home to the Leeds Iron Works and other factories. In that same spring McClellan campaigned against Richmond. It was capital of the Confederacy, but also the South's largest industrial centre, site of the famous Tredegar Iron Works and other heavy industries. Other places with manufacturing capabilities fell to the Union's onslaught, including Nashville (February 1862) and Memphis (June 1862), Tennessee, and the shipyards at Norfolk, Virginia (May 1862). Although McClellan failed to take Richmond, by the end of 1862 four of the

[134] Confederacy's twelve largest cities (New Orleans, Nashville, Memphis, and Norfolk) were in Federal hands. One by one, the Union armies captured other shipping or railroad centres containing industries, including Chattanooga, Tennessee (September 1863), Mobile, Alabama (August 1864), and Atlanta, Georgia (September 1864). Then came Sherman's 'March to the Sea'. As Grant summarized, the Georgia-Carolinas campaign had enabled Sherman 'to get into the interior of the enemy's country as far as he can, inflicting all of the damage you can against their war resources'. In the war's waning weeks, March–April 1865, Brigadier-General James H. Wilson led a column of 13,000 Union cavalrymen on a destructive 300-mile raid across Alabama and into eastern Georgia, ravaging the vital depots and industries at Selma, scorching central Alabama in the same way that Sherman had burnt the heart of Georgia. Thus by the end of the war, the Confederacy was deprived of much of its manufacturing capability, either destroyed or occupied by Union armies.[37]

As the war raged through its third year, Federal leaders refused to be distracted by Confederate guerrilla raids and focused on major campaigns. The war was mostly a conventional conflict and Lincoln and his generals insisted that Union forces hammer against the secessionists' conventional armies and resources.[38] Meanwhile, some, including Northern 'Peace Democrats' and die-hard Southern rebels, still held out hopes for an armistice. Avoiding a term like 'unconditional surrender', in July 1864 Lincoln gave directions to Horace Greeley, editor of the New York *Tribune*. The journalist was about to hold unofficial discussions in Canada with Confederate delegates. 'If you can find, any person anywhere professing to have any proposition of Jefferson Davis in writing, for peace, embracing the *restoration of the Union* and *abandonment of slavery*, whatever else it embraces, say to him he may come to me with you.' Nothing came from Greeley's meeting; likewise, no breakthrough resulted in February 1865 from Lincoln's conference with Confederate Vice-President Alexander Stephens at Hampton Roads, Virginia.[39]

Reunion and emancipation remained Lincoln's terms for ending the war. 'Restoration of the Union' foreclosed the continued existence of the Confederate States of America. If there was no entity called the Confederate States of America, the rebels' conventional armies could not survive. Anything else that remained to be 'negotiated' were such war-ending matters as when and how Confederates would turn in weapons before disbanding, arranging for the release of prisoners of war, and requiring any surviving Confederate ships to haul down their flags. Obviously, such a vague phrase as the 'abandonment of slavery' revealed no specifics as to the process of how slavery would be abandoned, or how long it might take. While vague, the phase meant that the institution was to be ended in some fashion; it required Davis and other

Southern leaders to give up the social and economic system that had ignited so much controversy since the Missouri Compromise of 1821. Not surprisingly, President Davis blanched when he learned of Lincoln's terms, seeing that they equalled unconditional surrender without using that dreaded phrase, even if there was a slim chance that Lincoln could persuade the Congress to appropriate money to pay slaveowners for their slave property.[40]

Sliding to oblivion, the Confederacy lived on for less than a year. By June 1865 all government offices and departments of the Confederate States of America had closed. Its Congress was dissolved and its president was imprisoned. Confederate armies were disbanded and their flags shredded or surrendered. To avoid arrest, some Confederate officers fled overseas to Mexico, Brazil or Egypt. Confederate ministers (ambassadors) to foreign nations held no portfolio. Confederate money was worthless in private or public commerce and its debt repudiated in America and Europe. Crippled by Lincoln's Emancipation Proclamation, the institution of slavery was abolished by the ratification of the Thirteenth Amendment to the US Constitution six months after the last Confederate army surrendered. There was no compromise on any of these issues. As a result of the Civil War, the Confederate States of America ceased to exist.

The war's casualties reflected the far-reaching nature of the conflict, especially for the Confederacy. Inexact records for the South and more accurate tabulations for the North indicate that a total of 620,000 American soldiers and sailors died during the war, some 360,000 Federals and probably more than 260,000 Confederates. Of those totals, more than 225,000 Yankees and 164,000 Rebels died of disease. In addition, more than 275,000 Northerners and 195,000 Southerners were wounded. The Confederate casualties represented 50 per cent of men in uniform killed, died of disease, wounded or missing.[41]

The Civil War ripped apart the social and economic fabric of the old Union, destroyed slavery and produced constitutional changes (the Thirteenth, Fourteenth and Fifteenth Amendments), the first steps toward a new society. Industries worked to fill military orders and railroads accommodated military schedules. Employing modern weapons and suffering significant casualties, large armies manoeuvred through the Southern countryside, damaging crops, railroads, businesses, cities and homes. Praising the sacred Union and promising a new birth of freedom on one hand, or pledging to uphold states rights and perpetuate slavery on the other, rival American governments sought to achieve national goals that could not be compromised. Northerners and Southerners fought to the bitter end in a conflict that can be viewed as the first modern war.

Notes

1. Adam Badeau, *Military History of Ulysses S. Grant*, 3 vols (New York, 1881), vol. 3, pp. 643–4. A valuable introduction to this topic is Mark Grimsley, 'Modern war/total war', in Steven E. Woodworth (ed.), *The American Civil War: A Handbook of Literature and Research* (Westport, Conn., and London, 1996), pp. 379–89. An assertive argument, answering the question in the negative, is Mark E. Neely, Jr, 'Was the Civil War a total war?' *Civil War History* 37 (1991), pp. 5–28; revised in Stig Förster and Jörg Nagler (eds), *On the Road to Total War* (Cambridge, England, 1997), pp. 29–51.

2. The largest individual American field armies of previous wars were those under George Washington during the American Revolution, numbering 20,000, and under Winfield Scott during the Mexican War (1846–8), at about 14,000. See Allan R. Millett and Peter Maskowski, *For the Common Defense* (New York, 1993), pp. 64, 146.

3. Gerald F. Linderman, *Embattled Courage: The Experience of Combat in the American Civil War* (New York, 1987), pp. 180–215.

4. As T. Harry Williams summarized: 'The Civil War was a war of ideas and, inasmuch as neither side could compromise its political purposes, it was a war of unlimited objectives.' Williams, 'Military leadership of North and South' in David Donald (ed.), *Why the North Won the Civil War* (Baton Rouge, La, 1960), p. 35. See also Richard A. Preston, Alex Roland, and Sydney F. Wise, *Men in Arms: A History of Warfare and its Interrelationships with Western Society*, 5th edn (Fort Worth, Tx., 1991), p. 217.

5. One of the best expositions delineating the gradual progression from a limited war toward total war is Mark Grimsley, *The Hard Hand of War: Union Military Policy toward Southern Civilians, 1861–1865* (Cambridge, England, 1995), esp. pp. 4–5, 205, 221–2. See also Grimsley, 'Conciliation and Its failure, 1861–1862' *Civil War History* 39 (1993), pp. 317–35.

6. Joseph L. Harsh, *Confederate Tide Rising: Robert E. Lee and the Making of Southern Strategy, 1861–1862* (Kent, O, 1998), pp. 11–13. Thirteen states, including Kentucky and Missouri, held seats in the Confederate Congress and stars in the Confederate flag. A survey of economic disparities is T. Harry Williams, 'The American Civil War' in J.P.T. Bury (ed.), *The Zenith of European Power, 1830–1870*, vol. 10 of *The New Cambridge Modern History* (Cambridge, England, 1960), pp. 632–5.

7. See the discussion in R. Ernest Dupuy and Trevor N. Dupuy, *The Encyclopedia of Military History* (New York, 1986), pp. 522–33. They single out the Thirty Years War (1618–48) as the first modern war.

8. Preston *et al.*, *Men in Arms*, pp. 164–73, 185–6, 217–21, quote on p. 217. See
    also, for example, Robert M. Epstein, *Napoleon's Last Victory and the Emergence of Modern War* (Lawrence, Ks, 1994); Gunther E. Rothenberg, *The Art of Warfare in the Age of Napoleon* (Bloomington, Ind., 1978).

9. Jack Coggins, *Arms and Equipment of the Civil War* (New York, 1962). For debates over the effects of rifles see Paddy Griffith, *Rally Once Again* (London, 1987), pp. 73–90, and Grady McWhiney and Perry Jamieson, in *Attack and Die: Civil War Military Tactics and the Southern Heritage* (Tuscaloosa, Ala, 1982), pp. 48–9, 57–8.

10. James M. McPherson, *Battle Cry of Freedom: The Civil War Era*, a volume in the *Oxford History of the United States* (New York, 1988), pp. 429–33, 600–1; E.B. Long, *The Civil War Day by Day, an Almanac* (New York, 1971), p. 705.

11. George E. Turner, *Victory Rode the Rails* (New York, 1953), pp. 45–8, 310–11; Edward Hagerman, *The American Civil War and the Origins of Modern Warfare* (Bloomington, Ind., 1988), pp. xi, 41–4, 58, 82–7, 103–5, 277, 280–5.

12. Brian Holden Reid, *The Origins of the American Civil War* (London, 1996), pp. 19–29, 64–6, 82–3, 172–3, 160–1, 304–5; James M. McPherson, *For Cause and Comrades: Why Men Fought in the Civil War* (New York, 1997).

13. Arguing the effectiveness of the Union blockade is Bern Anderson, *By Sea and By River: The Naval History of the Civil War* (New York, 1962), pp. 34–7, 65–6, 225–32. Arguing to the contrary are Frank L. Owsley, *King Cotton Diplomacy*, 2nd edn (Chicago, Ill., 1959), and Stephen R. Wise, *Lifeline of the Confederacy: Blockade Running during the Civil War* (Columbia, SC, 1988). Portraying the blockade's effectiveness is McPherson, *Battle Cry of Freedom*, pp. 313–14, 378–9, 380–8. For the rivers, see John D. Milligan, *Gunboats down the Mississippi* (Annapolis, Md, 1965), and Anderson, *By Sea and By River*, passim.

14. Frank Freidel, 'General Orders 100 and military government,' *Mississippi Valley Historical Review* 32 (1946), pp. 541–56; Richard S. Hartigan, *Lieber's Code and the Laws of War* (Chicago, Ill., 1983).

15. James E. Sefton, *The United States Army and Reconstruction, 1865–1877* (Baton Rouge, La, 1967); Joseph G. Dawson III, *Army Generals and Reconstruction: Louisiana, 1862–1877* (Baton Rouge, La, 1982).

16. Daniel E. Sutherland, 'Abraham Lincoln, John Pope, and the Origins of Total War', *Journal of Military History* 56 (1992), p. 567. See also Lance Janda, 'Shutting the gates of mercy: the American origins of total war, 1860–1880', ibid., 59 (1995), pp. 7–8.

17. See especially Neely, 'Was the Civil War a total war?' In contrast to Neely's contention that it was not a total war, see the conclusions in Robert A. Doughty

et al., *Warfare in the Western World: Military Operations from 1600 to 1871* (Lexington, Mass., 1996), pp. 322, 388, 456–8.

18. J.F.C. Fuller, *The Generalship of Ulysses S. Grant* (New York, 1929), p. 41; Fuller, *Grant and Lee: A Study in Personality and Generalship* (London, 1933; reprint, Bloomington, Ind., 1957), p. 31.

19. John B. Walters, 'General William T. Sherman and total war', *Journal of Southern History* 14 (1949), pp. 447–80, quotes on p. 457; John B. Walters, *Merchant of Terror: General Sherman and Total War* (Indianapolis, Ind., 1973); Sherman to Salmon P. Chase, 11 August 1862, in William T. Sherman, *Memoirs*, 2 vols (New York, 1875), vol. 1, p. 266. Gen. Sherman to Sen. John Sherman, 26 August 1862, in Rachel S. Thorndike (ed.), *The Sherman Letters* (New York, 1894), pp. 159–60; Sherman to Grant, 4 October 1862, *The War of the Rebellion: A Compilation of the Official Records of the Union and Confederate Armies*, 128 books in 80 volumes (Washington, DC, 1880–1901), series 1, vol. 17, pt 2, p. 261.

20. T. Harry Williams, *Lincoln and his Generals* (New York, 1952), pp. vii–viii, 3, 304–7; Williams, *History of American Wars from 1745 to 1918* (New York, 1981), pp. 202–3. In another work, Williams also hedged: 'Trite it may be to say that the Civil War was the first of the modern wars, but this is a truth that needs to be repeated. If the Civil War was not quite total, it missed totality by only a narrow margin.' Williams, *Americans at War* (Baton Rouge, La, 1960), p. 47. See also the qualification of 'total war' by James McPherson, *Drawn with the Sword: Reflections on the American Civil War* (New York, 1996), pp. 67–70.

21. Frank E. Vandiver, *Rebel Brass: The Confederate Command System* (Baton Rouge, La, 1956), pp. 61, 123, 125. Bruce Catton, 'The Generalship of Ulysses S. Grant', in Grady McWhiney (ed.), *Grant, Lee, Lincoln and the Radicals* (New York, 1966), p. 8. See also Catton, *America Goes to War* (Middletown, Conn., 1958), esp. pp. 14, 20. Russell F. Weigley, *The American Way of War: A History of United States Military Strategy and Policy* (New York, 1973), p. 150; Emory M. Thomas, *The Confederacy as a Revolutionary Experience* (Englewood Cliffs, NJ, 1971), p. 135; Phillip S. Paludan, *A People's Contest: The Union and the Civil War* (New York, 1988), p. 296. McPherson, *Battle Cry of Freedom*, p. 857; McPherson, *Abraham Lincoln and the Second American Revolution* (New York, 1990), pp. 65–91.

22. A convenient discussion of troop strengths is Long, *The Civil War Day by Day*, pp. 704–9.

23. Paul Van Riper and Harry W. Scheiber, 'The Confederate civil service', *Journal of Southern History* 25 (1959), pp. 448–70; Vandiver, *Rebel Brass*, pp. 14–15, 88–107, 115–21; Emory M. Thomas, *The Confederate Nation* (New York,

1979), pp. 134–5, 206–14, 265; Richard F. Bensel, *Yankee Leviathan: The* [139]
Origins of Central State Authority in America, 1859–1877 (Cambridge, England, 1990), pp. 113–18, 131–2, 146–51, 159, 167–72, 181–98.

24. McPherson, *Battle Cry of Freedom*, pp. 816–18; Bensel, *Yankee Leviathan*, pp. 113–18, 131–2, 146–51, 159, 167–72, 181–98; Paul Van Riper and Keith A. Sutherland, 'The Northern civil service' *Civil War History* 11 (1965), pp. 351–69.

25. Joseph T. Glatthaar, *Forged in Battle: The Civil War Alliance of Black Soldiers and White Officers* (New York, 1990); Glatthaar, 'Black glory: the African-American role in Union victory', in Gabor S. Boritt (ed.), *Why the Confederacy Lost* (New York, 1992), pp. 133–62; Dudley T. Cornish, *The Sable Arm: Negro Troops in the Union Army, 1861–1865* (New York, 1956). See also Allan Nevins, *The War for the Union*, 4 vols (New York, 1960–71), vol. 2, pp. 145–6.

26. Mark E. Neely, Jr, *The Fate of Liberty: Abraham Lincoln and Civil Liberties* (New York, 1991); Frank L. Klement, *Dark Lanterns: Secret Political Societies, Conspiracies, and Treason Trials in the Civil War* (Baton Rouge, La, 1984); George C. Rable, *The Confederate Republic: A Revolution Against Politics* (Chapel Hill, NC, 1994), pp. 143–4, 158–60, 250–2.

27. Patricia Lucie, 'Confiscation: constitutional crossroads', *Civil War History* 23 (1977), pp. 307–21; Grimsley, *Hard Hand of War*, pp. 68–71, 123; E. Merton Coulter, *The Confederate States of America* (Baton Rouge, La, 1950), pp. 251–4.

28. George C. Rable, *Civil Wars: Women and the Crisis of Southern Nationalism* (Urbana, Ill., 1989), and McPherson, *Battle Cry of Freedom*, 449–50, 480–5.

29. McClellan to Hill Carter, 11 July 1862, in Stephen W. Sears (ed.), *The Civil War Papers of George B. McClellan: Selected Correspondence, 1860–1865*, (New York, 1989), p. 352. See also Grimsley, *Hard Hand of War*, pp. 31–5, 74–5, 136–7, and Stephen W. Sears, *George B. McClellan, the Young Napoleon* (New York, 1988).

30. Marshall, quoted in Fuller, *Grant and Lee*, p. 252; Clifford Dowdey and Louis H. Manarin (eds), *Wartime Papers of R.E. Lee* (Boston, 1961), p. 106; Williams, *Lincoln and his Generals*, pp. 312–14; Gary W. Gallagher, *The Confederate War* (Cambridge, Mass., 1997).

31. Sutherland, 'Lincoln, Pope, and Total War', pp. 570–86; Grimsley, *Hard Hand of War*, pp. 85–92. In contrast to Pope, Confederate General Thomas J. 'Stonewall' Jackson was a marvellous tactical commander but like Pope he voiced some harsh rhetoric. Not content to maintain the defensive, Jackson wanted to 'invade his country [the North] and do him all possible damage in the shortest possible time'. Friends and enemies alike rated Jackson as audacious, relentless

and almost unmerciful. See Charles Royster, *The Destructive War: William Tecumseh Sherman, Stonewall Jackson, and the Americans* (New York, 1991), p. 40 and passim.

32. Sherman to Grant, 6 November 1864, *Official Records*, vol. 39, pt 3, p. 660. An excellent study of the campaigns is Joseph T. Glatthaar, *The March to the Sea and Beyond: Sherman's Troops in the Savannah and Carolinas Campaigns* (New York, 1985), esp. pp. xii, 119–55. John G. Barrett, *Sherman's March through the Carolinas* (Chapel Hill, NC, 1956), pp. 16, 25, 280–1, likewise concludes that Sherman's campaign deserved to be classified as 'total war'. See also Paludan, *A People's Contest*, pp. 291, 302. For other perspectives, see B.H. Liddell Hart, *Sherman: Soldier, Realist, American* (New York, 1929), pp. 425–31, and Royster, *Destructive War*, pp. 354–8.

33. Everard H. Smith, 'Chambersburg: anatomy of a Confederate reprisal', *American Historical Review* 96 (1991), pp. 432–55; Gary W. Gallagher (ed.), *Struggle for the Shenandoah: Essays on the 1864 Valley Campaign* (Kent, O, 1991), esp. pp. 1–18; Jeffry D. Wert, *From Winchester to Cedar Creek: The Shenandoah Campaign of 1864* (Carlisle, Penn., 1987); Philip H. Sheridan, *Personal Memoirs of P.H. Sheridan*, 2 vols (New York, 1888), vol. 1, p. 486.

34. Herman Hattaway and Archer Jones, *How the North Won: A Military History of the Civil War* (Urbana, Ill., 1983), pp. 501–37.

35. Ulysses S. Grant, *Personal Memoirs of U. S. Grant*, 2 vols (New York, 1881), vol. 1, pp. 368–9.

36. Ibid.; Janda, 'Shutting the gates of mercy: American origins of total war', p. 13.

37. Grant to Sherman, 4 April 1865, *Official Records*, series 1, vol. 32, pt 3, pp. 245–6; James P. Jones, *Yankee Blitzkrieg: Wilson's Raid through Alabama and Georgia* (Athens, Ga, 1976).

38. For introductions to the guerrillas, see Michael Fellman, *Inside War: The Guerrilla Conflict in Missouri During the American Civil War* (New York, 1989); Jeffry D. Wert, *Mosby's Rangers* (New York, 1990); Richard E. Beringer, Herman Hattaway, Archer Jones, and William N. Still Jr, *Why the South Lost the Civil War* (Athens, Ga, 1986), pp. 339–51, 430–2, 436–8, and Grimsley, *Hard Hand of War*, pp. 111–19.

39. Roy P. Basler *et al.* (eds), *The Collected Works of Abraham Lincoln*, 9 vols (New Brunswick, NJ, 1953–55), vol. 7, p. 435; McPherson, *Battle Cry of Freedom*, pp. 822–4.

40. For a sharply contrasting interpretation of these developments, see Neely, 'Was the Civil War a total war?' *Civil War History* 37 (1991), pp. 6–7. See also

Edward C. Kirkland, *The Peacemakers of 1864* (New York, 1927), pp. 253, 258; William C. Davis, *Jefferson Davis, the Man and His Hour* (New York, 1991), pp. 592–4. Lincoln's eleventh-hour proposal for compensated emancipation was outlined in a message to Congress, 5 February 1865, in Basler *et al.* (eds), *Works of Lincoln*, vol. 8, pp. 260–1.

41. James M. McPherson, *Battle Cry of Freedom*, p. 854; Long, *Civil War Day by Day*, pp. 710–11.

CHAPTER SIX

COMMAND AND LEADERSHIP IN THE CIVIL WAR, 1861–5

BRIAN HOLDEN REID

C ommand, and a proper sense of the duties that belong to the commander, are central to the conduct of war. Without a central directing brain, armies degenerate into violent mobs or apathetic hosts, and are unable to achieve the political and military objectives set for them. This chapter, therefore, concentrates on the structures and systems of command during the American Civil War, rather than on the personal qualities needed to be an effective commander, although these are hardly unimportant. The Emperor Napoleon, who inspired a cult in the United States in the years before 1865, was of the opinion that centralization of command in war was essential and that one bad general was better than two good ones. In war, he repeated, it is the *man* who counts. The experience of the Napoleonic Wars was to cast a spell over the American imagination before 1861, the full consequences of which have yet to be investigated by historians. The simple, dramatic and rather glamorous appeal of the great individual in battle – the great captain – overlooked the important fact that Napoleon waged war before the full effects of the Industrial Revolution had made themselves felt in continental Europe.

The American Civil War was the greatest conflict waged during the first (steam-driven) phase of the Industrial Revolution. Some of its features were anticipated in the Crimean War (1854–6), but during the great American civil conflagration they were magnified, mainly because of its scale and intensity. The broad developments that were to become so important in the first half of the twentieth century were the impact of the immense productiveness of the American economy, that could clothe and equip large numbers of men, the increased reliance on technology and machinery (especially the railways), the improvement of weapons, the growth of the power of the tactical defence, the spread of the 'empty battlefield' (as each side resorted to entrenchments, with a vacant space in between), and the lengthening of an army's 'tail' (its support echelons) in proportion to its 'teeth' (the fighting elements). All of these developments greatly complicated the duties of the commander in a technical sense during the mid-nineteenth century, and made his job more difficult.[1]

Paradoxically, a number of American social developments tended to conceal the significance of these structural changes in the art of war. The cult of Napoleon in the United States – the belief in the 'man of destiny' – experienced a transmutation that gave it a different character to similar cults in Europe. Napoleon's brother, Joseph Bonaparte, a former King of Spain, lived in Borderntown, New Jersey, while Marshal Grouchy (whom many blamed for Napoleon's defeat at Waterloo), was a resident of Philadelphia. Their presence gave the cult a boost. The political ambitions of General Andrew Jackson, the victor of the Battle of New Orleans (1815) over the British, were presented by his Democratic publicists with a distinctly Napoleonic hue. His enemies claimed that Jackson was 'a military chieftain' intent on establishing a military dictatorship; he was also alleged to nurse regal ambitions, and was known as 'King Andrew'. But the Democrats themselves stressed Jackson's homespun frontier background. The egalitarian aspects of the Napoleonic legend were stressed: how a man who had sprung from comparatively humble roots could command the destiny of nations. Jackson, the untrained son of the frontier, had crushed regular soldiers commanded by the Duke of Wellington's brother-in-law, Sir Edward Pakenham.[2] Jackson's example encouraged the widespread assumption throughout the antebellum period that command in war was something simple that could be undertaken successfully by anybody of spirit or intelligence. If one looked further back in American history, the Revolution had shown how citizen soldiers, led by the ineffable (former colonel of militia) General George Washington, could defeat regular armies. Washington himself became the exemplary model of the patriot-general.

The military experience of the Mexican War (1846–8) confirmed these views. Mexican soldiers were individually brave, but were no match for American armies composed mainly of volunteers. American forces were commanded by men of civilian distinction, mostly Democratic allies of President James K. Polk, including his former law partner, Gideon J. Pillow. However, the most senior army commanders, Zachary Taylor and Winfield Scott, were both Whigs, and Polk toyed with the idea that he should place Senator Thomas Hart Benton over them both with the rank of Lieutenant-General. Consequently, by the 1850s the notion had firmly taken root in the American imagination that warfare was a short and decisive thing, as the Mexican War had been, involving rapid and dramatic movements directed by charismatic

[144] personalities. Such simplistic views, that emphasized the romantic appeal of war, were to be contradicted by the Civil War.[3]

Moreover, this outlook tended to elevate the leaders rather than the commander. The infusion of large numbers of politically ambitious civilians into the US Army's ranks in 1846–7, meant that a good number of senior officers had already revealed a strong measure of skills as leaders: volunteer leaders were often fine public speakers, could rouse their men to follow them, and bind them to the cause and themselves. A good example of such a figure is the lawyer, Colonel Alexander W. Doniphan, who took 856 men of the 1st Missouri Volunteer Regiment, composed mostly of 'unwashed and unshaven' frontiersmen, on a 3,500-mile march comparable to Xenophon's *anabasis*, from Fort Leavenworth, Kansas, via Santa Fé, New Mexico, to Monterey, Mexico, winning two victories en route.[4]

Throughout the era of the Civil War, command and leadership were confused. Few able commanders were bad leaders, but a good leader could sometimes make a poor commander, especially at the higher levels. Stress on the leader as moral exemplar, furthermore, resulted in military attitudes which praised nerve and imagination at the expense of intricate preparation, and often ignored logistical reality. Enthusiasts for a Napoleonic style of warfare also failed to take into account that movement over the huge expanses of North America was just as likely to lead to disaster (as in Russia in 1812) as to crowning triumph (as at Austerlitz in 1805 or Jena-Aüerstadt in 1806).

Early difficulties

At the end of 1860 the United States Army consisted of 16,215 officers and men. In April 1861 after the bombardment of Fort Sumter, almost all the men remained loyal to the Union, although 313 officers resigned. The army was organized into 198 companies, 183 of which remained on the frontier, divided among 70 posts. Over the next four years the US Army grew to 27 times its initial strength, raising 1,696 regiments of infantry, 272 of cavalry and 78 of artillery. These forces were deployed in 16 Union armies, which were administered by 53 territorial departments. Each of the armies was based in a department, and the commander of the army doubled as the departmental commander. This basic structure was replicated in the Confederacy. On both sides, if an army commander moved out of the geographical confines of his department, he was still expected to administer its garrison affairs; nor did he automatically command the forces of the department into which his troops moved. This was a geographical rather than a formation system of command; generals commanded areas rather than forces; there was no real concept of army group level command, although for convenience, by 1864–5 more than one Union army was combined under the direction of Grant and Sherman.

The main challenge facing the commanders of both Union and Confederate armies in 1861–2 was making the conceptual leap from commanding companies (or at most battalions) to commanding sizeable field armies, sometimes exceeding 100,000 men. This demanded a certain kind of character. Major-General J.F.C. Fuller, who pioneered the modern system of analyzing Civil War commanders, has written that, 'Discipline makes soldiers, but it is personality which makes and sad to say sometimes unmakes, generals'.[5]

Given its small size in peacetime and a military role protecting the Indian frontier – in effect performing the duties of an imperial constabulary – the command philosophy of the US army was formulated amidst a range of what the British army calls 'small wars'. Consisting of tiny units scattered over huge distances, separated from the headquarters by inhospitable terrain, or impenetrable forests, as during the Seminole Wars (1835–41), the American army evolved a practice of devolving a lot of responsibility on to the shoulders of quite junior officers, who, in any case, were not permitted by the constraints of geography to consult their superiors. This practice was accentuated by the American staff system, which was still in its infancy. Regular staff officers were essentially administrators, and there was no conception of modern staff officers acting as the representative of the commander, giving orders in his name. Winfield Scott had put together the first truly professional US army in Mexico. He welded his headquarters into an efficient decision-making apparatus, but the staff did not take decisions on Scott's behalf; in one sense, this was unnecessary because Scott commanded an army of only 7,000 men. Although officers like Robert E. Lee, P.G.T. Beauregard and George B. McClellan became Scott's protégés, they lacked a sense of the staff as a cohesive grouping sharing a common operational ethos and training. There was, of course, no staff college to provide such training. Regular officers were educated at the United States Military Academy at West Point. If officers entered the artillery they would receive a further year of specialized training at the Artillery School of Practice at Fortress Monroe, Virginia.

The limitations of a West Point military education have often been remarked upon by historians. West Point provided an excellent technical education; but cadets received only one week's instruction on the higher levels of war, like strategy. Richard Ewell complained after the Civil War that officers in the 'old' army learned everything there was to know about commanding a company of dragoons on the western plains, but nothing else. In truth, this criticism tells us more about the deficiencies of post-graduate education in the US army rather than of the West Point system itself. It is not the function of cadet academies to equip generals to command armies. But in the 1830s and 1840s, West Point came under sustained attack as an anti-egalitarian nest of 'aristocratic' martinets. It was feared that such smug and narrowly educated men would stamp out the spontaneous 'genius' of the American people, which if untrammelled would produce those moral qualities that had brought victory in earlier American wars. Such a legacy of mistrust of West Point graduates would continue to exert its influence during the Civil War. It is therefore not surprising that this major gap in officer training and educa-tion was not filled until 1881 with the founding of the US Command and General Staff College at Fort Leavenworth, Kansas.

As the staff system was crude, so the command functions of the upper levels of the US army were rather vague. The heads of the staff bureaux based in the War Department in Washington DC, the Adjutant-General, Quarter-master-General, Judge Advocate, Chief Engineer, Inspector General, Paymas-ter General, Commissary of Purchases, etc. presided over their own separate domains. They tended to report directly to their political superior, the Secret-ary of War, and were appointed by dint of strict seniority. Consequently, by the end of the 1850s, many were septuagenarians and had sometimes directed their bureaux for up to thirty years. The system was hardly a dynamic one; indeed, it had become fossilized. Moreover, the role of the commanding general, the general-in-chief, had not been worked out, and this would have serious consequences. The general-in-chief commanded nothing; he did not direct a general staff responsible to him. His position was not acknowledged in the Constitution, as the president was Commander-in-Chief. Neither was his relationship with the Secretary of War defined. If the latter chose to assert himself, the general-in-chief was pushed to the sidelines, and this often led to unseemly squabbling. Moreover, the authority of the general-in-chief was weakened by the universal assumption in the United States that command in war equated to the field command of armies.[6]

Winfield Scott was the dominant personality of the 'old' army, and he still remained general-in-chief, at the age of seventy-five, until 1 November 1861, having been first appointed on 5 July 1841. His first reaction on the outbreak of the Mexican War in 1846 was to secure for himself a field command, which he gained on 24 November, although his authority was confined by President Polk to that sole command (he was not reappointed general-in-chief until 1851). In 1861 Scott was the only officer in the United States who had commanded an army successfully in the field. By his military methods, promotion of military professionalism, and the sheer strength of his personality as general-in-chief for nearly twenty years, Scott bequeathed a huge legacy to the Civil War generation, and it is appropriate to review it briefly.

Scott's military outlook had been developed from out of the challenges of the 'small wars' waged by the United States army before 1861. His methods were refined and taken forward by Civil War generals in an entirely different environment. Scott favoured offensive military action, and disliked the defensive; however, in battle, he preferred to avoid the main body of the enemy's strength and sought to strike an exposed flank. This led to an emphasis in all his plans on envelopment – moving around the side of the enemy's army to strike his rear and cause the maximum fear and dislocation. Scott also made effective use of waterways to gain strategic mobility. Once his army had attained freedom of manoeuvre, Scott displayed a taste for dividing his army in the face of the enemy, not only to bewilder him, but to attain the initiative, which he hoped never to relinquish.[7] Scott had adopted the motto, 'Be governed by circumstances', yet he sought to establish opportunism on the firm basis of detailed planning, and attempted to foresee every contingency, so that opportunities could be exploited as they arose. Consequently, he was sometimes criticized for slow and excessively methodical planning. But Scott retorted that if a durable plan was formulated that enjoyed the confidence of all, then a large measure of responsibility for its execution could be delegated to subordinates.[8]

The main disadvantage of Scott's approach was that his insufferable vanity and pomposity led him to make hasty, foolish judgments. Although he was not a graduate of West Point, he supported it enthusiastically and indeed tended to personify, in the eyes of the Academy's critics, its worst faults: rigidity, neurotic elitism, snobbery, hostility to American egalitarianism, and an inability to act speedily. Moreover, Scott was querulous in the extreme, and feuded with every other senior American general of his generation – Andrew Jackson, Alexander Macomb, Edmund P. Gaines and Zachary Taylor. His tactless and petulant behaviour set a peevish and quarrelsome example to be followed by the US officer corps.[9]

In 1861 Scott remained a dominant figure. He had attempted unsuccessfully to persuade Robert E. Lee to accept an invitation to command Union troops assembling around Washington. Eventually this was accepted by Irvin McDowell, a protégé of the Secretary of the Treasury, Salmon P. Chase.

[148] McDowell recommended himself to Scott because he had served in France and observed the French Army's staff procedures at first hand. During the spring of 1861, Scott was considering the scheme that the newspapers would later dub the 'Anaconda Plan'. His correspondence with other generals, but especially with George B. McClellan, then commanding the Department of Ohio, reveals the difficulties the new generation of generals experienced in adjusting their thoughts from the level of the captains they once had been. McClellan was inexperienced in high command and was excited by the chance of emulating Napoleon, directing operations of great sweep and dynamism. McClellan urged an advance up the Great Kanawha Valley from Ohio with 80,000 volunteers, which should push on to Richmond 'with the utmost promptness': his schoolboy essay in Napoleonic strategy concluded by advocating thrusts on Charleston, Pensacola, Mobile and New Orleans. In reply, Scott pointed out soberly that logistics, lack of training and neglect of water transport rendered McClellan's scheme hopelessly unrealistic.[10]

Similarly, in June 1861, the Confederate general, P.G.T. Beauregard, commanding forces around Manassas Junction, Virginia, urged on the Confederate President Jefferson Davis (a former West Point graduate and US Secretary of War 1853–7) a plan embodying 'bold and rapid movement' that would combine his forces with those of Joseph E. Johnston in the Shenandoah Valley, either before Washington, seizing Alexandria, or, withdrawing southwards and acting on interior lines, attempting 'to crush successively and in detail the several columns of the enemy'. Here is an example of an imaginative captain playing at being Napoleon, supposing that the enemy would do what he wanted, and neglecting not only logistics, but the capabilities of the troops under his command.[11]

As for McDowell, the plan he formulated for the summer campaign that the Lincoln administration insisted on, was much more sensible. Yet the government still hoped that rebel forces would be defeated, the city of Richmond occupied and the rebellion suppressed. His plan depended on a movement towards Manassas. Confederate forces in the Shenandoah would be distracted, and those isolated at Manassas would be enveloped. Yet it proved beyond the capability of his troops. The lack of organized, sizeable armed forces in 1861 made it enormously difficult to deal an overwhelming blow against the Confederacy. The command system at McDowell's disposal was very crude. William Howard Russell, the *Times* war correspondent, met McDowell in Washington DC on 16 July looking for two batteries of artillery. Russell observed, 'I was surprised to find the General engaged in such a duty, and took leave to say so.' McDowell's reply was illuminating: '. . . I am

COMMAND AND LEADERSHIP IN THE CIVIL WAR, 1861-5

obliged to look after them myself, as I have so small a staff, and they are all [149] engaged out with my headquarters.'[12] The Confederates laboured under comparable (perhaps greater) disadvantages, as they had to create a military system from scratch. Yet it was certainly more difficult to organize offensive operations than muster for the defensive. Even McDowell's substantial qualities as an administrator and planner could not overcome the structural weaknesses – especially lack of training – necessary to gain a Union victory in the first stage of the war.

Such frustrations raise the question of the moral dimension of command. As Union forces, in order to suppress a flagrant defiance of federal authority, had to move forward, take the offensive and occupy Southern territory, Northern generals faced a psychological burden not encountered by Confederates, who simply wished to remain in control of their own territory and institutions. Many Northerners were despondent at having to undertake such a distasteful duty. Major-General Ethan Allen Hitchcock, who in 1862 briefly advised the Secretary of War, Edwin M. Stanton, complained at the war's outbreak, 'Many friends urge my return to the Army. But I have no heart for engaging in a Civil War. . . . If fighting could preserve the Union (or restore it) I might consider what I could do to take part – but when did fighting make friends?' When after the defeat at Manassas a number of politicians demanded that the generals responsible should be shot, William T. Sherman complained that 'civilians are more willing to start a war than military men and so it appears now'. Sherman himself, later to emerge as one of the most resolute of Northern generals, suffered what amounted to a nervous breakdown in October and November 1861. The issue of putting down a rebellion was complicated by the social and political conservatism of a number of generals who believed that the Civil War should be waged for the restoration of the Union and not for the destruction of slavery. The way such generals interpreted war aims had an important influence on the command style they adopted.[13] The most important conservative military figure was Major-General George B. McClellan.

McClellan and limited war

When McClellan was called to Washington DC on 26 July 1861 he was treated like a conquering hero and feted by all. During the next six months his reputation would be gradually eroded. Nonetheless, during this period

[150]   he built up a record of substantial achievement. He proved himself a brilliant trainer of troops, an effective organizer, a tireless administrator and a charismatic leader. He built the Army of the Potomac, impressed his personality on the command, and was adored by his troops. However, these qualities in themselves did not guarantee success in high command, and once he moved into the field, McClellan revealed a number of significant deficiencies that were to contribute to his downfall. In November 1861 McClellan replaced Scott as general-in-chief. This promotion represented the apogee of McClellan's formal authority, but only served to weaken his position.

McClellan was a fitting heir to Scott, even though he had intrigued to bring about the latter's downfall. Although McClellan was a Democrat (while Scott had been a Whig) they both shared conservative views about the war's nature. McClellan believed that operations under his command should be undertaken in a gentlemanly spirit with a minimum of interference in civilian affairs and property. He intended to insulate Southern civilians from the movement of his armies. The aim was the restoration of the Union and a reconciliation of the sections, and this was to be achieved in the shortest possible time. Scott's Anaconda Plan had envisaged moving the main Union strategic thrust away from the political core of the Confederacy towards the Mississippi basin. McClellan's plan brought Virginia (which was Scott's native state) firmly into focus as the primary theatre. McClellan argued that all other operations were subsidiary to the Virginia campaign. He intended to make this truly decisive. It would demonstrate the futility of secession and the 'utter impossibility of resistance': his great army would advance on the Confederate capital and in seige operations comparable to those at Sevastopol (1854–5) during the Crimean War, seize Richmond and then the Confederacy would collapse, as Russia had shortly after the fall of Sevastopol. It was within the context of this outlook that McClellan's concern with increasing the professionalism of his army should be understood. While Lee would latch on to Scott's offensive outlook, McClellan developed Scott's interest in detailed planning and took it a stage further. Preparations would be so intricate, staff procedures so perfect, and the men so well trained, that his advance would be irresistible. McClellan would be able to control the battlefield and the object for which he was fighting: there would be no foolish temptation to consider any revolutionary steps such as the abolition of slavery, and the status quo would be restored with a minimum of destruction, discomfort and death.[14]

The only problem with this elegant scheme and stately view of the war's progress was that McClellan did not have the time necessary to put it into practice. McClellan was under considerable political pressure to defeat the

Confederacy at the earliest possible moment. In addition, McClellan reflected and shared some of the widespread illusions about the nature of the Civil War. For instance, he could never shake off the misconception that the war could be brought to an end by one strategic thrust. Here was an example of how his operational and tactical preferences were shaped by his political views or aspirations. The policy of conciliation could only succeed if McClellan and those like him (such as Don Carlos Buell, the commander of the Army of the Ohio) were able to seize rapid and complete victories. However, they were both temporarily incapable of seizing the opportunities that were offered to them on the battlefield.

In short, McClellan's tenure of command experienced a continuing tension between his role as general-in-chief and field commander which was exploited by his enemies. The most important critical forum established by his critics was the formation in December 1861 of the Congressional Joint Committee on the Conduct of the War. This served as a focal point for all the discontent with McClellan's performance that had bubbled up during the previous months. Harnessed by Congressional (and administration) critics, it blew towards McClellan like a hurricane by January and February 1862. It was clear that politicians of both parties had little sympathy with McClellan's efforts to impose professional standards on his army. Yet his problems were accentuated by the command structure that he had inherited from Scott. When Abraham Lincoln, the president, had queried whether McClellan could undertake the simultaneous duties of both field command and general-in-chief, the latter had replied confidently, 'I can do it all.'[15] Time would show that he could not.

The organization of an army is an immensely intricate task, and McClellan became aborbed in its detail. He neglected his duties as the government's principal strategic adviser. He produced no plans, and the president, dissatisfied with the general-in-chief, claimed that the war effort was 'stalled on dead center'. McClellan's health suffered because of over-work and he succumbed to typhoid. Lincoln convened councils of war and issued general orders in January and February 1862 in an attempt to get the Army of the Potomac to move, but to no avail. Nonetheless, McClellan's refusal to discuss his plans on the grounds of operational secrecy was high-handed and his credibility was damaged in the resulting controversy.[16]

In truth, McClellan was not acting as a general-in-chief should, but it is difficult to see how he could concentrate on these important duties when he was distracted by his tasks as a field commander. Everybody (including the president) persisted in judging him by his performance as commander of the

Army of the Potomac – and it was this latter consideration that brought him the most criticism. Nevertheless, McClellan had the intellect and vision to propound a grand strategic view and work out an operational method for fulfilling it. When eventually in February 1862 he drew up plans for the administration's perusal, they were impressive. He sought to launch 'combined and decisive operations' and not 'waste life in useless battles'. He argued in favour of an indirect approach on Richmond by shifting the Army of the Potomac to the peninsula between the James and York rivers, and advancing on the Confederate capital from the east. By avoiding the bulk of the Confederate main body in northern Virginia, he hoped to 'demoralize the enemy', and force him to come out of his defences and attack the Army of the Potomac. While standing on the defensive, McClellan hoped to inflict an 'American Waterloo' on the rebels. Yet it is noteworthy that McClellam hoped that such a decisive outcome could be produced with a minimum of fratricidal bloodshed. He seems to have unconsciously reflected anxieties among some Northern generals about the casualties resulting from any move into Southern territory because his plans are couched in and justified by sound military reasoning. But McClellan's cool military analysis was underwritten by looming fears that denote both a nervous lack of confidence in Northern troops compared with a romanticized notion of Southern martial ability, and a lack of self-esteem which transformed an avoidance of defeat into a triumph. McClellan's limited expectations of his army reinforced the limited aims he set himself both strategically and politically. Certainly, the compound of technical military reasoning and personal predilection lent a distinctly *defensive* tenor to his plan.[17]

McClellan did not gain any credit for the successes achieved on other fronts during his tenure as general-in-chief. These seemed to augur that the Confederacy would collapse by the summer. McClellan himself shared this ambivalence. His reaction to criticism was to centralize the system further, and thus to add to the burdens weighing on himself; it took longer to get decisions on urgent matters. He declined to appoint corps commanders, hoping to be able to direct twelve divisions himself unaided, and these appointments were eventually forced on him by the president. He neglected to appoint a commander of the Washington garrison, and Lincoln moved to install James S. Wadsworth, one of McClellan's critics. This dithering reduced McClellan's influence as general-in-chief, and Lincoln removed him on 11 March in Presidential War Order No. 3 on the grounds that he should concentrate on directing the Army of the Potomac.[18]

The Confederacy had experienced comparable problems to those of the Union. Jefferson Davis had resolutely refused to appoint a general-in-chief. His experience with Scott, when Secretary of War during the Pierce adminis-tration (1853–7) had not been a happy one, and he believed that the powers of the general-in-chief were an unconstitutional encroachment on the pres-idential war powers. The Confederacy's senior general was the Adjutant-General, Samuel Cooper, whom Steven E. Woodworth accurately judges as the president's 'chief military clerk'. Davis thus dealt with Confederate generals himself without an intermediary. The commander of the Confed-erate forces in Virginia, Joseph E. Johnston, resembled McClellan in his uncommunicativeness and unhelpfulness to politicians. If he had any plans, he did not divulge them. That Union generals were not alone in failing to comprehend the intricacies of offensive operations was shown in June 1862 in Johnston's over-elaborate, poorly co-ordinated and thoroughly muddled counter-offensive at Seven Pines (Fair Oaks). Johnston was wounded and was replaced by the president's military adviser, Robert E. Lee. Lee had only ever held staff positions before and had never commanded troops in battle.[19]

The essential difference between Lee and McClellan was that the former established cordial relations with his political masters, and that Lee's military outlook was offensive, not defensive. Although his methods have often been compared by historians to those of Napoleon, Lee was essentially Scott's pupil. He took the latter's methods and developed them further in scale and intensity. Given the Confederacy's overall strategic, industrial and logistical weakness when compared with the Union, Lee appreciated that time was not on its side. He was therefore prepared to accept great risks, was keen to disperse his force (sometimes for logistic reasons) and then concentrate at the decisive point, making the most of mobility. He would manoeuvre near the enemy to demoralize and confuse him rather than withdraw, as Johnston invariably did. Consequently, Lee was prepared to fight for the initiative, not wait for the inevitable accumulation of massive Union numerical and mater-ial superiority that, McClellan calculated, would overwhelm weaker Southern armies. Lee sought a *decision* in the Confederacy's favour; he did not believe the Confederacy could enjoy the luxury of attempting just to avoid defeat.

These dynamic methods imposed great physical and psychological strain on Lee. His chief of staff, Colonel R.H. Chilton, who had served under Lee on the Great Plains, was an amiable nonentity, who simply issued orders. This placed more work on Lee's shoulders, and it is perhaps not surprising that he relied heavily on oral orders. He never shied away from taking decisions, placed himself at the most convenient point where he could take them, and disdained councils of war. He had inherited Scott's view that, once the commanding general had issued orders, subordinates should carry them out in their own way. Over the next year he would modify this approach. For instance, in September 1862 he personally directed Confederate tactics at the Battle of Antietam. Soldiers largely responded to his cool leadership and record of success; aware of the effect of his presence at the front, he tended to ration his appearances to increase their tonic effect during dire emergencies. But unlike McClellan, Lee actually enjoyed the intellectual and moral challenges posed by field command.

The contrasting fortunes of Lee and McClellan indicate how important field command was for contemporaries in estimating the abilities of a commander. McClellan, for all his talents, was temperamentally unsuited for the moral challenges posed by the command of an army. He could plan but not carry through his ideas into practice. He was timorous and hesitant and was gripped by an obsession that he was greatly outnumbered by the Confederates; such a misconception led to the greatest possible misappreciation of the potential of his army by comparison with the Confederate, and fatal misjudgments about the current of battle. Certainly, the view that he was outnumbered was an important self-justifying link in the circular argument that underwrote his defensive schemes. In a very real sense, McClellan did not command. His interpretation of Scott's methods was simply to abandon his subordinates to fight their own battles. During the Seven Days' Battles (26 June–1 July 1862), Fitz-John Porter's Fifth Corps was left unsupported to bear the main burden of the fighting. Moreover, McClellan absented himself from the battlefield. While the Battle of Malvern Hill was raging, it was rumoured that he was on board a river steamer on the James River. His admirers dismissed rumours circulating in Washington DC to this effect as a vicious calumny. Yet although he was not relaxing (as critics claimed), he had virtually abandoned the battlefield, abdicated any semblance of responsibility for its movements, and was preoccupied with administrative trivia. During the Seven Days' Battles Union forces won a number of tactical successes, notably at Mechanicsville and Malvern Hill, but lacking a directing intelligence which could relate them to an over-arching operational design, the result was a major strategic defeat for the Union cause, and the dashing of the high hopes for McClellan's 'grand campaign'.

Nor did McClellan learn from experience. In the Antietam campaign in September 1862, he enjoyed the inestimable advantage of discovering Lee's entire plan and distribution of his forces from the famous 'lost order'. Yet due to laggard movements, over-caution and wasted time – not least the unaccountable waste of an entire day before McClellan launched his attack at Antietam on 17 September – Lee was allowed to concentrate his army and prepare for the Union attack. McClellan's disjointed efforts were repulsed and the opportunity to destroy Lee's army was frittered away through inertia. McClellan simply lacked the moral qualities of decisiveness and faith in his own judgment that contributes to dynamic action. He failed to harness the fighting power at his disposal and employ it to secure his military objectives. As a battlefield commander, McClellan still remained an ambitious captain bewildered by his weighty responsibilities; field command was not as easy as Scott had made it look in 1846–7. McClellan's two campaigns neither restored his fortunes nor resulted in his reappointment as general-in-chief. On 11 July 1862 that position had been offered by Lincoln to Henry W. Halleck after the fall of Memphis, Tennessee. Halleck accepted, but admitted that he did not know what his duties involved.[20]

Lee's experience was exactly the opposite. Success at field command resulted in the Army of Northern Virginia enshrining the hopes of the Confederacy, and Lee became influential as a result. The reason for his success was simple; he commanded confidently, although not as effortlessly as he sometimes made it look. He is sometimes criticized by historians for a certain meekness, yet Lee was a skilful manager of men. His loose leadership style suited the strong personalities of his subordinates. Although tensions existed within his army, for instance between his two corps commanders Stonewall Jackson and Longstreet, and between Jackson and his subordinates (especially with A.P. Hill), Lee managed to persuade his rather vain subordinates to work together. The Army of Northern Virginia was not crippled, as the Army of Tennessee had been throughout 1862–3, by petty and factious disputes between the commanding general, Braxton Bragg, and his subordinates, Leonidas Polk and William J. Hardee. In October 1863, most of the Army's generals signed a petition asking for Bragg's dismissal. This curious affair prevented the Army of Tennessee from benefiting from the success of the Chickamauga campaign, and demanded the personal attention of Jefferson Davis to sort out, which he did by siding with Bragg, who began an ill-advised purge of his critics. Southern generals – and here the experience of Scott's many quarrels was salutary – needed to be directed with tact. Lee had tact in abundance, but Bragg (and Stonewall Jackson, for that matter) sorely lacked it.[21]

Lee's force of character, and determination to secure the objectives he set himself, demonstrated that Scott's system could be made to work even with

[156]   untrained staffs and much larger armies (that were more difficult to command) than the small force that Scott himself had directed in Mexico. Nevertheless, Lee would modify it. In June 1862 Lee briefed his subordinates on his plans to relieve Richmond by striking at McClellan's lines of communications by a turning movement that would involve a junction with Jackson's troops from the Shenandoah Valley on the battlefield, among a number of other complex movements. Having outlined this concept, Lee then left the room so that his subordinates could discuss his plan and work out the movement details among themselves without reference to him. The errors that frustrated Lee's scheme to destroy McClellan's army proved to him that such a degree of latitude was excessive, and Lee never repeated the exercise.[22]

Moreover, the campaign indicated (despite an uncharacteristic lassitude) that Lee had found in Jackson an executive officer of incomparable talent. If McClellan had found a subordinate of similar energy his generalship might have prospered, but McClellan's protégés tended to mirror his own weaknesses. Jackson thrived when given responsibility and a long rein. Although very different in character from Lee, Jackson shared his military outlook, and the conviction that daring, deception and demoralizing manoeuvres that resulted from surprise could splinter Union numerical strength, and allow much more skilful Confederate forces to achieve local operational superiority and defeat Union forces in detail. In 1862 Confederate forces commanded by Lee and Jackson had the nerve to undertake operations based on calculated risks. Throughout the Seven Days Lee never once convened his subordinates in council. Such councils tend to take a cautious view and expend precious time, as Jackson discovered when he convened his only council of war in the Shenandoah Valley. 'That is the last council of war I will ever hold!' he exclaimed. Jackson could have spoken for Lee when he once snapped at an anxious staff officer. 'Never take counsel of your fears.'[23] In 1862–3 Lee was able to frame audacious plans guessing (correctly as it turned out) that Union commanders invariably took such ill-advised counsel.

The results for the Confederacy were a string of operational successes in the East but these could not be translated into a strategic dividend. The command system was part of the reason for this failure. Lee's victories increased his influence (which reached its height in May/June 1863), but not his power within the circles of the Davis administration (his suggestion, for example, that Beauregard command a new force on his right was ignored). By 1863 and 1864 Davis came to rely on Lee's advice; and needless to say, it was heavily influenced by his perspectives and responsibilities as an army commander. The appointment of Braxton Bragg as Davis's adviser 'Commanding the

Armies of the Confederate States' in February 1864 only accentuated the
muddle and ambiguity of the Confederate command system. Bragg's power
did not extend to Lee (who was his senior) or the Army of Northern Virginia.[24]

Lee was not general-in-chief and Davis's informal methods of working
while retaining all powers of decision in his own hands meant that Lee did
not have the time to devote to matters outside his department. Davis's
requests could also be importunate. For instance, at the height of Lee's
anxieties as to whether Grant had crossed the James River on 15 June 1864,
Davis asked him to recommend a successor to Leonidas Polk, who had been
killed at Pine Mountain, Georgia, the day before. Lee declined, pleading lack
of knowledge. Such opinions, expressed in his correspondence, used to be
adduced by some historians as evidence of Lee's parochialism.[25] But it is
the system that is at fault. It over-emphasized field command and expected
too much of its practitioners, and neglected to provide for the coordinating
duties of higher levels of command. Significantly, neither Joseph E. Johnston
nor P.G.T. Beauregard did more than Lee (in many ways much less) when
given command of the Department of the West in 1863 and 1864 respectively.
They assumed that their duties were purely advisory. Given such constraints,
Lee could not fulfil a role that the system was not designed to carry out.[26]

The rise of Grant

Yet if the command system was crude and in some important respects ineffect-
ive, how was victory gained in the Civil War? A successful system emerged in
the West, and it is now appropriate to turn to consider how and why the
solution reached here was so effective.

The huge expanse of the Western theatre accentuated a number of problems faced by commanders in 1862. The spreading out of forces to cover
these expanses led to enveloping fogs of war billowing over their campaigns.
It became more difficult for commanders to know what was going on; they
needed to exert themselves more energetically in order to grip more firmly
the operations continuing under their control. Consequently, there was an
increase in what military theorists used to term 'encounter battles' or, in contemporary parlance, 'meeting engagements'. Such actions occur when armies
collide into one another, each unaware of the presence of the other.[27]

Meeting engagements and surprise attacks were common by 1862. On
6 April, despite a chaotic approach march, Albert Sidney Johnston's Army of

[158]   Mississippi surprised Ulysses S. Grant's troops at Shiloh. Even though at least two of Grant's divisions (those of William T. Sherman and John A. McClernand) were aware of the presence of Confederate troops, and a third (that of Benjamin M. Prentiss) was formed in line when the Confederates attacked, Grant's army was surprised operationally and psychologically. Grant was thinking more in terms of attack than defence, and had neglected to carry out an order of his superior, Halleck, to entrench his position.[28] Fortunately, Johnston then lost control of the battle, and rode around like a brigade commander, directing regiments and siting cannon, showing a flair for leadership and exposing himself recklessly until he was mortally wounded.

Johnston thus lost the initiative and allowed Grant to galvanize himself and his command. Grant was handicapped by having to direct all of his six divisions himself rather than through two corps commanders. He spent much time 'passing from one part of the field to another, giving directions to division commanders'. But Grant did not lose control. On the second day of the battle, 7 April, he personally 'gathered up a couple of regiments, or parts of regiments, from troops near by and formed them in line of battle and marched them forward, going in front myself to prevent premature or long-range firing'. At Shiloh Grant displayed powers of leadership *and* the qualities of a first-rate commander. He ensured that his defensive line was not pierced, and then launched a counter-offensive in tandem with Don Carlos Buell's Army of the Ohio, which crossed the Tennessee River in his support. Grant also saw for the first time that Sherman displayed a comparable degree of confidence and aggressiveness.[29]

In his *Memoirs*, Grant praised Buell for his intelligence and bravery,[30] but during the campaign in Kentucky in the autumn of 1862, Buell showed that he lacked Grant's drive. In some ways, he conducted the campaign skilfully. Buell deftly shielded his supply base at Louisville and lines of communication. When he advanced it was in strength and he was well-supplied, unlike Braxton Bragg's Confederates, who found foraging difficult. But Buell was more interested in driving Bragg back than crushing him. His military outlook was essentially defensive. Like McClellan, Buell was more fearful of the enemy's moves against him than confident that his own moves would dispose of any threat. Freeman Cleaves judges correctly that Buell 'was willing to accept any alternative to tangling with the enemy'.[31] On 8 October Buell's Army of the Ohio in three 'wings' (really corps but not yet designated as such) collided with Bragg's troops at Perryville. Bragg attacked Buell's left under Alexander D. McCook, whose parched troops were searching for water.

The Union command system arranged before the battle was rather muddled. The week before, on 29 September, the Lincoln administration became so frustrated with Buell's slow progress that he was relieved of command. George H. Thomas, a stolid and stubborn loyal Virginian, was offered it but declined to accept it. So Buell remained in command for the duration of the campaign, with Thomas as his second-in-command. Thomas was a kind of executive officer, but lacked authority. Even under this pressure, Buell failed to grip the operations and impose himself on them. He did not go forward to see things for himself, and thus relied too heavily on the staff, whom he complacently assumed would inform him of 'intelligence of serious import'. He was wrong. The staff, taking their cue from their rather languid master, returned to headquarters for their lunch, leaving McCook to fight his own battle. Buell did not learn that a battle had commenced until after 4 p.m. The 'wing' of Thomas L. Crittenden, faced by only 1,200 Confederate cavalry, remained idle. The same fate seemed to face Bragg as the Confederates at Shiloh, but he was given time to disengage and withdraw back safely to Tennessee via the Cumberland Gap. Further orders for Buell's removal soon followed.[32]

Buell's successor, William S. Rosecrans, seemed more dynamic, and indeed he worked tirelessly on logistics and organization. His real skill was in strategic manoeuvre. Despite difficulties in coordination – signalling with flags was not easy in the wooded valleys of central and eastern Tennessee – he caught Bragg by surprise at Murfreesboro (31 December 1862–2 January 1863). Yet he, too, was at his best in defence, allowing Bragg to attack first. Rosecrans did not like fighting battles. Moreover, his technique of directing strategic manoeuvre over great distances risked dispersal and the destruction of his corps piecemeal. In September 1863, Rosecrans only just concentrated his corps in time before Bragg attacked at Chickamauga.

Rosecrans resembled McClellan in being well-prepared and methodical. Yet he also believed that the North's enormous material superiority rendered battle somehow obsolete. He assumed that if his management was meticulous enough, he could undertake strategic advances and win great battles bloodlessly. This was a delusion: intellect could not serve as a substitute for battle. Under the strain of operations when in contact with the enemy, Rosecrans neglected simple precautions. He did not take enough rest, and became overwrought through lack of sleep. It was a muddle over confused orders at Chickamauga, caused by Rosecrans losing his temper, that resulted in the gap opening in the Union line that led to Rosecrans's serious defeat. Rosecrans had also revealed a lack of confidence by continually convening councils of war to seek the advice or the approval of his corps commanders.[33]

Grant's style of command was the opposite of that adopted by McClellan, Buell and Rosecrans. After his first action at Belmont in November 1861, Grant learnt that his opponent was just as nervous of his moves as he was of the enemy's. From this experience stemmed Grant's confidence and aggressiveness. He realized that it was more important to concentrate on what he was going to do to the enemy than worry about what the enemy was going to do to him. Moreover, Grant concluded after Shiloh that 'I gave up all idea of saving the Union except by complete conquest'. Although later writers, such as his former military secretary and semi-official biographer, Adam Badeau, tended to exaggerate the 'totality' of his strategic ideas,[34] there can be no doubting Grant's commitment to the complete military defeat of the Confederacy. Also, he showed a taste and flair for confronting his enemies using a combination of manoeuvre *and* battle. He evolved this successful technique during the Vicksburg and Chattanooga campaigns.

The pivot of Grant's system was, of course, his own personality. He was modest, taciturn and of a tranquil nature. He could be very blunt, but rarely raised his voice. Unlike Rosecrans (or Sherman) he was not volatile or highly-strung. He appeared flat and uninspired, but the opposite was true. He adjusted his thoughts to meet the demands of the levels of military activity over which he rose to preside; he took decisions swiftly and assumed responsibility effortlessly. He spent much of his time in quiet contemplation. 'He talked less and thought more than any one in the service,' wrote Horace Porter, a former member of his staff. From this capacity for reflection, free from routine and petty distraction, grew Grant's overall grasp of the campaign.[35]

There was one feature of Grant's system that was unusual. He relied on a chief of staff. Lee had a chief of staff in 1862 but could not make much use of him. During the Peninsular campaign, McClellan's chief of staff was his father-in-law, Brigadier-General Randolph B. Marcy, and he had a negligible impact on operations. Throughout the Kentucky campaign, Bragg acted as his own chief of staff, which exacerbated his tendency to over-work and bad temper. In December 1862 Colonel George W. Brent became Bragg's acting chief of staff, but he lacked formal military training; his orders did nothing to clarify Bragg's instructions which simply listed units and their destinations without detailing tasks or their relative importance. During the Chancellorsville campaign in April–May 1863, Hooker had hoped to make effective use of his chief of staff, Daniel Butterfield, in coordinating the two wings of his army while Hooker went to the front. However, the experiment failed because the telegraph broke down and Butterfield became swamped. He was, in any case, much disliked and inspired confidence in no one save Hooker himself.[36]

Grant remained fresh by delegating urgent – but not operational – duties to his staff headed by his family lawyer, John A. Rawlins. Because of their specialist knowledge, Grant 'always invited the most frank and cordial interchange of views, and never failed to listen particularly to the more prominent members of his staff'.[37] Rawlins was forthright, impetuous and articulate. He tended to complement Grant, but lacked formal military training; he was certainly no Gneisenau, Blücher's brilliant chief of staff in 1813–14. His real significance was political. Rawlins dealt skilfully with politicians and journalists. These included Charles A. Dana, the Assistant Secretary of War, and Sylvanus Cadwallader of the *Chicago Tribune*, both of whom became powerful allies of Grant. Rawlins also served as a liaison with Grant's political mentor, Congressman Elihu B. Washburne, who had the ear of the president. Grant did not meet Lincoln until 1864. Rawlins also claimed that he served as a kind of moral guardian, protecting Grant from the evils of drink. The value of this function was probably exaggerated.[38]

Rawlins was not a chief of staff in the Prussian sense of enjoying real operational control. Sometimes Rawlins presented the staff view which Grant often ignored. Rawlins, in short, had a limited role to play. One of Grant's finest skills was as a writer. During the Vicksburg campaign, Grant's span of command grew enormously and he could not travel with his corps because they were so spread out. So he stayed behind the front line, going forward (like Lee) only when necessary, which increased the morale effect of such appearances.[39] The separation of the commander from the battle required that he supply precise written orders. Grant wrote fluently in lucid, unvarnished prose – his meaning was never in doubt. Grant was thus a commander, and he increasingly fulfilled Americans' expectations of what a commander should do. By the end of 1863 Grant had also forged a strong partnership with Sherman, based on close friendship. Yet it is indicative of how the Civil War system of command was based on personality rather than staff networks, that some of Grant's critics thought that his limited use of Rawlins indicated that he was in thrall of his staff.

Grant as general-in-chief

On 19 October after the Union setback at the Battle of Chickamauga, Grant was made commander of the Military Division of the Mississippi, directing all forces in the West. He was told by Halleck not to spend too much time on administration, because the command was designed to exploit Grant's skill at operations. In 1864 he moved to Washington DC to become general-in-chief with the rank of lieutenant general. Grant was the first officer to hold this rank since George Washington (Scott's had been held by brevet, that is, he enjoyed the rank but not the pay). Grant also interpreted this position to mean that he should take the field personally, rather than merely coordinate the movement of armies from a distance.

His predecessor, Halleck, had interpreted his position quite differently, and acted as a bureaucrat. He had played a major role in organizing and supplying the Union victories of 1863. But he acknowledged the centrality of army command in the American system; he made suggestions, briefed commanders on administration policy, but he did not command – let alone lead. He interpreted his role in the same way as the Confederates, Johnston and Beauregard, had done in 1863–4. Even this minimal role had been resented by some army commanders. Before Chancellorsville, Joseph Hooker had got permission to write directly to the president. After his defeat, when the privilege was removed, Halleck's relations with Hooker deteriorated, until the latter was replaced by the more cooperative George G. Meade.[40] By the spring of 1864 Halleck was the butt of universal ridicule. When he was reassigned as chief of staff, he continued to do what he had always done. This was an important contribution to the Union war effort because it allowed Grant to concentrate on what he did best – and what public opinion expected of him – namely, take an army into the field.

Grant's power was based on the close coincidence of his strategic views with President Lincoln's, and the unprecedented authority he was allowed to issue orders directly to the heads of staff bureaux without reference to the Secretary of War. This was a power that no previous general-in-chief had ever enjoyed.[41] Moreover, as Grant did not have to prove himself as a field commander, he was almost immune from harassment by Congressional bodies like the Joint Committee on the Conduct of the War. He enjoyed a moral authority that previous commanders in the East had lacked.

Yet Grant did not allow himself to be over-borne, as McClellan had in 1862. He understood the nature of the latter's difficulties. Experienced at army command – and after Chattanooga at directing three separate forces drawn from three different field armies – he appreciated the difficulties that arise from the movements of disparate forces. Consequently, he decided not to command the Army of the Potomac himself, and left Meade in post. Nonetheless, he would travel with it as a kind of superior army commander, and issue orders through Meade. Such a decision threatened to introduce duplication of effort and muddle into what was already a rather slack structure. Yet Grant and Meade cooperated well considering the circumstances (Rawlins became a great admirer of the latter). Grant's method was a pragmatic response to peculiarly American conditions, and was based heavily on the personalities involved. Grant was not an army group commander, because he directed the movement of armies far distant. But Grant's brisk and dynamic presence did something to increase the priority given to operations by Union commanders, rather than logistics and organization. As his friend Sherman commanded the Military Division of the Mississippi, Grant could count on a man he could trust.

The staffs were small. Grant's consisted of 15 officers. Halleck, when general-in-chief, had 24 officers at his disposal. Meade had his own staff, directed by Major-General A.A. Humphreys. Relations between these bodies were not warm. Yet despite antagonism, the system worked, although in operational terms it was not efficient, and its success was not as great as Grant had hoped. The great strength of the Union war effort remained in organizing and bringing to bear the greater resources of the North. Sherman eventually won a number of important victories in the West, but his success was facilitated by John B. Hood's quixotic decision to vacate the theatre of operations in Georgia and advance to the Ohio River. As Halleck had struggled, and failed, to coordinate simultaneous advances in 1863, Grant's personal contribution the following year was substantial. But Grant's methods failed to rectify widespread misconceptions about war. On the contrary, because Grant behaved like a superior army commander, he tended to reinforce them.

It is thus an error to claim, as T. Harry Williams did, that 'During the winter months of 1863–4, the United States created a modern command system'. Herman Hattaway and Archer Jones echo this judgment, claiming that, 'The contemporaneous Prussian general staff closely approximated that of the Union.'[42] It did not. Grant did not preside over a general staff responsible to him rather than to their respective commanders. Some commanders like Sherman (and to a lesser extent Meade) enjoyed his confidence, but many did not. Grant could not ensure that his less competent commanders carried out his instructions through the good offices of members of a Prussian-style general staff. In any case, such a body of trained staff officers imbued with a common ethos could not be created until the United States set up a staff college. Grant had put in place a system that was superior to the Confederate, but it was not modern, and it bore scant resemblance to the Prussian. As many American staff officers were drawn from business, they made excellent logisticians – better than the Prussians – but they were operationally inferior because they failed to understand the need for a true general staff revolution. Even McClellan, the self-conscious spokesman for American military professionalism, had failed to think this problem through to its logical conclusion.[43]

Yet the Union system, for all its imperfections, was much superior to the Confederate. The Confederate command system underwent hardly any modification during the war, except in terms of the generals that tried to direct it. The failure to appoint a figure like Grant to provide some central direction led to a series of rather piecemeal approaches, and an excessive centralization around Jefferson Davis with a resultant splintering of military effort. As Frank E. Vandiver summarizes: 'Richmond, to which all looked for guidance, was the nerve center of the Confederacy, but a nerve center lacking the power of coordination.' The only response of the Davis administration to military catastrophe in the winter of 1864–5 was to make Robert E. Lee general-in-chief while still remaining commander of the Army of Northern Virginia. Confederate leaders seemed to learn little from the military setbacks which the Confederacy endured.[44]

The command system that brought a Union victory relied on three related elements. First, the delegation of duties. Grant gave great latitude to his subordinates. He took the ethos of the 'old' frontier army and made it work under the quite different circumstances of a war of mass-involvement and great battles. Secondly, personal friendship was a vital lubricant for efficiency, especially between Grant and Sherman, and Sherman and Halleck. Sherman directed his three (rather small) field armies as a superior army commander, as Grant did in Virginia. Thirdly, Grant's system worked because of the telegraph. While travelling with the Army of the Potomac, his headquarters remained in the rear so that he could communicate with the other commands. But Grant's direction was minimal. After he had finally given permission to Sherman to undertake his 'March to the Sea', he knew nothing of the details of the operation, nor did he want to know. However, the telegraph could make committing errors easier. Grant had never been an admirer of George H. Thomas, directed by Sherman to guard his rear at Nashville, Tennessee, as Hood advanced recklessly northwards. In December 1864 Grant lost patience with Thomas's sluggish movements, especially as John M. Schofield was telegraphing privately that 'Many officers here are of the opinion that General Thomas is certainly too slow in his movements'. Fortunately, the final order for Thomas's dismissal arrived after his stunning victory at the Battle of Nashville, 15–16 December.[45]

Towards a 'modern' system?

Initially the Civil War was fought by North and South with command systems that were mirror images of one another. Both sections shared similar illusions about the nature of command, not least an over-emphasis on field command. So strong was this notion that Grant and Sherman were able to galvanize the Union command system in 1864 only by directing forces in the field themselves. Yet the Union system did develop, though not far enough to be accurately described as a modern command system. Although Grant and Sherman succeeded in organizing and directing the Northern war effort, their methods relied heavily on personalities rather than institutional innovation. Indeed, they relied more on the traditional methods of the United States army than is sometimes acknowledged.

The stress on the cooperation of key personalities is not surprising, as the Union army lacked a trained great general staff which owed its allegiance to a chief of staff rather than to individual field commanders. Grant and Sherman made the existing system work more efficiently and over a greater span than it was ever designed to operate. Once the exigencies of Civil War were no longer pressing, the system over which they presided could easily mutate back to meet the needs of Indian fighting on the Western frontier. Perhaps this explains why, in command terms, the Civil War seemed to have had little impact on the remainder of the nineteenth century.

Notes

1. Brian Holden Reid, *The American Civil War and the Wars of the Industrial Revolution* (London, 1999), pp. 22–8.

2. Dixon Wecter, *The Hero in America*, 2nd edn (1941; New York, 1972) pp. 199–203, 206; John William Ward, *Andrew Jackson: Symbol for an Age* (New York, 1953) pp. 122–3, 182–8.

3. Marcus Cunliffe, *Soldiers and Civilians: The Martial Spirit in America, 1775–1865* 3rd edn (1968; London, 1993), pp. 307–12; Brian Holden Reid, *The Origins of the American Civil War* (London, 1996), pp. 187–8.

4. Joseph G. Dawson III, ' "Zealous for annexation": volunteer soldiering, military government, and the service of Colonel Alexander W. Doniphan in the Mexican-American War', in Brian Holden Reid (ed.), *Military Power: Land Warfare in Theory and Practice* (London, 1997), pp. 10–30.

5. J.F.C. Fuller, *The Generalship of Ulysses S. Grant*, 2nd edn (1956; New York, 1992), p. 9.

6. Russell F. Weigley, *Quartermaster General of the Union Army: A Biography of M.C. Meigs* (New York, 1959), pp. 215–17; also see Holden Reid, *Origins*, pp. 340–2.

7. Timothy D. Jordan, *Winfield Scott: The Quest for Military Glory* (Lawrence, Ks, 1998), pp. 27, 208, 282; 65,77, 183; 39, 157–9, 191–7, 207; 29, 174–5; 207.

8. Ibid., pp. 47, 56, 113, 207.

9. Ibid., pp. 103, 187, 192.

10. McClellan to Scott, 27 April 1861, with an annotation by Scott 2 May 1861, *War of the Rebellion: The Official Records of the Union and Confederate Armies* (Washington, 1897), series 1, vol. 51, pt 1, pp. 338–9.

11. T. Harry Williams, *P.G.T. Beauregard: Napoleon in Gray* (1955; Baton Rouge, La, 1989), pp. 70–1.

12. William Howard Russell, *My Diary North and South*, ed. Eugene H. Berwanger (New York, 1988), p. 250.

13. E.A. Hitchcock, *Fifty Years in Camp and Field*, ed. W.A. Croffat (New York, 1909), p. 430; Lloyd Lewis, *Sherman: Fighting Prophet* (New York, 1929) p. 142; John F. Marszalek, *Sherman: A Soldier's Passion for Order* (New York, 1993), pp. 158–67.

14. T. Harry Williams, *Lincoln and his Generals* (New York, 1952), pp. 67–72; Stephen W. Sears, *George B. McClellan: The Young Napoleon* (New York, 1988), pp. 95, 99.

15. *Lincoln and the Civil War in the Diaries and Letters of John Hay*, ed. Tyler Dennett (1939: New York, 1988), p. 33. Lincoln then urged him to 'enlarge the sphere of his thoughts and feel the weight of the occasion'.

16. Williams, *Lincoln and his Generals*, pp. 56–63; Montgomery C. Meigs, 'On the conduct of the Civil War', *American Historical Review*, XXVI (1921), pp. 292–3; Sears, *McClellan*, pp. 138–43.

17. McClellan to Stanton, 3 February 1862, *The Civil War Papers of George B. McClellan: Selected Correspondence, 1860–1865*, ed. Stephen W. Sears (New York, 1989), pp. 163–9; Michael C.C. Adams, *Fighting for Defeat: Union Military Failure in the East, 1861–1865* (1978; Lincoln, Ne. and London, 1992), pp. 92–103, 129–31.

18. Brian Holden Reid, 'Rationality and irrationality in Union strategy, April
    1861–March 1862', *War in History*, I, no. 1 (March 1994), pp. 34–7.

19. Steven E. Woodworth, *Davis and Lee at War* (Lawrence, Ks, 1995), pp. 12, 129,
    132–6, 138–9.

20. Sears, *McClellan*, pp. 217–22, 303, 310, 314, 320; Williams, *Lincoln and his
    Generals*, pp. 165–9; Stephen E. Ambrose, *Halleck: Lincoln's Chief of Staff* (1962;
    Baton Rouge, La, 1990), pp. 61–2.

21. On the mutiny against Bragg, see Thomas L. Connelly, *Autumn of Glory: The
    Army of Tennessee, 1862–1865* (Baton Rouge, La, 1971), pp. 235–54, for a
    detailed account, and Steven E. Woodworth, *Six Armies in Tennessee* (Lincoln,
    Ne., 1998), pp. 139–40, for a shorter one.

22. Douglas Southall Freeman, *R.E. Lee: A Biography* (New York, 1934–5), II,
    pp. 109–12.

23. Quoted in Frank E. Vandiver, *Mighty Stonewall* (1957; College Station, Tx.,
    1988), pp. 199–200, 290.

24. Woodworth, *Davis and Lee at War*, p. 267; Judith Lee Hallock, *Braxton Bragg and
    Confederate Defeat* (Tuscaloosa, Ala, 1991), II, pp. 163–6.

25. The most extreme statement of this view is Thomas L. Connelly, 'Robert E. Lee
    and the Western Confederacy: a criticism of Lee's strategic ability', *Civil War
    History*, XV (1969), pp. 116–32.

26. Lee to Davis, 15 June 1864 (No. 781) in Clifford Dowdey and Louis H.
    Manarin (eds), *The Wartime Papers of R.E. Lee* (New York, 1961), p. 783; Craig
    L. Symonds, *Joseph E. Johnston* (New York, 1992), pp. 198–201; Williams,
    Beauregard, p. 242.

27. Philip Howes, *The Catalytic Wars: A Study of the Development of War, 1860–1870*
    (London, 1998), p. 30.

28. Bruce Catton, *Grant Moves South* (Boston, Mass., 1960), pp. 218–21.

29. Thomas L. Connelly, *Army of the Heartland: The Army of Tennessee, 1861–1862*
    (1967; Baton Rouge, La, 1986), pp. 160–1, 164–6; U.S. Grant, *Personal Mem-
    oirs* (London, 1886), I, pp. 342–3, 350–1; Kenneth P. Williams, *Lincoln Finds a
    General* (New York, 1952), vol. 3, pp. 348–9, 356, 360, 369, 383, 387, 390–
    1; Edward Hagerman, 'From Jomini to Dennis Hart Mahan: the evolution
    of trench warfare and the American Civil War', *Civil War History*, XIII (1967),
    p. 216.

30. Grant, *Personal Memoirs*, I, p. 358.

31. Freeman Cleaves, *Rock of Chickamauga: The Life of General George H. Thomas* (Norman, Oklahoma and London, 1948), p. 110.

32. Ibid., pp. 112–16; Williams, *Lincoln Finds a General*, vol. 4, pp. 128–33.

33. Holden Reid, *American Civil War and the Wars of the Industrial Revolution*, pp. 130–2.

34. Adam Badeau, *Military History of U.S. Grant* (New York, 1881), vol. 1, pp. 95–6, 226.

35. Horace Porter, *Campaigning with Grant* (New York, 1897), pp. 13–16, 63–4.

36. Grady McWhiney, *Braxton Bragg and Confederate Defeat* (1969; Tuscaloosa, Ala., 1991), pp. 229, 342; Stephen W. Sears, *Chancellorsville* (Boston, Mass., 1996), p. 194–6.

37. Porter, *Campaigning with Grant*, pp. 8, 37–8, 102–3.

38. Brian Holden Reid, 'The commander and his chief of staff: Ulysses S. Grant and John A. Rawlins', in G.D. Sheffield (ed.), *Leadership and Command: The Anglo-American Experience Since 1861* (London, 1997), pp. 17–36.

39. On Lee's calculated use of his appearances at the front, see N.A. Trudeau, '"A mere question of time": Robert E. Lee from the wilderness to Appomattox Court House', in Gary Gallagher (ed.), *Lee: The Soldier* (Lincoln and London, 1996), p. 528.

40. Edwin B. Coddington, *The Gettysburg Campaign* (New York, 1968), pp. 42–4, 94–102, 130–3, 214–17, 221, 223.

41. See Bruce Catton, *Grant takes Command* (Boston, 1968), p. 139, for Lincoln's injunction to Stanton to 'leave him [Grant] alone to do as he pleases'.

42. Williams, *Lincoln and his Generals*, p. 291; Herman Hattaway and Archer Jones, *How the North Won* (Urbana and Chicago, Ill., 1983), p. 285.

43. Edward Hagerman, *The American Civil War and the Origins of Modern Warfare* (Bloomington, Ind., 1988), pp. 34–5, 50–1.

44. Frank E. Vandiver, *Rebel Brass: The Confederate Command System* (Baton Rouge, La, 1956), pp. 18–20.

45. Cleaves, *Thomas*, pp. 257–60.

CHAPTER SEVEN

THE EXPERIENCE OF THE CIVIL WAR: MEN AT ARMS

ANDREW R. HAUGHTON

In 1982 Marvin R. Cain published a plea for an assessment of motives and men in American Civil War historiography – a 'Face of Battle' for the soldiers of the Union and the Confederacy. Reflecting upon the preoccupation of previous generations of historians first with the causes of the war, and then with its consequences, Cain suggested that the 'human equation' had been neglected, and even as an increasing body of literature had addressed the daily lives of common soldiers in the war, analysis of their attitudes, behaviour and motives had remained superficial and incomplete.[1] The construction of a detailed and comprehensive 'Face of Battle' for the Civil War is beyond the scope and brevity of this chapter, indeed, a sizeable tome would be required to give proper attention to such a complex subject. However, a number of historians over the past twenty years have made suggestions as to why the men who fought for blue or grey were willing to go to war, risk death or disablement, and stick it out until one side or the other could no longer continue. This chapter is, in part, a survey of the questions that have been posed, the answers that have been offered, and the problems that remain unsolved in analyzing the hopes and fears of the men who experienced the sharp end of the Civil War. In conjunction with this historiographical analysis the key areas of debate will be reassessed through an overview of Civil War armies, the battlefield environment, and the daily pressures endured by 'Billy Yank' and 'Johnny Reb'.

Any assessment of such a large and diverse body of men as made up the armies of the North and South must begin with a caveat. Every observation concerning the common soldier of the Civil War can be applied to only a portion of the aggregate. Studies of this type are based upon highlighting factors which pertained to a significant number of the participants, which are repeated time and again in their letters and diaries, but which could not possibly hold true for each and every man involved in the conflict. Indeed, both armies, Union and Confederate, encompassed the complete spectrum of their society, from the wealthiest Boston Brahmin to immigrant labourers, from university professors to young men who had barely completed their schooling. One contemporary observer marvelled at the incredible variety of men serving in the Confederate army early in the war, noting that 'numbers of wealthy planters serve as privates side by side with the professional man, the shopkeeper, the clerk, the labourer; and all go through ordinary fatigue duties incident to camp life'.[2] The first experience of the Civil War for most volunteers was, therefore, the shock of being thrown into a large and varied society in the confined space of a camp of rendezvous.

Why soldiers fought

Soldiers arrived at the various camps of rendezvous – normally organized by state authorities and conducted under the auspices of the state militia – with little more than a willingness to fight for their country or their cause. Few had any personal experience of war, but relied instead on what they could recall from school textbooks and the stories of romance and glory that found an audience through popular literature. Earl J. Hess has suggested that, by dis-seminating a romanticised view of historical figures and events – particularly those of the classical and Napoleonic period – antebellum literature 'inad-vertently prepared young men to accept and even to embrace the idea of going to war'.[3] Many young volunteers did indeed set out for the camps of rendezvous filled with thoughts of the excitement and drama of war. One soldier remembered riding off with his best friend to enlist in the Confeder-ate army, like 'two modern Don Quixotes setting out to seek adventure', and the prospect of a short and heroic war appealed to many, just as it would for the young men of Europe in 1914.[4] John F. Lucy's comment that 'going to war seemed a light-hearted business' is as applicable to the America of 1861 as it was to the Britain of 1914, for few had any idea of what to expect, but many revelled in the hope and expectation of demonstrating their courage and ability on the battlefield, and worried only that they would miss the great battle that would decide the conflict.[5]

'Initial motivation', as John Lynn has described the impulse to enlist and fight, was however, more complicated than simple *rage militaire*, particularly for those who had employment, homes and families, which they left behind to enlist.[6] In his explanation of motivations in the Civil War, *For Cause and*

Comrades, James McPherson found that 'in explaining to family members and friends their motives for enlisting, far more volunteers mentioned patriotism and ideology than adventure and excitement'. Indeed McPherson contends that 'ideological convictions' were crucial in prompting men on both sides of the Mason-Dixon line to volunteer. The problem for any study of the ideological motivations of Civil War soldiers is that the volunteers themselves were often vague in their definitions and understanding of ideological and psychological values. McPherson himself warns that the motives of many volunteers 'were mixed in a way that was impossible for them to disentangle in their own minds'.[7] Michael Barton has proposed a delineation between ideological terms, such as freedom, democracy, equality and individualism, and psychological terms, including patriotism, religion and achievement. Barton found that the psychological terms were used more frequently in the letters and diaries of Civil War soldiers, and that most also expressed an admiration for high moral standards.[8] However, ideology, patriotism, religion and morality were often interwoven in the mind of the volunteers in a way such as to make the connections between them indistinguishable and irrelevant. Patriotic sentiment in the North, for example, was heavily based upon the pride many felt in their democratic system of government, which protected the freedom of every American to do as he wished under the law, ensured freedom of religion, and prevented degeneration into lawlessness and immorality. What can be said with some degree of certainty is that patriotism and ideology underpinned the initial motivation of many in both the North and the South – both sides claimed to be the true heirs to the principles of the American Revolution, and each accused the other of betraying that inheritance – and drew many to the colours in spite of family, friends and 'gloomy forebodings'.[9]

For some volunteers, North and South, pride in their government, nation or section developed into a strangely possessive affinity, and led to strong indignation in the face of any threat to the *status quo*. Wilbur J. Cash, in his attempt to comprehend the 'Southern mind', contended that Confederate motivation throughout the war was based upon a conviction on the part of every Southerner 'that nothing living could cross him and get away with it'.[10] The South had seceded in the first place to preclude domination by the North, and consequent loss of control over their own institutions and laws. Fighting for their independence was the next logical step for many Confederate volunteers, and references to potential enslavement to the North should the Confederacy be defeated were common not only in Southern newspapers and political debates, but also in the letters of the volunteers themselves. There

[172]   were not many Americans who remained unaware of the political situation following the tumultuous election of Abraham Lincoln, and maintenance of their freedom and independence was paramount in the motivation of many Southerners. Indignation was, however, far from being a Southern monopoly. Southern dominance of the US Senate, Supreme Court and, in the form of James Buchanan, presidency in the 1850s had engendered a sense of injustice in the more populous North which was exacerbated by controversial, pro-Southern legislation such as the Fugitive Slave law and the Kansas-Nebraska Act.[11] The perception of Southern leaders as arrogant and high-handed was, for many in the North, confirmed by the secession of the Southern states when the election of 1860 did not go in their favour. The attack upon Fort Sumter was the final straw that brought Northern indignation to the fore, and prompted resolutions by political bodies, local communities and individuals across the Northern states to 'stand by the stars and stripes wherever they float, by land or sea'.[12] As Reid Mitchell as put it, 'one way to sum up Union war motivations succinctly was to say, the South needed to be taught a lesson.'[13]

Most Americans in the 1860s felt a very real affinity and allegiance toward their community, section and, for the Northerners, their country. 'The consciousness of duty was pervasive in Victorian America', and many felt a binding moral duty to defend the flag of their nation or – as in the case of Robert E. Lee – their state in the crisis.[14] More than this, to fail in their moral duty to nation or state was perceived by many as failing their community. Thomas Hopkin Deavenport was fairly typical in the mixture of duty, honour and the wish to be worthy of his family, community and country (in this case, the South) which prompted him to enlist. 'I felt that I had no right to enjoy blessing[s] purchased by others,' he recalled when explaining his enlistment. Remarking that he would consider himself unworthy of his family, ancestors and patriotic heritage, Deavenport 'determined, if in my power to prevent it, my country should never be enslaved, or if she were, that she should never clank her chains in my ears and say it was your cowardice that led me to this'.[15] This wish to demonstrate one's honour, duty and courage was thus interwoven with a spirit of community and patriotic sentiment in both North and South that propelled men into the army camps of 1861, and gave them a solid motivational basis for the sustained conflict that few anticipated.[16] As much as 'going to war seemed a light hearted business' in 1861, most of those in blue or grey enlisted for reasons with more depth and resonance than the pursuit of glory or excitement.

Before concluding this survey of the motives that led so many Americans to volunteer in 1861 one final point – often ignored in more recent studies of initial motivation – deserves some attention. In his broad survey of soldier life in the Union army, *The Life of Billy Yank: The Common Soldier of the Union*, Bell Wiley remarked that, preposterous as it may seem, many were attracted by the paltry $13 paid to the private soldier, and by the prospects for promotion. 'The first months of the war were marked by depression,' he reminded readers, 'and unemployment recurred periodically until 1863.'[17] While some saw the war as steady pay and employment for a short time, others grasped the opportunity to escape their mundane existence, establish their independence and manhood, and use their courage and ability to achieve greater standing in their community through a display of their bravery and martial qualities. More than a few nursed hopes of returning home at the end of the war as officers. Arthur B. Carpenter, for example, was 'becoming increasingly disenchanted with everyone and everything' in the turbulent spring of 1861; 'he did not particularly care for his work in his uncle's shoe business but found no other jobs available.' Combined with a patriotic wish to defend his government and flag, Carpenter's boredom and lack of prospects led him to enlist over the objections of his family, and by October 1861 he was as a sergeant in the 19th Regiment, US Infantry, drawing good pay and enjoying his incipient military training.[18]

Life in camp

Thousands of men all over America found their way to the public recruitment meetings that took place in almost every village, town and city. At these meetings local politicians and civic leaders would encourage men to join up – sometimes offering themselves as leaders for the company or regiment they hoped to form – and, once a sufficient number had been enlisted, the men would be directed to report to a camp of rendezvous on a certain date. In the South, where the authorities faced an acute scarcity, men were often invited to bring rifles or equivalent weapons with them. These camps were usually placed in a central and readily accessible location, often close to a major town in the state, but they served a very limited purpose. The volunteers were organized into the companies for which they had enlisted – giving them a strongly local character – and were then combined into regiments of eight to ten companies each, commonly amounting to around 1,000 men. Initially very little else was done at these camps, but in those units commanded by more organized and influential men, they often received their clothing and

[174] equipment at this stage. As military organization improved in the early months of the war the issuance of equipment and weapons became more common. In the Confederate states, where the authorities were still in considerable confusion in the spring of 1861, and where supplies of uniforms, equipment and weapons were especially scarce, men often went without such essentials for a prolonged period. In early 1862, some volunteer regiments were still training without weapons, and many Southerners continued to wear civilian apparel, attracting the name 'butternuts' because of the distinctive colour of their homespun clothing.[19] The Union soldiers were little better off in the first months of war. William T. Sherman recalled the conglomeration of troops he found upon his arrival in Washington DC in the summer of 1861: 'their uniforms were as various as the States and cities from which they came; their arms were also of every pattern and calibre; and they were so loaded down with overcoats, haversacks, knapsacks, tents, and baggage' that it required up to fifty wagons to move a regiment from one place to another.[20]

The first wave of volunteers on both sides were quickly moved up to the frontier, massing most conspicuously in Washington and northern Virginia, but rushing also to threatened points in Kentucky, Missouri and at Pensacola on the Gulf coast. These men would be trained where they stood, while making regular forays to reconnoitre enemy positions – often only a few miles distant. Most volunteers, however, found themselves delivered from their camp of rendezvous to a 'camp of instruction', although, in some cases, this was the same place and only the designation changed. The camps of instruction varied considerably in their climate, environment, size and discipline. Camp Moore in Louisiana, for example, was notorious for its poor location, the ubiquity of its insect population, and the prevalence of disease among its inhabitants. Frank L. Richardson, of the Thirteenth Louisiana, later remembered it as being 'more like a camp of destruction than instruction'.[21] Disease was common and expected in all camps, the exposure of men previously unfamiliar with diseases such as mumps and measles made that unavoidable. Equally endemic in the camps was ill-discipline. Few volunteers had any prior military experience – the regular army had a pre-war strength of only 15,000; the Mexican War, fought fifteen years previously, furnished some experienced volunteers, but even the forces involved in that conflict were dwarfed by Civil War armies; some immigrant volunteers had received training or experience in Europe, but again, there were not sufficient numbers of them to make a serious impact; and the militia system, by which citizens were expected to gain some military education, had long since fallen into disuse in all but a handful of states.

Some contended that Southerners held an advantage due to a natural martial spirit born of rural life, but this was considerably exaggerated, and neglected the fact that most Northerners came from similar farming back-grounds.[22] Indeed, Peter Maslowski has suggested that the case was quite the reverse, and 'that Southerners were consistently in worse mental condition and consistently enjoyed army life less than Northerners'.[23] Whether or not this is overstating the case, initial reaction to the discipline and training that was imposed upon the volunteers in the camps of instruction was decidedly mixed. As with any large body there were those who took to military life with ease, and those who found it utterly insufferable. Between these extremes, most men got on as best they could, enjoyed the camaraderie and positive features of camp life, and gradually adapted to the new regimen they found themselves under. With the benefit of hindsight, many looked back upon the early days of the war with some fondness. Thomas Hopkin Deavenport was one Confederate who could reflect upon the hardships of later campaigns and refer to the first year of the war as 'our easy days'. 'We worked a heap, drilled much and stood guard not a little,' he recalled, 'we had good tents with brick chimneys, biscuits, beef and coffee in abundance. We thought it was poor fare. We have since learned better.'[24]

Most volunteers found camp life difficult at first, but quickly adapted to the routine that was set for them. Those units with efficient commanders would drill from four to five hours a day, answer several roll calls, and perform dress parade in the early evening. The remainder of the day would be spent on guard duty, cleaning weapons, preparing for dress parade, or doing general fatigue duties around camp. Soldiers filled their spare time by playing cards, writing letters to their friends and family, reading any newspapers available, and indulging in the prime occupation of all soldiers in camp – rumour-mongering. Most soldiers eventually received a uniform, a weapon, and some items of equipment. Federal soldiers were better fed than any other military force in the western world; Confederate victuals were a little more capricious in both quantity and quality.[25] Yet, whatever their rations, the men of both Union and Confederacy lacked discipline and any form of training when they arrived at camps of instruction, and the process of instilling basic obedience to orders was the single most pressing problem for the new officers, and undoubtedly the greatest annoyance for enlisted men throughout the first year of the war. 'It took years to teach the educated privates in the Army that it was their duty to give unquestioning obedience to officers,' remembered an erstwhile Confederate in his memoir, and it was no exaggeration to describe the time frame in terms of years rather than months.[26]

The underlying problem for both sides was that their officers, in most cases, knew little or nothing more than the men they were expected to command. This was manifest when the commandant of Camp Curtain, a camp of instruction in Pennsylvania, promulgated strict rules and routines for the units in camp. The orders were based upon a 'faulty assumption', according to William J. Miller, 'they assumed that the inexperienced officers would or could enforce them'. With little idea of how to conduct themselves, much less control their men, it took months before the officers were able to execute the rules with any expectation of success.[27] The degree of discipline in a given unit varied widely depending on the experience and competence of its commander; even so, it was the exception rather than the rule in 1861 to find a unit which measured up to the standards of officers trained at the US Military Academy. As late as July 1862, Sherman issued an admonition to his officers stipulating that 'all officers of this command must now study their books; ignorance of duty must no longer be pleaded'.[28] However, discipline did eventually improve with experience, and this was amply demonstrated on the battlefields of Virginia, Kentucky and Tennessee in 1862 and 1863 where both sides repeatedly suffered appalling casualties.[29]

Tactical conditions

The explanation for the high casualty figures arising from Civil War combat, particularly in 1862–3, is the subject of some controversy. In *Attack and Die: Civil War Military Tactics and the Southern Heritage*, Grady McWhiney and Perry D. Jamieson have pointed to the failure of Confederate commanders to comprehend and adapt to the introduction of new technology – specifically, to the invention of the Minié bullet. At the time of the Mexican War, when most of the US Military Academy graduates who would lead armies in the Civil War received their only experience of combat, muzzle-loading smoothbore muskets were by far the most common infantry weapon. The inaccuracy of smoothbore muskets dictated that effective fire could only be delivered by a close-order line, and training and tactics were arranged accordingly. Rifled muskets, while more accurate, had an extremely slow rate of fire because, to utilize the rifling in the barrel, the ball had to be an extremely tight fit, and was consequently difficult to load. The Minié bullet, an oblong projectile small enough to drop easily down the barrel, but with a hollow base which expanded to fit the rifling of the barrel when fired,

changed the tactical situation completely. Infantrymen could now fire accur- [177]
ately over a far greater range, making fire zones larger and transferring
battlefield dominance to the defensive. However, not only did Civil War
commanders fail to properly adapt to these new circumstances, but Confederate commanders destroyed their armies in repeated frontal assaults in the
misguided belief that the offensive remained superior in spite of the prevalence of rifled muskets.[30] The explanation for this Southern predilection for
the offensive was, according to the McWhiney–Jamieson thesis, not merely
a misunderstanding of the tactical situation – after all, Federal army commanders had also fought in Mexico, but did not attack as much in Civil War
battles – but a Celtic heritage which pervaded Southern culture and inspired
a dedication to the charge, the ancient tactics of the Celts.[31] For McWhiney
and Jamieson, the Civil War battlefield is dominated by the Southern charge,
and its crushing repulse at the hands of the rifled musket – Pickett's Charge
during the Battle of Gettysburg might therefore be considered as the apo-
theosis of the *Attack and Die* thesis.

In contrast, Paddy Griffith has argued that Civil War battlefields were not
dominated by the rifled musket at all, and the superiority of the defensive was
instead exaggerated by the failure of the attackers to exploit their opportunities. Griffith based this proposition on his belief that discipline in Civil War
armies remained poor, and they were consequently unable to carry through
the Napoleonic tactics that would have brought decisiveness to the battlefield. Without the competence to force a breakthrough, Civil War battles
degenerated into costly fire-fights, 'casualties mounted' according to Griffith,
'because the contest went on so long, not because the fire was particularly
deadly'. Griffith thus concludes that the American Civil War was in fact the
last Napoleonic War, rather than the first modern war – although the Americans failed to copy correctly Napoleonic tactics, and thus failed to achieve the
decisive battles the French had won fifty years earlier.[32] Griffith's battlefields
are dominated by these indecisive fire-fights, and by the poor fire discipline
of the men which leads to them.

Combining parts of both the above theses, though it was written before
either, Thomas V. Moseley has produced perhaps the most balanced por-
trayal of the Civil War battlefield, and of the combat effectiveness of the troops
involved. Moseley certainly finds evidence to support Griffith's contention
that the fire discipline of the Civil War soldier was not all that might have
been expected, and cites, by way of example, a memorandum circulated among
officers of the Army of the Potomac in April 1864, which indicated that 'there
are men in this army who have been in numerous actions without ever firing

[178] their guns, and it is known that muskets taken on the battle-fields have been found filled nearly to the muzzle with cartridges'.[33] Moseley concludes that 'it was the exception, not the rule, if an officer could control the delivery of his fire' on the battlefield, maintaining that few exerted much influence on proceedings once a fire-fight had commenced. On the other hand, Moseley makes it clear that the rifled musket and other technological innovations made a significant impact upon Civil War combat, and hastened the deterioration of cohesion and control, particularly in attacking units.[34]

In point of fact, most units in the Civil War were well disciplined and poorly trained, and it was this combination as much as the destructive power of rifled muskets that created high casualties in the battles of 1862–3. In battle after battle attacking forces, arrayed in close-order linear formations, were able to break through the lines of their opponents, usually following a brief fire-fight and a close-range charge.[35] It was at this point that a number of factors would come into play to prevent exploitation of this success and the battle of annihilation that all Civil War commanders sought. The key to the problems encountered after an initial breakthrough was the loss of command and control on the part of the attacking forces, and the ability of defenders to adapt quickly and fall back to new positions, often augmented by additional infantry and increased artillery support. The Confederate attack upon the Federal right wing at the Battle of Murfreesboro is a good example. Having initially surprised and routed the better part of two Federal divisions, the Confederates were then slowed by a dense brake of cedars and underbrush which broke up their close-order lines and made coordination between regiments very difficult. By this point Southern corps and division commanders were taking an increasingly peripheral role, but brigade and regimental leaders remained in the thick of the action and crucial to the continuing momentum of the attack. The difficulties of communicating orders to commanders spread across long lines in dense woods led to increasing dislocation, and regiments would advance ahead of their supports, becoming exposed to flanking fire from the Federal forces falling slowly back in their immediate front. Fire-fights were constantly breaking out, forcing one side or the other falling back to find supporting units, thus slowing the Confederate advance and allowing Federal commanders time to rush forces to the threatened point and reorganize. Ultimately, though the Southerners continued to advance through most of the day, any possibility of annihilating the Union army was lost in the early hours of the battle when the assault became mired by difficult terrain, Federal resistance, and Confederate loss of command and control.[36] Of course, not every assault conformed to this pattern; the Battle of Antietam, for example, was marked more by the repulse of frontal assaults by lines of rifled muskets rather than the breakthroughs and fire-fights described above. Every battle is to some degree unique, and any generalization on tactics in the Civil War has to take into account the different circumstances and object-ives on the part of the protagonists. What is clear is that a sufficient number of men were prepared to go forward into the hail of musket and artillery fire to produce bloody repulses, partial breakthroughs and hugely destructive fire-fights.[37]

The reasons why men fight are as complex and debatable as the tactics they employed. For the man in the ranks battle was as awesome and confus-ing as it was for the brigade and divisional commanders desperately trying to coordinate their forces. Most battles took place across a broad expanse which encompassed woodlands, rivers and small farms. Soldiers themselves remarked on the contrast between the battles they had read of, where entire armies would be arrayed on open plains, and the intimate fighting that took place between trees and underbrush on the American battlefield. The 'fog of war', dispensed by thousands of muskets and dozens of cannon, further obscured men who habitually went to ground until it was their time to advance. 'I have taken part in two great battles', reported one Federal officer, 'and heard the bullets whistle both days, and yet I had scarcely seen a Rebel save killed, wounded, or prisoners.'[38] Both sides also employed the tactic of having their men lie down during a fire-fight while they prepared for a final assault, further adding to the concealment of troops on the battlefield, and, of course, increasing the tension for those awaiting the assault – not being able to see the enemy was often more stressful than having his lines in view not only because of a fear of the unknown, but also because the lack of a target removed the emotional satisfaction gained from firing.[39] 'If you wish to know how a soldier feels in a battle such as that you must ask someone else,' one Confederate said recalling the Battle of Perryville, 'if you ask me if I was scared, I answer I don't know that I was scared before we got in the thickest of the fight.'[40]

Primary group loyalty

To explain how so many volunteers not only survived such conditions, but repeatedly advanced into enemy fire in battle after battle, historians have examined the concepts of combat motivation proposed by sociologists in the aftermath of the Second World War, the Victorian moral principles and community ties that first propelled men into the ranks of the Union and Confederate armies, and the leaders they followed into fire zones so intense they attracted names like Devil's Den and Bloody Angle. 'The Cause' was, of course, fundamental not only to bringing men into the ranks, but also to combat and sustaining motivation. Yet not all Union and Confederate troops fought for the cause – after 1862, for instance, increasing numbers of conscripts augmented the strength of both sides – and those who did often referred to other psychological supports which helped them in moments of crisis when ideological convictions seemed distant. The most physically immediate stimulus to the infantryman of the Civil War was the men on either side of him. In terms of training and tactics, both sides remained committed to close order throughout the first three years of war, despite the impact of rifled muskets, and this was in part due to the belief that close order made it easier for volunteers to maintain cohesion and discipline. While men were often unable to see their enemy, they seldom lost contact with the men of their squad, company and regiment. As long as the regiment remained in place, men were loathe to fall to the rear and not only lose the respect of their comrades, but to fail those with whom they had shared the travails of camp life, marching and previous combat experiences. Civil War soldiers were bound to their comrades in much the same way as the GIs of the Second World War would cite the primary group as crucial to their combat motivation, and were as keen not to let their comrades down.[41]

Nevertheless, primary group loyalty in the Civil War must be addressed within its historical context. In the studies of combat motivation that have emerged over the past ten years, Gerald Linderman, Reid Mitchell, James McPherson and Earl J. Hess have highlighted the importance of duty and honour in the American mind, and the strength of the ties between the troops at the front and the communities from which their units had been formed. 'The community never entirely relinquished its power to oversee its men at war', and the values represented by those at home – the values for which men had volunteered in the first place – were continually reinforced by those ties. Men were well aware that any show of cowardice, any failure to fulfil one's duty as it was perceived by comrades and community, would mean disgrace and scorn among friends and even family. Of course, the possibility of disgrace never crossed the mind of some, but they were nonetheless eager to maintain their honour and demonstrate their courage – virtues closely interwoven with Victorian perceptions of masculinity and morality.[42] These links to the community back home also acted to reinforce the commitment of soldiers to the war where the letters they received commended them, and the knowledge that those at home were relying upon and supporting a soldier [181] acted as a powerful stimulus to remain in the ranks when under fire.[43] As George Reeves and Joseph Frank have pointed out, the bond between community and soldier was crucial for the latter's self-esteem, and acted as an emotional support not only in the midst of combat, but also in the difficult transition from civilian life to a military existence.[44]

In some cases, however, men would receive letters begging them to return, often because a soldier's wife found herself in financial difficulties, or sometimes due to simple loneliness, and this no doubt severely impaired the morale of men who received such missives.[45] In the historical context of nineteenth-century America, the primary group to which the soldier owed his loyalty might be extended to the community he had left behind, so close and influential were the connections between home and the front. These connections also reinforced the concepts of duty and honour which were inextricably caught up in the relationship of the individual to his comrades because, for many, the social values of the community had merely been shifted to a new location – a location where pressure made those values all the more intense.

Another central feature of American culture in the nineteenth century was a commitment to religion, and many mentioned their religious beliefs as sustaining them in the most difficult moments of battle. Although some were deeply devout, and trusted in God to see them through the battle, or to ensure that they would be victorious, religious belief was more commonly expressed in a resigned fatalism. A common entry in the diaries or letters of soldiers, particularly upon the death of a friend or relative, was 'man proposes and God disposes'. This balance between a belief in free will and divine omnipotence led men to the acceptance of their fate, an acceptance supported by a widespread belief that killing others in battle would not preclude entry to Paradise when death should finally come.[46] The importance of religion is exemplified in the baptism of the Confederate commanders Joseph E. Johnston and John B. Hood in 1864, an individual act that was perhaps not entirely free from the awareness of flagging morale in the Southern army at that time.

Importance of leadership

Leadership was a crucial component in combat motivation. References to commanders steadying their men under fire, leading by example, and all but physically moving their commands forward are strewn through the battle reports of officers and the letters of enlisted men.[47] Their importance to combat motivation is perhaps best demonstrated by the performance of commands when they had lost a high proportion of officers, or when a respected commander was lost in the heat of battle. In such circumstances units seldom succumbed to complete disintegration, but loss of a key leader often contributed to a loss of nerve that detracted from combat effectiveness. This was especially the case early in the war, and is perhaps exemplified in the Confederate collapse at the Battle of Mill Springs when General Felix Zollicoffer, who had been held in great esteem by his troops, was killed during the battle. This was repeated at the Battle of Shiloh where, although the impact of the death of Albert Sidney Johnston did not lead to a precipitate collapse, many of his subordinates considered his death on the field to have been the turning-point in the battle.[48]

Greater familiarity with combat dulled the impact of such events as the war went on. Indeed, one commander believed that familiarity with battle was the key to developing competent soldiers and effective armies. 'Put a plank six inches wide five feet above the ground and a thousand men will walk it easily,' Union General George Thomas remarked in the summer of 1863, 'raise it five hundred feet and one man out of a thousand will walk it safely. It is a question of nerve we have to solve, not dexterity.' Thomas believed that only through becoming accustomed to violence and battle could the Union create veteran soldiers, and suggested that this had been George McClellan's greatest failure during his period in command of the Army of the Potomac – 'McClellan's great error was in his avoidance of fighting . . . his troops came to have a mysterious fear of the enemy.'[49] This is very close to the thesis proposed by Michael C.C. Adams in *Our Masters the Rebels*. Noting the widespread – and greatly exaggerated – belief among Northern volunteers that the South enjoyed a peculiarly martial tradition, Adams traces Northern fear of the Cavalier Southerners through the Army of the Potomac's fortunes and misfortunes against the Confederate Army of Northern Virginia. Indeed, according to Adams, not until the arrival of Ulysses S. Grant from the western theatre were the soldiers and officers of the Army of the Potomac able to overcome their inferiority complex.[50]

For Adams the Army of the Potomac lost its nerve almost before the conflict began, and certainly in the aftermath of the first Battle of Bull Run. By contrast, Gerald Linderman contends that declension was gradual, and most volunteers suffered a loss of nerve – or rather, a loss of belief in the values which had brought them into the Union and Confederate armies – later in the war. Linderman's thesis is based upon the premise that courage was the single, determining quality at the centre of the male outlook in the 1860s, the core value of the Civil War volunteer. Courage was the highest virtue of the Victorian male, and it formed the cornerstone of a cultural philosophy which lauded duty, honour, chivalry and masculinity. Courage had underpinned the initial motivation of Civil War volunteers, and it was just as important in combat motivation. However, it quickly became clear that courage was not sufficient to ensure victory, or even to attain glory. The volunteers saw that brave men were often killed or maimed as a result of their valour, while the less courageous survived. Nor was it any safeguard against ignominious death through diseases such as dysentery or measles. By 1863 the lustre of courage had become tarnished, or, in Linderman's phrase, 'embattled', and the volunteers had become disillusioned, 'the very nature of combat did not fit, and could not be made to fit, within the framework of soldier expectations'. The result was that men began to go to ground at every possible opportunity, the construction of entrenchments became commonplace, and it was no longer considered cowardly to use available cover. By the spring of 1864, the Civil War was being fought in a manner that would have appalled the volunteer of 1861, and the distinction between courage and cowardice had become blurred to the point of irrelevance.[51]

This is certainly a provocative thesis, but Linderman has been criticized on a number of points. James McPherson, for example, while finding much to recommend in *Embattled Courage*, found that the concepts of duty, honour, courage and belief in the cause for which they were fighting persisted to the end of war. Michael C.C. Adams confessed that he was 'not convinced that courage was the one over-arching quality, the cement, holding together the white male's philosophy of individual character', and also pointed to Linderman's failure to offer a satisfactory analysis of Victorian social attitudes. Yet perhaps the most interesting idea in Linderman's thesis is in his exploration of how motivation and tactics – why men fight and how men fight – become interwoven, how they act upon one another to alter the nature of conflict.

That the tactical nature of the war changed significantly between 1861 and 1864 is beyond dispute: the battlefield became increasingly static and dominated by entrenchments or field fortifications; sniping became widespread; contact between opposing armies was extended from a day or two in 1862–3 to weeks, exemplified in the Wilderness, Petersburg and Atlanta campaigns.[52] This was, however, as much to do with manpower resources, strategy, increasingly competent tactical thinking on the part of commanders like Sherman and Johnston, as with the disillusionment of the men under their command. In the Confederate Army of Tennessee, for instance, there was a significant tactical change between the Battle of Missionary Ridge – which was essentially a siege operating in much the same way as was the case in the eighteenth century – and the opening of the Atlanta campaign. The tactical development experienced by that army was, however, due to a change in its commander and the lessons learned by its officers and men in the battles of late 1863 rather than the fall of the concept of courage. Moreover, despite an increase in desertion (particularly on the part of the Confederate army) the vast majority of Civil War soldiers did not leave the army in 1864 – in fact, more than half of the Union volunteers whose term of service expired in 1864 reenlisted. Clearly, these men remained highly motivated even in 1864–5.

The motivations which drew men into the army, and which sustained them in combat, also contributed to their morale, supporting them through long periods away from home and family, through the monotony of camp life, and through up to four years of warfare. These motives were augmented by the improved discipline of the soldiers, and by the pride they came to have in their units – although, in some cases, infusions of conscripts to replace the killed and wounded severely hampered unit pride and cohesion.[53] They were also aided by the darker side of discipline, strict laws against desertion and frequent executions to dissuade potential offenders. For Southerners there was the added incentive of defending their homes against increasingly de-structive Federal invasions; while many Northerners expressed an intention to see the job through to its completion. Indeed, many would have identified with sentiments expressed by a First World War officer almost seventy years later: 'at no time in the war', Robert Graves recalled, 'did any of us allow ourselves to believe that hostilities could possibly continue more than nine months or a year more, so it seemed almost worth taking care.'[54] On both sides men fought on in the hope of an imminent – but honourable – return to the homes and communities they had left behind. Perhaps the final differen-tiating factor between the Union and Confederate soldier, the thing that prompted Southerners to desert in large numbers in the early months of 1865, was the prospect of success. In his study of the final Confederate campaign in the West, Wiley Sword has concluded that Hood's army finally gave way to fear in the Battle of Nashville and its immediate aftermath. 'Yet it was not the fear of fighting', he asserts, 'but only a fear of wasting their lives, of too long being abused in the field and sacrificed to no sensible purpose.'[55] As Richard Beringer and others pointed out in explaining *Why the South Lost the Civil War*, Confederate morale was closely tied to their military success throughout the war, so when success no longer seemed remotely possible, the motivation that had sustained Confederate soldiers through four years of conflict was [185] outweighed by the prospect of sacrificing their lives for a cause already lost.[56] The Civil War thus came to an abrupt end in April and May 1865, *in part* because of the reluctance of so many Southerners to continue the fight.

'The Civil War,' writes Peter Parish, 'like any other war, reflected the society in which it took place.'[57] Civil War soldiers shared many of the same experiences as the troops of other conflicts, ancient and modern; they were motivated by their cause, religion, loyalty to comrades and community, by duty, honour, courage, good leadership, and by the hope of victory. Yet their experience of war – their attitudes to it and their endurance of it – was permeated by a unique mixture of ideology, morality and motives that determined not only *why* men fought, but also had a significant influence over *how* they fought. The historiography of the common soldier of the Civil War has, over the past twenty years or so, come to reflect the complex and often incongruous nature of its subject, bringing greater depth to our understanding of the war as a whole, and the influence of the private soldier on its great events – and, of course, on the decision-making process which brought them about. Ultimately, the 'Face of Battle' for the Civil War is reflected as much in its historiography as in the writings of the men who fought. They were, in many cases, no more certain of the juxtaposition of one factor or another in sustaining their will to fight. Future academic interpretations might have to move into this 'grey area' rather than be coloured black and white.

Notes

1. Marvin R. Cain, 'A "face of battle" needed: an assessment of motives and men in Civil War historiography', *Civil War History*, XXVIII (1982), pp. 5–27.

2. Anonymous, 'A month with the "rebels"', in Henry S. Commager (ed.), *The Blue and the Gray: The Story of the Civil War as told by Participants* (New York, 1950), p. 64. The Union army was perhaps even more diverse than that of the Confederacy due to the greater numbers of immigrants in its ranks; see William L. Burton, *Melting Pot Soldiers: The Union's Ethnic Regiments* (Ames, Ia, 1988).

3. Earl J. Hess, *The Union Soldier in Battle: Enduring the Ordeal of Combat* (Lawrence, Ks, 1997), p. 2.

4. John S. Jackman Journal, January –, 1863, Manuscripts Reading Room, Library of Congress, Washington DC.

[186]   5. John F. Lucy, *There's a Devil in the Drum* (London, 1938), quoted in Trevor
            Wilson, *The Myriad Faces of War: Britain and the Great War, 1914–18* (Cambridge,
            1988), p. 53.

          6. In his construction of the model of combat effectiveness, Lynn divides motiva-
            tion into 'initial', 'combat' and 'sustaining motivation'. John A. Lynn, *The Bayo-
            nets of the Republic: Motivation and Tactics in the Army of Revolutionary France,
            1791–94* (Oxford, 1996, Westview Press edn), p. 22.

          7. James M. McPherson, *For Cause and Comrades: Why Men Fought in the Civil War*
            (New York, 1997), pp. 27–8.

          8. Michael Barton, *Goodmen: The Character of Civil War Soldiers* (University Park,
            Pa, 1981), pp. 33–40.

          9. John D. Billings, 'Hardtack and coffee', in Philip Van Doren Stern (ed.), *Soldier
            Life in the Union and Confederate Armies* (Bloomington, In., 1961), p. 13.

         10. Wilbur J. Cash, *The Mind of the South* (New York, 1941; Pelican edn, 1973),
            pp. 64–5.

         11. James M. McPherson, *Battle Cry of Freedom: The American Civil War* (New York,
            1988; Penguin edn, 1990), pp. 6–275; Brian Holden Reid, *The Origins of the
            American Civil War* (London, 1996) pp. 154–7, 182–4.

         12. William Garrett Piston, 'The 1st Iowa Volunteers: honor and community in a
            ninety-day regiment', *Civil War History*, XLIV, (1998), p. 7.

         13. Reid Mitchell, *The Vacant Chair: The Northern Soldier leaves Home* (New York,
            1993), p. 15.

         14. McPherson, *For Cause and Comrades*, pp. 22–3.

         15. Thomas Hopkin Deavenport Diary/memoir, p. 1, Civil War Collection, Ten-
            nessee State Archives and Library, Nashville, Tennessee. (Hereafter referred to
            as TSLA.)

         16. Reid Mitchell, *Civil War Soldiers: Their Expectations and Experiences* (New York,
            1988), highlights the importance of patriotism, duty and community in the
            motivations of Civil War soldiers; Gerald Linderman, *Embattled Courage: The
            Experience of Combat in the American Civil War* (New York, 1987), which focus-
            ing more upon combat and sustaining motivation, presents an interesting thesis
            emphasizing centrality of courage in Victorian culture, and the corollary of this
            attitude for the initial motivation of Civil War volunteers.

         17. Bell I. Wiley, *The Life of Billy Yank: The Common Soldier of the Union* (Baton
            Rouge, La, 1978), p. 38.

18. Thomas R. Bright, 'Yankees in arms: the Civil War as a personal experience', [187]
Civil War History, XIX, (1973), pp. 197–218.

19. For an insight into Confederate organizational problems in the first months of
the war, see Thomas L. Connelly, *Army of the Heartland: The Army of Tennessee,
1861–62* (Baton Rouge, La, 1967), pp. 3–58.

20. William T. Sherman, *Memoirs of General William T. Sherman* (New York, 1984;
first published, 1875), p. 178. For similar remarks concerning the Confederate
troops in northern Virginia around the same time, see General Joseph E.
Johnston, *Narrative of Military Operations during the Civil War* (New York, 1990;
first published, 1874), p. 16.

21. Frank L. Richardson, 'The war as I saw it', *Louisiana Historical Quarterly*, II,
(1923), p. 92; Ruben A. Pierson's letter to his wife, from Camp Moore, 21 July
1861, Pierson Family Papers, Kuntz Collection, Howard–Tilton Memorial
Library, Tulane University, New Orleans.

22. On pre-war American military experience and the debate over the Southern
martial tradition, see Edward M. Coffman, *The Old Army: A Portrait of the American Army in Peacetime, 1784–1898* (New York, 1986); Marcus Cunliffe, *Soldiers
and Civilians: The Martial Spirit in America, 1775–1865* (London, 1968);
John Hope Franklin, *The Militant South* (Cambridge, Mass., 1956); R. Don
Higginbotham, 'The martial spirit in the antebellum South: some further
speculations in a national context', *Journal of Southern History*, LVIII, (1992),
pp. 3–26; Robert E. May, 'Dixie's martial image: a continuing historical
enigma', *Historian*, LX (1978), pp. 213–34; William K. Riker, *Soldiers of the
States: The Role of the National Guard in American Democracy* (Washington DC,
1957).

23. Pete Maslowski, 'A study of morale in Civil War soldiers', *Military Affairs*,
XXXIV, (1970), p. 128.

24. Deavenport Diary/memoir, p. 6, TSLA.

25. For first hand account of life in the camps of Union and Confederate armies, see
Commager, *Blue and the Gray*, pp. 267–337, 407–516. Bell Wiley's works on
The Life of Billy Yank and *The Life of Johnny Reb: The Common Soldier of the Confederacy* (Baton Rouge, La, 1943) are extremely informative, and have recently
been supplemented by James I. Robertson, *Soldiers: Blue and Gray* (New York,
1988). There are no works which explicitly compare Civil War soldiers to their
other soldier contemporaries, although John R. Elting, *Swords Around a Throne:
Napoleon's Grande Armée* (London, 1989), and J.G. Fuller, *Troop Morale and
Popular Culture in the British and Dominion Armies, 1914–18* (London, 1990), provide useful material for general comparisons.

26. Carlton McCarthy, 'Detailed minutiae of soldier life in the Army of Northern Virginia', in Van Doren Stern, *Soldier Life*, p. 300.

27. William J. Miller, *The Training of an Army: Camp Curtain and the North's Civil War* (Shippensburg, Pa, 1990), pp. 13–18.

28. General Orders No. 62, Fifth Division, Army of the Tennessee, 24 July 1862, *War of the Rebellion: A Compilation of the Official Records of the Union and Confederate Armies* (Washington DC, 1880–1901), series 1, XVII, pt 2, p. 119. (All subsequent references to Series 1.)

29. Mark A. Weitz, 'Drill, training, and the combat performance of the Civil War soldier: dispelling the myth of the poor soldier, great fighter', *Journal of Military History*, LXII (1998), pp. 263–89. Further details on discipline and casualties after the first year of the war can be found in battle histories, such as Peter Cozzens, *No Better Place to Die: The Battle of Stones River* (Chicago, 1991); and unit histories like Terry L. Jones, *Lee's Tigers: The Louisiana Infantry in the Army of Northern Virginia* (Baton Rouge, La, 1987), or Alan T. Nolan, *The Iron Brigade: A Military History* (Indianapolis, In., 1994).

30. Grady McWhiney and Perry D. Jamieson, *Attack and Die: Civil War Military Tactics and the Southern Heritage* (Tuscaloosa, Ala, 1982), p. 48 and passim.

31. McWhiney and Jamieson, *Attack*, pp. 141–91. For a critical appraisal of the figures and argument in *Attack*, see Richard E. Beringer *et al.*, *Why the South Lost the Civil War* (Athens, Ga, 1986), pp. 458–81. On the alleged Celtic heritage in the Southern states, see David Hackett Fischer, *Albion's Seed: Four British Folkways in America* (Oxford, 1989), and the symposium which considered Fischer's thesis the following year and was published in *William & Mary Quarterly*, XLVIII (1991), pp. 223–309.

32. Paddy Griffith, *Battle Tactics of the Civil War* (New Haven, Conn. 1989), p. 190 and passim. Griffith's work has received rather mixed reviews; see Albert Castel's appraisal in *Civil War History*, XXXV (1989), pp. 335–8, Herman Hattaway in the *Journal of Military History*, LVIII (1994), pp. 155–6, and Perry Jamieson in *Journal of American History*, LXXVII (1990), pp. 314–15.

33. Circular, Army of the Potomac, 19 April 1864, *War of the Rebellion*, XXXIII, p. 908.

34. Thomas Vernon Moseley, 'The evolution of American Civil War infantry tactics', PhD dissertation, University of North Carolina at Chapel Hill (1968), pp. 383–99 and passim.

35. Moseley, 'Infantry tactics', pp. 334–8. See also the various battle studies that have been produced on the battles of 1862–3, and the battle reports of Union and Confederate commanders in *War of the Rebellion*.

36. Cozzens, *No Better Place to Die*, pp. 81–143 and passim.

37. Beringer *et al.*, *Why the South Lost the Civil War*, pp. 167–68; McPherson, *Battle Cry*, pp. 538–67.

38. George R. Agassiz (ed.), *Meade's Headquarters, 1863–65: Letters of Colonel Theodore Lyman from the Wilderness to Appomattox* (Boston, Mass., 1922), p. 101, and quoted in Hess, *The Union Soldier in Battle*, p. 9.

39. In the Franco-Prussian War many officers found that they could not properly assault enemy lines because their men would go to ground under fire, and, although they continued to return fire, they could not be moved. This does not appear to have been as great a problem in the Civil War, but was instead seen as a valuable tactic in assaulting enemy lines. For observations on tactical problems in the Franco-Prussian War, see A. von Boguslawski, *Tactical Deductions from the War of 1870–1871* (Minneapolis, Ma, 1996; first published, 1872), pp. 47–62; John A. English and Bruce I. Gudmundsson, *On Infantry* (London, 1994, revised edn), pp. 1–35.

40. Carroll Henderson Clark memoirs, p. 26, TSLA.

41. McPherson, *For Cause and Comrades*, pp. 77–82. On primary group loyalty as a concept, and its prominence among American soldiers in the Second World War, see S.A. Stouffer *et al.*, *Studies in Social Psychology in World War II* (Princeton, NJ, 1949; 2 vols); S.L.A. Marshall, *Men Against Fire: Battle Command in Future War* (New York, 1947); Anthony Kellett, *Combat Motivation: The Behavior of Soldiers in Battle* (Boston, Mass., 1982).

42. Mitchell, *The Vacant Chair*, p. 25.

43. Mitchell, *The Vacant Chair*, p. 29.

44. Joseph A. Frank and George A. Reeves, *'Seeing the Elephant': Raw Recruits at the Battle of Shiloh* (Westport, Conn., 1989), passim. This is generally regarded as one of the best monographs on combat motivation in the Civil War, and is handicapped only by its limitation to a single battle. See Marvin Cain's review in *Civil War History*, XXXVI (1990), pp. 351–2.

45. Wiley, *The Life of Johnny Reb*, p. 210.

46. Samuel J. Watson, 'Religion and combat motivation in the Confederate armies', *Journal of Military History*, LVIII (1994), pp. 31–55; McPherson, *For Cause and Comrades*, pp. 62–76.

47. There are examples of the influence of leadership on combat motivation throughout the official records of the war. For some examples, see the report of Colonel George C. Porter, Sixth Tennessee Infantry (Confederate), 16 October

[190]

1862, *War of the Rebellion*, XVI, pt 1, pp. 1114–15; report of Major G.W. Kelsoe, Ninth Tennessee Infantry (Confederate), 12 October 1862, ibid., XVI, pt 1, p. 1116; report of Brigadier-General Joseph B. Carr, commanding First Brigade, Second Division, III Corps, Army of the Potomac, 1 August 1863, ibid., XXVII, pt 1, p. 544; report of Captain L.R. Stegman, 102nd New York Infantry, 6 July 1863, ibid., XXVII, pt 1, p. 865.

48. Connelly, *Army of the Heartland*, pp. 98, 166.

49. Peter Cozzens, *This Terrible Sound: The Battle of Chickamauga* (Chicago, 1992), pp. 422–3.

50. Michael C.C. Adams, *Our Masters the Rebels: A Speculation on Union Military Failure in the East 1861–65* (Cambridge, Mass., 1978), p. 6 and passim.

51. Linderman, *Embattled Courage*, p. 134 and passim.

52. Edward Hagerman, *The American Civil War and the Origins of Modern Warfare: Ideas, Organization, and Field Command* (Indianapolis, In., 1988), pp. 243–98; Beringer *et al.*, *Why the South Lost the Civil War*, pp. 236–335; Albert Castel, *Decision in the West: The Atlanta Campaign of 1864* (Lawrence, Ks, 1992), passim; Bruce Catton, *Grant Moves South* (Boston, Mass., 1960), p. 119 and passim; Joseph T. Glatthaar, *The March to the Sea and Beyond: Sherman's Troops in the Savannah and Carolinas Campaigns* (New York, 1985), pp. 156–74.

53. Nolan, *The Iron Brigade*, pp. 263–82; Larry J. Daniel, *Soldering in the Army of Tennessee: A Portrait of Life in a Confederate Army* (Chapel Hill, NC, 1991), p. 132.

54. Robert Graves, *Goodbye to All That* (London, 1931), p. 176.

55. Wiley Sword, *The Confederacy's Last Hurrah: Spring Hill, Franklin, and Nashville* (Lawrence, Ks, 1992), p. 377.

56. Beringer *et al.*, *Why the South Lost the Civil War*, pp. 424–42; for a contrasting interpretation, see Gary W. Gallagher, *The Confederate War* (Harvard, Mass., 1997).

57. Peter Parish, *The American Civil War* (London, 1975), p. 128.

CHAPTER EIGHT

FIGHTING FOR FREEDOM: AFRICAN-AMERICAN SOLDIERS IN THE CIVIL WAR

SUSAN-MARY GRANT

In 1897, over thirty years after the end of the American Civil War, a very special monument to that war was unveiled opposite the State House in Boston. Designed by the Irish-born sculptor Augustus Saint-Gaudens, it depicted in profile the figure of Robert Gould Shaw, the twenty-five-year-old white officer of the North's showcase black regiment, the Massachusetts 54th (Colored), leading his men through Boston on their way to South Carolina in 1863. It was an unusual and in many ways seminal piece of sculpture. Not only was it the first American monument focused on a group rather than a single figure, it was the first example of a monument portraying blacks as heroes. Saint-Gaudens had worked very hard to avoid representing the black troops in any kind of stereotypical manner, portraying them instead in a more accurate, but unprecedented, way as noble patriot soldiers of the American nation. Both in its novelty and in its sentiment the Saint-Gaudens monument remains, according to Robert Hughes, 'the most intensely felt image of military commemoration made by an American'.[1]

Impressive though it was – and indeed still is – the Saint-Gaudens monument in no way reflected the general mood of the American people towards those black troops who had fought in the conflict. By 1897 the American nation had all but forgotten that black troops had ever played a role in the Civil War. Saint-Gaudens completed his monument at a time when segregationist legislation – 'Jim Crow' – was beginning to bite in the South, but the exclusion of black troops from the national memory of the Civil War began long before 1897. In the Grand Review of the Armed Forces which followed the cessation of hostilities very few blacks were represented, despite the fact that many of the black Union regiments had fought longer and harder than some of the white regiments on parade that day. Relegated to the end of the procession in 'pitch and shovel' brigades or intended only as a form of comic relief, neither the free black soldier not the former slave was accorded his deserved role in this most poignant national pageant.[2] The reasons for this were not wholly racist. Those troops who marched down Pennsylvania Avenue on 23–4 May 1865 represented Northern armies which had not included black units, notably the Army of the Potomac and those under Sherman's command. In addition, having enlisted later than many of the white troops the African-American units had time left to serve, and so many of the black regiments were still on duty in the South when their white comrades were parading in Washington.[3] Nevertheless, the limited role taken by black troops – however explicable the grounds for it – did not bode well for the future. Rather than a war fought for liberty, in which the role of the African-American soldier was pivotal, the image of the American Civil War as a 'white man's fight' became the national norm almost as soon as the last shot was fired, and remained so until the late twentieth century. Indeed, although Brooks Simpson is undoubtedly right to observe that Americans today are much more aware of the 'role taken by African-Americans in fighting for their freedom during the Civil War' it remains the case that the black soldier is still not regarded as a central figure of that conflict.[4] This is in some ways unusual, given that the American Civil War became a war for liberation, for emancipation, for freedom and for a Union in which slavery had no place. From another angle, however, it is not unusual at all. There is, after all, more than one kind of freedom. The paradox of the African-American soldier lies in the fact that he was not simply fighting for freedom from slavery for his own race during the Civil War but for a much broader and more demanding kind of freedom; freedom not just for a race but for a nation.

Early frustrations

The relationship between the black soldier and the 'land of the free' has always been ambiguous. The pattern of involvement for black troops in America's wars from colonial times up to the nineteenth century followed a depressingly similar pattern. Encouraged to enlist in times of crisis, the African-American soldier's services were very clearly unwelcome in times of peace. Despite this, however, the link between fighting and freedom for African-Americans was forged in the earliest days of the American nation, and once forged proved resilient to all attempts to break it. During the colonial era, South Carolina enacted legislation that offered freedom to slaves in return for their military services, although Virginia remained welded to a strict policy of forbidding slaves to bear arms or from serving in the militia except as 'drummers and trumpeteers'.[5] Despite such mixed messages, by the conclusion of the American Revolution – in which some 5,000 out of the 300,000 troops in Washington's Continental Army were black – military service was regarded as a valid and successful method of achieving freedom for the slave as well as an important expression of patriotism and loyalty to the new nation. During the War of 1812 the future president Andrew Jackson rallied black troops to America's cause with the words: 'As sons of Freedom you are now called upon to defend your most estimable blessings. As Americans, your country looks with confidence to her adopted citizens. . . .'[6] Long before the Civil War, therefore, the African-American tradition of equating military service not just with freedom but with citizenship of the American nation was firmly established.

It was not surprising, therefore, that when hostilities commenced between North and South in 1861 blacks throughout the North, and some in the South too, sought to enlist. However, free blacks in the North who sought to respond to Abraham Lincoln's call for 75,000 volunteers found that their services were not required by a North in which slavery had been abolished but racist assumptions still prevailed. Instead they were told quite firmly that the war was a 'white man's fight' and offered no role for them. The notable northern black leader, Frederick Douglass, himself an escaped slave, summed the matter up succinctly:

> Colored men were good enough to fight under Washington. They are not good enough to fight under McClellan. They were good enough to fight under Andrew Jackson. They are not good enough to fight under Gen. Halleck. They were good enough to help win American independence but they are not good enough to help preserve that independence against treason and rebellion. They were good enough to defend New Orleans but not good enough to defend our poor beleaguered Capital.[7]

Douglass further recognized that unless the issue not just of arming free blacks but of freeing the slaves was addressed, the Union stood little chance of success. Until 'they shall make the cause of their country the cause of freedom', he asserted, 'until they shall strike down slavery, the source and center of this gigantic rebellion, they don't deserve the support of a single sable arm, nor will it succeed in crushing the cause of our present troubles.'[8] The Union, however, showed little sign of wanting the support of any sable arms. In the early months of the conflict the *National Intelligencer* reinforced the view that the war 'has no direct relation to slavery. It is a war for the restoration of the

Union under the existing constitution.'[9] Yet under the pressures of war it became increasingly difficult to maintain such an exclusionary and limited policy. This was particularly true for those generals in the field who found themselves having to deal with not only the free black population but a growing number of slaves who, dislocated by the war, were making their way through to Union lines. Whilst the Federal Government prevaricated on the question of arming blacks for a variety of legal, political and military reasons – not least of which was the desire not to upset the loyal but slaveholding border states – the Union generals found themselves faced with a problem that required more immediate resolution. Consequently, the first moves both toward arming blacks and freeing slaves during the American Civil War came not from Washington but from the front line.

An important precedent as far as the slaves were concerned was set very early in the conflict. In 1861 Benjamin F. Butler, in charge of Fortress Monroe in Virginia, declared that all slaves who escaped to Union lines were 'contraband of war', and refused to uphold the terms of the Fugitive Slave Law which bound him to return them to their owners. Butler's policy did not have much impact on attitudes in the North, but it did reinforce the views of those like Douglass who felt that slavery was of great military use to the Confederacy – and therefore damaging to the Union – and who consequently felt that the Civil War was likely to turn into a war for freedom if it lasted any length of time at all. For this reason, Butler's actions did find limited favour in Washington, and the Joint Committee on the Conduct of the War, founded in December of 1861, strongly supported both emancipation and the arming of blacks.[10]

Perhaps predictably, however, the first moves to arm blacks and free slaves proved clumsy. In Missouri, John C. Frémont, the commander of the Department of the West, unilaterally declared martial law in August, 1861, and declared all slaves owned by Confederate sympathizers to be free. Lincoln insisted that Frémont modify his announcement to bring it into line with the 1861 Confiscation Act, which removed slaves only from those actively engaged in hostilities against the Union. Then in late March 1862 Major General David Hunter, on taking over control of the Department of the South from Sherman, also declared martial law, emancipated all slaves held in Georgia, South Carolina and Florida, and forced as many escaped male slaves as he could find into military service. Not only was Hunter's announcement also rejected by Lincoln, but the aggressive manner in which he went about recruiting blacks for the Union army served only to alienate the very people whom he was attempting to help. The fact that he was also unable to pay them only made matters worse. Thomas Wentworth Higginson, the white officer in charge of what became the 1st South Carolina Volunteers (and later the 33rd US Colored Infantry), had cause to lament Hunter's rashness. Higginson praised the military ability of the black troops under his command, noting that 'they take readily to drill, and do not seem to object to discipline; they are not especially dull or inattentive; they seem fully to understand the importance of the contest, and of their role in it.' The troops did, however, express suspicion of the Federal government, and this Higginson put down to the 'legacy of bitter distrust bequeathed by the abortive regiment of General Hunter, – into which they were driven like cattle, kept for several months in camp, and then turned off without a shilling, by order of the War Department.'[11]

More successful were the efforts of Jim Lane in Kansas. A former US Senator and a Brigadier General in the Union army, Lane chose simply to ignore the War Department and raised a black regiment, the 1st Kansas Colored Volunteers, in 1862. This regiment was finally recognized the following year, by which time it had already seen active service against the Confederacy. The War Department did sanction the recruitment of black troops in August 1862, when General Rufus Saxton, the military commander in charge of the sea islands off South Carolina was authorized to 'arm, equip, and receive into the service of the United States' up to 5,000 black volunteers. Black regiments were not properly raised, however, until after Lincoln's Emancipation Proclamation of 1 January 1863. Massachusetts, Connecticut and Rhode Island were the first states to raise black regiments, and in May 1863 the War Department established the Bureau of Colored Troops, headed by C.W. Foster, with the remit of organizing the training and administration of the new black regiments. Both Northern free blacks and freed slaves in those parts of the South now under Union control were recruited into these regiments, all of whom (with the exception of the Connecticut and two of the Massachusetts regiments) came under the new designation 'United States Colored Troops' (USCT), whether they were Infantry (USCI), Cavalry (USCC) or Heavy Artillery (USCHA).

Military necessity

The reasoning behind the decision to raise black regiments was not necessarily along the idealistic lines that men such as Frederick Douglass would have welcomed. In part, it was seen by some as a war measure. The belief that slavery underpinned the Confederate war effort persuaded some Northerners of the need to remove this support from the South. Foreign opinion also

[196] played a part, although it was less important than was once thought. Above all, the war had not been going well for the Union throughout 1862, and the decision to allow blacks to join the Union army coincided with the first draft in the North. Yet in some ways this worked in the blacks' favour. One soldier observed, with some irony, that '[j]ust in proportion as the certainty of a draft increased, did the prejudice against Negro soldiers decrease. It was discovered that Negroes were not only loyal persons and good mule drivers, but exceedingly competent to bear arms.'[12] Even if prejudice did not decrease, racist objections to the arming of blacks could easily be countered on the grounds that it was better that a black soldier die than a white one. Such attitudes were summed up accurately if cruelly in a poem written by Lt. Col. Charles Halpine, under the pen name of 'Private Miles O'Reilly', entitled 'Sambo's Right to Be Kilt' which ran:

> The men who object to Sambo
> Should take his place an' fight'
> And it's better to have a naygur's hue
> Than a liver that's wake an' white.
> Though Sambo's black as the ace of spades,
> His finger a trigger can pull,
> And his eye runs straight on the barrel-sights
> From under his thatch of wool!
> So hear me all, boys, darlings, –
> Don't think I tippin' you chaff, –
> The right to be kilt I'll divide wid him,
> And give him the largest half![13]

Abraham Lincoln sought to convey a rather more positive version of the message in his famous letter to James Conkling, written in August 1863, in which Lincoln defended his emancipation decision in the face of criticism that he was changing the nature of the war. 'You say you will not fight to free negroes. Some of them seem willing to fight for you,' Lincoln noted, 'but no matter . . . I thought that whatever Negroes could be got to do as soldiers leaves just so much less for white soldiers to do, in saving the Union.' This was Lincoln appealing to the practical side of the question, but in conclusion he made a more incisive observation on the future of the nation and the role of African-Americans in it when he argued that:

> there will be some black men who can remember that, with silent tongue and clenched teeth, and steady eye, and well-poised bayonet, they have helped mankind on to this great consummation; while, I fear, there will be some white

ones unable to forget that, with malignant heart, and deceitful speech, they have strove to hinder it.[14]

For many blacks, Lincoln's latter point was the important one, and they were initially confident that their acceptance, however reluctantly granted, by the Union army offered them the opportunity both of short-term military glory and longer-term acceptance into the nation as a whole. As Frederick Douglass put it, 'once let the black man get upon his person the brass letters U.S., let him get an eagle on his button, and a musket on his shoulder and bullets in his pocket, and there is no power on earth which can deny that he has earned the right to citizenship in the United States.'[15] George E. Stephens, a Philadelphia cabinetmaker and volunteer in the 54th Massachusetts Colored Infantry (the famous 'Massachusetts 54th'), argued that the Union army was 'the proper field for colored men, where they may win by their valor the esteem of all loyal men and women – believing that "Who would be free, themselves must strike the blow."'[16]

Corporal James Henry Gooding, a former seaman and another volunteer in the Massachusetts 54th, similarly reminded his people that 'their position is a very delicate one; the least false step, at a moment like the present, may tell a dismal tale at some future day.' It was essential, Gooding argued, that the black soldier be seen to be active in this regard, and he warned blacks throughout the Union 'not to trust to a fancied security, laying comfort to your minds, that our condition will be bettered because slavery must die. It depends on the free black men of the North, whether it will die or not.' If blacks left it to whites to effect emancipation, Gooding concluded, 'language cannot depict the indignity, the scorn, and perhaps violence, that will be heaped upon us; unthought of laws will be enacted and put in force, to banish us from the land of our birth.' He stressed the need for blacks to grasp the opportunity now being offered in a letter to the New Bedford *Mercury:*

> Our people must know that if they are ever to attain to any position in the eyes of the civilized world, they must forego comfort, home, fear, and above all, superstition, and fight for it; make up their minds to become something more than hewers of wood and drawers of water all their lives. Consider that on this continent, at least, their race and name will be totally obliterated unless they put forth some effort now to save themselves.[17]

Gooding anticipated, optimistically, that 'if the colored man proves to be as good a soldier as it is confidently expected he will, there is a permanent field of employment opened to him, with all the chances of promotion in his favor.' The 1st Arkansas Colored Regiment had an equally optimistic view of the future following the Emancipation Proclamation. They gleefully marched into battle singing, to the tune of 'John Brown's Body':

> We have done with hoeing cotton, we have done with hoeing corn,
> We are colored Yankee soldiers, now, as sure as you are born;
> When the masters hear us yelling, they'll think it's Gabriel's horn,
> As it went sounding on.
>
> They will have to pay us wages, the wages of their sin,
> They will have to bow their foreheads to their colored kith and kin,
> They will have to give us house-room, or the roof shall tumble in!
> As we go marching on.
>
> Father Abraham has spoken, and the message has been sent,
> The prison doors he opened, and out the prisoners went,
> To join the sable army of the 'African descent,'
> As we go marching on.[18]

Not everyone shared such optimism. One black New Yorker argued that it would be foolish for blacks to heed the Union's call to arms since the race had 'nothing to gain, and everything to lose, by entering the lists as combatants.' To respond to the Union's call for troops, he asserted, would be simply to repeat the errors of previous generations of blacks, who had 'put confidence in the words of the whites only to feel the dagger of slavery driven deeper.' Given the virulent racism of the North, he concluded, free blacks were in 'no condition to fight under the flag which gives us no protection.'[19] Initially, the pessimistic view appeared to be the more accurate one. The white response to the raising of black regiments was far from positive, and indeed in some ways inspired a backlash against the whole idea of emancipation. Despite the relative success of racist arguments in favour of blacks rather than whites being killed, most whites did not believe that blacks would make effective soldiers, seeing them as, at best, cannon fodder.

'Blooding' of black troops

Both white and suspicious black attitudes began to change only with the battlefield successes of several of the black regiments. Even before its official recognition by the War Department, Jim Lane's black regiment had performed well in Missouri, prompting one journalist to write that it was 'useless to talk any more about negro courage. The men fought like tigers, each and every one of them.'[20] Skirmishes between Thomas Wentworth Higginson's 1st South Carolina and the rebels, and between Benjamin Butler's 2nd Louisiana Native Guards (later the 74th US Colored Infantry) and Confederate cavalry and infantry regiments were equally decisive in terms of proving that the black troops could and would fight, but as mere skirmishes they did little to alter the northern public's perception of the colored regiments. The first major engagement for the black regiments came in the spring of 1863, with an assault on Port Hudson on the Mississippi in Louisiana. The assault itself was misconceived, and the Union army suffered a defeat, but for the black troops who had fought there Port Hudson proved a turning-point of sorts. This was recognized by some white troops as well as by black. Before the actual assault, white private Henry T. Johns expressed his belief that the black regiments would perform well, and that consequently whites would 'give them a share in *our* nationality, if God has no separate nationality in store for them.'[21] In the aftermath of the battle, Johns's optimism seemed justified. One lieutenant reported that his company had fought bravely, adding 'they are mostly contrabands, and I must say I entertained some fears as to their pluck. But I have none now.' The New York *Times* was similarly impressed:

> Those black soldiers had never before been in any severe engagement. They were comparatively raw troops, and were yet subjected to the most awful ordeal than even veterans ever have to experience – the charging upon fortifications through the crash of belching batteries. The men, white or black, who will not flinch from that will flinch from nothing. It is no longer possible to doubt the bravery and steadiness of the colored race, when rightly led.[22]

If further proof were required that the black soldier had potential one of the Civil War's most bloody engagements, the Battle of Milliken's Bend in June 1863, came shortly after the Port Hudson defeat. Here, too, raw black recruits found themselves facing substantial Confederate forces. In the black units engaged, casualties ran to 35 per cent and for the 9th Louisiana Infantry (later the 5th US Colored Heavy Artillery) alone casualties reached 45 per cent. The cost was clearly high but, as at Port Hudson, white commanders declared themselves impressed with the behaviour under fire of the black troops. Charles A. Dana, the Assistant Secretary of War, concluded that 'the sentiment in regard to the employment of negro troops has been revolutionized by the bravery of the blacks in the recent Battle of Milliken's Bend. Prominent officers, who used in private sneer at the idea, are now heartily in favor of it.'[23]

At the same time as black soldiers were proving their valour on the Mississippi at Port Hudson and Milliken's Bend, the North's most famous coloured regiment, the Massachusetts 54th, was preparing to set off from Massachusetts toward its first major campaign and a place in the history books. Fort Wagner, on the northern tip of Morris Island in South Carolina, was the main defence both for Charleston and for Battery Gregg which overlooked the entrance to Charleston Harbour. The taking of the fort would have been a significant prize for the Union forces, enabling them to attack Fort Sumter – where the Civil War had begun in April 1861 – and, it was hoped, Charleston itself. Originally, the plan had been to use the 54th in a minor supporting role, but its commander, Robert Gould Shaw, recognized the importance of taking an active part in the forthcoming engagement and campaigned vigorously for his regiment to be given a more prominent role in the attack. Shaw was successful, and the 54th received orders to head the attack on the fort on 18 July 1863. Shaw and his men regarded this as an honour, although Major General Truman Seymour, in agreeing to Shaw's request, expressed the opinion that it was a good idea to 'put those d . . . d niggers from Massachusetts in the advance; we may as well get rid of them one time as another.'[24]

As with Port Hudson, the attack on Fort Wagner, one of the most heavily defended and impregnable of the Confederate forts, was doomed to failure, and the Union forces sustained heavy casualties. The Massachusetts 54th lost over half its men, including Robert Gould Shaw who was shot through the heart as he took the parapet of the fort. His troops held the ground he had reached for barely an hour. To add insult to injury, the Confederates refused to return Shaw's body to his family, as was normal procedure for senior ranks. When Shaw's father requested that his son's body be returned, a Confederate officer is reported to have denied the request with the words, 'We have buried him with his niggers.' In the face of this deliberate insult, Shaw's father merely responded that, 'We hold that a soldier's most appropriate burial place is on the field where he has fallen.'[25] Following the disaster of Fort Wagner the Massachusetts 54th and her sister regiment, the 55th, did achieve military victories against the Confederacy, but in the more general battle against racism Fort Wagner, like Port Hudson, was a significant, although not complete, success. One white Union soldier, who had expressed extreme hostility toward black troops prior to the 54th's attack on the fort, felt compelled to declare afterwards that in his opinion the '54th Mass Infantry "colored" is as good a fighting regiment as there is in the 10th Army Corps Department of the South.' Yet his objections to fighting alongside black troops remained.[26]

More positively, at the end of the Civil War, the New York *Tribune* reminded its readers that to the 'Massachusetts Fifty-fourth was set the stupendous task to convince the white race that colored troops would fight, – and not only that they would fight, but that they could be made, in every sense of the word, soldiers.' From the outset, much had been riding on this particular regiment. Raised by Governor John Andrew of Massachusetts and numbering the sons of noted abolitionists and prominent Bostonians among its ranks – not only Robert Gould Shaw but two of Frederick Douglass's sons fought in the 54th – much more than military success was at stake when the Massachusetts 54th marched out of Boston, to cheering crowds, in the spring of 1863. As the New York *Tribune* put it:

> It is not too much to say that if this Massachusetts Fifty-fourth had faltered when its trial came, two hundred thousand colored troops for whom it was a pioneer would never have been put into the field, or would not have been put in for another year, which would have been equivalent to protracting the war into 1866. But it did not falter. It made Fort Wagner such a name to the colored race as Bunker Hill has been for ninety years to the white Yankees.[27]

Thanks in part to the bravery of the Massachusetts 54th, therefore, by the end of 1863 the Union army had recruited some 50,000 African-Americans – both free blacks and former slaves – to its ranks. By the end of the war this number had risen to some 186,000, of which 134,111 were recruited in the slave states. African-American troops comprised 10 per cent of the total Union fighting force, and some 3,000 of them died on the battlefield plus many more of disease and in the prisoner of war camps, if they made it that far. By 1865, black troops had taken part in 39 major battles, some 449 engagements, and twenty-one of them had received the Congressional Medal of Honor.[28] Toward the end of 1863 Henry S. Harmon, a soldier in the 3rd USCI, felt confident enough to declare that 'you can say of the colored man, we too have borne our share of the burden. We too have suffered and died in defence of that starry banner which floats only over free men. . . . I feel assured that the name of the colored soldier will stand out in bold relief among the heroes of this war.'[29]

The propaganda success of the assaults on Port Hudson, Milliken's Bend and Fort Wagner were, however, only part of the story as far as African-American troops were concerned. The fact that blacks had shown that they could fight in no way diminished the prejudice they experienced in the Union army. Nor did it resolve the crux of the issue which was that the war, for many of the black troops, was in essence a very different conflict from that experienced by the whites. In purely practical terms, the conditions experienced by African-American troops were far inferior to those experienced by some white ones. It is important not to overstate this, however, as racism alone was not always the root cause. The fact was that by the time the African-American regiments were raised and sent into the field the Civil War had been going on for almost two years. Fresh recruits, therefore, of whatever colour, found themselves facing a rebel army which had much more combat experience. At Milliken's Bend, for example, the most experienced officers had been in uniform for less than a month. Even worse, some of the black troops had received only two days of target practice prior to going into battle, and in a war where fast reloading was crucial for survival, they simply lacked the necessary skill. When the 29th USCT arrived at Camp Casey in 1864, for example, they were issued with the .58 calibre Springfield Rifled Musket. They were not, however, given any training in how to use this beyond basic parade evolutions. In such circumstances it was unsurprising that the troops struggled under battlefield conditions.[30] Similarly, the racist comments of Major General Seymour notwithstanding, in the attack on Fort Wagner it was not necessarily the case that the Massachusetts 54th was sent in on a suicidal mission. Throughout the Civil War, Bay State regiments fought in the front line of some of the very worst battles, and consequently Massachusetts had some of the highest combat casualties of any of the Union states. In this regard the Massachusetts 54th was continuing the tradition of the Bay State troops in July 1863, which would hardly have been a comfort to them.

Second class soldiers

Unfortunately, deliberately prejudicial policies compounded the more general problems that the African-American regiments faced after 1863. Most obviously, blacks were never promoted on a par with whites. Benjamin Butler, in mustering in the Louisiana regiments, had created a mixed officer class. Jim Lane in Kansas did likewise, and since he was acting against orders anyway he never troubled himself to defend his actions. However, when Governor Andrew sought to appoint black officers to the 54th and 55th Massachusetts, he was told that white officers only would be accepted. Similarly, when Jim Lane's Kansas regiments were officially recognized, its black officers were not. In the South Nathaniel P. Banks, on taking over from Butler, promptly set about removing – by fair means and foul – all the black officers, usually by forcing them to resign following a deliberate campaign of humiliation. In many cases the argument used to defend such blatant racism was that the blacks concerned lacked the necessary literacy and military knowledge to cope with high command. In many cases, particularly as far as the contraband regiments were concerned, there was an element of truth to the charge. Unfortunately, white officers had no more experience, and were no more capable in this regard, than the blacks. The only difference was that the white officers were not being put under the microscope to the same extent. By 1865 only one in 2,000 black troops had achieved officer rank, mostly as chaplains or physicians.

The African-American regiments also received a greater proportion of fatigue duty than many of the white regiments. This meant not only that they were not receiving essential fighting experience, but the nature of the duties required of them meant that their uniforms become worn out very quickly, giving them the appearance of labourers rather than of soldiers. The quality of weapons distributed to the black regiments was also not always on a par with those the white regiments received, although again it is important to bear in mind that adequate weaponry – and more importantly the ability to use it – was a problem for many regiments, both black and white. Medical care for the black regiments was equally discriminatory, and a particular problem given the high rate of combat casualties in these regiments. Many of the black troops, being relatively new to the field, had little immunity to the diseases that infected the camps, and the problem was compounded by a white assumption that blacks were not as susceptible to disease as whites. Finding surgeons to work with black troops was also difficult. Again, racism alone does not account for this. By 1863 there was a general shortage of physicians in the Union army, and those that could put up with the rigours of camp life had long ago been employed by regiments formed earlier in the war.

Poor morale problems and combat stress also affected the black regiments to a greater degree, in part because some of them suffered under the leadership of unprincipled officers. Several of the Virginia regiments reported low morale, and members of the 38th USCT almost rebelled because of the treatment they received from their officers.[31] This, however, was nothing in comparison to the treatment black troops suffered at the hands of some of the Confederate regiments. Depressingly, but perhaps unsurprisingly, a greater proportion of wartime atrocities were directed at the coloured regiments. The most notorious incident occurred in April 1864, at Fort Pillow, north of Memphis. A force of some 1,500 Confederates, under the command of Major General Nathan Bedford Forrest – later to found the notorious Ku Klux

Klan – demanded the surrender of the fort which was manned by about 500
Union troops, half of them black. In the fighting that ensued some 66 per
cent of the black troops were killed as opposed to 33 per cent of the whites.
The Fort Pillow incident was investigated by the Joint Committee on the
Conduct of the War, which concluded that a massacre had taken place and
that most of the garrison had been murdered after it had surrendered. Northern
public opinion rallied to the black troops in the wake of Fort Pillow, but,
as with Port Hudson and Fort Wagner, it was a high price to pay for the
recognition of valour.[32]

Of all the discriminatory policies to impact on the African-American
regiments, the most damning related to pay. At the outset, however, there
was no indication that the War Department intended to pay black troops
less than white. When Governor Andrew was granted permission to raise the
Massachusetts 54th, for example, he was instructed to offer $13.00 per month
plus rations and clothing, along with a bounty of $50.00 for signing up and
$100.00 on mustering out. In 1863, the army paymaster actually gave the
33rd Colored Infantry the standard pay. Unfortunately, in June of that year
the War Department decided that black troops were entitled to only $10.00
per month, of which $3.00 should be deducted for clothing. The reasoning
was that the raising of black regiments came under the Militia Act of 1862,
which specified the lower rate of pay on the grounds that it had not anticipated combatant blacks. Even before this, however, the promised $50.00
bounty was slow in coming, and in some cases never appeared at all.

For many blacks, the problem went far beyond a simple insult. Their families depended on the money. The matter prompted an angry backlash from
both black troops and many of their officers. Robert Gould Shaw was one
who refused to take any pay unless his men received the full $13.00 per month,
but this was a sacrifice that his troops found harder to make than he did.
Governor Andrew, embarrassed at the turn of events, offered to make up the
difference out of his own pocket, but the 54th would not let him. There was
a principle at stake. James Henry Gooding of the 54th wrote in some anger to
the New Bedford *Mercury*, reminding its readers 'that the colored men generally, as a class, have nothing to depend upon but their daily labor; so, consequently, when they leave their labors and take up arms in defence of their
country, their homes are left destitute of those little necessities which their
families must enjoy as well as those of white men; and as the city has passed a
resolution to pay them a sum, they would rather their families received it than
become objects of public charity.'[33] One of his comrades concurred: 'Now it
seems strange to me that we do not receive the same pay and rations as the
white soldiers. Do we not fill the same ranks? Do we not cover the same space

of ground? Do we not take up the same length of ground in a graveyard that others do? The ball does not miss the black man and strike the white, nor miss the white and strike the black.' Corporal John B. Payne, of Gooding's sister regiment the Massachusetts 55th, likewise declared: 'I am not willing to fight for anything less than the white man fights for. If the white man cannot support his family on seven dollars per month, I cannot support mine on the same amount.'[34]

The issue of pay went beyond prejudice alone. It represented the crux of the problem for those African-American regiments who fought in the Civil War, and threw into sharp focus many of the inconsistencies and contradictions that lay at the heart of Union war aims. The Union had, from the very start of the war, been faced with two distinct yet linked problems: the role of the free black and the future of the slave. Equality and emancipation were not synonymous, but at the same time one could not be addressed without affecting the other. The question over the rights of citizenship for the free Northern black went hand in hand with the larger and more troubling question of slavery – for many the root cause of the conflict. Northern blacks were very well aware of this and, unlike Northern whites, could not and would not avoid the wider implications of the Civil War. Thomas D. Freeman, of the Massachusetts 54th, described not just the financial difficulties that his regiment were facing but summed up the wider problem in a letter to his brother-in-law in 1864:

> the Regiment in general are in Good Health but in Low Spirits and no reason why for they have all to a man done there duty as a soldier it is 1 Year the 1st Day of April since I enlisted and there is men here in the regiment that have been in Enlisted 13 Months and have never received one cent But there bounty and they more or less have family . . . we are not Soldiers but Labourers working for Uncle Sam for nothing but our board and clothes . . . we never can be Elevated in this country while such rascality is Performed Slavery with all its horrors can not Equalise this for it is nothing but work from morning till night Building Batteries Hauling Guns Cleaning Bricks clearing up land for other Regiments to settle on . . . now do you call this Equality if so God help such Equality.[35]

Lincoln's reasons for hesitating over emancipation were valid ones, but he knew that the matter had to be addressed. The question was when and how. The Emancipation Proclamation, when it came on 1 January 1863, was not perfect. Lincoln knew that it would have to be confirmed via a constitutional amendment. But it did irrevocably commit the Union to a policy of attacking slavery, and made it impossible to deny to blacks the right to fight as full members of the citizen army of the Union.

For many African-Americans, including Frederick Douglass, the Emancipation Proclamation was long overdue, and the discrimination suffered by the black soldiers represented a troubling omen for the future. George E. Stephens voiced his anger over the matter: 'After we have endured a slavery of two hundred and fifty years we are to pay for the privilege to fight and die to enable the North to conquer the South – what an idea! to pay for the privilege to fight for that tardy and at best doubtful freedom vouchsafed to us by the government.' He returned to this theme a few months later, and expanded on the relationship between pay and patriotism. 'The matter of pay seems to some of those having slaveholding tendencies a small thing,' he noted, 'but it belongs to that system which has stripped the country of the flower of its youth. . . . Like as the foaming waves point the mariner to the hidden rocks on which his storm-driven ship will soon be lost, this gross injustice reveals to us the hidden insidious principles on which the best hopes of the true patriot will be dashed.' For Stephens the matter was a simple one, and he reminded the readers of the *Anglo-African* of it starkly: 'Our destiny is united with that of the country – with its triumph we rise, with its defeat we fall.'[36]

Leading African-American spokesman like Stephens saw the Civil War very much as a war for emancipation long before it became apparent to them that Lincoln shared this view and was far ahead of a Northern public who, like James Conkling, regarded it as a war for the restoration of the Union as it had been, with slavery intact. William H. Johnson, of the 8th Connecticut Infantry, was arguing that the Civil War was a war for freedom long before Lincoln issued the Emancipation Proclamation and the Union began recruiting blacks. Writing from North Carolina in 1862 he expressed the 'hope to meet the enemy again, fight, conquer him, end the rebellion, and then come home to our Northern people, to freemen who look South with joyous hearts, and behold not a single Slave State – but only free territory, from Maryland to Texas.' He was confident that the Union armies would, ultimately, 'defeat the rebels, and hang slavery'.[37]

Second class citizens

Frederick Douglass, too, had been arguing that the Civil War had to be linked to the cause of freedom from the earliest days of the war. What Douglass meant by freedom, however, went far beyond George Stephens's

vision. Rather than the destiny of the black man being linked to the Union's
success in the Civil War, Douglass was more of the opinion that the future of
the American Republican experiment itself rested on the triumph of the black
soldier and the freed slave. For Douglass, the evil of slavery had corrupted
the white man as much as it had degraded the slave, and the Civil War was
an opportunity not just to end the institution but to rededicate the nation to
the principles set out in the Declaration of Independence. Freedom for both
white and black depended not just on a Union victory but on a complete
reassessment of the national ideal. Speaking in Boston in 1862, he advised
his audience:

> My friends, the destiny of the colored American, however this mighty war shall
> terminate, is the destiny of America. We shall never leave you. The allotments
> of Providence seem to make the black man of America the open book out
> of which the American people are to learn lessons of wisdom, power, and
> goodness – more sublime and glorious than any yet attained by the nations of
> the old or the new world. Over the bleeding back of the American bondsman
> we shall learn mercy. In the very extreme difference of color and feature of the
> negro and the Anglo-Saxon, shall be learned the highest ideas of sacredness
> of man and the fullness and protection of human brotherhood.[38]

Ultimately, the problem facing both African-American soldiers and their
non-combatant spokesmen in the North was that their vision of the meaning
of the Civil War clashed with that of the majority of whites. For blacks, the
Civil War offered an opportunity not just to end slavery, but to redefine
American national ideals. Their determination to fight in the face of hostility
and prejudice left their dedication to these national ideals in no doubt
whatsoever. In this regard, African-Americans during the Civil War had a far
more expansive, optimistic and demanding vision of the nation's future than
many whites did. They had proved themselves to be 'patriot soldiers' to a
far greater extent than some whites. As George Stephens noted only a few
months after Fort Sumter fell, 'this land must be consecrated to freedom, and
we are today the only class of people in the country who are earnestly on the
side of freedom.'[39]

This message was reiterated time and again in the course of the conflict.
Following the Emancipation Proclamation, James Henry Gooding declared
that the 'American people, as a nation, knew not what they were fighting for
till recently.' In the aftermath of the New York City Draft Riots of 1863,
George Stephens took the opportunity to remind white Americans that
'even while your mob-fiends upheld the assassin knife, and brandished the
incendiary torch over the heads of our wives and children and to burn their

homes, we were doing our utmost to sustain the honor of our country's flag, to perpetuate, if possible, those civil, social, and political liberties, they, who so malignantly hate us, have so fully enjoyed.'[40] That black troops were showing much more dedication to the nation's ideals than many whites in the midst of the Civil War cannot have been a message that whites wished to hear.

Yet, at the war's conclusion the future did, initially, look promising, and several of the black regiments received a heroes' welcome. The Massachusetts 54th was honoured at a reception in Boston in September 1865, and the Boston *Evening Transcript* reported the event in glowing terms:

> The Fifty-fourth Massachusetts Regiment, the pioneer State colored regiment of this country, recruited at a time when great prejudices existed against enlisting any but so-called white men in the army, when a colored soldiery was considered in the light of an experiment almost certain to fail, this command – which now returns crowned with laurels, and after two hundred thousand of their brethren, from one end of the traitorous South to the other, have fought themselves into public esteem – had such a reception today as befitted an organization the history of which is admitted to form so conspicuous a part of the annals of the country.[41]

The paper's optimism proved to be premature. When Joseph T. Wilson, a veteran of Port Hudson, came to write his history of black troops in the American army in 1887, he concluded sadly that their 'devotion has been not only unappreciated, but it has failed to receive a fitting commemoration in the pages of national history.'[42] Ultimately, to the detriment of the black soldier and his role in the Civil War, whites simply chose to ignore not only the sacrifice of the African-American regiments but the implications of their involvement in America's greatest national crisis. The opportunity to reconstruct the United States on the basis of full racial equality was thrown away. Instead, the reconciliation of the North and South was based on an increasingly selective interpretation of what the Civil War had been about. In the Gettysburg Address, Lincoln had expressed the hope that the nation might experience 'a new birth of freedom', yet North and South increasingly looked to the past, and not to the future, when contemplating the recent conflict. Increasingly over the years, the Civil War became less about changing than preserving the American nation. If the Union had been preserved in an altered form, there were many African-Americans who could have been forgiven for not appreciating the difference between the old Union and the new. As the African-American writer and activist Frances Harper saw it, post-war whites continued to regard her race as 'good enough for soldiers, but not [209] good enough for citizens'.[43]

On Memorial Day in 1871, speaking at the Tomb of the Unknown Soldier at Arlington, Frederick Douglass observed with sadness the call 'in the name of patriotism to forget the merits of this fearful struggle, and to remember with equal admiration those who struck at the nation's life, and those who struck to save it.'[44] In the end, the need to find some common ground between North and South encouraged the growth of a patriotism that could not acknowledge the sacrifices of the African-American soldier. This was a patriotism in which the pride of those black troops who had fought and died for a Union that chose to betray them had no valid place.[45] By the time Douglass spoke the process of constructing monuments to the Civil War was beginning, a process that gathered momentum during the 1880s and 1890s. Few of the monuments acknowledged the role taken by African-American troops in the conflict. The explanation for this, again, goes beyond racism alone. The link between the figure of the black soldier and the emancipation issue was too unsettling for a nation which, it was clear by the 1890s, had failed to live up to both Lincoln's and Douglass's expectations. As both North and South devoted themselves to the practicalities of reunion, any reminder of the causes of the Civil War proved unwelcome.[46] Equally unwelcome was any reminder that African-American troops had willingly fought not just for freedom for their race but in defence of a Union which, once reestablished, continued to deny them the full benefits of citizenship. Saint-Gaudens's monument, therefore, was destined to be, and was until only recently to remain, one of only a very few commemorative sites that acknowledged the sacrifice of African-American troops in the American Civil War.[47]

On 31 May 1997, 100 years after Saint-Gaudens's monument was first unveiled, a rededication ceremony was held at the site. The day included an historical re-enactment of Shaw's troops leaving for the South and a speech by General Colin Powell in which he drew parallels between the Union's decision to raise black regiments during the Civil War and the contemporary army's leading role in the fight for racial equality in America today. Despite Colin Powell's words, however, despite the many thousands of books written to date on the American Civil War and despite the cinematic success of a Hollywood film about the Massachusetts 54th, *Glory,* the war continues to be regarded by many as a white man's war. For many, the importance of Saint-Gaudens's monument lies not in the black troops that are represented by it, but in the sacrifice of the regiment's white colonel, Robert Gould Shaw, whose death inspired Ralph Waldo Emerson to reflect:

So nigh is grandeur to our dust,
So near is God to man,
When Duty whispers low, *Thou must,*
The youth replies, *I can.*[48]

To acknowledge this in no way diminishes either the heroism or the tragedy of Shaw's death on the ramparts of Fort Wagner. Yet the very poignancy of this Boston youth's untimely end has served to obscure, to a great extent, the cause for which he gave his life, and the equally tragic deaths of those black troops who fought alongside him. The significance of the African-American soldier in America's most bloody conflict to date continues to be downplayed, since neither the race nor the nation achieved the kind of freedom that so many, both black and white, had fought and died for.

Notes

1. Robert Hughes, *American Visions: The Epic History of Art in America* (New York, 1997), pp. 209–10. For an extended discussion of Augustus Saint-Gaudens's approach to the monument, see Kirk Savage, *Standing Soldiers, Kneeling Slaves: Race, War, and Monument in Nineteenth-Century America* (Princeton, NJ, 1997), pp. 193–203.

2. Stuart McConnell, *Glorious Contentment: The Grand Army of the Republic, 1865–1900* (Chapel Hill, NC and London, 1992), p. 8.

3. On this subject see Brooks D. Simpson, 'Quandaries of command: Ulysses S. Grant and black soldiers', in David W. Blight and Brooks D. Simpson (eds), *Union and Emancipation: Essays on Politics and Race in the Civil War Era* (Kent, Oh. and London, 1997), pp. 133–4. Sherman's divisions did have black labourers marching ahead of the soldiers during the Grand Review. On this, see Charles Royster, *The Destructive War: William Tecumseh Sherman, Stonewall Jackson, and the Americans* (1991; paperback reprint, New York, 1993), p. 413.

4. Simpson, 'Quandaries of command', p. 123.

5. Brian Holden Reid, *The Origins of the American Civil War* (London, 1996), p. 25.

6. Andrew Jackson quoted in Robert W. Mullen, *Blacks in America's Wars: The Shift in Attitudes from the Revolutionary War to Vietnam* (New York, 1973), p. 15.

7. Frederick Douglass, 'The black man's future in the Southern states', an address delivered in Boston, 5 February 1862, in Louis P. Masur, *The Real War Will*

Never Get in the Books: Selections from Writers during the Civil War (New York and [211] Oxford, 1993), p. 110.

8. Frederick Douglass quoted in Dudley Taylor Cornish, *The Sable Arm: Negro Troops in the Union Army, 1861–1865* (New York, 1966), pp. 5–6.

9. *National Intelligencer*, 8 October 1861.

10. Phillip Shaw Paludan, *A People's Contest: The Union and Civil War, 1861–1865*, 2nd edn (Lawrence, Ks, 1996), p. 65.

11. Thomas Wentworth Higginson, *Army Life in a Black Regiment* (Boston, Mass., 1962), p. 15. *Army Life* was first published in 1869.

12. Quoted in Edward A. Miller, Jr, *The Black Civil War Soldiers of Illinois: The Story of the Twenty-ninth U.S. Colored Infantry* (Columbia, SC, 1998), p. 5.

13. Quoted in Ervin L. Jordan, Jr, *Black Confederates and Afro-Yankees in Civil War Virginia* (Charlottesville, Va and London, 1995), p. 266.

14. Abraham Lincoln to James C. Conkling, 26 August 1863, in Roy F. Basler (ed.), *The Collected Works of Abraham Lincoln*, 2nd printing (New Brunswick, NJ, 1988), vol. 6, pp. 409–10.

15. Frederick Douglass quoted in James M. McPherson, *Marching Toward Freedom: The Negro in the Civil War, 1861–1865* (New York, 1967), p. 68.

16. George E. Stephens to the New York *Weekly Anglo-African*, 7 August 1863, in Donald Yacavone (ed.), *A Voice of Thunder: The Civil War Letters of George E. Stephens* (Urbana and Chicago, Ill., 1997), p. 254.

17. Corporal James Henry Gooding to the New Bedford *Mercury*, 3 March 1863, in Corporal James Henry Gooding, *On the Altar of Freedom: A Black Soldier's Civil War Letters from the Front*, ed. Virginia M. Adams (Amherst, Mass., 1991), pp. 4, 13.

18. Marching Song of the First Arkansas Colored Regiment, quoted in Mullen, *Blacks in America's Wars*, pp. 23–4. There were seven verses in all.

19. Quoted in McPherson, *Marching Toward Freedom*, p. 10.

20. Chicago *Tribune*, 10 November 1862, quoted in Joseph T. Glatthaar, *Forged in Battle: The Civil War Alliance of Black Soldiers and White Officers* (New York, 1991), p. 122.

21. Johns quoted in Leon F. Litwack, *Been in the Storm So Long: The Aftermath of Slavery* (1979; reprint New York, 1980), p. 70.

22. New York *Times*, 11 June 1863, quoted in Glatthaar, *Forged in Battle*, p. 130.

23. Charles A. Dana quoted in Glatthaar, *Forged in Battle,* p. 135.

24. Seymour to Maj. Gen. Quincy A. Gillmore, quoted in Glatthaar, *Forged in Battle,* p. 137.

25. On the reaction to Shaw's death, see George M. Fredrickson, *The Inner Civil War: Northern Intellectuals and the Crisis of the Union* (1965; New York, 1968), pp. 152–6.

26. George M. Turner, to various members of his family, 15 December 1861; 19 June 1862; 13 August 1862; 28 July 1863; and 2 May 1864, in Nina Silber and Mary Beth Sievens (eds), *Yankee Correspondence: Civil War Letters between New England Soldiers and the Home Front* (Charlottesville, Va and London, 1996), pp. 84–7.

27. New York *Tribune,* 8 September 1865.

28. Figures taken from Paludan, *A People's Contest,* p. 214.

29. Henry S. Harmon, Corporal, Co.B, 3rd USCI, Morris Island, South Carolina, to the *Christian Recorder,* 23 October 1863. The letter appeared in the paper on 7 November 1863. Edwin S. Redkey, (ed.), *A Grand Army of Black Men: Letters from African-American Soldiers in the Union Army, 1861–1865* (New York and Cambridge, 1992), p. 36.

30. See Miller, *The Black Civil War Soldiers of Illinois,* pp. 43–4.

31. Jordan, *Black Confederates,* p. 271.

32. For a discussion of the killing of black prisoners of war at the Battle of the Crater in 1864, see Miller, *The Black Civil War Soldiers of Illinois,* pp. 77–88.

33. Corporal James Henry Gooding to the New Bedford *Mercury,* 21 March 1863, in Gooding, *On the Altar of Freedom,* p. 7. The letter appeared on 24 March.

34. Unnamed private to the *Christian Recorder,* March 1864; Corporal John H.B. Payne in the *Christian Recorder,* 11 June 1864, both in Redkey, *A Grand Army of Black Men,* pp. 48, 208.

35. T.D. Freeman to William, 26 March 1864, in Silber and Sievens (eds), *Yankee Correspondence,* pp. 47–8.

36. Yacovone, *A Voice of Thunder,* pp. 281–2, 321, 288.

37. Redkey, *A Grand Army of Black Men,* p. 18.

38. Frederick Douglass, 'The black man's future in the Southern states', an address delivered in Boston, Massachusetts, 5 February 1862, in Masur, *The Real War Will Never Get in the Books,* p. 111.

39. George E. Stephens writing in November 1861, to the *Weekly Anglo-African*, in Yacovone, *A Voice of Thunder*, p. 141.

40. Gooding, 11 May 1863, *On the Altar of Freedom*, p. 19; George E. Stephens to the *Weekly Anglo-African*, August 1863, Yacovone, *A Voice of Thunder*, pp. 250–1.

41. Quoted in Luis F. Emilio, *A Brave Black Regiment: History of the Fifty-Fourth Regiment of Massachusetts Volunteer Infantry, 1863–1865* (1894; New York, 1992), p. 334.

42. Joseph T. Wilson, *The Black Phalanx: African American Soldiers in the War of Independence, the War of 1812 and the Civil War* (1887; New York, 1994), p. 462.

43. Frances E.W. Harper, 'We are all bound up together', from *Proceedings of the Eleventh Women's Rights Convention* (1866), in Karen L. Kilcup (ed.), *Nineteenth-Century American Women Writers: An Anthology* (Cambridge, Mass. and Oxford, 1997), p. 157.

44. Frederick Douglass quoted in David W. Blight, '"For something beyond the battlefield": Frederick Douglass and the struggle for the memory of the Civil War', *Journal of American History* 75, 4 (March 1989), p. 1160.

45. On this subject see S.-M. Grant, '"The charter of its birthright": the Civil War and American nationalism', in *Nations and Nationalism* 4, 2 (1998), pp. 163–85.

46. On this point, see Savage, *Standing Soldiers, Kneeling Slaves*, pp. 179–81 and passim.

47. On 18 July 1998, 'The Spirit of Freedom', the centrepiece of a memorial to all African-American troops who had fought in the Civil War, was dedicated in Washington DC.

48. Ralph Waldo Emerson, 'Voluntaries'. This poem appeared in the *Atlantic Monthly* in October 1863. Reprinted in Richard Marius (ed.), *The Columbia Book of Civil War Poetry* (New York, 1994), pp. 79–84.

.

PART THREE

THE RACE FRONT

CHAPTER NINE

THE FIGHT FOR BLACK SUFFRAGE IN THE WAR OF THE REBELLION

ROBERT COOK

On 11 April 1865, at the end of a day of celebrations in Washington following the Confederate surrender at Appomattox, President Abraham Lincoln appeared at a second-storey window of the White House and delivered a short speech on the thorny problem of restoring the Southern states to their normal relations within the Union. Towards the end of his address (which was, in large measure, a vigorous defence of his wartime reconstruction policy in Louisiana), Lincoln confessed that it was unfortunate that the Unionist-controlled state government in New Orleans in which he had invested so many of his hopes had so far failed to give the vote to loyal blacks. 'I would', he said, 'myself prefer that it were now conferred on the very intelligent, and on those who serve our cause as soldiers.'[1] Granted that this was an endorsement of partial rather than impartial or universal suffrage, it was nonetheless a remarkable comment – the first public avowal by a president of the United States that African-American men should, at least under certain circumstances, enjoy the same fundamental political privileges as their white counterparts.[2] What is even more remarkable in view of the pervasive racism of the era, is that by the end of a brutal civil war black suffrage had become a major debating point for political elites and ordinary citizens alike. For a growing number of Americans by the spring of 1865 the notion that black men should be given the ballot was no longer as preposterous as it had once seemed. Why was this the case and how optimistic were the supporters of this cause entitled to be as the process of post-war Reconstruction began in earnest?

Black suffrage before 1860

Many historians have written justifiably about the virulence of white racism in the United States during the first half of the nineteenth century. The federal census counted 4.4 million blacks in 1860, nearly 14 per cent of the Republic's total population. Of these 3.9 million were slaves in the upper and lower South. The remaining half a million were divided almost equally between free blacks (many of whom were former slaves) resident in the North and South. Life for most antebellum blacks was harsh – not only for the majority of bondsmen and women but also for free blacks whose horizons everywhere were constrained by racial prejudice, poverty and legal discrimination. Even in the North where African-Americans worked mainly as menial labourers in the city and countryside, they enjoyed few rights and were generally regarded by the dominant population as innately inferior and as temporary sojourners in the white Republic. Although social and economic trends linked to the growth of a national and international market contributed significantly to the demise of suffrage qualifications for white males after 1787, the fiercely competitive politics of the Jacksonian period did not embrace blacks. Indeed, there is much evidence to suggest that a relatively democratic antebellum political system was constructed in part by defining certain groups as beyond the pale of political society. Certainly, most blacks and Indians (as well as women and minors) were excluded from the suffrage during this period and the regnant Democratic party solidified its main constituents (white yeoman farmers, slaveholders and working men) by appealing to their deepest racial fears and prejudices.

Most states went out of their way to disfranchise free blacks during the early decades of the nineteenth century. Ohio provided for a racially exclusive franchise in 1802. In 1821 New York withheld the vote from all blacks save those few who held more than $250 worth of property and who had lived in the state for three years. And in 1838 Pennsylvania, previously tolerant of limited black voting, disfranchised all African-Americans when local Democrats claimed that ignorant blacks had defeated Jacksonian candidates in that year's autumn elections. Because the federal Constitution gave the individual states control over suffrage qualifications within their own borders, the die appeared to be cast. By 1860 blacks could vote in only five New England states (Massachusetts, Vermont, Maine, Rhode Island and New Hampshire) and, on a limited basis, in New York.

On the whole, matters were made worse for antebellum blacks by the rapid rise of sectional tensions associated with slavery expansion after 1830. As the peculiar institution strengthened its grip on southern society and the national government, slaves found manumission harder to secure, free blacks below the Mason-Dixon Line were subject to increased harassment and legal restraints, and their northern counterparts witnessed the passage of a tough new Fugitive Slave Act which, potentially at least, rendered their own freedom vulnerable to the activities of slavecatchers, US marshals and federal judges. The 1850s was a particularly harsh decade for Northern blacks. Several thousand of them fled to Canada to avoid seizure under the new federal law and the rest were constantly reviled and abused for the race's unwitting role in the burgeoning political conflict between North and South. For the first time large numbers of blacks contemplated leaving the United States. Their disillusionment seemed entirely justified when, in March 1857, the US Supreme Court ruled in the case of Dred Scott *v.* Sandford that blacks could not be considered national citizens under the law.

Depressing though the racial situation was in this period, it was by no means entirely hopeless. In the North at least, particularly in large urban centres like Philadelphia and New York, free blacks managed to found community institutions such as churches, schools and fraternal lodges which imparted real meaning to their lives, nurtured the development of a uniquely African-American culture and identity, provided genuine leadership training, and enabled them to survive the kind of sustained white assaults which afflicted urban blacks in the Jacksonian period. Inevitably, the mayhem, murder and property destruction which accompanied these 'riots' could be profoundly corrosive of community morale. In 1842, after a predominantly Irish mob had reacted violently against black efforts to commemorate the anniversary of British West Indian emancipation, Robert Purvis, one of Philadelphia's leading black citizens, wrote: 'I am convinced of our utter and complete nothingness in public estimation . . . [and] despair black as the face of Death hangs over us – And the bloody Will is in the heart of the [white] community to destroy us.'[3] Such understandably bleak responses to white supremacist violence, however, did not prevent Philadelphia blacks, like their peers in other parts of the North, from asserting their perceived rights as men and equal citizens. In this respect, no other issue was more important to free blacks than their fight for the suffrage.

By the mid-nineteenth century the advent of adult white male suffrage had made the ballot the most conspicuous and valued badge of first-class citizenship in the United States. Turnout in antebellum elections reached historic levels in large measure because white males regarded the vote as a potent weapon in the ongoing struggle to protect the nation from those designing and corrupt individuals who, in the eyes of a politically polarized electorate, would undermine the precious liberties of the people in their quest for personal aggrandizement. Throughout the United States the physical act of going to the polls constituted an assertion of citizenship and a positive contribution to the welfare of the Republic. Unsurprisingly, therefore, the majority of disfranchised Northern free blacks made attainment of the ballot a central feature of their evolving campaign for equal rights.

After 1830 numerous 'colored people's' conventions met to press government for the abolition of slavery and the enfranchisement of African-Americans. Antebellum black leaders such as the New York Presbyterian minister, Henry Highland Garnet, and the slave-born abolitionist, Frederick Douglass, had no doubt that racism and slavery were intrinsically connected and that attainment of the vote would contribute significantly to the downfall of the peculiar institution, not only by proving that blacks were capable of acting as responsible citizens but also by bringing their influence to bear on the major political parties of the day. Battling against inchoate prejudices rooted in scientific racism, biblical exegesis and contemporary power relations, the conventions passed numerous resolutions demanding the right of black men to vote. The language of such resolutions and of many speeches delivered by contemporary leaders was often gendered and nativist – the ballot was critical to the black male's concept of manhood and drunken, ignorant Irishmen were invariably deemed to be unworthy of the franchise – but it was generally patriotic and couched in the rhetoric of natural rights. African-Americans repeatedly declared themselves to be loyal to the Republic and therefore deserving of the same political rights as their white counterparts. 'America is my home, my country, and I have no other,' intoned Henry H. Garnet in February 1848 in a statement designed in part to undercut the colonizationist argument that blacks should return to Africa.[4] Although passage of the Fugitive Slave Act two years later rendered most blacks more ambivalent about the United States, Frederick Douglass was still able to announce at a pro-suffrage convention ·in September 1855 that 'We love our country'. 'The more unitedly', he told whites, 'you can attach us to your institutions, the more reason you give us to love your government, the more you strengthen the country in which we live.'[5]

Black efforts to achieve the ballot before the Civil War went beyond mere rhetoric. Pro-suffrage petitions were addressed to legislatures and delivered in person to legislative committees. Black leaders allied themselves with progressive whites (primarily political abolitionists) in order to pressurise white politicians into acknowledging the existence of black suffrage as a legitimate political issue. Relatively sophisticated organizations were set up by state and local community leaders to distribute pro-suffrage literature, most notably in New York in the autumn of 1860 after the Albany legislature had provided for a popular referendum on black enfranchisement. The fact that eight black suffrage referenda were held in five different Northern states between 1846 and 1860 is an indication that these tactics were surprisingly successful. The cause appealed to significant numbers of whites, particularly evangelical Protestants involved in the New England diaspora after the Revolution. An awareness that a small but vocal fraction of their party demanded black enfranchisement on religious and humanitarian grounds forced pragmatic Northern Whigs and Republicans to provide their constituents with an opportunity to vote on the issue. Consistent Democratic attempts to fan the flames of popular racism made positive endorsements of black suffrage suicidal outside areas of radical strength such as upstate New York and the Western Reserve around Cleveland, Ohio, but even the most moderate of major party leaders understood that a safety valve had to be found for antislavery and pro-suffrage sentiment.

If one ignores an anomalous vote in favour of black ballots in Wisconsin in 1849, nearly a third of all people voting in the antebellum suffrage referenda expressed a willingness to enfranchise African-Americans.[6] Although a minority of these voters were certainly abolitionists, the majority were ordinary Whigs and Republicans who believed that their party stood for more than federal support for internal improvements or simple opposition to the expansion of slavery into the Western territories. In Iowa perhaps as many as a fifth of Republican voters participating in the 1857 gubernatorial election favoured black suffrage in a referendum in which 86 per cent of whites voting on this issue opposed it.[7] At least half of all New York Republicans who voted for Abraham Lincoln in the November presidential election may have supported extending the franchise to all black males. Pro-suffrage majorities in Western counties (the centre of the heavily evangelized Burned-Over district) were overridden by white supremacist votes in the eastern and southern portions of the state, not least heavily Democratic New York City.[8]

The significance of these statistics should not be overstated. Even though a base of white support clearly existed for black suffrage in the antebellum North, it was not, even with the growth of the anti-Southern and antislavery Republican party in the mid-1850s, sufficiently large to bring major victories. Many Republican leaders on the radical wing of the party were willing to pay more than lip-service to the idea that blacks were as entitled to vote as whites but even they understood the force of Democratic and popular racism well enough not to push the point. Under pressure from their opponents most centrists were content, like Abraham Lincoln during his famous Illinois senate campaign in 1858, to cite the Declaration of Independence, assert that free blacks were entitled to basic civil rights short of the ballot, and focus the voters' attention on the alleged Slave Power conspiracy to subvert republican liberties and institutions. Little wonder then that on the eve of the Civil War even those black leaders most sympathetic to the Republicans had become disillusioned by the new party's apparent readiness to defer to grass-roots prejudice. Speaking at Framingham, Massachusetts, on 4 July 1860 the Illinois black leader, H. Ford Douglass, criticised the Republican presidential candidate, Abraham Lincoln, for refusing to sign a pro-suffrage petition two years earlier. 'I am a colored man,' insisted Douglass. 'I am an American citizen; and I think that I am entitled to exercise the elective franchise.'[9]

Loyalty, citizenship and suffrage in the Civil War

Forthright words though these were it took the outbreak of civil war in April 1861 to turn suffrage extension into an issue of central political importance for whites as well as blacks. There were three closely connected reasons for this transformation: black participation in the struggle to defeat the Confederacy; radical Republican attempts to ensure that African-American loyalty to the Union was rewarded with a recognition of full citizenship; and the evolving federal effort to restore the seceded states to their proper relations within the Union.

Most blacks may have had mixed feelings about their homeland at the time of the secession crisis but several leading figures recognized that the impending clash between the two sections offered the race an opportunity to reassert its demands for abolition and equal rights by dint of proven devotion to the United States. Foremost among them was Frederick Douglass who, having become disillusioned with temporizing Republicans during the recent suffrage campaign in New York, spent much of the winter of 1860–1 debunking the idea of attempting to fashion another humiliating compromise with seditious slaveholders. For him the only answer to secession was an unambiguous assertion of federal power. After the Confederates attacked Fort Sumter in April 1861 Douglass rejoiced openly at the enemy's foolishness and threw himself immediately into the task of generating a popular hatred of the South which, he truly believed, could only redound to the benefit of African-Americans. With slaveholders the ultimate negative reference group for Northern whites, surely patriotic blacks were entitled to believe that they might at last be recognized as first-class citizens in their own country?

It was not long before the dream of a more inclusive American nationality began to evaporate. The Lincoln administration's desire to conciliate War Democrats and loyal slaveholders in the border states resulted in a conservative policy on slavery during the first year of the Civil War. Grass-roots racism meant that spontaneous African-American offers to fight for the Union were rejected brusquely by Northern politicians and administrators. This response appeared to bolster the view of one black New Yorker that it was pointless for African-Americans to fight in the defence of a nation which oppressed them: 'We of the North must have all rights which white men enjoy; until then we are in no condition to fight under the flag which gives us no protection.'[10]

If black cynicism in the early stages of the Northern war effort was fully justified, the exigencies of war ultimately fulfilled the millennial hope of Frederick Douglass and other reformers that sacrifice on the battlefield would redeem the nation's sins, particularly the ultimate sin of slaveholding. In September 1862 the failure of Union armies to make significant headway against the Confederacy finally induced President Lincoln to issue a preliminary emancipation proclamation. Citing military necessity rather than any moral imperative, the document declared that from 1 January 1863 all slaves belonging to rebel owners would be free under United States law. The measure was far from popular with conservatives (and contributed to a revival of Democratic fortunes in the 1862 Congressional elections) but Lincoln held firm and signed the historic Proclamation at the beginning of the new year. Importantly, the document also provided for the enlistment of former slaves into the armed forces of the Republic, a move which had long been called for by many Northerners impatient with what they saw as the government's overly cautious response to the rebellion. When Congress passed a non-racial conscription act shortly afterwards, Douglass and other race leaders responded positively to the government's belated recognition of black resources by acting as recruitment agents or serving as non-commissioned officers in segregated units. By the end of the war 179,000 black troops had served in the Union armies and navies, making a substantial contribution to the final defeat of the Confederacy in 1865. Liberated slaves constituted the largest proportion of this total but nearly a fifth of black troops serving in the Union armies were free blacks from the Northern states.[11]

Powerful evidence of elite and grass-roots black support for the Union during the Civil War indicated the determination of most African-Americans to assert their manhood and devotion to a new Union purged of slavery and discrimination. Through their brave deeds on the battlefield and continued political agitation, they expected to earn and receive the civil rights enjoyed by the white male citizens of the Republic.

From the beginning of 1863 African-Americans and some of their more radical white allies hastened to add suffrage extension to a political agenda still headed by the demand for the unqualified abolition of slavery in the United States. Five weeks after promulgation of the Emancipation Proclamation, Frederick Douglass told an audience in New York City that it was difficult to grasp the significance of the president's action. 'The change in the attitude of the Government is vast and startling,' he said. 'For more than 60 years the Federal Government has been little better than a stupendous engine of Slavery and oppression, through which Slavery has ruled us, with a rod of iron.' As further evidence of the dramatic shift in official attitudes to his race, Douglass also noted a recent decision of US Attorney General Edward Bates that blacks were citizens of the United States. As a result of this opinion, contended Douglass, he spoke not only as a coloured man and an American but as 'a colored citizen, having, in common with all other citizens a stake in the safety, prosperity, honor, and glory of a common country.'[12] Although Douglass neglected to mention that Bates had distinguished between citizenship and suffrage, it was not long before he was making the connection from A to B. Before a predominantly white audience in Brooklyn in May 1863 he asserted that a just realignment of the relationship between whites and African-Americans was critical to the nation's future well-being. Noting that the term 'Negro' was currently 'the most pregnant word in the English language', he advocated the black man's 'most full and complete adoption into the great national family of America'. Proper integration demanded 'the most perfect civil and political equality, and that he shall enjoy all the rights, privileges and immunities enjoyed by any other members of the body politic.'[13]

Douglass's effortless shift from citizenship to suffrage was a natural one for an expert political agitator, particularly a black one, to make but it was probably based on a wilful misreading of the Attorney General's opinion which had been delivered on 29 November 1862. In that decision Edward Bates, a conservative Republican from Missouri, had rejected Chief Justice Taney's ruling in the Dred Scott case that blacks could not be considered citizens of the United States. Asserting that ancient and contemporary authorities supported a broad definition of national citizenship, Bates undermined Taney's decision by contending, firstly, that all free persons born in the United States were citizens of the United States and, secondly, that the Court's controversial definition of citizenship was largely 'dehors the record' and therefore of no authority as a legal decision.[14] While Bates emphasized that he did not concur with the Aristotelian notion that political rights flowed naturally from citizenship (how could he after defining women and children as well as free blacks as citizens?) his ruling made the citizenship portion of the Dred Scott decision a dead letter.

Edward Bates was no friend of black suffrage and would emerge from the war a committed opponent of those Republicans who vaunted what he called 'the absurd theory of the exact equality of all men'.[15] However, his liberal definition of citizenship was meat and drink not only to black leaders like Frederick Douglass but also to progressive Republicans at the heart of the Lincoln administration. Foremost among these humanitarian radicals was the Secretary of the Treasury, Salmon P. Chase. A churchgoing Episcopalian, committed opponent of Southern slavery, and a supporter of black suffrage as early as 1843, Chase had been one of the supreme architects of the Republican coalition in the 1850s. In this capacity he had sometimes subordinated the fight against racial prejudice to the broader struggle against the Slave Power. Many contemporaries regarded him as an arrogant and aloof figure driven by an overweening ambition for the highest political office. The charge was by no means unjust but it should not be allowed to disguise the fact that Chase possessed a keen moral sense and a remarkably prescient awareness that the fate of the Republic was closely bound up with that of African-Americans.

In common with most radical Republicans, Salmon Chase struggled not only with his own racial prejudices (which inclined him towards a paternalistic attitude towards blacks) but also with the white supremacist assumptions of most Northern voters. Even while holding strong antislavery views, therefore, he could delude himself into thinking that blacks might be better off in Africa. Colonization proved to be attractive to many politicians in antebellum America and Chase was not unusual in regarding voluntary emigration as one solution to the problem of race relations in the United States. But while he gave a cautious welcome to President Lincoln's scheme to colonize blacks in Central America as late as November 1861, wartime events convinced him that slavery, the engine of the rebellion, had to be destroyed; that blacks were morally entitled to equal rights under the law; and, crucially, that because Southern slaves were the only substantial loyal population in the South, liberated blacks ought to be enfranchised in order to counter the baleful influence of their former masters. By August 1862 Chase could be heard in cabinet suggesting that eventually loyal blacks in the border slave states might be allowed to vote. For him, proven devotion to the Union – not race or colour – should be the principal qualification for manhood suffrage.

Of course, the powerful minister was well aware that the Dred Scott decision constituted a major obstacle to franchise extension at a time when the process of Reconstruction was already beginning in Union-occupied areas of the South. If the government did not consider blacks to be national citizens then clearly it would find it difficult to convince anyone that the race should enjoy the same political privileges as whites. When, on 5 August 1862, a black skipper was detained off the coast of New Jersey on the grounds that only US citizens were allowed to captain vessels engaged in the coasting trade, Chase seized the opportunity to ask Attorney General Bates to consider the simple question: 'are colored men Citizens of the US, and therefore Competent to command American vessels?'[16]Although, as shown above, Bates answered in the affirmative without endorsing black suffrage, Chase knew all along that male citizenship and suffrage were closely equated in the public mind and that therefore an official declaration that free blacks enjoyed national citizenship was likely to prove a potent weapon in the nascent struggle to influence Reconstruction. Like Frederick Douglass, the secretary would make the leap from citizenship to suffrage with consummate ease.

Black suffrage and wartime Reconstruction

Had the issues of Reconstruction and black ballots not become intertwined during the middle of the Civil War, it is far from clear that the suffrage issue would have become a matter for widespread political debate by early 1865. True, the heroic performances of black regiments such as the 54th Massachusetts at Fort Wagner, South Carolina, in July 1863 earned African-Americans the grudging respect of many Northerners, including racist Union troops, but in themselves such glorious deeds would not have been translated automatically into franchise extension. It was the growing realization, promoted strenuously by radical Republicans, that most white Southerners were likely to prove ambivalent Unionists, even after military defeat, that finally brought the suffrage question centre stage.

In this respect Salmon Chase was ahead of the game. Seeking to build on Bates's opinion during 1863 the secretary took every opportunity to dissem-

inate his belief that blacks were fellow human beings worthy of respect. Rightly
conscious of the way in which language was used to depersonalize the mass
of black slaves encountered by the Union armies, he insisted that federal
officials abandon the initially popular label of 'contraband' in favour of 'freedmen, Afric-Americans, blacks, negroes, [or] colored citizens'.[17] More importantly, perhaps, he laboured to enshrine black suffrage as a central feature of
government Reconstruction policy in the state of Louisiana which began to
emerge as the focal point for a potentially disastrous split between radical
and non-radical Republicans in Washington and in the country at large.

In late January 1863, several months after Union forces had occupied
New Orleans and the surrounding sugar parishes, Major-General Nathaniel
P. Banks, the federal commander of the Department of the Gulf, laid the foundations for a controversial labour system designed to keep Louisiana's slaves
at work on the sugar plantations. Slave-born blacks who did not enlist were
to perform paid work in the fields at wage rates determined by the government. While the new system gradually came under attack from radicals for
allegedly bolstering a status quo based on coercion, President Lincoln chose
to regard it as an acceptable form of apprenticeship and pressed on with his
own policy of restoration. Suspicious of imposed solutions and desirous of
encouraging self-reconstruction on the part of Southern whites, Lincoln told
Banks in August 1863 to make haste in creating a free state government
in New Orleans. While he expressed a desire that local blacks should be
liberated and educated by the new regime, the president's missive made no
mention of black suffrage. Why should it have done? Was it not the case that
Louisiana blacks were a downtrodden race, degraded (perhaps through no
fault of their own) by slavery, and therefore incapable of voting as enlightened citizens of a modern, free-labour republic? Even if Lincoln had privately
favoured franchise extension at this stage, his political sixth sense would have
told him that Northern voters would not accept it.

Chase's determination to make loyalty the cornerstone of federal Reconstruction policy gathered pace in late 1863 as Lincoln prodded his military
commanders in New Orleans to redouble their efforts to hold elections for a
new state legislature prior to the meeting of a constitutional convention that
would expunge slavery from the state's organic law. The Ohioan's enthusiasm
for black suffrage was not shared by any white Louisiana Unionists (or,
for that matter, his own faction of treasury agents in New Orleans) but his
commitment to franchise extension gelled neatly with the vociferous demand
of local free blacks for political suffrage. Uniquely (because of its former
status as a French and Spanish port in the eighteenth century), New Orleans

possessed a large population of around 11,000 free blacks (mainly light-skinned mulattos), significant numbers of whom were wealthy, well-educated, and enrolled in the armed forces of the United States. When election preparations finally got underway in late 1863 the 'gens de couleur' agreed to petition the local military commander for the vote and, if unsuccessful, to take their case to Washington. Shortly afterwards Chase wrote to the president of the Free State Committee in New Orleans, Thomas Durant, making known his wish that 'colored citizens' should be registered to vote in the forthcoming elections. This policy was, he said, in full conformity with the Attorney General's opinion on black citizenship and required on the grounds of justice and the security of the Union.[18]

In spite of being a former slaveholder, Durant understood the political advantages of acting in conformity with a powerful patron in Washington and ingratiating himself with the assertive creole population of New Orleans. Consequently, when he responded to Chase on 4 December, he expressed himself in favour of enfranchising free-born blacks as 'an act well founded in justice'.[19] As Durant's letter made its way to Washington President Lincoln finally delivered a Proclamation of Amnesty and Reconstruction designed to speed up the process of restoration and emancipation in the occupied South. Whenever 10 per cent of Southern white voters in a rebel state had taken an oath of future loyalty to the Union they were invited to form a free state government which would abolish slavery and dispatch delegates to Congress. Significantly, there was no provision in this document for either limited black suffrage or the extension of even basic civil rights to blacks. Undaunted, Chase used Durant's support for franchise extension to elicit what appears to have been the first endorsement of this policy from the White House. As Chase explained events to Durant at the end of 1863, the secretary told the president of Durant's views whereupon he (Lincoln) 'said he could see no objection to the registering of such citizens [the "gens de couleur"], or to their exercise of the right of suffrage.'[20]

This was clever work on Chase's part – prodding one of the South's leading Unionists to endorse at least limited suffrage for blacks and then using that endorsement to secure Lincoln's acquiescence in franchise extension in Louisiana. The secretary's efforts, however, to promote reform did not stop here. At the close of his communication with Durant he ventured the hope that the forthcoming Louisiana constitutional convention would go beyond suffrage for free-born blacks and adopt the principle of 'universal suffrage of all men, unconvicted of crime, who can read and write, and have a fair knowledge of the Constitution of the State and of the United States.'[21]

Here was a bold declaration in favour of impartial suffrage for all races –
including not only the 'gens de couleur' but also the freedmen who would be
liberated by the new constitution. In order that his views should reach a wider
public Chase also wrote to Horace Greeley, editor of the New York *Tribune*,
suggesting that the influential Republican editor should indicate his support
for black suffrage. In spite of his record as a pragmatic reformer Greeley agreed
that the issue should be aired in public. '"Conservatism" will howl at the
thought of "Negro Suffrage",' he responded on 31 December. 'But we shall
have to keep it horrified for a while yet.'[22]

At this stage Chase's views ran ahead of those held by Durant and his free
black allies in New Orleans. Few white Louisiana Unionists or 'gens de couleur'
were enthusiastic about admitting tens of thousands of recently liberated
bondsmen to the body politic. They were certainly anathema to the sugar
planters of southern Louisiana whose views exerted a significant influence on
the military government. As a result the Banks regime, lacking as it did any
instructions to the contrary from Lincoln, made no attempt to register any
blacks during the winter of 1863–4 and began to throw its weight behind
the moderate Unionist faction headed by Durant's rival, Michael Hahn. Outraged, the predominantly mulatto creoles dispatched a two-man delegation
to Washington with a petition praying for the enfranchisement of free blacks
in Louisiana.

By the time Arnold Bertonneau, a rich wine merchant, and J.B. Roudanez,
a plantation engineer, arrived at the capital in March they discovered that
radical Republicans in Congress were already worried about the apparent
conservatism of Lincoln's Ten Per Cent plan. The latter, it was alleged,
made it too easy for rebels to regain power and offered no security for loyal
citizens, including the former slaves. As early as January 1864 one of Chase's
longtime allies in Ohio, Representative James M. Ashley, attempted to place
onto the House agenda a bill providing for the enrolment of all loyal male
citizens over the age of twenty-one. His effort failed but it was nonetheless an
important statement that radicals did not see partial suffrage as an adequate
solution to the problem of reestablishing Southern loyalty to the Union. Keen
to make universal or impartial suffrage a fundamental element of Reconstruction, Senator Charles Sumner of Massachusetts, a staunch supporter of black
civil rights and another Chase ally, persuaded the two creoles to adapt their
petition to suit the broader national goals of the radical Republicans. Whereas
the original document had called for the enfranchisement of 'coloured' men
who were free before the Civil War (i.e. the 'gens de couleur'), the revised
petition requested the suffrage for all Louisiana blacks 'whether born slave or

free, especially those who have vindicated their right to vote by bearing arms.'[23] On 12 March Bertonneau and Roudinez were granted an audience at the White House. As Chase's meeting with the president in December had already revealed, Lincoln was now personally in favour of some form of suffrage for African-Americans (quite probably because he sensed that support for reform was gaining momentum within the Republican Party and genuinely respected the role which blacks were now playing in the war). The following day he took positive action to spur suffrage reform in Louisiana by writing a brief letter to the state's new Unionist governor, Michael Hahn, who had been elected on 22 February against the opposition of Durant and his ally in the New Orleans customs house, Benjamin Flanders. The pro-Chase Flanders camp (which had been outraged by Major General Banks's insistence that elections should be held under the unreformed antebellum constitution) had downplayed the issue of black suffrage during the campaign but Hahn's supporters had made use of Durant's alliance with the 'gens de couleur' to appeal to the racism of local white Unionists. In his letter to the governor Lincoln asked if the forthcoming constitutional convention might not provide for partial suffrage extension to blacks. 'I barely suggest for your private consideration' he wrote,

> whether some of the colored people may not be let in – as, for instance, the very intelligent, and especially those who have fought gallantly in our ranks. They would probably help, in some trying time to come, to keep the jewel of liberty within the family of freedom. But this is only a suggestion, not to the public, but to you alone.[24]

Although the historian LaWanda Cox has asserted that this letter reveals the gap between the radicals and Lincoln on black rights to have been smaller than often supposed, it is clear that, unlike the radicals, the president was not prepared to insist on partial suffrage – still less on impartial or universal suffrage – as a fundamental condition of Reconstruction. Initially, his views had minimal impact on events in Louisiana. The Banks-Hahn administration did attempt to enrol mulattoes for the constitutional convention elections but legal restrictions, the extent of white supremacist feeling and the tentative wording of Lincoln's letter curtailed the effort. When the lilywhite convention met during the spring and summer of 1864 the delegates took care to meet Lincoln's non-negotiable demand for emancipation. However, the furthest they were prepared to move on suffrage (and Lincoln's wishes were made known to key members of the convention) was to make provision for the state legislature to enfranchise blacks at some point in the future.

While debate over Reconstruction remained an issue confined largely to political elites, African-American leaders believed that events were moving in the desired direction. Determined as ever to assert their rights they lost no opportunity in the early months of 1864 to press the suffrage issue on a Northern public preoccupied with the progress of the war. In April Frederick Douglass spoke in Boston at a dinner held in honour of the two New Orleans creoles, Roudanez and Bertonneau. Present were many members of the anti-slavery elite of Massachusetts, among them the Republican governor, John A. Andrew, and the veteran abolitionist, William Lloyd Garrison. Douglass urged his mainly white listeners to strike while the iron was hot. 'We are in a malleable state now, we are melted,' he insisted. '[B]ut let the arm of this rebellion be broken, let their weapons be flung away, and I fear that again we shall mistake prosperity for righteousness, and forget those brave negroes who are standing up in defense of the government.' The gentlemen of Massachusetts, he urged, should exert their influence immediately 'for the complete, absolute, unqualified enfranchisement of the colored people of the South . . .'.[25]

The black abolitionist leader's insistence on the need for haste may well have been influenced by an awareness that the franchise question was nearing the top of the Republican agenda. Although James Ashley's black suffrage proposal had been shelved in January, 22 out of 31 Senate Republicans had recently voted to strike the word 'white' from a House bill providing for elections in Montana Territory. By no means all of those moderates who voted for the measure regarded it as a test case for southern Reconstruction. There was, after all, no doubt that Congress had the constitutional authority to impose suffrage qualifications on a federal territory and there were few African-Americans living in Montana at the time. However, Charles Sumner, who led the fight to enfranchise all adult male citizens in the territory, clearly intended that the vote should be regarded as a precedent for the upcoming debate over a congressional alternative to Lincoln's Ten Per Cent plan. The refusal of roughly a third of House Republicans to support the Senate's actions eventually forced the upper chamber to withdraw from its amendment but in May Sumner tried to attach franchise extension to a bill to amend the charter of Washington, DC. This time he failed to secure majority backing from co-partisans in the Senate. In June Congress finally passed the Wade-Davis Reconstruction bill. No provision was made for black suffrage in part because pragmatic radicals like Benjamin Wade of Ohio recognized the extent of opposition to the measure from conservative and moderate Republicans and chose to prioritize legislative control of reconstruction policy over equal rights. Only Sumner and four other Senate radicals backed a motion to make impartial suffrage a central feature of congressional reconstruction.

By the summer of 1864 it appeared that the country was not ready for black suffrage. While war-driven events meant that there was significant support for the measure among Republicans in Washington, there was manifestly little unity on whether franchise extension should take the form of partial, impartial or universal suffrage and even less on the divisive constitutional question of whether the policy could actually be imposed on the rebel states. In the country at large there was minimal enthusiasm for the issue among whites. Indeed, with a crucial presidential election looming – one which would determine whether the war was fought to a victorious conclusion – conservative Republicans were appalled that radicals in their own party would endanger the war effort through their advocacy of allegedly impractical measures. 'It is amazing to me', wrote a splenetic Henry J. Raymond, the editor of the pro-Lincoln New York *Times*,

> to see men forcing the country into new contests as negro suffrage & negro rights of all kinds in the midst of the greatest contest the world has seen for a hundred years & while that, too, is undecided. For our sanguine expectations of victory will be blasted hopelessly, if these new issues are permitted to distract the public mind & divide loyal men.[26]

Raymond was right to fear divisions among the Union ranks. By mid-1864 the paucity of Union successes on the battlefield had combined with opposition to the president's lenient Reconstruction policy to promote a concerted movement against Lincoln's renomination by the Republican-dominated Union Party coalition. Initially, Salmon P. Chase had hoped to benefit from the groundswell of dissent, but the president's impressive grass-roots popularity and control of the patronage had put paid to Chase's covert candidacy at the beginning of the year. Abolitionists on the radical wing of the New England Anti-Slavery Society, however, were in no mood to stomach four more years of the Railsplitter and many of them united with dissident Democrats and German-American radicals to nominate John C. Frémont for president in May 1864. The Cleveland convention cheered a letter from Wendell Phillips calling for land and the ballot to be given to Southern loyalists, black and white. It also adopted a platform advocating Congressional control of Reconstruction and the adoption of a constitutional amendment to 'secure to all men absolute equality before the law'.[27] Pro-suffrage men like Parker Pillsbury were far from happy with the vagueness of this latter clause but the presence of Democrats at the convention meant that it was the most radical plank they could achieve.

In the event black suffrage played only a minor role in the 1864 election campaign. The Democrats did try to use Republican backing for franchise extension to convince white voters that their opponents stood for racial amalgamation. But Lincoln, renominated by his party in June, had made no public endorsement of black rights beyond emancipation and the Union platform remained predictably silent on the issue. As a result, when the tide of war turned in favour of the North after the fall of Atlanta in September, Peace Democrats and Frémont supporters alike found their causes in terminal decline. Lincoln's triumphant reelection in November appeared to make him master of events.

The coming question: black suffrage at the close of the Civil War

During the first week of October, 144 black delegates, some of them Union soldiers, gathered at the National Colored Men's Convention in Syracuse, New York, to establish the National Equal Rights League. The organization's principal objective was to lobby for equal suffrage across the United States. 'We want the elective franchise in all the States now in the Union,' read an address drafted by Frederick Douglass. John Rock, a black Massachusetts lawyer who had once cast doubt on the Republican commitment to equal rights, underscored the importance of the suffrage but added that it was crucial for blacks to recognize that there were now only two parties in America: the Democrats, who represented despotism and slavery, and the Republicans, who stood for freedom and the Union. Such polarized and partisan rhetoric was tested to the limit during the winter of 1864–5 when the tangled issues of Reconstruction and black suffrage were debated in Congress. Once again, events in Louisiana played an important role in the final outcome.

By the time Congress reconvened in early December it was evident that the war was virtually won. However, the president and Congressional leaders were determined to secure passage of a constitutional amendment to secure the final and complete abolition of slavery, widely understood to be the main cause of the rebellion. Equally important was Lincoln's desire to push ahead with his lenient plan of Reconstruction, ideally with the support of Republicans in Congress. The request of senators and representatives from Louisiana to be seated was likely to prove a major test for executive policy, not least because the New Orleans legislature had declined to mandate any form of black suffrage during the autumn, thereby infuriating local blacks (both 'gens de couleur' and freedmen) and the radical Republican and abolitionist critics of the Hahn-Banks administration. Knowing the president's personal wish for limited black suffrage, Governor Hahn had urged franchise extension but to no avail. In common with Hahn, both Lincoln and Banks (whom the president ordered to Washington to lobby for the admission of Louisiana) were prepared to endorse suffrage for intelligent blacks and those who had fought for the Union. But crucially none of them tolerated the imposition of such a measure on any state. The Constitution appeared not to allow it and, besides, any attempt to force the measure on Southern whites might damage the prospects for a speedy Reconstruction and, quite possibly, endanger the Union Party coalition in the North. Large numbers of Republicans in Washington, moderates as well as radicals, rejected such conservatism as likely to threaten the security of the Union after the war. Traitors must be punished; loyal Southerners (black and white) should be allowed to protect themselves through the ballot box; and Congress was empowered under the Constitution to guarantee a republican form of government to every state in the Union.

Against a background of strident black and abolitionist calls for suffrage reform during early 1865, Congress debated a new Reconstruction bill which radicals hoped would inject some much-needed steel into the government's southern policy. At first it seemed that an intra-party compromise between the president and radical Republicans might be possible. The original version of James Ashley's Reconstruction bill proposed to recognize the Unionist government of Louisiana while enfranchizing blacks in other Southern states. Lincoln liked much of what he saw in the bill but, as recounted by his secretary, John Hay, thought one or two sections 'rather calculated to conceal a feature which might be objectionable to some'. Among these was the provision for black voting and jury service. According to Hay, Banks agreed with the president. 'What you refer to', the general told Lincoln, 'would be a fatal objection to the Bill. It would simply throw the Government into the hands of the blacks, as the white people under that arrangement would refuse to vote.'[28]

The administration's reluctance to impose even limited franchise extension on Southern whites combined with the radicals' enthusiasm for reform to destroy any hopes of compromise. Ashley's bill eventually died in the House and a radical filibuster in the Senate led by Charles Sumner prevented the recognition of Louisiana. Stalemate on these issues did not prevent Congress from creating a Freedmen's Bureau to oversee the transition from slave to free labour in the South or, even more momentously, from passing the Thirteenth Amendment to extirpate slavery from the national domain. However, the plain fact is that by the spring of 1865, black suffrage had not yet received official endorsement from the federal government.

As the Civil War drew to a close the Republican Party was seriously split over black suffrage. Much support existed for the measure among radicals and moderates. Although the fear of grass-roots racism caused most (but by no means all) Republicans to maintain a pragmatic silence on the controversial topic of enfranchizing Northern blacks, the notion that the ballot could be an important weapon in the hands of the loyal freedmen appealed to supporters of laissez-faire as well as state intervention within the ruling party. If blacks did not merit the franchise as equal men or because of their service to the Union, then they might well be entitled to it on the grounds of national security. Such arguments were debated increasingly seriously in the Northern press during the opening months of 1865 and even garnered the grudging support of conservative Republicans such as Samuel Bowles, whose Springfield *Republican* endorsed impartial suffrage nearly a month before Appomattox.[29] Given the momentum on this issue generated by blacks and their antislavery allies and the Northern public's war-driven attachment to Abraham Lincoln and the Republican Party, it is not impossible that a decisive commitment to partial or even impartial suffrage on the part of the White House in early 1865 could have made the measure an intrinsic feature of post-war Reconstruction policy. To the last, however, the president's attitude to the reform remained a cautious one. Influenced by his own border state Whiggery, a temperamental dislike of extreme measures, an astute awareness of white racism among the voters, and a genuine respect for the role that blacks had played in defeating the Confederacy, Lincoln found himself, in his last public address, willing to declare a personal preference for partial suffrage but still unable to demand this as a condition of restoration. Convinced that the South's military defeat might not prove to be the end of the rebellion, radicals like Chase were still vigorously pressing their views on Lincoln in the final week of his life. 'I am now convinced that universal suffrage is demanded by sound policy and impartial justice alike,' wrote the new Supreme Court chief justice anxiously on 11 April.[30] Three days later, on the morning before the president's assassination, Chase was driving over to the White House to discuss the role of universal suffrage in Reconstruction when he abruptly changed his mind on the grounds that 'my talk might annoy him [Lincoln] and do harm rather than good'.[31]

Chase's sense that the president may have had a bellyful of his conversation could well be taken as an indication that Lincoln was equally satiated with radical demands for black suffrage. However, even this interpretation does not necessarily mean that franchise extension was dead in the water by April 1865 and that only Andrew Johnson's excessively lenient attitude to the white South and the Republicans' alleged need for black votes in the North were responsible for the Party's decision to commit itself to black suffrage after 1867. Given his own personal preferences and his proven capacity for intellectual growth on racial matters, it is likely that, had Lincoln lived, early evidence of post-war Confederate obstructionism would have wrought an intra-party consensus on limited suffrage by the end of 1865. There was much left for veteran campaigners like Frederick Douglass to do but at the end of the Civil War African-Americans had sound reasons for thinking that their contribution to the nation's survival would not be in vain.

Notes

1. A. Lincoln, 'Last public address', 11 April 1865, in R.P. Basler (ed.), *The Collected Works of Abraham Lincoln* (New Brunswick, NJ, 1953), vol. 8, p. 403.

2. Wartime supporters of black suffrage considered several forms of franchise reform. At the conservative end of the scale partial suffrage involved the imposition of certain tests on potential black voters alone (e.g. literacy tests, military service, payment of taxes). Impartial (or equal) suffrage required such tests to be applied to blacks and whites alike. The most radical reformers favoured universal suffrage which would confer the ballot on all adult males regardless of colour.

3. R. Purvis quoted in N. Salvatore, *We All Got History: The Memory Books of Amos Webber* (New York, 1997), p. 24.

4. J. Schor, *Henry Highland Garnet: A Voice of Black Radicalism in the Nineteenth Century* (Westport, Conn., and London, 1977), p. 92.

5. F. Douglass, 'We ask only for our rights' (4 September 1855) in J.W. Blassingame (ed.), *The Frederick Douglass Papers; Series I: Speeches, Debates, and Interviews*, vol. 3 (New Haven and London, 1985), p. 93.

6. T.L. McLaughlin, 'Grass-roots attitudes toward black rights in twelve non-slave-holding states, 1846–1869', *Mid-America* 56 (1974), p. 176. The Wisconsin referendum should be treated as anomalous because large numbers of voters ensured the defeat of black suffrage in 1849 by refusing to vote on the issue.

7. R.J. Cook, *Baptism of Fire: The Republican Party in Iowa, 1838–1878* (Ames, Ia, 1994), p. 93.

8. P.F. Field, 'Republicans and black suffrage in New York state: the grass roots response', *Civil War History* 22 (1975), pp. 142–3.

9. H.F. Douglass cited in J.M. McPherson (ed.), *The Negro's Civil War: How American Blacks Felt and Acted During the War for the Union* (New York, 1991), p. 6.

10. Douglass quoted in McPherson, *The Negro's Civil War*, p. 34.

11. D.W. Blight, *Frederick Douglass' Civil War: Keeping Faith in Jubilee* (Baton Rouge, La, and London, 1989), p. 164.

12. F. Douglass, 'The Proclamation and the Negro army' (6 February 1863) in Blassingame (ed.), *Douglass Papers*, vol. 3, pp. 549–50.

13. F. Douglass, 'The present and future of the colored race in America' (15 May 1863) in Blassingame (ed.), *Douglass Papers*, vol. 3, pp. 570–2.

14. E. Bates to S.P. Chase, 29 November 1862, in J.M. McClure, L. Johnson, K. Norman and M. Vanderlan (eds), 'Circumventing the Dred Scott decision: Edward Bates, Salmon P. Chase, and the citizenship of African-Americans', *Civil War History* 43 (1997), p. 309.

15. H.K. Beale (ed.), *The Diary of Edward Bates 1859–1866* (Washington, DC, 1933), p. 445.

16. S.P. Chase to E. Bates, 24 September 1862, in McClure *et al.*, 'Dred Scott decision', p. 288.

17. Chase to J.M. McKaye, 25 July 1863, Salmon P. Chase Papers (UPA microfilm edition), reel 28, frame 25.

18. Chase to T.J. Durant, 19 November 1863, Chase Papers, reel 29, frames 913–14.

19. Durant to Chase, 4 December 1863, Chase Papers, reel 30, frame 182.

20. Chase to Durant, 28 December 1863, Chase Papers, reel 30, frame 635.

21. Chase to Durant, 28 December 1863, Chase Papers, reel 30, frame 636.

[238]   22. H. Greeley to Chase, 31 December 1863, Chase Papers, reel 30, frame 726.

23. T. Tunnell, *Crucible of Reconstruction: War, Radicalism and Race in Louisiana 1862–1877* (Baton Rouge, La, and London, 1984), p. 78.

24. A. Lincoln to M. Hahn, 13 March 1864, in Basler (ed.), *Collected Works*, vol. 7, p. 243.

25. F. Douglass, 'Representatives of the Future South' (12 April 1864) in J.W. Blassingame and J.R. McKivigan (eds), *The Frederick Douglass Papers*, I, IV (New Haven, Conn., and London, 1991), pp. 27–8.

26. H.J. Raymond to J.R. Doolittle, 30 April 1864, J.R. Doolittle Papers, Library of Congress (mic).

27. J.M. McPherson, *The Struggle for Equality: Abolitionists and the Negro in the Civil War and Reconstruction* (Princeton, NJ, 1964), p. 270.

28. T. Dennett, *Lincoln and the Civil War in the Diaries and Letters of John Hay* (New York, 1988), pp. 244–5.

29. Springfield [Mass.] *Weekly Republican*, 11 March 1865, p. 2.

30. Chase to Lincoln, 11 April 1865, in Basler (ed.), *Collected Works*, vol. 8, p. 401n.

31. D. Donald (ed.), *Inside Lincoln's Cabinet: The Civil War Diaries of Salmon P. Chase* (New York, London and Toronto, 1954), p. 264.

CHAPTER TEN

'WHAT DID WE GO TO WAR FOR?' CONFEDERATE EMANCIPATION AND ITS MEANING[1]

BRUCE LEVINE

During the first month of the Civil War, Jefferson Davis presented to the Confederate Congress a straightforward justification for secession and a now-classic explanation for the war's origins. Over the decades, Davis explained, the South's slave labour force had 'convert[ed] hundreds of thousands of square miles of wilderness into cultivated lands covered with a prosperous people,' while 'the productions in the South of cotton, rice, sugar, and tobacco . . . had swollen to an amount which formed nearly three-quarters of the exports of the whole United States and had become absolutely necessary to the wants of civilized man.' 'For the full development and continuance' of such achievements, Davis stressed, 'the labor of African slaves was and is indispensable.' Naturally, then, 'with interests of such overwhelming magnitude imperiled,' secession was necessary.[2]

After decades of scholarly struggle, the prevailing interpretation today of the war's causes follows Davis's speech in placing slavery at centre stage. And yet, just four years later, Confederate President Jefferson Davis was advocating the large-scale emancipation of the most able-bodied male slaves of the South in exchange for their taking up arms and fighting on behalf of the Confederacy against Union forces. To every slave ready to accept such an offer, Davis's government proposed to say, 'Go and fight; you are free.'[3] That policy has attracted a considerable amount of attention over the years.[4] Much of it has tended to place a question mark over the centrality of slavery to the Confederate cause. Did these events not demonstrate, after all, that other values – cultural, political, philosophical – proved more important (or, at least, more enduring) than attachment to a plantation system based on unfree labour? A hundred years ago the public obtained its first look at many of the documents produced in the course of the Confederacy's debate about arming and freeing its slaves. A quarter of a century ago, a documentary collection focused entirely on that subject appeared.[5] The intervening years have not dispelled the cloud of confusion that hangs over the meaning of this story.[6] These anniversaries provide a convenient occasion for reconsidering the matter.

Once it became clear that the war would be no glorious and swiftly con- summated adventure, the Union's overwhelming numerical superiority in adult white males led individual Confederate loyalists to look for other sources of military manpower.[7] But an important turning-point came during the second half of 1863, when the Confederacy suffered devastating blows in the war's western theatre. The fall of Vicksburg, Mississippi, and Port Hudson, Louisi- ana, in July of 1863 completed the Union's conquest of the Mississippi River, the South's chief inland water route, thereby physically splitting the Con- federacy and opening the way for the penetration of Union forces deeply into the heartland of the cotton kingdom. Lee's stunning and immensely costly defeat at Gettysburg that same month deepened a sense of foreboding among highly placed Confederate leaders.[8] These reversals posed much more urgently than before the question of manpower and possible sources thereof. In the fall of 1863, the Alabama legislature endorsed the enlistment of slaves as soldiers.[9]

The first fully argued Confederate proposal for arming and freeing slaves came in December 1863, from the pen of Major-General Patrick Cleburne, an energetic, courageous and highly regarded division commander in the Confederate Army of Tennessee, a man known for the clinical detachment of his judgment. Cleburne's beleaguered army, its ranks already plagued by low morale and its officer corps riven with dissension, had in November come face-to-face with the enemy's numerical superiority. Union reinforcements that month breached the siege of Chattanooga, after which the augmented force simply burst out of that city's confines, hurling Braxton Bragg's troops from its seemingly impregnable position on nearby Missionary Ridge.[10]

Afterwards, as the Army of Tennessee licked its wounds in winter quarters in north-west Georgia, Patrick Cleburne considered the hard lessons to be learned and the grim choices to be faced.[11] In a careful and lengthy memor- andum, Cleburne pointed to the lopsided relationship of forces between Confederate and Union armies, as a result of which 'our soldiers can see no end ... except in our own exhaustion; hence, instead of rising to the occasion, they are sinking into a fatal apathy, growing weary of hardships and slaughter which promises no results.'

Cleburne therefore proposed 'that we immediately commence training a large reserve of the most courageous of our slaves, and further that we guarantee freedom within a reasonable time to every slave in the South who shall remain true to the Confederacy in this war.' This alone would supply the Confederacy with the combat forces so sorely required. Nor did Cleburne shrink from the further implications of this proposal. 'If we arm and train him and make him fight for the country in her hour of dire distress, every consideration of principle and policy demand that we should set him and his whole race who side with us free.'[12]

This was a remarkable recommendation, to say the least. More remarkable still was the aftermath. When Cleburne circulated his memo among the officers in his command, four brigade commanders, ten regimental commanders and one cavalry division commander added their signatures to his. Encouraged by this support, Cleburne then invited all general officers, including the newly appointed commander, Joseph E. Johnston, to meet with him the evening of 2 January 1864 at the headquarters of General William Hardee. There Cleburne read the memo aloud to a mixed reception. Informed of these events, Secretary of War James Seddon ordered Johnston to suppress 'not only the memorial itself, but likewise all discussion and controversy respecting or growing out of it.' Johnston quickly complied, as did Cleburne.[13]

But though discussion of Cleburne's proposal was suppressed, and Cleburne himself died in battle before the year was out, the further deterioration of the Confederacy's situation kept alive the idea that Cleburne had raised.[14] The fall of Atlanta in September 1864 had not only great military significance, demonstrating that the balance of forces in the field had irrevocably tilted in favour of the North. It also ensured the reelection of Lincoln and a landslide Congressional victory in the North for a Republican party determined to employ that military superiority to prosecute the war down to the unconditional surrender of the South. Sherman's occupation of Savannah in December sharpened the Confederate sense of desperation. 'Demoralization is rife in our armies,' came a report from southwestern Georgia in early 1865, 'and among the people at home the sign of succumbing may be seen. . . . treason is stalking the land.'[15]

From that point onward, the Confederate government received a steady stream of reports testifying to the collapse of morale both in army and on the home front. Stationed near Petersburg, Sgt Alexander W. Cooper felt 'compelled by inexorable duty' to inform Jefferson Davis that 'the elements from which you have heretofore drawn your armies is exhausted', leaving the ranks filled with 'the mere dreggs [sic] of the noble armies that have so far sustained the Confederacy.'[16] A report from Sherman's path affirmed that 'we must be overrun if an adequate force is not thrown into the field to check the Yankees.'[17] Assessing the relationship of forces in the field in November 1864, Robert E. Lee summarized, simply, 'The inequality is too great.'[18] From

[242] Greenville, Meriwether County, in western Georgia came this alarming assessment of popular morale: 'If the question were put to the people of this state, whether to continue the war or return to the union, a large majority would vote for a return.' Indeed, this writer added, he 'almost inclined to believe that they would do it if *emancipation* was the *condition.*'[19] With matters in such a state, it was no wonder that in early November a lower South newspaper discovered 'a growing disposition within the Confederacy to make soldiers of the negroes'.[20] Governor William Smith of Virginia now endorsed the proposal, followed shortly afterward by Governor Henry W. Allen of Louisiana.[21]

Jefferson Davis publicly embraced limited manumission as a war measure in a message to the Confederate Congress on 7 November 1864. He proposed that the government purchase outright 40,000 slaves and train them to serve as military labourers. Because performing such duties at the front would require not mere submission but positive motivation ('loyalty and zeal'), Davis urged that such slave labourers be promised eventual freedom and the right to enjoy that freedom after the war within their home states. And while he expressed the cautious view that black *troops* were not yet needed, he did open the door to that eventuality, asserting that 'should the alternative ever be presented of subjugation or of the employment of the slave as a soldier, there seems no reason to doubt what should then be our decision.' Davis's Secretary of State and closest cabinet adviser, Judah P. Benjamin, endorsed emancipation not only for such slaves but also for their families.[22]

On 10 February, Mississippi congressman Ethelbert Barksdale introduced a measure in the Confederate House of Representatives calling for the arming of slaves. A legislative committee reviewed and reported favourably upon it within a matter of days.[23] Further support now came, on 18 February 1865, from Robert E. Lee, newly appointed Confederate general in chief. In a letter to Barksdale intended for broader circulation, Lee endorsed the proposal to make slaves into soldiers. 'I think the measure not only expedient but necessary,' Lee wrote, urging in addition that 'those who are employed should be freed. It would be neither just nor wise, in my opinion, to require them to serve as slaves.'[24] Supporting letters and petitions came flooding in from Confederate officers and enlisted men alike.[25]

On 20 February, in secret session, the House passed Barksdale's resolution in a close vote.[26] The Senate at first balked, but after the Davis administration successfully appealed to the Virginia legislature to instruct its senators to support the measure, the Confederate upper house reconsidered and passed the House bill by another narrow majority on 13 March. The new law stipulated that 'nothing . . . shall be construed to authorize a change in the relation which the said slaves shall bear to their owners, except by consent of the owners and of the States in which they reside.' What Congress withheld, Davis tried to reintroduce on his own initiative. Slaves enrolled in the newly created units would become free men not after completing their service but as soon as they enlisted – with their masters' consent.[27]

In military terms, the measure was fruitless. The Confederate War Office issued the necessary orders only on 23 March 1865, just two weeks before Appomattox. But such orders, however belated, have understandably attracted the attention of generations of historians anxious to determine what this extraordinary chapter in Southern history signified about the nature of the Confederacy and its evolution.

Most commentators have treated the proposal to emancipate slaves in return for military service as prima facie evidence of a weak (or, at least, a weakened) commitment to the economic interests and institutions – plantation agriculture based on unfree black labour – of the Southern elite. Some have argued that a firm commitment to those interests had, in fact, never been central to the Confederate cause. Others contended that it had but that the socio-economic stakes had declined in importance during the war years, to be replaced by a nationalistic commitment to Southern independence for its own sake. Still others, declining to characterize the Confederate leadership as a whole in such terms, have nonetheless presented the proposal's chief architects in this light.

This general understanding of the proposal's significance originated in the Confederacy's wartime debate itself. Planter resistance to the Confederate government's interference with their slave property, especially through impressment, was notorious. 'They give up their sons, husbands, brothers and friends,' caustically observed one Confederate congressman, 'and often without murmuring; but let one of their negroes be taken, and what a houl [sic] you will hear.'[28] The response to the Cleburne-Davis policy was naturally even shriller. Planter critics saw it as an abandonment – indeed, a betrayal – of their core interests. The Charleston *Mercury* responded to Jefferson Davis's November 1864 message to Congress by recalling that 'the mere agitation in the Northern States to effect the emancipation of our slaves largely contributed to our separation from them.' And now, the *Mercury* added in tones of incredulity, 'before a Confederacy which we established to put at rest forever all such agitation is four years old, we find the proposition gravely submitted that the Confederate Government should emancipate slaves in the States.'[29] Virginia's Robert M.T. Hunter, president pro tempore of the

Confederate Senate, asked in amazement, 'What did we go to war for, if not to protect our property?'[30] Where was the logic, demanded these critics and many others, in defending slavery with measures that dissolved it?[31]

Regarding the proposal as subversive led logically to viewing its supporters as, at best, indifferent to the defining institutions of the Old South's economy and society. Generals Braxton Bragg and W.H.T. Walker of the Army of Tennessee denounced Patrick Cleburne and his co-thinkers as leaders of an 'abolition party' who 'should be watched'.[32] Even the already sainted Robert E. Lee found his loyalty questioned when he endorsed Davis's plans months later. An enraged Charleston *Mercury* attributed Lee's position to 'a profound disbelief in the institution of slavery' that could be traced back through the political opinions of 'some of the strongest and most influential names and individuals in Virginia.'[33] Closer to home, the Richmond *Examiner* also questioned Lee's standing as 'a good southerner'.[34] Belief that the debate pitted those who prioritized the Confederacy's socio-economic foundations against pure Southern nationalists attached primarily to independence per se drew additional strength from at least some of the proposal's defenders and their public justifications. Following republican rhetorical practice, the latter tended to elevate the claims of patriotic duty over selfish preoccupations with wealth and property.[35]

This understanding of the proposal's meaning was powerfully reinforced in the post-war era, when the Confederacy's apologists, with Jefferson Davis and Alexander Stephens in the lead, sought retrospectively to minimize the centrality of slavery to the Southern cause.[36] In 1869, the journalist Edward A. Pollard, previously associated with the ardently secessionist Richmond *Examiner*, specifically introduced the Davis administration's manumission plans as evidence that the Confederate leadership as a whole had harboured little enthusiasm about slavery. That programme of 'Negro enlistments and consequent emancipation,' Pollard contended, demonstrated that slavery had been merely 'an inferior object of the contest – surely not the chief cause and end of the war, as Northern writers have been forward to misrepresent.' That hierarchy of Confederate priorities, he continued, also explained 'the easy assent which the South gave to the extinction of Slavery at the last'.[37]

Modern scholars with little sympathy for such post facto apologias have reaffirmed that slavery was indeed the cornerstone of the old South and that its defence was central to secession and the creation of the Confederacy. But many of them have had difficulty reconciling that general view with the particular proposal to arm and free Confederate slaves. Robert F. Durden dealt with the problem by minimizing the extent of the support for the Cleburne-

Davis measures, stressing the furious resistance to the enterprise mounted by so many planters and the Confederate Congress's consequent refusal to offer manumission to prospective slave soldiers, even at the eleventh hour. But in characterizing the Cleburne-Davis camp, Durden did attribute to it a fundamental difference with slavery's last-ditch defenders. The latter, Durden held, were paralysed by 'parochialism and racial conservatism'. But the existence of the former, Durden believed, did reveal 'that there was yet a reservoir of good will between the white and black races in the South, which reservoir was nearly tapped by the Confederacy.'[38]

By no means all modern accounts of the Confederacy's debate give this much credit to Cleburne, Davis and company. But some of the finest historians of the old South have argued that the arming-and-emancipating project reflected a relative disinterest in the fate of slavery and disregard for core planter interests. The drive to preserve a separate southern nation, in their view, had become for some central leaders of the Confederacy an end in itself, one worth achieving even at the expense of the economic and social institutions for the sake of which the Confederacy had originally been constituted.[39] So, as Paul D. Escott saw it, the debate ranged those who recognized that 'slavery was the basis of the planter class's wealth, power, and position in society' and therefore 'found the idea of voluntarily destroying that world, even in the ultimate crisis, . . . almost unthinkable,' against those, like Davis, for whom 'from the first days of the war . . . [the] paramount goal was the attainment of independence'.[40] For Emory Thomas, too, 'the debate over arming the slaves was a debate over the South's entire racial attitude.' Davis and his allies prized 'independence over all other considerations'; at the end their 'struggle had but one goal: independence, the ability to exist as a people.'[41] Other able students of the South have come to similar conclusions.[42]

A fresh look at the Cleburne-Davis plan's details, its most candid justifications, and its broader social context, especially in light of the scholarship of the last couple of decades on slavery and emancipation, points to a different conclusion. This reevaluation challenges the view that the Confederacy's internal debate on this issue represented the clash of fundamentally distinct sets of values. It denies that the eventual, albeit belated, promulgation of the Cleburne-Davis plan meant the triumph of nationalist-political over planter-economic priorities. It argues instead that the dispute was primarily a tactical one, expressing only differing assessments of how best to defend the plantation system and how best to assure the continued availability of the relatively malleable and inexpensive labour that chattel slavery had previously provided. According to this analysis, advocates of arming and emancipating slaves championed a shrewder and more farsighted calculation of planter interests in the face of extremely adverse conditions. Because of the extent and ferocity of planter resistance, even at the Confederacy's eleventh hour, their plans could be implemented only by a regime in Richmond that was increasingly freed from planter control precisely by the conditions of a failing war effort.

A central premise of General Patrick Cleburne's thinking in late 1863 was that slavery was already a dying institution. As Union forces entered plantation districts, slaves abandoned their masters by the thousands in pursuit of freedom. This made its swiftest headway and left its deepest imprint on slavery in the western theatre – specifically, in the Union's seizure of the black-belt Mississippi River Valley, culminating in the summer of 1863 with the conquest of Vicksburg, Mississippi, and Port Hudson, Louisiana. By then, the Lincoln administration had recognized the military logic of the situation, incorporating emancipation into its war aims and recruiting black former slaves into its armed forces – some 180,000 by the war's end. Black Union troops had already played important and visible roles in the taking of Port Hudson, just as they did at the battles of Milliken's Bend and Fort Wagner.[43] One Louisiana-born infantryman, proud of having volunteered for units raised in two states, attributed 'the protracted duration of the war' to the role that former slaves were playing in and for the Union army. 'Seward', this soldier noted, 'has boldly laid down the proposition of an irresistible conflict between free and slave labour.' In light of how the armed struggle itself had evolved, the Union's secretary of state now 'no doubt often recalls this, as the most sage remark of his life'.[44]

The impact of these developments on slavery was not limited to those districts actually occupied by Union troops, as W.E.B. Du Bois argued sixty years ago, and as modern scholars have amply documented.[45] Even within the unoccupied Confederacy, the obviously declining coercive power of owners emboldened and enabled black field workers to demand improvements in their conditions and implicit but no less momentous alterations in their status – and to withhold their labour until their demands were met. Owners were thus compelled to bid, to bargain, more and more openly for the services of those who were nominally still their own property.

The unavoidable reality, in short, was that slavery was dissolving and that the ex-slaves were themselves becoming principal instruments of the planters' ruin. The year 1864, when Sherman's army crossed from Tennessee into north-west Georgia and then took Atlanta and Savannah, carried this inescapable dynamic into the eastern sector of the Confederacy.[46] From the path of Sherman's army, thus, came warnings that if the slaves were 'left as they are', the Confederates would soon 'be compelled to fight them in the ranks of our enemies',[47] that 'in a very short time every able bodied negro' here 'will either be a soldier in the Yankee Army or employed in some way to contribute to our destruction.'[48] Even as Patrick Cleburne was composing his memorandum, a journalist in Atlanta reported 'often hear[ing] such remarks as that slavery is doomed'.[49]

Cleburne's Army of Tennessee, veteran of the western theatre (it had formerly been known as the Army of Mississippi) and retreating before Sherman's troops ever since Chattanooga, witnessed all these developments at first hand. As Cleburne observed, 'Slavery, from being one of our chief sources of strength at the commencement of the war, has now become, in a military point of view, one of our chief sources of weakness.' 'All along the lines slavery is comparatively valueless to us for labor,' he specified, 'but of great and increasing worth to the enemy for information. It is an omnipresent spy system, pointing out our valuable men to the enemy, revealing our positions, purposes, and resources.' The slaves' obvious pro-Union partisanship created 'fear of insurrection in the rear' and 'anxieties for the fate of loved ones when our armies have moved forward.' And when federal troops advanced, the slaves became 'recruits awaiting the enemy with open arms', and those who donned Union blue had proved able 'to face and fight bravely against their former masters'.[50] Cleburne and those Southern leaders who endorsed his proposal then or later sought to harness the military power of the slaves on behalf of the Confederacy while preserving key aspects of antebellum economic and social arrangements. Some of them, especially at first, hoped that the number of those slaves actually freed could be limited.[51] Before long, however, the logic of the continual disintegration of slavery demonstrated the impossibility of so restricting the quantitative scope of emancipation. The firmer and enduring hope was, by whatever means were necessary, to preserve the existence of a separate Confederate state and government in order to be able after the end of the war to dictate and thereby limit the *qualitative* scope – the nature and degree – of emancipation.

Robert E. Lee couched his support for the measure in just such terms. On 11 January 1865 – some five weeks before writing his better-known letter to Barksdale – Lee wrote to Virginia state legislator Andrew Hunter to affirm his belief that 'the relation of master and slave, controlled by humane laws and influenced by Christianity and enlightened public sentiment' was 'the best that can exist between the white and black races'. Unfortunately, developments beyond the control of the master class now made impossible the survival of that ideal relationship; slavery as such was doomed. The question at hand had therefore shifted to the manner it which it would die and exactly what relationship would take its place. The choice, Lee explained, was 'whether slavery shall be extinguished by our enemies and the slaves used against us, or use them ourselves at the risk of the effects which may be produced upon our social institutions.' The penetration of Union forces into the Confederacy threatened to 'destroy *slavery in a manner* most pernicious to the welfare of our people.' 'Whatever may be the effect of our employing negro troops,' he added, 'it cannot be as mischievous as this. If it ends in subverting slavery it well be accomplished by ourselves, and we can devise the means of alleviating the evil consequences to both races.'[52]

The Davis administration developed this theme further in November 1864, when it first floated the trial balloon of emancipation. At that time Judah P. Benjamin theorized about just what kind of emancipation might occur and what role free blacks would play in a post-war Confederacy. The Richmond government, Benjamin made clear, looked forward to no kind of inter-racial democracy or the end of plantation society. Benjamin thought that 'ultimate emancipation' would follow only after 'an intermediate state of serfage or peonage' of unspecified duration. '[W]hile vindicating our faith in the doctrine that the negro is an inferior race and unfitted for social or political equality with the white man,' thus, the South could still 'modify and ameliorate the existing condition of that inferior race by providing for it *certain* rights of property, *a certain degree* of personal liberty, and legal protection for the marital and parental relations.'[53]

The same line of reasoning found still fuller and clearer exposition in a communication written in February 1865. It would be difficult to depict the writer, John Henry Stringfellow of Virginia, as a long-time doubter of slavery's value or legitimacy or even as a single-minded Southern nationalist who placed slavery second to regional pride and independence. During the 1850s Stringfellow had helped lead the effort to impose slavery upon the Kansas territory. As speaker of the territory's pro-slavery House of Representatives in 1855, he sponsored a resolution declaring it 'the duty of the pro-slavery party, the Union-loving men of Kansas Territory, to know but one issue, Slavery; and that any party making, or attempting to make, any other [issue] is and should be held as an ally of Abolition and Disunionism.'[54] Stringfellow returned to Virginia in 1858; in 1865 he resided in the town of Glenn Allen in Henrico County, just north of the Confederate capital. There he got wind of Davis's proposal and committed his thoughts to paper two days before the Confederate Congress took up the matter.

Stringfellow began by reaffirming the virtues of slavery, doing so in the ardent terms of a Calhoun or Fitzhugh. He had 'always believed, and still believe[d], that slavery is an institution sanctioned, if not established, by the Almighty, and the most humane and beneficent relation that can exist between labor and capital.' Yet, he added,

> If the war continues [as at present], we shall in the end be subjugated, our negroes emancipated, our lands parceled out amongst them, and if any of it be left to us, only an equal portion with our own negroes, and ourselves given only equal (if any) social and political rights and privileges.

On the other hand, he continued, 'If we emancipate, our independence is secured, the white man only will have any and all political rights,' he alone will 'retain all his real and personal property, exclusive of his property in his slave,' he alone will 'make laws to control the free negro.' The latter, meanwhile, 'having no land [,] must labor for the land owner . . . on terms about as economical as tho owned by him.' To make the point absolutely clear, Stringfellow returned to it a few pages later. '[I]f we emancipate,' the slaveowner of today will 'have all his labour on his farm that he had before,' while the former slave, 'having no home & no property to buy one with,' will have to 'live with & work for his old owner for such wages as said owner may choose to give, to be regulated by law hereafter as may suit the change of relation.' And yet again:

> In my judgment the only question for us to decide is whether we shall gain our independence by freeing the negro, we retaining all the power to regulate them by law when so freed, or permit our enemies through our own slaves to compel us to submit to emancipation with equal or superior rights for our negroes, and partial or complete confiscation of our property for the benefit of the negro.[55]

Examined so closely and in its actual context, the Confederate plan for emancipation thus ceases to be an incomprehensible, pointless, even self-defeating act of desperation. It also ceases to appear a fundamental reversal of traditional slaveowner priorities, much less of previous notions about race. It rested, instead, upon a shrewd and cold-blooded appraisal of the slaveholders' actual situation and real options after the middle of 1863. Given the almost certain demise of slavery, one way or the other, Cleburne, and later Davis, Benjamin, Lee and others, asked: what is the next-best state of affairs from the planters' point of view? They concluded: a minimum degree of personal liberty for black labourers whose real alternatives would be severely limited by the planters' monopoly of land and their control of the state apparatus. Preserving Confederate independence thus meant preserving a South in which political power remained securely in the hands of white planters and farmers – power that alone would allow them to 'make laws to control the free negro' and 'to regulate [their wages] by law'. To retain that supreme political power in friendly hands, and thereby ensure the best possible conditions for plantation agriculture, many things, even full-fledged slavery itself, could be compromised.

Cleburne had urged his policy on Confederate politicians in precisely these terms. 'It is said slaves will not work after they are freed,' his memo noted, but 'we think necessity and wise legislation will compel them to labor for a living.'[56] Confederate Congressman Arthur St Clair Colyar of Tennessee spoke with Cleburne in Atlanta shortly afterward. Colyar's account of that conversation reported that Cleburne 'considered slavery at an end'. But that observation was, for Cleburne, only the beginning, not the end, of wisdom concerning black labour's future status. '[I]f the Yankees succeed in abolishing slavery,' Cleburne had continued, 'equality and amalgamation will finally take place.' On the other hand, 'if we take this step now, we can mould the relations, for all time to come, between the white and colored races; and we can control the negroes, and . . . they will still be our laborers as much as they now are; and, to all intents and purposes, will be our servants, at less cost than now.'[57]

This project was by no means *sui generis*. It bore a strong family resemblance to a series of revolutions-from-above attempted by various contemporaneous regimes in Europe. Confronting the instability or economic inadequacy of the social and political arrangements upon which their reign depended, especially in the face of challenges from within (popular resistance) or without (invasion of the German states by Napoleonic armies, Russia's defeat in the Crimean War), one ruling group after another sought to modify those arrangements. Each attempted to do so in ways that would reinforce its own supremacy while preserving intact as much as possible the wealth and power of those elite social strata upon which the rulers depended. These manoeuvres usually required concessions at least to some segments of the lower classes while limiting their real civil and political rights. Serf emancipation east of the Elbe, despite the considerable variation in the way it occurred there, conformed to this general characterization.[58] Otto von Bismarck continued the project in Germany in the second half of the century by accelerating industrialization and strengthening national unity while resisting the expansion of popular democratic rights and preserving much of the power of the Junkerdom.[59]

In the history of the American South, the Cleburne-Davis proposal and the understanding that it represented of planter society's needs and actual options constituted an equivalently important moment in the evolution of elite programmatic thought. It has been suggested that planter leaders were utterly unready in mid-1865 to formulate a practical programme for post-slavery society. Robert F. Durden thought the white South's post-war record showed it had 'forgot[ten] all about the uncharacteristic flirtation with unorthodoxy' represented by the Cleburne-Davis plan.[60] On both counts, the opposite seems much closer to the truth. Touring the deep South within a few months of Appomattox, Carl Schurz already discerned broad agreement among the planters that while 'slavery in the old form *cannot* be maintained' it was necessary 'to introduce into the new system that element of physical compulsion which would make the negro work' for them – i.e., 'to make free labor compulsory by permanent regulations.' Thus, Schurz discovered, 'although the freedman is no longer considered the property of the individual master, he is considered the slave of society, and all independent State legislation will share the tendency to make him such.'[61] As is well known, Schurz's report anticipated political developments soon to come, as one Southern legislature after another wrote precisely the programme he had outlined into law in the form of the so-called Black Codes.[62] But just how could so many planters and their allies have reached the same programmatic conclusions so quickly? The foregoing analysis of the Cleburne-Davis plan and the thinking behind it provides a partial answer to this question. The idea of coupling nominal emancipation with aggressive state action to keep the freedmen property-less and to compel them to labour hard and cheaply for the white landowners was already in the minds of Cleburne, Benjamin, Davis, Lee and others before the end of the war.[63] In this sense, the years-long, escalating debate may well have served as a programmatic rehearsal for reconstruction for the planter elite and its champions.[64] Military defeat, to be sure, dashed hopes that an independent Confederate government might control and limit the extent of emancipation. Schurz had noted the political re-adjustment corresponding to that fact: a widespread 'anxiety to have their State governments restored *at once*, to have the troops withdrawn, and the Freedmen's Bureau abolished' – that is, to reestablish planter-friendly political rule in the southern states of the restored federal union.[65]

These observations, of course, beg the next question: from what sources did inspiration for the wartime proposal (and post-war Black Codes) arise? Answers point back to multiple examples of aggressive state action to assure the availability of a cheap and malleable labour force. Some Southern leaders, including George Fitzhugh and J.D.B. DeBow, found precedent for granting limited civil but no political rights in the laws and practices of the ancient and medieval Mediterranean world.[66] Notoriously, English rulers over the course of centuries had used political power both to dispossess small producers and (in the form of vagrancy and other laws) to compel them to labour for others in targeted sectors in return for minimal compensation.[67] In Ireland, 'penal laws' that restricted the economic options of Catholics combined with market forces and social structure to produce a similar result.[68] As the Irish-born Confederate General Patrick Cleburne assured Arthur Colyar in January, 1864, 'writing a man "free" does not make him so, as the history of the Irish labourer shows.'[69] More recent precedents could be found nearby. In the US South, state laws had long imposed sundry restrictions on the economic options of technically free black residents. Apprenticeship laws imposed a form of semi-slavery on free black youths, and adults were subjected to various forms of debt peonage.[70]

A related object lesson, a negative one from the planter standpoint, was to be found in the record of emancipation in the British West Indies during the 1830s. There, a post-emancipation programme of 'apprenticeship' that had narrowed the occupational options of former slaves was quickly abandoned. The destruction of the plantation system, it was widely reported then and later, had been the inevitable result. What was needed, a convention of US cotton planters later argued, specifically invoking the West Indian experience, was 'some well regulated system of labor, . . . devised by the white man'.[71] Judah P. Benjamin, who had been born in the West Indies and who apparently retained an intellectual interest in things British throughout his life, was already a young man when emancipation came to the Empire.[72] Benjamin's biographers depict him as the Davis administration's first and most vigorous champion of a new departure on the subject of slavery.[73] Perhaps memories of the West Indies' aborted 'apprenticeship' plan helped Benjamin to see thirty years later that there could be more than one path leading out of slavery.

Many scholars have explored yet another possible inspiration for the Confederate leadership's late wartime policies. This was the antebellum and wartime campaign to reform, or 'humanise', chattel slavery, to make it conform more closely to the paternalist ideal of a reciprocal, 'organic', mutually beneficial and universally appreciated relationship between masters and servants, superiors and inferiors.[74] Championed by secular figures (including T.R.R. Cobb, Henry Hughes, and even Robert Toombs), this movement found its most numerous and consistent advocates among Protestant ministers (notably Calvin H. Wiley, James Henley Thornwell, George Foster Pierce and James

A. Lyon) who urged such measures as easing restrictions on slaves' religious practice and education and legalizing and practically reinforcing their marriages and family lives. The reformers pressed their case with increased vigour and urgency in the late wartime years. As it happens, Jefferson Davis had a long and intimate familiarity with the paternalist programme. His family's cotton plantations in Davis Bend, Mississippi, had for decades operated according to a school of 'slave management' that sought to win the loyalty and cooperation of its labourers by granting them across-the-board material improvement, incentives and an unusual degree of both personal and communal self-government within the framework of continuing bondage.[75] Perhaps these experiences plus the strictures of the reform movement helped prepare Davis to accept more quickly than most members of his class the idea that unfree labour might take a variety of forms.

But some scholars have pushed this line of reasoning a crucial step further. The reform movement's existence and strength, they suggest, shows that even before the war the South had been moving to reshape slavery along the general lines subsequently enunciated in the Cleburne-Davis plan – and would have continued along that same path had not war and military defeat intervened.[76] It is always risky to venture onto such hypothetical terrain, but doing so can clarify issues of causation. The movement to reform or 'humanize' slavery, whether advocated in frankly pragmatic terms or as the expression of secular or religious ideology, arose in response to the palpable ills of the slave-labour system. Reformist agitation grew in volume and support as challenges to planter power mounted from below (i.e., from among the slaves) and from outside the South.[77] If we correct 'the evils and abuses connected with slavery,' Rev. James A. Lyon thus argued in 1863, 'the slave will not be so likely to make his escape' or 'to engage in insubordinate schemes and insurrectionary enterprises,' and 'we can defend the institution against the wily assaults of the world.'[78]

Until the war, however, threats to the slave-labour system had rarely appeared potent enough to give reformers the leverage they needed to enact their full programme. For every legislative advance they could boast, there was a counterbalancing instance of frustration, defeat and rollback.[79] Even in 1861 and 1862, the idea of replacing full-fledged chattel slavery with state-enforced peonage was rarely heard. It was still being discouraged – indeed, suppressed – by the Davis administration as late as January 1864. The momentous changes that Confederate leaders finally accepted in 1864–5 became thinkable only when imminent military defeat brought Southern society's general social crisis to a head and left them alternatives that seemed far worse.

As noted earlier, many writers have exaggerated the differences in basic outlook and interests between proponents and critics of the Cleburne-Davis plan, mistaking a programme designed to salvage as much of plantation society as possible for one that turned its back on planter interests entirely. But to assert that the same kind of programme would have been adopted even without the war-spawned social and political crisis rejects one error only to embrace its mirror-opposite. Such an assertion substantially underestimates the planter majority's attachment to chattel slavery per se, its aversion to legislative reforms thereof, and its enraged resistance to exchanging chattel slavery for state-sponsored peonage. It also overlooks the massive war-spawned crisis of slave society required to induce the more far-sighted planters and their political representatives to accept such a programme at the eleventh hour.

Even then, it is worth noting, the half-hearted and very incomplete approval wrested from the Confederate Congress was forthcoming only because the exigencies and progress of the war had released the Richmond government as a whole from the effective control of planters who still had slaves to lose. War Bureau chief R.G.H. Kean thus recorded in late November 1864 that 'the [Congressional] representation of the planters are strongly averse' to 'the suggestion of the employment of negroes as soldiers.' Support for such a measure, Kean observed, tended rather to come from those Confederate Congressmen 'who represent imaginary constituencies' – i.e., from those parts of the Confederacy already occupied by Union troops and in most cases now subject to the terms of the Emancipation Proclamation.[80] A careful modern study by Thomas B. Alexander and Richard E. Beringer reached a similar conclusion. Interestingly, the slavery-reformer Henry Hughes's pantheon of heroes evidently included Caesar and Napoleon.[81] Perhaps Hughes recognized that enacting significant change in the nature of bondage would require the kind of government autonomy from the nation's socially dominant class historically associated with those two names. An even more appropriate hero would have been Otto von Bismarck. In relation to the East Elbian Junker landlords, as Friedrich Engels remarked, the Iron Chancellor 'had acted in their own best interest', albeit 'against the steady opposition of these Don Quixotes'.[82]

The real meaning of Confederate emancipation can be disclosed only when that policy is examined in its specific context. In the mind of the Confederate leadership, it was part of an attempted revolution-from-above designed to safeguard as well as possible core planter interests in extremely adverse circumstances. Only such critical circumstances made it possible to propose, much less impose, such a plan. And only the climax of the general crisis of slave-labour society – in the form of unconditional surrender and militarily imposed abolition in the spring of 1865 – made a programme of half-way emancipation a palatable one for the planter class as a whole during the era of Reconstruction.

Notes

1. The author is indebted to the assistance and suggestions of many friends and colleagues, notably Jonathan Beecher, Ira Berlin, David Brundage, Mark Cioc, Stanley Engerman, Eric Foner, William W. Freehling, Charles Hedrick, Peter Kolchin, Leslie Rowland, Patricia Sanders, Buchanan Sharp, Bruce Thompson and Lynn Westerkamp. He would also like to thank the staffs of the National Archives Textual Reference Division; the Kansas State Historical Society; the Rare Book, Manuscript, and Special Collections Library at Duke University; and the Hargrett Rare Book and Manuscript Library at the University of Georgia. Research for this chapter was supported by a faculty research grant from the University of California, Santa Cruz.

2. James D. Richardson (ed.), *A Compilation of the Messages and Papers of the Confederacy, Including the Diplomatic Correspondence, 1861–1865* (Nashville, Tenn., 1906), vol. 1, pp. 64–8. Confederate Vice President Alexander Stephens had, if anything, put the matter even more bluntly in a speech delivered in Savannah the previous month. The Confederacy, he explained, was dedicated to preserving 'the proper status of the negro in our form of civilization'. Where Jefferson had talked of human equality, 'our new government is founded upon exactly the opposite idea; its foundations are laid, its cornerstone rests, upon the great truth that . . . slavery – subordination to the superior race' – was the 'natural and normal condition' of the African. Augusta, Georgia, *Constitutionalist*, 30 March 1861.

3. The words belonged to Davis's secretary of state and closest cabinet advisor, Judah P. Benjamin. Quoted in Robert F. Durden, *The Gray and the Black: The Debate over Confederate Emancipation* (Baton Rouge, La, 1972), p. 194.

4. Articles dedicated specifically to this subject include N.W. Stephenson, 'The Question of arming the slaves', *American Historical Review*, 18 (January 1913), pp. 295–308; Thomas Robson Hay, 'The South and the arming of the slaves', *Mississippi Valley Historical Review*, 6 (June 1919), pp. 34–73; Charles H. Wesley, 'The employment of negroes as soldiers in the Confederate Army', *Journal of Negro History*, 4 (July 1919), pp. 239–53; Bill G. Reid, 'Confederate

opponents of arming the slaves, 1861–1865', *Journal of Mississippi History*, 22 (October 1960), pp. 260, 264; and Barbara C. Ruby, 'General Patrick Cleburne's proposal to arm Southern Slaves', *Arkansas Historical Quarterly*, 30 (Fall 1971), pp. 193–212. Popularized accounts include Stephen E. Ambrose, 'By enlisting negroes, could the South still win the war?', *Civil War Times*, 3 (January 1965), pp. 16–21; and Steve Davis, 'That extraordinary document: W.H.T. Walker and Patrick Cleburne's Emancipation Proposal', *Civil War Times*, 16 (December 1977), pp. 14–20. The subject is also addressed in many other works, many of which will be discussed below.

5. The year 1998 was the centenary of the publication of *The War of the Rebellion: A Compilation of the Official Records of the Union and Confederate Armies* (Washington, DC, 1898) – hereafter cited as *O.R.* – in which the world first glimpsed a number of the documents generated by this controversy. In 1972, Robert F. Durden's *The Gray and the Black* reprinted much of the documentary record.

6. Emory M. Thomas, review of Durden, *Journal of Southern History*, 39 (May 1973), pp. 300–1.

7. W.S. Turner to Hon. L.P. Walker, 17 July 1861, in *Freedom: A Documentary History of Emancipation, 1861–1867*, ser. 2, *The Black Military Experience*, ed. Ira Berlin, Joseph P. Reidy and Leslie S. Rowland (Cambridge, 1982), p. 283; C. Vann Woodward and Elisabeth Muhlenfeld (eds), *The Private Mary Chesnut: The Unpublished Civil War Diaries* (New York and Oxford, 1984), p. 213. See also C. Vann Woodward (ed.), *Mary Chesnut's Civil War* (New Haven, Ct, 1981), pp. 255, 340.

8. Richard Taylor, *Destruction and Reconstruction: Personal Experiences of the Late War* (1879; rpt, New York, 1955), p. 281; O.G. Eiland to Jefferson Davis, 20 July 1863, in Berlin *et al.*, *The Black Military Experience*, p. 284.

9. Bell Irvin Wiley, *Confederate Negroes, 1861–1865* (Baton Rouge: La, 1938), p. 149; Edward Younger (ed.), *Inside the Confederate Government: The Diary of Robert Garlick Hill Kean* (New York and Oxford, 1957), p. 96; *O.R.*, ser. 4, vol. 2, p. 767.

10. A sketch of Cleburne's life written by his long-time commanding officer, William J. Hardee, appeared as an appendix to John Francis Maguire, *The Irish in America* (London, 1868), pp. 642–53.

11. Irving A. Buck, 'Negroes in our army', *Southern Historical Society Papers*, 31 (1903), p. 215; and Thomas L. Connelly, *Autumn of Glory: The Army of Tennessee, 1862–1865* (Baton Rouge, La, 1971), pp. 235, 274–81, 290–1. Capt. Buck was Cleburne's adjutant.

12. *O.R.*, ser. 1, vol. 52, pt 2, pp. 586, 589–90.

13. Connelly, *Autumn of Glory*, pp. 318–20; Buck, 'Negroes in our army', p. 217;
    O.R., ser. 1, vol. 52, pt 2, pp. 593–9, 606–7. Cleburne himself evidently
    respected Seddon's orders to cease agitation on the matter. And at Cleburne's
    order, Capt. Irving Buck destroyed all but one copy of the original memo.
    R.G.H. Kean, head of the Bureau of War, believed that few not present at the
    meeting at Hardee's headquarters had learned of the incident. Following its
    suppression, the text of Cleburne's memo disappeared from sight until 1890,
    when a copy was discovered in the papers of a member of Cleburne's staff.
    Letter from A.S. Colyar to A.S. Marks, 5 February 1864, in *The Annals of
    the Army of Tennessee and Early Western History*, vol. 1 (May 1878), p. 52; Buck,
    'Negroes in our army', pp. 216–17; Younger (ed.), *The Diary of R.G.H. Kean*,
    pp. 177–8; J.B. Jones, *A Rebel War Clerk's Diary at the Confederate State Capital*, ed.
    Howard Swiggett (New York, 1935), vol. 2, p. 146; and Connelly, *Autumn of
    Glory*, p. 319.

14. Younger (ed.), *The Diary of R.G.H. Kean*, p. 182.

15. Samuel Clayton to Jefferson Davis, 10 January 1865, in *O.R.*, ser. 4, vol. 3,
    p. 1011.

16. Alexander W. Cooper to Jefferson Davis, 25 December 1864, in the Jefferson
    Davis Papers, Rare Book, Manuscript, and Special Collections Library, Duke
    University.

17. C.B. Leitner to Jefferson Davis, 31 December 1864, Letters Received by the
    Secretary of War, National Archives, letter L 40 1865.

18. Lee to Davis, 2 November 1864, in Durden, *The Gray and the Black*, p. 68.

19. H. Kendall to Jefferson Davis, 16 September 1864, original emphasis, Letters
    Received by the Secretary of War, National Archives, letter K 73 1864.

20. New Orleans *Picayune* of 3 November 1864, in Durden, *The Gray and the Black*,
    p. 80. See also *O.R.*, ser. 1, vol. 48, pt 1, p. 1321; and Younger (ed.), *The Diary
    of R.G.H. Kean*, p. 183.

21. *O.R.*, ser. 4, vol. 3, pp. 915–16; ser. 1, vol. 41, pt 3, p. 774.

22. *O.R.*, ser. 4, vol. 3, p. 959.

23. Wilfred Buck Yearns, *The Confederate Congress* (Atlanta, Ga, 1960), pp. 97–8.

24. Lee to Barksdale, 18 February 1865, in Durden, *The Gray and the Black*,
    pp. 206–7.

25. In addition to individual letters cited earlier, see Jones, *Rebel War Clerk's Diary*,
    p. 451; and Durden, *The Gray and the Black*, pp. 205, 215–24.

[258]   26. *Journal of the Congress of the Confederate States of America, 1861–1865* (Washington, DC, 1905), vol. 7, pp. 612–13; Yearns, *The Confederate Congress*, p. 97.

27. *Journal of the Confederate Congress*, vol. 4, pp. 585, 670–1; Yearns, *The Confederate Congress*, p. 98; *O.R.*, ser. 4, vol. 3, pp. 1161–2.

28. Paul Escott, *After Secession: Jefferson Davis and the Failure of Confederate Nationalism* (Baton Rouge, La, 1978), pp. 246–7.

29. The *Mercury* of 3 November 1864, in Durden, *The Gray and the Black*, p. 98.

30. Shelby Foote, *The Civil War: A Narrative* (New York, 1974), vol. 3, p. 766.

31. Durden, *The Gray and the Black*, pp. 232–3; James M. McPherson, *For Cause and Comrades: Why Men Fought in the Civil War* (New York and Oxford, 1997), p. 171; Reid, 'Confederate opponents of arming the slaves', p. 267; *O.R.*, ser. 4, vol. 3, pp. 1009–10.

32. Connelly, *Autumn of Glory*, p. 320.

33. The *Mercury* of 3 February 1865, in Durden, *The Gray and the Black*, pp. 235–6.

34. Quoted in Escott, *After Secession*, p. 254.

35. Thomas Robson Hay, 'The South and the arming of the slaves', *Mississippi Valley Historical Review*, 6 (June, 1919): 48–9; *O.R*, ser. 1, vol. 52, pt 2, pp. 586–92.

36. Stephens gave pride of place to differences over states rights. The Confederacy, he declared, was the creature not of a 'Pro-Slavery Party' but rather of those with 'strong convictions that the Federal Government had no rightful or Constitutional control or jurisdiction' over such local matters as slavery. Alexander Stephens, *A Constitutional View of the Late War Between the States; its Causes, Character, Conduct and Results* (Philadelphia, Pa, 1868), vol. 1, p. 11. Davis attributed the war to transcendent sectional competition. If slavery provided the 'occasion' for the conflict, he insisted, it was 'far from being the cause'. The war was, instead, 'the offspring of sectional rivalry' that preceded and existed quite independently of slavery; the same rivalry 'would have manifested itself just as certainly if slavery had existed in all the states or if there had not been a negro in America.' Jefferson Davis, *The Rise and Fall of the Confederate Government* (1881; rpt, New York, 1958), vol. 1, pp. 78–9.

37. Edward A. Pollard, *Life of Jefferson Davis with a Secret History of the Southern Confederacy* (Atlanta, Ga, 1869), p. 453.

38. Durden, *The Gray and the Black*, pp. viii, 253.

39. Early presentations of this view appeared in Charles H. Wesley, *The Collapse of the Confederacy* (1937; rpt New York, 1968), p. 166; Reid, 'Confederate opponents of arming the slaves,' pp. 260, 264.

40. Escott, *After Secession*, pp. 254–5.

41. Thomas, *The Confederate Nation, 1861–1865* (New York, 1979), pp. 291–4, 299.

42. Laurence Shore, *Southern Capitalists: The Ideological Leadership of an Elite* (Chapel Hill, NC, 1986), p. 93; Richard E. Beringer, Herman Hattaway, Archer Jones and William N. Still, Jr, *Why the South Lost the Civil War* (Athens, Ga, 1986), p. 391; William C. Davis, *Jefferson Davis: The Man and his Hour* (New York, 1991), p. 598; Lawrence N. Powell and Michael S. Wayne, 'Self-interest and the decline of Confederate nationalism', in *The Old South in the Crucible of War*, ed. Harry P. Owens and James J. Cooke (Jackson, Miss., 1983), p. 32; Eli N. Evans, *Judah P. Benjamin The Jewish Confederate* (New York, 1988), p. 287; Craig L. Symonds, *Stonewall of the West: Patrick Cleburne and the Civil War* (Lawrence, Ks, 1997), p. 182. While noting anomalous cases, Clarence Mohr agreed that the debate generally ranged 'traditionalists', for whom secession was 'merely a tactic to defend chattel bondage', against 'Rebel patriots who reversed the priorities and saw political independence itself as the transcendent war aim'. Mohr, *On the Threshold of Freedom: Masters and Slaves in Civil War Georgia* (Athens, Ga and London, 1986), pp. 275, 277.

43. *Freedom: A Documentary History of Emancipation, 1861–1867*, ser. 1, vol. 1, *The Destruction of Slavery*, ed. Ira Berlin, Barbara J. Fields, Thavolia Glymph, Joseph P. Reidy and Leslie Rowland (Cambridge, 1985), pp. 38–40; James M. McPherson, *Battle Cry of Freedom: The Civil War Era* (New York, 1988), pp. 637, 664.

44. Edward Pollard to Jefferson Davis, 13 January 1865, National Archives, Letters Received by the Secretary of War, letter P 16 1865.

45. 'In a certain sense, after the first few months everybody knew that slavery was done with; that no matter who won, the condition of the slave could never be the same after the disaster of the war,' DuBois wrote. As accustomed means of enforcing slave obedience disintegrated, 'there was a certain feeling and appre-hension in the air on the part of the whites', and 'the rigor of the slave system in the South softened as war proceeded.' W.E.B. DuBois, *Black Reconstruction in America* (1935; rpt, Cleveland: World Publishing Co., 1964), p. 59. See also Armstead Louis Robinson, 'Day of Jubilo: Civil War and the demise of slavery in the Mississippi Valley, 1861–1865' (PhD dissertation, University of Rochester, 1976), pp. 546–9; Thomas, *Confederate Nation*, pp. 236–40; Mohr, *On the Threshold of Freedom*, pp. 210–34; and especially Berlin *et al.*, *The Destruction of Slavery*, pp. 663–818.

[260]   46. Joseph P. Reidy, *From Slavery to Agrarian Capitalism in the Cotton Plantation South: Central Georgia, 1800–1880* (Chapel Hill, NC 1992), pp. 128–35.

47. C.B. Leitner to Jefferson Davis, 31 December 1864.

48. H. Kendall to Jefferson Davis, 16 September; original emphasis.

49. Editorial in the Memphis *Appeal*, refugeeing in Atlanta, 23 December 1863, in Durden, *The Gray and the Black*, p. 45. Simultaneously, Margaret Daily of Georgia was confiding in her diary, 'I tremble for the institution of slavery; it is well nigh done for.' Bell Irvin Wiley, *Confederate Women* (Westport, Conn., 1975), p. 154.

50. *O.R.*, ser. 1, vol. 52, pt 2, pp. 586–92.

51. Durden, *The Gray and the Black*, pp. 79, 120–2, 246.

52. Lee to Andrew Hunter, 11 January 1865, in *O.R.*, ser. 4, vol. 3, pp. 1012–13, emphasis added.

53. Benjamin to Frederick A. Porcher, 21 December 1864, in *O.R.* ser. 4, vol. 3, pp. 959–60; emphasis added.

54. Clippings from the *Kansas Chief*, 23 January 1879; and the *Atchison Daily Globe*, 16 July 1894 and 13 May 1905, Kansas State Historical Society; Michael B. Ballard, *A Long Shadow: Jefferson Davis and the Final Days of the Confederacy* (Jackson, Miss. and London, 1986), p. 12. Stringfellow's Kansas resolution is quoted in F.B. Sanborn (ed.), *The Life and Letters of John Brown* (1885; rpt, New York, 1969), p. 176.

55. *O.R.*, ser. 4, vol. 3, pp. 1069–70.

56. *O.R.*, ser. 1, vol. 52, pt 2, p. 591.

57. A.S. Colyar to Col. A.S. Marks, 30 January 1864, in *The Annals of the Army of Tennessee and Early Western History*, vol. 1 (May, 1978), pp. 50–2. Marks was Colyar's cousin and a colonel in Cleburne's division. See Thomas Robson Hay, *Pat Cleburne, Stonewall Jackson of the West* (Jackson, Tenn., 1959), pp. 45–6.

58. Hans Rosenberg, *Bureaucracy, Aristocracy and Autocracy: The Prussian Experience, 1660–1815* (1958; rpt, Boston, Mass., 1966), pp. 202–28; Werner Conze, 'The effects of nineteenth-century liberal agrarian reforms on social structure in Central Europe', in *Essays in European Economic History, 1789–1914*, ed. F. Crouzet, W.H. Chaloner and W.M. Stern (New York, 1969), pp. 53–81; Elisabeth Fehrenbach, 'Verfassungs- und sozialpolitische Reformen und Reformprojekte in Deutschland unter dem Einfluss des Napoleonischen Frankreich', *Historische Zeitschrift*, 228 (April 1979), pp. 289–316; G.T.

Robinson, *Rural Russia under the Old Regime* (1932; rpt, Berkeley, Ca, 1960), pp. 88, 92–3. See also Terence Emmons, *The Russian Landed Gentry and the Peasant Emancipation of 1861* (Cambridge, 1968); Alfred J. Rieber, 'Alexander II: A revisionist view', *Journal of Modern History*, 43 (1971), pp. 42–58; and Peter Kolchin, 'Some controversial questions concerning nineteenth-century emancipation from slavery and serfdom', in *Serfdom and Slavery: Studies in Legal Bondage* (London: Ser. 1, 1996), pp. 43–67.

59. Hans-Ulrich Wehler, *The German Empire, 1871–1918* (Leamington Spa, 1985), esp. pp. 24–31, 52–62.

60. Cf. W.R. Brock, *Conflict and Transformation: The United States, 1844–1877* (Harmondsworth, 1973), pp. 306–7; James L. Roark, *Masters without Slaves: Southern Planters in the Civil War and Reconstruction* (New York, 1977), p. 107; Durden, *The Gray and the Black*, p. viii.

61. 'Report on the condition of the South', in *Speeches, Correspondence and Political Papers of Carl Schurz*, ed. Frederic Bancroft (1913; rpt, New York, 1969), vol. 1, pp. 279–374. Quotations on pp. 311, 316, 321, 359, 371–2; emphases added. Subsequent testimony before Congress's Joint Committee on Reconstruction confirmed the prevalence of this thinking throughout the former Confederacy. See, for example, *Report of the Joint Committee on Reconstruction*, pt 2, pp. 123–4, 126, 177; pt 3, pp. 5–7, 15, 24–5, 36, 175, 184.

62. Dan T. Carter, *When the War Was Over: The Failure of Self-Reconstruction in the South, 1865–1867* (Baton Rouge, La, 1985), p. 216; Eric Foner, *Reconstruction: America's Unfinished Revolution, 1863–1877* (New York, 1988), pp. 198–209; Theodore Brantner Wilson, *The Black Codes of the South* (Alabama, 1965), pp. 61–80; Daniel A. Novack, *The Wheel of Servitude: Black Forced Labor After Slavery* (Lexington, Ky, 1978), pp. 1–8; William Cohen, 'Negro involuntary servitude in the South, 1865–1940', *Journal of Southern History*, 42 (February 1976), pp. 35–50; Pete Daniel, 'The metamorphosis of slavery, 1865–1900', *Journal of American History*, 66 (June 1979): 88–99.

63. Berlin *et al.*, *The Black Military Experience*, p. 281.

64. Six days after Judah P. Benjamin speculated about emancipated slaves passing through a 'stage of serfage or peonage', Georgia planter William B. Hodgson contemplated the implications of a Union victory he considered imminent. He noted in his journal that while 'slavery as it has existed may be modified', still 'the European race' must remain able to 'contract the labor of the African under some forms.' Therefore 'a state of serfage, or ascription to the soil is a necessity from which there is no escape.' Hodgson Journal, p. 22, Charles Colcock Jones, Jr, Collection (Ms 215), Hargrett Library, University of Georgia; Mohr, *On The Threshold of Freedom*, p. 292.

65. Schurz, 'Report on the condition of the South', p. 359.

66. See Carter, *When the War Was Over*, p. 186; M. I. Finley, *Ancient Slavery and Modern Ideology* (Harmondsworth, 1980), pp. 142–7; Marc Bloch, *Feudal Society*, tr. L.A. Manyon (Chicago, 1964), vol. 1, pp. 256–60. The relationship between the intellectual and political life of the planter elite and training in the classics in Southern institutions of higher learning deserves further study. See Jennifer Tolbert Roberts, *Athens on Trial: The Antidemocratic Tradition in Western Thought* (Princeton, NJ, 1994), pp. 262–75, 281–3; Roberts, 'Athenian Equality: A Constant Surrounded by Flux', in *Demokratia: A Conversation on Democracies, Ancient and Modern*, ed. Josiah Ober and Charles Hedrick (Princeton, NJ, 1996), pp. 187–202; and Wayne K. Durrill, 'The power of ancient words: classical learning and social change at South Carolina College, 1804–1860', unpublished manuscript.

67. Karl Polanyi, *The Great Transformation: The Political and Economic Origins of Our Time* (Boston, Mass., 1957), pp. 86–8; Christopher Hill, *The Age of Revolution, 1603–1714* (New York, 1961), pp. 207–8; Hill, *Reformation to Industrial Revolution*, vol. 2 of the *Pelican Economic History of Britain* (Baltimore, Md, 1969), pp. 268–74; Buchanan Sharp, 'Common rights, charities and the disorderly poor', *Reviving the English Revolution*, ed. Geoff Eley and William Hunt (London, pp. 107–38).

68. J.C. Beckett, *Making of Modern Ireland, 1603–23* (New York, 1966), pp. 158–59, 172–6; J.G. Simms, 'The Establishment of Protestant Ascendancy, 1691–1714', in *A New History of Ireland*, vol. 4, *Eighteenth-Century Ireland, 1691–1800*, ed. T.W. Moody and W.E. Vaughan (Oxford, 1986), pp. 19–20; J.L. McCracken, 'The social structure and social life, 1714–60', in Ibid., p. 34–9; L.M. Cullen, 'Economic development, 1750–1800', in Ibid., pp. 163–80; R.F. Foster, *Modern Ireland, 1600–1972* (London, 1988), pp. 154–5, 205–11; S.J. Connolly, 'Eighteenth-century Ireland: colony or *Ancien Regime*?', in *The Making of Modern Irish History: Revisionism and the Revisionist Controversy*, ed. D. George Boyce and Alan O'Day (London, 1996), pp. 15–33.

69. Col. A.S. Colyar to Col. A.S. Marks, 30 January 1864, in *The Annals of the Army of Tennessee and Early Western History*, I, no. 2 (May, 1978), p. 52.

70. In addition to the works by Theodore B. Wilson, Daniel Novack and Eric Foner cited above, see Ira Berlin, *Slaves without Masters: The Free Negro in the Antebellum South* (New York, 1974), pp. 225–6, 381–2; and Barbara Jeanne Fields, *Slavery and Freedom on the Middle Ground: Maryland during the Nineteenth Century* (New Haven, Conn., 1985), pp. 35–8, 79–80.

71. Thomas C. Holt, '"An Empire Over the Mind": emancipation, race, and ideology in the British West Indies and the American South', from *Region, Race, and*

Reconstruction: Essays in Honor of C. Vann Woodward, ed. J. Morgan Kousser and James M. McPherson (New York, 1982), pp. 283–313; O. Nigel Bolland, 'Systems of domination after slavery: The control of land and labor in the British West Indies after 1838', *Comparative Studies in Society and History*, 23 (October 1981), pp. 591–619; Joe B. Wilkins, 'Window on freedom: the South's response to the emancipation of the slaves in the British West Indies, 1833–1861' (PhD diss., University of South Carolina, 1977); Eric Foner, *Nothing but Freedom: Emancipation and Its Legacy* (Baton Rouge, La and London, 1983), pp. 41–3.

72. Evans, *Judah P. Benjamin*, p. 5.

73. Pierce Butler, *Judah P. Benjamin* (1907; rpt, New York, 1980), pp. 348–9; Robert Douthat Meade, *Judah P. Benjamin, Confederate Statesman* (New York, 1943), pp. 305–6; Evans, *Judah P. Benjamin*, pp. 5, 233–6, 249–50, 259–75. In his 21 December 1864, letter to Frederick A. Porcher, Benjamin claimed to have been turning the matter over in his mind throughout the previous year. *O.R.*, Ser. 4, vol. 3, pp. 959–60.

74. See Bell I. Wiley, 'Movement to humanize the institution of slavery during the Confederacy', *Emory University Quarterly*, vol. 5 (December 1949), pp. 207–20; Donald G. Mathews, 'Charles Colcock Jones and the Southern Evangelical Crusade to form a biracial community', *Journal of Southern History*, 41 (August 1975), pp. 299–320; Anne C. Loveland, *Southern Evangelicals and the Social Order, 1800–1860* (Baton Rouge, La, 1980), pp. 206–18; Bertram Wyatt-Brown, 'Modernizing Southern slavery: the proslavery argument reinterpreted', in *Region, Race and Reconstruction: Essays in Honor of C. Vann Woodward* (Baton Rouge, La, 1981), pp. 27–50; Mohr, *Threshold of Freedom*, pp. 235–71; Eugene D. Genovese and Elizabeth Fox-Genovese, 'The social thought of antebellum Southern theologians', in *Looking South: Chapters in the Story of an American Region*, ed. Winfred B. Moore, Jr, and Joseph F. Tripp (New York, 1989), pp. 31–40; Eugene D. Genovese, *The Slaveholders' Dilemma: Freedom and Progress in Southern Conservative Thought, 1820–1860* (Columbia, SC, 1992), pp. 58–64; William W. Freehling, 'Defective paternalism: James Henley Thornwell's mysterious antislavery moment', in Freehling, *The Reintegration of American History: Slavery and the Civil War* (New York, 1994), pp. 59–81; Drew Gilpin Faust, *The Creation of Confederate Nationalism* (Baton Rouge, La, 1988), pp. 58–81.

75. Janet Sharp Hermann, *The Pursuit of a Dream* (New York, 1981), pp. 3–34.

76. Wiley, 'Movement to humanize slavery', p. 220; Wyatt-Brown, 'Modernizing Southern slavery', pp. 32, 37, 40; Faust, *Creation of Confederate Nationalism*, p. 80.

77. James Oakes, *Slavery and Freedom: An Interpretation of the Old South* (New York, 1990), p. 165; Robinson, 'Day of Jubilo', pp. 522–71.

[264]   78. Lyon, 'Slavery, and the duties growing out of the relation', *Southern Presbyterian Review*, 16 (July 1863), pp. 14, 31. Lyon specified that 'the family constituted amongst the slaves, as God designed it should be, will serve as hostage for the good behavior of its several members, and will act with more potency than all fugitive slave laws, in bringing the fugitive back to his home' (p. 31).

79. Loveland, *Southern Evangelicals and the Social Order*, pp. 187, 202–4, 209–11, 214–16. William W. Freehling details such setbacks in the case of James Henley Thornwell, a founder of the journal in which Rev. Lyon's words appeared. See Freehling, 'Defective paternalism', pp. 73–5, 78–9; and Marilyn J. Westerkamp, 'James Henley Thornwell, pro-slavery spokesman within a Calvinist faith', *South Carolina Historical Magazine*, 87 (January 1986): esp. pp. 57–61. Donald G. Mathews earlier made the same point about the experience of Charles Colcock Jones, probably the leading antebellum religious advocate of slavery reform. Before the war, Mathews wrote, Jones 'could not demonstrate convincingly that his plan would serve the interests of the planter class', while 'there was no way within the antebellum South to create a constituency that could compel the masters to change.' Mathews, 'Charles Colcock Jones and the Southern Evangelical Crusade to form a biracial community', pp. 317–18.

80. Younger (ed.), *The Diary of R.G.H. Kean*, p. 177. See also Jones, *A Rebel War Clerk's Diary*, vol. 2, pp. 353, 416.

81. Wyatt-Brown, 'Modernizing Southern slavery', p. 36.

82. Engels, *The Role of Force in History: A Study of Bismarck's Policy of Blood and Iron* (1888; New York, 1968), p. 96.

CHAPTER ELEVEN

SLAVERY AND EMANCIPATION: THE AFRICAN-AMERICAN EXPERIENCE DURING THE CIVIL WAR

DAVID TURLEY

There is a central paradox that articulates the experience of very many African-Americans during the era of the Civil War. Without the transforming upheavals of war they would not have been able to gain their freedom as rapidly as they did, but often they pursued that freedom and began to give it content by means they had adopted within the constraints of slavery before the war. The 4 million black slaves in 1861 were subjected to a system commanding the loyalty of the majority of the Southern white population whether they were directly implicated in slaveholding or not. The natural increase of slaves had underpinned an enormous expansion in staple crop agriculture, especially in cotton, during the first half of the nineteenth century. Slaves migrating with their masters and an internal slave trade averaging perhaps 200,000 per decade between 1820 and 1860 placed labour resources where and when they were most needed. Economic success was impossible without good commodity prices for the staples the slaves produced. Working the slaves hard, moving them when necessary and closing off exits from slavery by tighter manumission laws enabled owners to take advantage of prices in the cotton market above the long-term trend for much of the 1830s and for almost all of the pre-war decade. Confidence in the long-run economic returns of slave agriculture was registered in the rising prices of prime slaves well into 1860. The system showed little sign of evolving in the direction of free labour on the eve of the war; if freedom was to come, so far as the majority of Southern whites was concerned, it would be as the result of a sharp rupture with what had gone before.[1]

Slavery in the antebellum South

Slaves, however, had long known that whatever aspirations their masters had toward total control were beyond full achievement. They could sometimes get away with working inefficiently, breaking tools, pretending illness, feigning stupidity, or protesting at circumstances through running away for a period. Moreover, the majority of slaves lived and worked within groups of twenty or more of their fellows. They were able to form partially distinct cultural communities through ties of family and kin, common religious activity and cultural practices. Whatever comfort and protection was thus provided, these communities had a more general significance. They underlined the potentially awkward agency of slaves, individually and collectively, in their dealings with masters and their agents.[2]

Slave initiative was also manifested in an 'informal economy' of fishing, hunting, the rearing of birds and animals, production of foodstuffs on garden plots and the making of handicrafts. In these activities different slave families sometimes worked together. Often, no doubt, when production in the 'informal economy' yielded a surplus beyond the needs of the slave families they entered into exchange with the master, enabling him to control the process and even present it as an aspect of his munificence. However, exchange off the plantation also took place and has to be construed in a different sense. It reduced the master's control of slave consumption and sometimes drew the slaves into a cash economy, allowing them to accumulate modest property and experience and limited economic freedom within the structure of slavery.[3]

Slaves caught up in the internal slave trade embodied this element of instability in slavery with peculiar intensity. Perhaps one in five underwent major family separations, provoking alienation even in older parts of the South amongst those left behind as well as in the recently opened up areas of the expanding economy. Especially in the rougher frontier regions of the South, but even elsewhere amongst the disaffected, many owners had constantly to reestablish and then maintain their authority over slaves who had only recently become their property or who resented what had happened to their kin. Slaveowners expressed a muted anxiety about the system's potential for social instability in counterpoint to their confident assertions of its economic success. When the war began Southerners initially tried to impose even more rigorous control on their labourers. As the conflict developed, many African-Americans had to improvise forms of behaviour to deal with unprecedented circumstances. But, alongside those improvisations, the objective of so many, to seek a freer life, took forms similar to those shaped in the pursuit of living space under slavery.[4]

By April 1865 some half a million ex-slaves were involved in free labour activity in former Confederate territory under the sanction of Union author-ities. Many more were technically still enslaved at the time of Appomattox, in the South and in the loyal states of Delaware and Kentucky which only acceded to emancipation on the ratification of the Thirteenth Amendment in December 1865. Large numbers, however, had managed to negotiate looser economic relations with their owners in return for staying with them. Yet others had escaped to the free states in the North. Thus, as the fighting ended, perhaps a million blacks had already experienced a significant transforma-tion in their legal and/or real status or circumstances. This estimate does not take into account the tens of thousands dislodged by Union forces or who flocked after them and had found only temporary places of rest. It is appro-priate, therefore, to begin detailed discussion of the African-American experi-ence of the war by considering how blacks dealt from within with the gradual dissolution of the Confederacy. The chapter will then turn to the ways in which they maintained a livelihood, especially in relation to the land. Finally, the freedmen's military experience will be reviewed.

Slavery in the Confederacy

At the beginning of the war the majority of white Americans in both North and South were agreed on one thing: no dramatic rupture should occur in regard to slavery. Most Confederates accepted the view of their Vice-President, Alexander H. Stephens of Georgia, that the 'corner-stone' of the government 'rests upon the great truth, that the negro is not equal to the white man; that slavery-subordination to the superior race is his natural and normal condition.' The Lincoln administration proclaimed that the war was about restoration of the Union and initially promised not to interfere with the South's institutions. Many whites also seem to have assumed that slaves had very little idea of the significance of the conflict. This was to underestim-ate the extent and efficiency of the 'grapevine' which spread news and rumour in the slave quarters and between plantations. An experienced journalist accompanying Union troops in Missouri in 1862, after questioning a number of slaves, concluded: 'The darkeys understand the whole question and the game played.'[5]

Parts of the Confederacy, like Texas, remained largely distant from the fighting for the whole of the war and there 'the war didn't change nothin'. . . . It was the endin' of it that made the difference.' Elsewhere the element of instability within slavery assumed more serious proportions but produced a complex set of responses amongst African-Americans. They did not universally anticipate the approach of a longed-for freedom. Some reported fears of how the Yankees might treat them. A Tennessee bondsman in 1861 had been told by his owner that Union forces would 'Sell them to Cuba'. Some gave credence, with justification, to rumours that Yankee soldiers on first encountering slaves had treated them as enemies. Until substantial numbers of African-Americans could sift and talk over the news and stories that came to them, uncertainty in face of the unknown was bound to be paramount for some. Samuel Elliott of Liberty County, Georgia, was typical of many thousands in admitting, 'At the beginning of the rebellion I did not know anything about the war.' He was perhaps also representative in how he began to find out. 'Mrs Somersall boys told me the War had commenced and we would all be free.' To uncertainty about Northerners might be added contradictory feelings about members of the white families who owned them. Familiarity kept some house servants close to their owners and slaves might feel sympathy when the war brought death or disability to individuals they had known for years. Yet, as many later recalled, such grievous blows could make the remaining whites behave towards them with even greater unpredictability than before.[6]

Yet many blacks in the Confederacy did feel from an early stage their hopes rising that the attainment of freedom was nearer. As Mack Duff Williams of South Carolina testified, 'I sympathized with the Union cause, because that was the party I believed would give me my liberty.'[7] Slaves like Williams, however, had no immediate prospect of freedom. When the masters and their sons left for the war they experienced the removal of a familiar authority to be replaced sometimes by a more rigorous and unmediated regime of work and discipline. The overseer or remaining family members who enforced it could strain to the limit the compromises with necessity the slaves had normally made. Thus precisely at the time when their hopes might be rising slaves could experience with greater intensity the constraints of their situation.

When slaves had had to cope with deep frustrations before the war they had not infrequently resorted to flight. As an increasing number of slaves came to appreciate that their masters were under direct assault, the temptation to try to escape was enhanced. The advance of Union forces meant the chances of reaching free communities successfully were greater than in peacetime. Then only a small minority had successfully followed the North Star to Canada. One delighted fugitive explained his successful escape: 'It used to be five hundred miles to git to Canada from Lexington, but now it's only eighteen miles! *Camp Nelson* is now *our* Canada.' The pattern of slaves' behaviour indicated they had seized upon the hope of a general turn in their fortunes. Sometimes the sense of turning fortune was aided by the actions of the masters. Samuel Elliott spent eleven months as a waiter in the company of his master in military service. 'I came home with him. I told my son what was going on. He with 11 more ran off and joined the Army [the Yankee Army] on St Catherine Island.'[8]

Elliott's military labour as a personal servant prompted thoughts of freedom. So too did other slaves' experiences of work for the army. Owners came to fear that they might not get back labourers who had served a turn with the military forces. Various reasons encouraged military labourers to attempt escape. The initial patriotic intent of their masters in hiring them out was usually that they should aid in the construction of coastal and river fortifications and defensive works to protect the main towns and cities. Frequently the urgency of this work arose from the approach of enemy forces. Yet the proximity of Union troops was precisely the temptation which might lure the slaves away. Working as teamsters as well as labourers bondsmen had the opportunity to travel across the surrounding country, survey the lie of the land and plan how best to get to Union lines. The harsh reverse side of working for the army – sufficiently unpleasant at any rate to provoke complaints and debate about the conditions in which the hired or impressed bondsmen lived and worked – could provide the determination the fugitives needed to make the most of the opportunities that came their way.[9]

The practice of impressment of slave and eventually free black labour by the Confederate authorities occurred when they could not attract enough hired labourers. It was widely detested by the workers themselves in addition to producing tensions between masters and military officials and the War Department and state governments seeking to protect the interests of local slaveowners. Masters not only disliked loss of control over their own agricultural and sometimes artisan labour but suspected that impressed labourers were treated with less regard than hired slaves. Slaves knew how hard they had to work: 'They have a perfect horror of working on entrenchments,' commented one Virginia legislator. The conditions were widely known to be so harsh that 'I feel certain if they hear of another impressment, we will lose nearly all our men.' Many of the impressed were soon unable to work, an engineer officer revealed. 'Most of them have run away – many are sick – and some are dead.' In such circumstances runaways escaped to their owners and were not handed back or fled to the enemy. By February 1864 in the Confederate District of West Louisiana the shortage of impressed labourers to construct works in defence of the Red River Valley was so great that the local military commander sent cavalry in pursuit of runaways, even when it meant slaves being seized back from their owners. The only sweetening of a bitter pill for the dragooned labourers was the provision of huts, rations and medical attention. For many, during the last months of the war, not even these compensations were possible. At the start of 1865 the commander of the 3rd Military District of the Department of North Carolina and Southern Virginia, though convinced 'I need labor always now especially,' contemplated 'releasing all slaves, especially in view of the complaints I learn relative to clothing them. That is not my fault. I have done all in my power to provide Clothing for negroes; even to overstepping the limits of my authority. It has been literally due to want of money & material.' In March 1865 at Danville, Virginia, the food being issued to the labourers 'was inadequate to maintain their physical strength to a degree sufficient for them to perform the labour required.' They consequently ran off.[10]

Another profoundly disruptive process was 'refugeeing', the term applied to transfer of slaves from areas under threat from Union troops to places more distant. This was analogous to, and caused as much anguish as, migration with owners and the internal slave trade had done before the war. In those earlier years slaves had sometimes tried to take their fate into their own hands in escaping back to old haunts or leaving slavery behind altogether. They attempted similar actions while being 'refugeed'. The early stages of a 'refugeeing' journey were the most likely time for slaves to make off. Mary Williams Pugh of Louisiana decided to add her people to her parents' and take them to Texas. 'The first night we camped Sylvester left – the next night at Bayou B. about 25 of Pa's best hands left & the next day at Berwick Bay nearly all of the women & children started – but this Pa found out in time to catch them all except one man & one woman. Altogether he had lost about 60 of his best men.'[11] In some cases losses by flight were so disastrous that masters decided to turn back and hope for the best so far as the Yankees were concerned. The use of Confederate troops in Washington County, Mississippi, in 1863 to move slaves out of the path of the Yankees led to slaves taking to the hills where they 'laid out for over a week' until the troops had gone. Some went over to the Yankees.[12]

Particularly courageous fugitives returned to slave territory in the hope of liberating others. The Superintendent at the Union encampment of Fortress

Monroe in Virginia in charge of 'contrabands', that is, slaves of rebel owners who had fled from Confederate military labour, had encountered runaways with the daring to have returned 200 miles to aid others. In one incident, helped by Yankee troops near Smithfield, Virginia, in August 1864, the rescuers with fugitives and soldiers came under fire from 'a force of irregular appearance, numbering about 100'. They had to scatter over marshes resulting in the loss of nearly all the fugitives and even some of the troops. In consequence of these missions of liberation Confederate authorities gave strict orders to their forces: 'When you take Negroes with arms evidently coming out of the enemie's [sic] camp proceed at once to hold a drum head court martial and if found guilty hang them on the spot.' Recaptured fugitives were quite frequently executed.[13] Despite the risks, flight was extensive, occurring in phases as news of Union advances spread. Initially the incidence was significant in Northeast Virginia in 1861 and 1862; then around the Union enclaves in North Carolina in 1862. After Union forces achieved control of the length of the Mississippi Valley in the summer of 1863 river towns drew in thousands from the surrounding country. Similar flight happened in Southeast coastal regions with Yankee occupation of islands and mainland bridgeheads.

Reacting to changed circumstances

The majority of African-American slaves, none the less, remained in Confederate territory until the war ended. But they were not passive. In the many instances when the master was no longer present on the place, the readjustment of manager–slave relations could give opportunities to shift the balance towards slightly better conditions or a little more autonomy. Towards the end when shortage of food became a serious problem in some areas of the South, slaves cowed overseers and took plantation animals to eat. The proximity of Union troops or the widely understood possibility of flight put pressure upon those in charge of slaves to find ways of keeping them at work. Many slaves understood this or benefited from it if masters kept to new agreements. In the autumn of 1864, on Colonel Thomas Jones's place in De Soto County, Mississippi, Nat Green was offered wages to stay on. He agreed and worked through the winter and spring but finally had to appeal to the provost-marshal of freedmen to try to get his pay. Owners also attempted to hold labourers to the land or induce runaways to return by agreeing a division of the crop with them. In the winter of 1862–3 a Mississippi slaveholder 'contracted with my negroes to work for half of the cotton, and the corn still to be raised for the use of the place. . . . A portion of them remained and fulfilled the contract during the years 1862, 3 and 4.' Masters, anticipating the end of the system, let slaves go well before the arrival of the Northerners. This happened to Alfred Scruggs near Huntsville, Alabama, as early as 1862. He set to work hauling wood with a team loaned him by his master and used what he made to acquire a team of his own in 1863. He also had sufficient resources to rent 40 acres 'and raised a crop of cotton and corn that year'. He rented annually from two other local whites up to the end of the war 'hauling working and making money in any way I could in an honorable manner.' A slave from Sumner County, Tennessee, remaining in bondage, was hired out by his owner but also worked for himself. He was given 'a half Saturday at times to work for myself', leased a small plot of land and cleared it with the help of another slave. Sharing the proceeds the two raised about 4 acres of corn in the summer and autumn of 1862. These cases exemplify the element of continuity in wartime with the practices of the earlier 'informal economy'.[14]

The erosion of the old order within the Confederacy gave greater force to African-Americans' desire to take control of their lives. Yet fugitives to Union lines discovered that how they were received drastically shaped their initial experience of freedom. Their reception was more incalculable than the changing legal framework would indicate. Congressional sanction in the first Confiscation Act (August 1861) of General Benjamin Butler's designation of fugitives who had been sent to work directly on the Confederate war effort as 'contrabands' excluded any claims by masters to their labour. It could not guarantee that local military commanders would accept fugitives' claims that they had been so used or refuse demands of masters professing loyalty for the return of their runaways. The circumstances of a fugitive might be more immediately determined by the responses of ordinary soldiers. Initially most Union soldiers did not see themselves as members of an army of liberation. They arrested and returned fugitives in the normal course of duty. Some, however, had their dislike of this activity fostered by knowledge of congressional passage of an additional article of war in the spring of 1862. An Illinois soldier in Kentucky protested at the return of an alleged fugitive (though in Kentucky the owner could presumably claim loyalty – a matter of indifference to the soldier). 'The Regemut feel indignut about it. the most of us enterd [sic] the service with the understanding that there was to be an end to such dirty work.' Troops also acted directly. In the spring of 1862 a Missouri

slaveowner saw two runaways with a Union regiment and attempted to recover them with the aid of a letter from a senior officer. The troops surrounded
and drove him off by stoning him, pursuing him and putting him 'under a
guard of Soldiers & ropes were called for to hang us'. Fugitives knew that
they might reduce the unpredictability of their reception through offering
useful information; they then got a guarantee of protection.[15] As Union forces
penetrated deeper into the South it became impractical to distinguish between
slaves used to help the enemy and those who merely belonged to owners in
rebel states; the numbers became too great. The Second Confiscation Act of
July 1862 removed all entitlement to fugitives' labour from any rebel owner.
Runaways of owners in the loyal border states were still under threat even
if they claimed their masters were in rebellion. So were slaves whose masters had pledged allegiance to the United States in the already conquered
and later exempted areas of the South before and after the Emancipation
Proclamation. In general, though, by 1863 distinctions of status amongst
African-Americans became increasingly blurred outside the heartlands of the
Confederacy. Once slaves had reached Union territory, what degrees of
freedom meant in a practical sense depended upon the relation of the blacks
to the land, their circumstances as military labourers or family dependants in
contraband camps and the nature of military service for the 180,000 who
experienced it.

The behaviour of blacks coming under Union authority when they had a
choice suggests they mostly wanted to continue with the kind of work they
knew, but to have more say over its rhythm and content and over the disposition of family labour. The extent to which they could achieve their inclina-
tions to greater economic as well as personal freedom depended on a number
of factors. Were masters or their agents still in the vicinity? What limitations
or possibilities did government policy present? What were the attitudes of
local civilian and military officials, missionaries and reformers? Were there
any resources the ex-slaves themselves controlled or could obtain? Did the
Confederates still pose a threat? Since these variables combined with differing effects in different areas it is best to approach the issue of black aspirations and their fulfilment by considering distinct localities.

Areas in northern Virginia and some Tidewater districts came very early
under control of the Union. Apart from employing males of prime age as
military labourers and some women as cooks and laundresses, military commanders turned their attention to occupying the rest of the black population
and reducing the costs of maintaining them. These areas of mixed farming,
often with worn-out soils, were unattractive to possible outside Northern

[274] lessees. Management, therefore, of these lands abandoned by Confederate sympathisers fell to military officials. Superintendents of Contrabands (later Negro Affairs) were appointed and early in 1862 authorised to allow blacks 'to cultivate the Ground and use the property of Rebels in arms against the Government, or who have abandoned their homes.' There was initial difficulty when the ex-slaves were offered only very low wages and 'little was accomplished by it'. But in 1863 they were supplied with livestock and tools and guaranteed protection against Confederate raids. 'Instead of issuing them rations, they were furnished with such subsistence as they needed, and it was charged against their share of the crop. That year they much more than supported themselves, and generally had enough to supply their wants until the following Spring.' In 1864 the system was extended, the crop share required as rent varying according to the fertility of the soil and what other forms of assistance were granted. African-Americans working in this way had some leeway. In the First District of Virginia and North Carolina 18 day schools and 11 night schools had been established by the end of 1864 supported by a number of Northern benevolent associations. The Superintendent, Charles B. Wilder, whose outlook had been formed in Massachusetts abolitionism, believed that the system used in his district had successfully spread a spirit of independence and inculcated the work ethic amongst the ex-slaves while preparing them for citizenship. Elsewhere, in and around Norfolk, Virginia, former slaves constituted 'the main industrial force of the District'. They also worked at fishing and catching oysters, farmed abandoned land under some supervision on a crop-share arrangement and did part-time wage labouring for white farmers to supplement returns from their own farming.[16]

From May 1863 onwards a project with a different emphasis was undertaken on abandoned lands in northern Virginia. Its most notable feature was the establishment of Freedman's Village as well as a number of farms. In part funded from a levy on all employed freed people in the District of Columbia it was inhabited mainly by women and children. There was a school run by the American Tract Society with 400 pupils and an establishment to look after the old and infirm. But the only form of employment was a 'Tailor Shop' where some of the women produced clothes but only covered the costs of the materials and their 'fair wages'. The five government farms near Arlington had implements, subsistence and maintenance covered by government departments and the labourers were paid monthly wages ranging from $2 to $10 per month but received no share of the crops. Criticism of the Village's mode of operation and of the supposed losses to the government from the farms revealed a strand of Northern white opinion convinced that African-

American dependence on government provision for any length of time told against 'any improvement in the character or conduct of the Adults'. Farming operations had to be subject to the discipline of economic success. Even within Union areas of Virginia there were different but limited possibilities open to freed people seeking an element of economic freedom on the land. Only a few thousand African-Americans were involved.[17]

There were about 15,000 African-Americans under Union control on the Sea Islands off the South Carolina coast after the occupation of late 1861. Their situation has intrigued observers and scholars because it revealed with exceptional clarity not only the preferences of the de facto freed people but also the interplay and conflicts of interest and perspective between them and other actors involved in this early process of reconstruction. Those other actors – Treasury Department agents, military officers and soldiers, reformers, missionaries, Northern entrepreneurs and, indirectly, Confederate raiders – competed to influence the circumstances shaping the lives of the ex-slaves. Because the masters had fled this gave some initial latitude to the great majority of their slaves who had refused to accompany them. The Army and Navy put some to work but most stayed on or about their plantations. There they prepared the ground for food crops, especially corn, and by April 1862 were also to be found 'in the potato field planting sweet potatoes, swinging their hoes in unison timed by a jolly song'. Although some of the Treasury Department agents charged with handling the 1861 cotton crop enlisted blacks in dealing with it, the freed people were unwilling to begin work on the next crop. They refused to enter the fields with 'no clothes, no tobacco, no molasses, no bacon, no salt, no shoes, no medicine &c', all items they had expected from their masters. Their priority was food cropping of the kind they had engaged in on their plots under slavery. Staple crop production was initially a matter of negotiation of terms. 'We only wanted to know if we were sure of our pay, it is so hard living without clothes a whole year, & we get sick putting sea water in our hominy, & haven't had our salt for so many months.'[18] During the course of 1862, however, government plantation superintendents claimed to notice a greater willingness to work in cotton. One of them, Edward Philbrick, believed it showed the labourers beginning to act on the civilizing basis of economic self-interest. Yankee entrepreneurs, including Philbrick, were on hand with offers to lease the cotton estates for the next year. Reformer and missionary advocates of the freed people feared what treatment the African-Americans might receive as wage labourers from lessees. Government policy, however, limited the alternatives. Most military and civil officials in the Sea Islands believed that black improvement, a moral and economic objective, required the inculcation of the habit of 'steady labor'. But individual cultivation or fishing was not deemed to produce the right effect. Wage labour, whether for government or private entrepreneurs, was the correct solution because it was believed to promote blacks' understanding of the link between work and reward. It would 'demonstrate to the world . . . that the cotton and rice fields of the South can be cultivated by the labor of freedmen.' Wage work combined with the schooling and religion of Northern missionaries was considered the basis for African-American progress. Since much of the wage labour was to cultivate cotton it also maintained the existing economic pattern and, in the case of government-run plantations, brought benefit to the Treasury.[19]

Some whites, including Saxton, the military commander on the islands and a believer in the virtues of wage labour, assumed, however, that the African-Americans should also work their own grounds. Blacks themselves had no doubt that 'the possession of land by our people either individually or collectively . . . will give us the claim of home; and no life gives to a people that spirit of independence as the tillage of the soil.' They raised food crops from plots at the same time as labouring on the estates. When Philbrick and his associates began to run some of the estates the slaves soon gained the confidence to voice complaints about the low level of wages and to claim that Philbrick had promised to turn over blocks of land to them at a dollar an acre. This spirit of assertion was despite recurrent harsh treatment of the African-Americans on the part of some Union soldiers. Their best chance of acquiring more land might have come from land sales under the Direct Tax Act (1862) under which land forfeit to the United States for non-payment of taxes by rebels was put on the market. Eventually the government allowed very little of it to be set aside for purchase by the former slaves and they were unable to compete on the open market with buyers like Philbrick.[20]

Revealing as these developments were, they involved a small minority of former slaves. Most of those in Union territory en route to freedom were in southern Louisiana and the Mississippi Valley. Often masters were still in place after Union occupation because they had proclaimed their loyalty to the United States and assumed they should remain in control of their slaves. Confirmed in this view by the recognition of exempted areas in the Emancipation Proclamation, they found collaborators in Union military commanders anxious to maintain plantation production. They pledged their authority to the 'protection and inviolability of the rights of property'. But slaves, Yankee troops and abolitionist officers such as John W. Phelps in command at Fort Parapet above New Orleans disturbed these intentions. Slaves of loyal masters saw no necessity for this to affect their intentions and joined those of rebel owners in moving to Union lines where they were protected and employed by the soldiers. Slaves remaining on the estates sometimes refused to continue as before. A Louisiana owner complained that he found some of his bondsmen 'in a state of insurection[sic] . . . some of them would not work at all & others wanted wages.' Nearby blacks drove an overseer off the estate. Not only owners but officers trying to enforce Butler's orders were convinced that disorder was fomented by troops with the encouragement of their camp commander, Phelps. He allegedly allowed his men 'to range the country, insult the Planters and entice negroes away from their plantations.' In conflict with Butler and after an inconclusive reference of the controversy to the War Department, Phelps resigned his commission.[21] Butler's successor in the Department of the Gulf, Nathaniel P. Banks, determined to bring order to the labour system. His regulations of January 1863 and February 1864 set wage rates, standards of treatment and conditions and promised some education for children. But they placed limits on the movement of the labourers, punished poor discipline by loss of wages and held back payment of half of earnings to the end of the year to ensure consistency of work. Many blacks protested, unavailingly, that 'the beneficent intentions of the government, if it has beneficent intentions,' were being undermined.[22]

Beginning in 1863 in the Mississippi Valley the Lincoln administration leased out, seized or abandoned plantations to Southern loyalists or incoming Yankees. To help absorb the growing number of black fugitives, lessees were encouraged to employ the freed people gathered in contraband camps as wage labourers. The policy was particularly directed to drawing into self-supporting work the women, children and older freed people unsuitable for military recruitment and who were regarded as a burden by the military authorities. Despite government regulations on conditions and terms of employment, one observer reported them as victims of lessees who were 'only adventurers, camp followers, "army sharks," as they are termed' concerned purely with profit. Wages often went unpaid and conditions were similar to those under slavery. 'The poor negroes are everywhere greatly depressed at their condition.' Other lessees, however, appeared as ' liberal minded philanthropic Gentlemen' desiring to make a profit but with a regard for black rights. In other cases the lessee might have been driven off by Confederate raids or simply neglected the property so that 'the negroes subsisted mainly on the corn and meat obtained from the country around.' The government did also make some effort in the Mississippi Valley to lease farms to blacks, many of them as small as five acres 'farmed with hoe alone'. According to an experienced official, if they also foraged and cut wood, 'I doubt if any . . . have, for months, required or received any aid from the Government.' Where they were near army camps they sold produce to the soldiers and some of the women became cooks, laundresses or prostitutes. Yet the administration placed limits on the ex-slaves' ability to accumulate land. The Proclamation of Amnesty and Reconstruction, issued in December 1863, and intended to undermine Southern white support for the Confederacy, allowed former rebels to resume property rights (except for slaves) on swearing an oath of loyalty and accepting wartime laws and proclamations in relation to slavery. But its effect was a rapid resumption by pre-war owners in the early months of 1864 of two-thirds of the plantations leased in the Mississippi Valley in 1863, including places on which ex-slaves had been left to their own devices.[23]

Substantial numbers of African-Americans looked for security and hoped for some opportunities in Southern towns and cities under Union rule. They encountered very variable material conditions. Around Norfolk, Virginia, an American Missionary Association school superintendent reported 'hundreds of Colored families' living in 'cheap houses & sheds' and suffering high levels of mortality. Fugitives able to carry property away with them or who had accumulated a little capital were in a better position to make their way. Samuel Larkin moved from northern Alabama to Nashville, bought horses and made a living hauling stores for local merchants. Nashville, however, exemplifies the contradictory circumstances African-Americans faced in this transitional period. The local black community supported a coloured hospital and schools were established 'taught by colored people who have got a little learning somehow'. But, as late as the summer of 1864, the local Union commander was overseeing the return of fugitives to claimants.[24]

Border slave states remaining within the Union, particularly Kentucky, imposed some of the toughest restraints on blacks in pursuit of freedom. Especially in the first two years of the war, slaves worked under tightened slave codes for a class of owners prepared to use all the political influence they could muster to ensure protection of their interests in return for their Unionism. These states were exempted by the Emancipation Proclamation and some military commanders helped secure the return of escapees to loyalists claiming them. Subordinate officers occasionally refused and even when obedient often found the task distasteful. Slaves, therefore, could find allies in maintaining freedom but must have experienced a pervasive uncertainty. The ebb and flow of the battle lines and Confederate guerrilla attacks added to their anxieties. They could be hunted down and killed. Avoiding these fates resolved into a choice, at best, between running for the North or seeking federal protection in becoming military labourers or soldiers. Progressively in 1863–4 Union authorities in the loyal slave states ignored the Unionism of owners in taking in fugitives as labourers and in responding to Washington's sanctioning of black recruitment in Maryland and Missouri in 1863 and in Kentucky in the spring of 1864. The changing circumstances of Union military success from the summer of 1863[25] and the shift towards antislavery politics within both loyal and proximate ex-Confederate states made it easier to do so.

Even in these circumstances the process of securing freedom was far from smooth. Males from Kentucky who became military labourers or recruits often left their families behind. They 'are most shamefully and inhumanly treated by their masters in consequence of their husbands having enlisted in the union army.' Mere suspicion that men were contemplating enlistment could lead to their harsh treatment. Some blacks in the border states did manage to loosen the constraints of forced labour before local emancipations occurred by exploiting the relative scarcity of prime field labour after military labour and black recruits had been taken. They worked in the fields under informal wage agreements or for a share of the crop. Masters could renege on these unrecorded agreements but workers complained to the military authorities in some instances.[26]

The absorption of many of the men by military labour or soldiering meant that much other work was done by women, children and older blacks – if work was available. When not cultivating abandoned land in groups or labouring for lessees, they worked from contraband camps. Visitors to some of the early camps in 1862–3 glimpsed 'misery and wretchedness . . . [amongst the blacks] herded together in masses.' Crises of overcrowding recurred whenever Union military progress shook African-Americans loose from their old locations. The organization of health measures and food supplies brought improvements and the camp superintendents established forms of work so that the former slaves, even 'the disabled men with the women and children . . . should as far as practicable support themselves.' In strict accountancy terms, this was unlikely to have been achieved but the imperative to labour was impressed on the contrabands. When there was no work in the camps along the Mississippi in 1863, Adjutant-General Lorenzo Thomas encouraged the ex-slaves to return to their old places. He assumed that former masters realized slavery was at an end and would employ them for wages. In consequence some critics charged that the camps were sustaining the old system. A year later, in more favourable circumstances, workers were able to be filtered out of camps to jobs in towns like Vicksburg 'so far as required by its virtuous industry'.[27]

Military opportunities

Initially military labour was a practical response by commanders faced with fugitives reaching their lines. Soon politicians and soldiers began to see significant advantages to employing black labour; it contributed in support work to the Union war effort what had been removed from the Confederacy; it freed white troops from ancillary work so that they were available for fighting. Many labourers gladly escaped to military work. But the army also impressed many thousands into labour. In Tidewater Virginia and North Carolina, for example, in 1864, African-Americans had promises made to them that were not kept. 'They left in great haste, some of them not bidding farewell to their families. They have not been paid for some time, have no money and but few clothes and are I judge in a poor way.' The construction of the fortifications at Nashville in 1863 used very large numbers (3,000). The scale of the operation clearly defeated any efforts at proper treatment; 'they worked well, and through all that were cheerful, although in the fifteen months they have been employed at that fort . . . about 800 have died.' In the District of Columbia and other places the government made provision for the unemployed – women, children and the sick – by deducting $5.00 per month from the wages of teamsters and labourers working for the army. As a measure it saved the government money but it also calmed the anxieties of the labourers about their families.[28]

Becoming soldiers and sailors expressed most dramatically African-Americans' break from their earlier circumstances. This appeared particularly true for the three-quarters of the 180,000 serving blacks who had formerly been slaves. They were in the process of becoming citizens and in a position directly to contribute to the liberation of their fellows still held in the South. In terms of their psychology and their effect on others, this was a profound aspect of black military involvement. But the possibilities of choosing some new kinds of action were interlaced with forms of compulsion and limited by constraints as to their practice and meaning. At the beginning of the war Northern free blacks willing to take part in the struggle had been refused by the civil and military authorities. Officially only with the passage of the Militia Act in July 1862 was the legal basis for recruitment laid. Even the actions of whites sympathetic to black desires to engage militarily in the struggle underlined the often ambiguous character of the black military experience.

In the spring of 1862 General David Hunter on the Sea Islands sought permission from the War Department to recruit a black regiment, perhaps to try to give reality to his proclamation under martial law of emancipation in neighbouring mainland areas over which he had no actual control. Lincoln shortly reversed the proclamation and Secretary Stanton provided no supplies for Hunter's putative black soldiers. In the mean time, however, Hunter sent white troops, without warning or explanation, to round up likely black soldiers, provoking suspicion and distress amongst their families and flight into the woods on the part of prospective recruits. Recurrently thereafter such impressment tactics persuaded some African-Americans that they did not want to be soldiers. Despite its initial reluctance the government moved progress-ively towards taking in black recruits. Continued military reverses, difficul-ties in filling recruitment quotas and later the logic of the Emancipation Proclamation encouraged, from August 1862, the establishment of the 1st South Carolina Volunteers drawn largely from Sea Islands freedmen and under the command of the Boston abolitionist, Thomas Wentworth Higginson. Even after the Proclamation they were not yet, however, treated equally or full participants in the whole range of military activities. They were con-sidered as uniformed military labourers to be used primarily 'for fatigue duty'. The commander of a North Carolina black regiment was moved to complain of insults to his soldiers by officers from other units. He was critical too that their menial work 'throws them back where they were before and reduces them to the position of slaves again.'[29] Moreover, under the Militia Act, black troops were paid less than white soldiers – $10.00 per month with a possible clothing deduction of $3.00 – as against $13.00 plus a clothing allowance of $3.50. Black soldiers bitterly resented such discrimination. Officers of black regiments pointed out that they had been 'forced to put in their hands arms almost entirely unserviceable and in other respects their equipments have been of the poorest kind.' Many of the non-commissioned officers in particu-lar were also keen to have black commissioned officers 'whose hearts are truly loyal to the rights of man'. As striking as the instances of discrimination was the determination of African-Americans to protest against them either directly themselves or through sympathetic officers. The most extensive and deter-mined of these protests demanded equal pay. Individual and group protests culminated in the 54th and 55th Massachusetts black regiments refusing any pay, including the offer of their state government to make up the difference. They could thus deny that they were 'holding out for money, not from principle.' But Congress so delayed in enacting legislation for equal pay – the measure passed on 15 June 1864 – that near mutinies occurred in both Massachusetts regiments.

Such powerful feelings expressed the black troops' awareness of the dis-crepancy between white behaviour towards them and their sense of their position and the worth of their actions. The soldiers had a deep pride in what they had achieved. In 1864 Sergeant George Hatton of 1st Regiment, United States Colored Troops expressed it simply: the African-American 'has proved . . . that he is a man.' They were conscious that once they had got into combat their conduct, especially at Port Hudson, Milliken's Bend and Fort Wagner in the spring and summer of 1863, but also in dozens of other incidents, dramatically improved their reputation as soldiers. Some of them acted openly as liberators as when troops from the 1st Louisiana Native Guards visited plantations in St Bernard Parish, commandeered horses, mules and wagons and carried off blacks to New Orleans. Protest against discriminatory treatment was thus intimately linked to the increasingly assertive roles soldiers were playing. A sense of a shift in power relations invigorated the Missouri black soldier, Spotswood Rice, as he wrote to his daughter's owner about coming to get her back. 'I will have bout a powrer and autherity to bring hear away and to exacute vengencens [sic] on them that holds my Child.' Some of them began to extend this assertiveness to claiming full citizenship and the means to exercise it. Soldiers asked for 'a general system of education . . . for our moral and literary elevation' and sometimes contributed funds towards unit libraries. In a Louisiana black regiment 'the cartridge box and spelling book are attached to the same belt.' The other necessary instrument was the franchise. The initial impetus came from free Northern blacks, most of them having been denied it under their state constitutions, though some petitions also emerged from the South. Only in Louisiana, however, was it a major political question in 1864–5 within the context of Lincoln's reconstruction proposals for the state based on a loyalty oath taken by one tenth of those who had voted in 1860. Despite private indications from Lincoln that he was prepared to see some blacks possess the franchise 'for instance the very intelligent, and especially those who have fought gallantly in our ranks' the new Louisiana constitution excluded them. Protests focused on the fighting efforts of black troops and on the literacy many of these same troops had acquired in the army. They refused to accept proposals which drew any distinctions according to race or between the mulatto elite and the mass of the black population based upon education. The stand on principle ensured that non-whites remained excluded. The Lincoln administration was not prepared to intervene further.[30]

Clearly the African-American experience during the Civil War was very varied. Blacks sometimes found more room to exercise choices than they had previously, though the ways in which they did so were often familiar – flight, plot agriculture, small-scale marketing. They also chose to assert their human priorities against the tendency of slave owners and Northern civil and military authorities to ignore them. Some gained new work arrangements from hard-pressed masters, well short of complete autonomy, but giving families more control over their daily lives and use of labour. Military labourers and soldiers reminded whites that they needed security for their families or communities. Their local actions demonstrated a desire for a negative freedom from bondage but also for the opportunity to shape individual and community economic and cultural life. Above all, soldiers achieved a dignity as agents and pride in helping shape the course of events. But achievements were intertwined with constraints; the meaning for many African-Americans of their experience during the war was ambiguous. That very ambiguity prompted them to become political beings for the first time to seek a more positive outcome. The army fostered in the most ideologically conscious black soldiers the actions of citizens in pursuit of citizenship. There was no guarantee that government or army would respond sympathetically. But, finally, no assessment of African-American experience can ignore the incalculable but deeply emotional sense of transformation in individuals. Higginson caught a glimpse of it in his account of the reading of the Emancipation Proclamation on the Sea Islands. 'The very moment the speaker had ceased . . . there suddenly arose, close beside the platform a strong male voice (but rather cracked and elderly), into which two women's voices instantly blended, singing, as if by an impulse that could no more be repressed than the morning note of the song sparrow – "My Country, 'tis of thee/ Sweet land of liberty/ Of thee I sing." '[31]

Notes

1. Michael Tadman, *Speculators and Slaves. Masters: Traders, and Slaves in the Old South* (Madison, Wi. 1996), pp. 106, 289–90; Robert William Fogel, *Without Consent or Contract: The Rise and Fall of American Slavery* (New York, 1989), pp. 63–5, 70–1.

2. John W. Blassingame, *The Slave Community: Plantation Life in the Antebellum South* (New York, 1979); Eugene D. Genovese, *Roll, Jordan, Roll: The World the Slaves Made* (New York, 1974); Herbert G. Gutman, *The Black Family in Slavery and Freedom, 1750–1925* (New York, 1976); Albert J. Raboteau, *Slave Religion: The 'Invisible Institution' in the Antebellum South* (New York, 1978); Peter J. Parish, *Slavery: History and Historians* (New York, 1989).

[284]

3. Ira Berlin and Philip D. Morgan (eds), *Culture and Cultivation: Labor and the Shaping of Slave Life in the Americas* (Charlottesville, Va, 1993), pp. 1–45, 138–99, 243–99.

4. Leon F. Litwack, *Been in the Storm So Long: The Aftermath of Slavery* (London, 1979), pp. 4, 13.

5. Ibid., pp. 16, 23–7.

6. Ibid., p. 6; Ira Berlin *et al.* (eds), *Freedom: A Documentary History of Emancipation 1861–1867*, series 1, vol. 1, *The Destruction of Slavery* (Cambridge, 1985), doc. 81, p. 269; doc. 37, p. 147; *Been in the Storm*, p.10.

7. *Destruction of Slavery*, doc. 330, p. 812.

8. *Been in the Storm*, p. 51; *Destruction of Slavery*, doc. 37, p. 146.

9. Ibid., docs 274A, 281, 282, pp. 713–14, 727, 728–9.

10. Ibid., docs 266, 269, 276, 283, pp. 701, 703, 719–20, 729–30.

11. Ira Berlin *et al.*, *Slaves No More: Three Essays on Emancipation and the Civil War* (Cambridge, 1992), p. 15; Litwack, *Been in the Storm*, pp. 32–6.

12. *Destruction of Slavery*, doc. 311, p. 775.

13. Ibid., docs 12, 17, 101 note, pp. 89, 98, 300.

14. Litwack, *Been in the Storm*, p. 14; *Destruction of Slavery*, doc. 122, p. 326; Ira Berlin *et al.* (eds), *Freedom: A Documentary History of Emancipation 1861–1867*, series 1, vol. 3, *The Wartime Genesis of Free Labor: The Lower South* (Cambridge, 1990), doc. 156, pp. 671–2; *Freedom: A Documentary History of Emancipation 1861–1867*, series 1, vol. 2, *The Wartime Genesis of Free Labor: The Upper South* (Cambridge, 1993), docs 112, 89, pp. 445–6, 387–8.

15. *Destruction of Slavery,* docs 131A, 201, 165, 86, pp. 354, 525, 429–30, 275–6.

16. *Upper South,* docs 4, 5, 28, pp. 116–17, 121 note, 177–82.

17. *Upper South*, docs 63, 77, pp. 298–9, 338–42.

18. Willie Lee Rose, *Rehearsal for Reconstruction: The Port Royal Experiment* (New York, 1964); *Lower South*, docs 19, 8, pp. 183, 185, 127–8; James M. McPherson, *The Negro's Civil War: How American Negroes Felt and Acted during the War for the Union* (New York, 1965), p. 120.

19. *Lower South*, docs 40, 8, 53, 36, pp. 279–80, 142, 317, 262.

20. *Lower South*, doc. 41, pp. 282–3; Edwin S. Redkey (ed.), *A Grand Army of Black Men: Letters from African-American Soldiers in the Union Army, 1861–1865*

(Cambridge,1992), Letter 92, p. 216; McPherson, *Negro's Civil War*, p. 122; *Lower South*, doc. 47B, pp. 301–2; McPherson, *Negro's Civil War*, p. 113; *Lower South*, docs 41–47A, pp. 281–99.

21. *Destruction of Slavery*, docs 61, 66B, 62, pp. 204–5, 220, 221 note, 208; Ira Berlin *et al.* (eds), *Freedom: A Documentary History of Emancipation 1861–1867*, series 11, *The Black Military Experience* (Cambridge, 1982), docs 9–10, pp. 62–5.

22. McPherson, *Negro's Civil War*, pp. 128–30.

23. *Lower South*, doc. 196, pp. 794–6; *Black Military Experience*, doc. 194, pp. 488–9; McPherson, *Negro's Civil War*, pp. 124–5; *Lower South*, doc. 177, pp. 732–3; McPherson, *Negro's Civil War*, pp. 126–7; Berlin *et al.*, *Slaves No More*, pp. 152–4.

24. *Upper South*, docs 30–1, 97, pp. 185–6, 403; McPherson, *Negro's Civil War*, pp. 141–2; *Destruction of Slavery*, doc. 120, p. 324.

25. *Destruction of Slavery*, docs 202A, 202C, 202E, 202F, 202G, pp. 528–9, 530–8; *Upper South*, doc. 41, pp. 204–6; *Black Military Experience*, doc. 85, pp. 228–30; *Upper South*, doc. 190, p. 611; *Destruction of Slavery*, docs 227, 228A, 228B, pp. 601–4.

26. *Destruction of Slavery*, docs 235, 237, 150A, 150B, pp. 613, 615, 387–9; *Upper South*, doc. 125, pp. 467–9.

27. McPherson, *Negro's Civil War*, pp. 122–3; *Upper South*, docs 18, 226 note, pp. 150, 693; *Lower South*, doc. 212, p. 845.

28. *Upper South*, docs 20, 36, 102, 55, pp. 157, 191–2 and note, 416, 270–3.

29. McPherson, *Negro's Civil War*, pp. 19–22, 28–35; Litwack, *Been in the Storm*, p. 64; *Black Military Experience*, docs 2, 198A–202, pp. 49–50, 491–502; McPherson, *Negro's Civil War*, pp. 201–3; Redkey, *Grand Army*, Letters 102–3, 89, pp. 233–4, 211; McPherson, *Negro's Civil War*, pp. 197–201.

30. Litwack, *Been in the Storm*, pp. 64–76; McPherson, *Negro's Civil War*, pp. 183–92, 228–34; *Black Military Experience*, docs 299A–B, 248, 252, pp. 689–90, 615, 618; McPherson, *Negro's Civil War*, pp. 276–85.

31. Thomas Wentworth Higginson, *Army Life in a Black Regiment* (New York, 1984 edn), p. 60.

PART FOUR

THE IDEOLOGICAL FRONT

CHAPTER TWELVE

CAPITALISM AND THE CIVIL WAR

JOHN ASHWORTH

W ithout doubt the Civil War stands as the severest political crisis, the primary single event in the history of the American Republic. Of equal importance, nevertheless, was a long and slow process which was occurring over the entire nineteenth century: the growth of the American economy to a position of world leadership. The frail and internationally insignificant economy of 1800 had by 1900 become the greatest economic power the world had yet seen. In the midst of this process, however, the United States had been convulsed by sectional agitation, the secession of the Southern states, war on an unprecedented scale, and the emancipation of 4 million slaves – a sequence of events that occurred with bewildering rapidity. An obvious question thus arises: what was the relationship between the process and the events, between the economic transformation and the political cataclysms, in short between American capitalism and the Civil War?[1]

Although apparently simple, this question is in reality complex and subtle. Several sets of problems should be noted at the outset. First, it is important to determine which years and which parts of the country are being considered. Is it claimed that the war years themselves witnessed a transformation of the national economy? Or rather that they set in motion or continued trends which, over many years, would more gradually alter the trajectory of American capitalism? And is it the economic effects upon the North, the South, or the nation as a whole which are to be measured? Clearly there is no reason to assume that the impact of the war was geographically uniform.[2]

Even more fundamentally, it is not clear what is meant by American capitalism. Are we concerned merely with the economy in a narrow sense? Such an approach has the attraction of (relative) simplicity but in actuality the war's impact was much larger. For the struggle had major political consequences in that a class of slaveholders, dominant in the antebellum republic, saw its national power shattered; the economic consequences would be of some significance. Similarly the war years generated a set of ideological changes or shifts which, although frequently ignored by economic historians, also had an impact upon the American economy. It is therefore appropriate, in considering the war's effects upon the economy, to separate them into the more narrowly or directly economic, and the political / ideological, recognizing that a capitalist economy necessarily has an ideological underpinning as well as a political superstructure. At the same time, however, we should remain alert to the complex and, it is safe to say, not fully understood, processes of interaction between politics, economics and ideology.

An even more basic problem concerns the very term 'capitalism', itself the subject of much controversy and debate. While it is not necessary here to consider all the competing definitions, three must be noted. Many historians, economists and social scientists in effect equate 'capitalism' with commerce. On this view production for the market is the key feature of a capitalist economy. This definition has huge implications for our understanding of the United States in the nineteenth century and in particular for the analysis of slavery in the Old South. For it is immediately obvious that plantation slavery in the South was irreducibly commercial. Production of cotton, by far the most important crop in the final antebellum decades, was almost entirely for distant and primarily for international markets. The entire slave system was fuelled by the demand for raw cotton and other crops, and the commodification of slaves themselves was an essential feature of the system. In these respects, therefore, the South was at least as 'capitalist' as the North.[3]

An alternative definition, however, casts doubt upon Southern capitalism. Derived essentially from the Marxist tradition, this narrower, more restrictive definition requires the commodification of labour power, in effect the existence of wage labour on a large scale. On this view the antebellum South, many of whose spokesmen trumpeted forth their hostility to what was polemically termed 'wage slavery', had a commercial but scarcely a capitalist economy. While some Southerners did of course work for wages, by almost any criterion wage work on the land came a poor third to slavery and the various forms of farming carried out either by family farmers or tenants. It is true that in the cities and in the manufacturing establishments of the South wage labour was more prominent than on the land or in agriculture but one of the striking features of the Southern economy was its inability to urbanize or industrialize on a significant scale.[4]

It is not necessary here to determine the relative merits of these definitions. Indeed since the postbellum South was a region in which the wages system was similarly eclipsed – this time primarily by share-cropping and tenant

farming – it might seem as though the definitional problem is of little consequence. As we shall see, such is not the case. Instead it is necessary to keep
in mind the distinction between capitalism-as-commerce and capitalism-
as-wage-labour.

A third definition features most prominently in the work of Charles and
Mary Beard and their followers, perhaps the leading advocates of the view
that the Civil War promoted American capitalism. Here capitalism is in effect
industrialism. This definition also has major implications for our understanding of the Civil War and its economic impact. Before the war both sections
were primarily agricultural, although parts of the North could reasonably
be described as industrial. In the postbellum decades, although the South continued to lag behind in this process, the nation became an industrial giant,
indeed the foremost industrial power on the face of the earth. The Beards
themselves argued that the war played a crucial role in this process; for them
it facilitated the transformation from agrarianism to industrialism. Alongside
capitalism-as-commerce and capitalism-as-wage-labour we must therefore
place capitalism-as-industrialism.[5]

Southern war economy

When both sides went to war, they expected it to be of short duration and
foresaw little economic disruption. Both predictions proved hopelessly
wrong. Every significant feature of the Union and Confederate economies
was touched by the four years of bitter conflict. This was particularly true of
the South which was driven by economic as well as military necessity to
employ ever more drastic measures and even to consider the arming of its
slave population, an idea which would have astounded every white Southerner a few years earlier. Indeed for the Confederacy the war years were ones
of increasingly severe economic dislocation, and for the overwhelming
majority of her white citizens, of unwontedly severe hardship.[6]

The Confederate economy was plagued by problems from the outset.
Although the Northern embargo and blockade were not entirely successful,
they reduced the cotton trade by perhaps as much as 90 per cent. (A further
difficulty arose since 1860 had seen a bumper cotton crop and the British
market was all but glutted.) As a result, and since Southerners had, on the
outbreak of war, repudiated at least US$300,000,000 in debts to Northern
banks and merchants, the Confederacy was starved of credit and capital. This

made imports the more difficult to finance. Except in New Orleans, banks suspended specie payments for the duration of the conflict. Faced with declining revenues and mounting expenditure, the Confederate government had little choice but to issue paper money in the form of treasury notes, which eventually totalled well over a billion dollars. Inevitably the money depreciated with the declining economic and military fortunes of the Confederacy so that rapid inflation and hoarding of foodstuffs occurred on an ever-greater scale. Indeed a vicious cycle was created as the Confederate government authorized army officers to seize foodstuffs and pay for them at confiscatory prices; the result was yet more hoarding and a still deeper food crisis.[7]

With military reversals came disruption of supplies. The railroad network, which had in any case lacked trunk lines from the outset, was starved of funds and materials for essential repairs and maintenance, partly because materials could not be imported and partly because they were needed elsewhere for the war effort. Thus even when food and other supplies were available they could not be distributed. Although there was a small shift out of agriculture in the South, with the government itself taking over the operation of factories for the processing of, for example, salt and the production of guns and other armaments, the enormous profits available from successful blockade-running probably diverted productive capital out of manufacturing. On the land, circumstances dictated a similar shift away from cotton towards grain and meat. This diversification was perhaps in the longer-term interests of Southern agriculture and of the Southern economy as a whole, but, once again, it was on too small a scale to do more than slightly mitigate the full effects of the economic hardship.

Whilst it would be wrong to conclude that all Southerners were economically injured by the war – given the windfall gains available to blockade-runners and successful speculators – there can be little doubt about its overall macroeconomic impact. It is no exaggeration to say that Southern agriculture, by far the most important sector in the Southern economy, was pauperized by 1865. The value of Southern real estate fell by half while the value of farms, farm products and livestock in the older states of the Confederacy (that is, all except Arkansas, Texas and Florida) did not regain the levels of 1860 until 1900 (by which time the value of farms in the North had doubled). In the decade of the Civil War, Southern per capita output fell by 39 per cent.[8]

The combination of the war and the ending of slavery, together with a probable reduction in the world demand for cotton jointly produced these effects. The abolition of slavery was itself an act of confiscation of revolutionary proportions with catastrophic effects upon aggregate Southern wealth. It is likely that the loss of somewhere between one-and-a-half and two billion dollars' worth of slave property represented about 30 per cent of total Southern wealth.

Nor were these effects of limited duration. On the contrary, Southern agriculture, and the Southern economy as a whole sank into a position of weakness relative to the nation as a whole from which they would not recover until well after the Second World War. Despite the shift out of agriculture during the war, the South's share of the nation's manufacturing output which had been a mere 7.2 per cent in 1860 fell to 4.7 per cent in 1870 and would not regain even the modest antebellum level until the end of the century. Indeed a central feature of the Confederate wartime economy – its fatal shortage of credit and capital – persisted as a characteristic and a chronic problem in the postbellum South.[9]

By most criteria, therefore, Southern capitalism was anything but furthered by the Civil War. Commodity output was severely damaged and Southern industrialization, lagging far behind the North in 1860, slipped still further behind. Only if we define capitalism so as to exclude slavery can it be said to have been furthered by the wartime experience. As we shall see later, this effect was of major proportions, though not perhaps primarily in the South. For the ending of Southern slavery did not produce wage labour in the region so much as a bewildering array of labour systems, including share-cropping, tenant farming, the crop-lien system and other contractual agreements, generally designed to give as little true freedom to the freedmen as possible and to perpetuate racial inequality throughout the region. Thus the South emerged from the Civil War as a backward economic region, characterized by low wages, low productivity, underdevelopment and a chronic shortage of productive capital. Most Republicans had hoped that the war and Reconstruction would together remake the South in the image of the North. By the mid-1870s, if not earlier, it was apparent that this project lay in ruins.[10]

Northern war economy

Those who have claimed that the Civil War promoted American capitalism, however, have not based their case on the Southern experience. For the impact of the war upon the North was, of course, very different. The war years gave a great boost to certain industries in the North and produced institutional changes that were beneficial to Northern capitalism during the war itself and for many years thereafter. Nevertheless and quite apart from the sacrifices entailed by the military struggle, some groups in the North suffered severe deprivation. It is perhaps ironic that under the Republicans, ostensibly the party of 'free labor', labour lost heavily. In fact a relatively large number of labour unions came into existence in the war years – at least ten national unions as well as local ones were created between 1863 and 1866 – but these were essentially defensive reactions to a deteriorating environment. Although the war effort should have made labour comparatively scarce, this effect was offset by the arrival of some 800,000 immigrants. Wages actually rose by perhaps 50 per cent during the war but failed to keep pace with prices. In the first two years of the war wages rose 20 per cent but prices rose by 50 per cent. The following year prices rose even faster and the result was the organization of unions and the outbreak of strikes in the winter of 1863–4. By the end of the war prices were perhaps more than two-thirds higher than on the eve of conflict. Meanwhile, federal troops and martial law had been employed to defeat strikers.[11]

The cause of the price rise was, of course, the emission of paper money. In part the North shared the experiences of the Confederacy. With the disruption of the export trade, cotton now had to be imported and a large balance of payments deficit quickly emerged. This put pressure on the currency. Simultaneously, the government had the problem of financing the war. Increased taxation was one method and this was indeed adopted but Lincoln's Secretary of the Treasury, Salmon P. Chase, determined to rely primarily upon the sale of government bonds. (Ultimately about 80 per cent of the cost of the war would be funded in this way.) Once again the federal government's experience mirrored that of the Confederacy. Having issued Treasury notes, Chase found that with every military reversal the tendency to hoard specie was strengthened and by December 1861 the government lacked the funds to redeem its own notes in specie. Hence when the banks suspended specie payments at that time, the government did likewise.[12]

Released from the obligation to have currency convertible into specie, Chase was now able, after Congressional prompting, to issue treasury notes that would be acceptable for virtually all public and private debts and which would therefore circulate as legal tender. Hence the birth of the famous 'Greenbacks'. In all $450,000 in Greenbacks were issued and this resulted in a doubling of the pre-war stock of money in the United States. Almost immediately the Greenbacks fell in value, and with every military reversal further downward pressure was exerted on them (as a result of the fear that the notes would be repudiated in the event of a Confederate victory). More fundamentally, however, the amount of paper money in circulation had increased far more rapidly than the supply of goods and services in the economy so that there was too much money chasing too few goods, the classic recipe for inflation.[13]

To this extent the Northern experience paralleled that of the Confederacy. But the outcomes were entirely different. Whereas in the South the supply of banking capital fell in the Civil War decade by more than 70 per cent, the financial network in the North acquired a new maturity and sophistication. Not only had the government financed the war successfully (if controversially), it had also, through the National Banking Acts of 1863 and 1864, placed the banking system on a far more secure basis than ever before. Once again fiscal crisis had been the midwife of change. The banks chartered were required to accept federal supervision and taxation and to meet clearly defined specie reserve requirements. Moreover they had to agree only to issue notes against federal bonds. Before long the state banks, whose notes often circulated at rates far below their face value and who were now increasingly unable to compete with the newer national banks, were under threat and the United States possessed a banking system – and a currency – far more appropriate to the needs of the industrial era.

Thus although the financial changes and innovations of the Civil War era inevitably injured many, the overall impact was probably beneficial to the economic development of the North. Similarly the Union government produced other wartime initiatives. The fiscal crisis gave rise to a revision of the tariff which, although intended to raise revenue, in fact gave considerable protection to American industry. The average rates rose from 19 per cent to 47 per cent by the conclusion of the war. Lincoln and his party also continued the liberalization of land policy that had been underway in the final antebellum decades, with the passage of the Homestead Act of 1862. Although speculators made windfall gains, the Act did promote the establishment of family farms in the West. The federal government continued to offer land grants not only to railroad companies, as it had done before the war, but also to states that established agricultural colleges. Finally, the war saw the introduction of a federal income tax.[14]

This was a bold economic programme and, partly as a consequence, large sectors of the Northern economy experienced significant growth rates in the war years. In addition to the direct and intended effects of the federal government's programme were the unintended consequences of the war: spiralling inflation, a great shortage of cotton, an army of over a million men to feed and clothe. These together inevitably gave a boost to some Northern industries. Thus the iron industry boomed as a result of inflation, wartime needs and the protection afforded by the tariff. Woollen manufacturing also surged ahead, as consumers sought to substitute wool for cotton. In agriculture, an additional factor was the poor run of European harvests, increasing the demand for American wheat. Despite the absence of many farmers, more was produced than ever before. The number of sheep reared doubled and the trend towards mechanization in agriculture, already visible in the 1850s, continued in the war years.[15]

The war years were thus a time of considerable prosperity for many Northerners. Stockholders in railroads and telegraph companies enjoyed high dividend yields and the merger of some companies created oligopolies or monopolies which, whilst small compared to the corporate mammoths of the late nineteenth century, were large enough to cause considerable disquiet among sections of the Northern public. Moreover new industries, destined to be of enormous importance in the future, like the oil industry, emerged during the war. In dozens of cities streetcars made their first appearance, again anticipating the changes of the gilded age.[16]

Thus the war years produced an effect on the Northern economy that contrasted sharply with its impact on the South. However, it is important to compare Northern economic performance not merely with that of the Confederacy, where the conclusions are scarcely in doubt, but with that of the North, or the entire nation, before and after the war. Here the picture is far less clear. Although Charles Beard was in no doubt that the exigencies of war were critical in the history of Northern capitalism, some historians have accused him of projecting the experiences of the First World War, when the United States boomed, back into the nineteenth century. His claim that the Civil War played a special role is therefore very much open to question.[17]

For Beard, industrialization was the key concern. Here the data requires careful analysis. It is true that agriculture did decline in importance in the national economy in the 1860s but this was as a result of the collapse of Southern agriculture, not of any absolute, or even relative, decline in the North. Indeed in the 1860s agriculture in the North expanded more rapidly – in terms of total output – than other sectors. In manufacturing, experience varied from industry to industry. Although the woollen industry expanded, cotton manufacturing not surprisingly fell back sharply. In some industries prices and profits rose, while production fell. Should this be viewed as a success for capitalists or a failure for capitalism? In any event the index of manufacturing productivity was almost static for the war years.[18]

Moreover, it is important to place the experience of the 1860s in historical perspective. Here it seems that there is little reason to see the war decade as a watershed. Annual growth in commodity output in the two decades before the war was higher than in the two decades after 1870. When value added in manufacturing is considered, no obvious conclusion emerges. The rate of growth was 7.8 per cent for the years 1840–60 but 6 per cent for the final three decades of the century. On the other hand the *per capita* rate was somewhat higher in the latter period, though this may have merely represented a catching up after the war decade. As far as the North's absolute growth performance is concerned, between 1840 and 1860 per capita income rose at an average annual rate of 1.3 per cent; for the next two decades the figure was 1.75 per cent and for the last two of the century 1.9 per cent. In sum, either there was no acceleration in growth after the war, or if the rate of growth did increase it appears to have been part of a longer process. The data do not therefore give obvious support to the claim that the war has a privileged status in the history of American capitalism.[19]

It is therefore far more to difficult to draw up an economic balance sheet for the North during the war, and for the United States as a whole, than for the South. Whereas the war years were ruinous for large swathes of Southern agriculture and of little benefit to Southern manufacturing, in the North the processes of industrialization and mechanization continued, though probably without breaking sharply with the past. The change in the American banking system and the raising of the tariff walls were of considerable importance but each decade in the late nineteenth century saw developments that were probably of similar significance. In short there is no obvious reason to single out the war experience or the war decade as critical to the success or the development of American capitalism.[20]

Effects of the war

Nevertheless, it is important to consider other factors. Among the chief effects of the war was, of course, the ending of slavery in the South. Its effects on the South have already been noted. But it has been argued that slavery was an impediment to Northern capitalism. On this view slavery blocked Northern development because it 'strangled the home market for industrial capital'. This effect was attributable to the relative self-sufficiency of the plantations as well as the difficulty that planters allegedly experienced when seeking to introduce labour-saving machinery. Slaves were considered unfit to use such machinery and they lacked the purchasing power to give a boost to the regional economy equivalent to that supplied by Northern free farmers.[21]

Even if these constraints did operate, however, it is important not to exaggerate their importance. First, Southern slavery was, in some respects, beneficial to Northern capitalism. Exports of cotton and other staple crops obviously benefited Northern mercantile interests in the antebellum decades; Northern merchants themselves played a key part in the early stages of indus-trialization. Equally, Southern (as well as Northern) exports facilitated and underwrote loans into the North, which were then used for capital projects to improve the regional infrastructure. Even if by 1860 these advantages no longer offset the disadvantages entailed by Southern slavery (and this has not been demonstrated) Southern slavery was only a partial, rather than a total liability to the North. In other words, we are dealing with a net rather than a gross loss.

Second, and more important, it is abundantly clear that Northern capital-ism had not come to a grinding halt in 1860, immobilized by the existence of Southern slavery. The experience of the 1850s, probably the very decade when the North was progressing most rapidly, is the strongest possible evid-ence to the contrary. The Northern economy of 1860 in no sense faced crisis or stagnation. With a huge area of land open – including California – a grow-ing population, and a favourable international environment, it did not need the South Atlantic states to expand into, still less the territory or states in the Southwest.

Finally, and more generally, we must guard against an implicit functional-ism, in which changes are assumed to be optimal for the dominant social order. At a practical level, it is surely clear that the postbellum South was scarcely ideal for the development of capitalism in the South or the North. In other words, after the war one set of sub-optimal conditions replaced another.[22]

Yet one important possibility remains. It is still conceivable that the war and the elimination of slavery played a key role in the development of Amer-ican capitalism, at least if capitalism entails wage labour. For the acceptance of wage labour was almost certainly facilitated by the war. This happened to some degree in the South in the obvious sense that some former slaves became wage-earners, but more importantly, perhaps, in the North and in the nation as a whole, where an important ideological change or shift took place. This effect is normally overlooked or ignored by economic historians; it therefore merits a closer look.

What was the relationship between the wages system and the Civil War? More than anyone else it was Abraham Lincoln who took responsibility for presenting the war to the Northern electorate and his views can be taken as representative of the Republican party, now the dominant political force in the nation. As is well known, Lincoln announced that the war was a test of democracy not merely in the United States but the world over:

> And this issue embraces more than the fate of these United States. It presents to the whole family of man the question whether a constitutional republic or democracy – a government of the people by the same people – can or cannot maintain its integrity against its own domestic foes. It presents the question whether discontented individuals, too few in number to control administration according to organic law in any case, can always, upon the pretences made in this case, or on any other pretences, or arbitrarily without any pretence, break up their government, and thus practically put an end to free government upon the earth. It forces us to ask: Is there in all republics this inherent and fatal weakness? Must a government, of necessity, be too strong for the liberties of its own people or too weak to maintain its own existence?

But for Lincoln democracy was not simply a form of government. Instead it was the political underpinning of a social system. At the heart of this social system lay mobility:

> This is essentially a people's contest. On the side of the Union it is a struggle for maintaining in the world that form and substance of government whose leading object is to elevate the condition of men – to lift artificial weights from all shoulders; to clear the paths of laudable pursuit for all; to afford all an un-fettered start, and a fair chance in the race of life. Yielding to partial and temporary departures, from necessity, this is the leading object of the government for whose existence we contend.

If democracy required social mobility then social mobility in turn required the wages system: Lincoln explained the process by which mobility occurred:

> The prudent, penniless beginner in the world, labors for wages awhile, saves a surplus with which to buy tools or land for himself, then labors on his own account another while, and at length hires another new beginner to help him. This, say its advocates, is free labor – the just and generous and prosperous system, which opens the way for all – gives hope to all, and energy, and progress, and improvement of condition to all.

Thus it is not too much to claim that Lincoln believed the Civil War was being fought in order to preserve the wages system. As he put it, 'this progress, by which the poor, honest, industrious, and resolute man raises himself, that he may work on his own account, and hire somebody else' was 'the great principle for which this government was really formed.'[23]

At the end of the war the Union cause had received a tremendous boost. Now the ideals expressed by Lincoln and the Republicans had become dominant not merely in the North but in the nation as a whole. Indeed the entire ideology of Americanism had been redefined so that it stressed mobility and growth with the wages system playing an essential role. Historians have generally ignored or underestimated this effect, perhaps because they have also underestimated the hostility to the wages system that existed in antebellum America, North as well as South. But by the end of the war the values of Lincoln and his Republican party had become the values of the North, and of the nation as a whole. This is not to say that the South had been converted. It had not. But after the war the power of the South was so reduced that it could not prevent the nationalization, as it were, of Northern values. We should remind ourselves that this had not been possible before the War, where the South had wielded considerable power politically and where Southern thought had played a key role in the formulation and the formation of the American democratic tradition.

How important was this for the future development of American capitalism? Here it is, once again, difficult to be precise. A more willing acceptance of the wages system cannot be given a financial value: one cannot quantify the effect upon per capita or national income and wealth. Instead, however, we may make several tentative observations. The United States since the Civil War has exhibited an extraordinary attachment to capitalist values. Across the political spectrum from right-wing Republicans to the liberal reformers of the Progressive, New Deal and Great Society eras, the core values of popular capitalism have gone largely unchallenged. Within the political mainstream a social democratic challenge has been rare, a socialist one non-existent. It is as if the creed that was forged in the 1850s by the Republican party in opposition to slavery, and which acquired enormous prestige with the victory of the Union armies, has been powerful enough to withstand the challenges to the capitalist system that in many other countries proved fatal or at least highly damaging. Plainly many other factors have been present and it is not possible to establish the proposition firmly but there is still reason to believe that in this sense the war indeed played a major role in establishing and protecting capitalism in the United States.

Notes

1. The classic view of the Civil War as a key stage in the growth of American capitalism is to be found in Charles and Mary Beard, *The Rise of American Civilization* 2 vols (New York, 1927), esp. vol. 2 pp. 54, 166 and Louis Hacker, *The Triumph of American Capitalism* (New York, 1940), esp. p. 339. This thesis stimulated a historiographical debate in which two of the major contributions were Thomas Cochran, 'Did the Civil War retard industrialization?' *Mississippi Valley Historical Review* XLVIII (1961), pp. 197–210 and Stanley Engerman, 'The economic impact of the Civil War', *Explorations in Economic History* III (1966), pp. 176–99. Both these essays were reprinted in Ralph Andreano (ed.), *The Economic Impact of the Civil War*, 2nd edn (Cambridge, Mass., 1967), which contains many other valuable contributions, some of which are cited below. Special mention should be made, however, of an essay original to that volume by Stephen Salsbury, 'The effect of the Civil War on American industrial development', pp. 180–7, which seeks to rehabilitate the Beard-Hacker thesis and defend it from the damaging criticisms of Cochran, Engerman and others. In this connection see also Harry N. Scheiber, 'Economic change in the Civil War era: an analysis of recent studies', *Civil War History*, XI (1965), pp. 396–411. Some of the older economic histories, which contain chapters on the Civil War, are still valuable, such as Harold U. Faulkner, *American Economic History* (8th edn, New York, 1960) and Reginald C. McGrane, *The Economic Development of the American Nation* (Boston, Mass., 1950). One should also refer to more general works by economic historians, some of which include important observations about the Civil War such as Robert Fogel, *Without Consent or Contract*, 4 vols (New York, 1989–92) and Roger L. Ransom, *Conflict and Compromise: The Political Economy of Slavery, Emancipation and the American Civil War* (New York, 1989), which contains an excellent discussion of this topic, pp. 253–88.

2. It is probably fair to say that these distinctions have not always been fully taken into account by historians. See, however, Salsbury, 'Effect of the Civil War', in Andreano, *Economic Impact of Civil War*, pp. 184–6.

3. This is the more widely accepted view of the Old South. It received a classic expression in Robert Fogel and Stanley Engerman, *Time on the Cross*, 2 vols (Boston, 1974).

4. This view is to be found in the works of Eugene D. Genovese, especially *The Political Economy of Slavery: Studies in the Economy and Society of the Slave South* (New York, 1967). It is also found in John Ashworth, *Slavery, Capitalism and Politics in the Antebellum Republic, Volume I, Commerce and Compromise, 1820–1850* (Cambridge, 1995).

5. Beards, *Rise of American Civilization*, vol. 2, p. 105.

6. On the Confederacy see E. Merton Coulter, *The Confederate States of America 1861–1865* (Baton Rouge, La, 1950), Emory M. Thomas, *The Confederate Nation, 1861–1865* (New York, 1979), and the excellent essay in William L. Barney, *Flawed Victory: A New Perspective on the Civil War* (Lanham, Md, 1980), pp. 81–120, which is equally valuable on the North during the war.

7. For the topics covered in this and the next paragraph see Eugene M. Lerner, 'The monetary and fiscal programs of the Confederate Government, 1861–1865', *Journal of Political Economy*, LXII (1954), pp. 506–22; Lerner, 'Money, wages, and prices in the Confederacy', *Journal of Political Economy*, LXIII (1955), pp. 20–40 reprinted in Andreano (ed.), *Economic Impact of Civil War*, pp. 31–60. An older work is John C. Schwab, *The Confederate States of America: A Financial and Industrial History of the South During the Civil War* (New York, 1901), which is not fully superseded by Richard C. Todd, *Confederate Finance* (Athens, Ga, 1954). On the blockade and its effects see William M. Robinson, Jr, *The Confederate Privateers* (New Haven, Conn., 1928). James L. Sellers, 'Economic incidence of the Civil War in the South', *Mississippi Valley Historical Review*, XIV (1927), pp. 179–91 is a valuable article, reprinted in Andreano (ed.), *Economic Impact of Civil War*, pp. 98–108.

8. Engerman, 'Economic impact' in Andreano (ed.), *Economic Impact of Civil War*, p. 180; Jeremy Atack and Peter Passell, *A New Economic View of American History*, 2nd edn (New York, 1994), pp. 373–4; Eugene Lerner, 'Southern output and agricultural income, 1860–1880', *Agricultural History*, XXX (1959), pp. 117–25, reprinted in Andreano (ed.), *Economic Impact of Civil War*, pp. 109–22.

9. Atack and Passell, *New Economic View*, pp. 373–4, 378; Gavin Wright, *Old South, New South: Revolutions in the Southern Economy* (New York, 1986); Stephen Decanio, 'Productivity and income distribution in the postbellum South', *Journal of Economic History*, XXXIV (1974), pp. 422–46.

10. On economic conditions in the postbellum South, see, in addition to works already cited, three by Roger Ransom and Richard Sutch: 'Debt peonage in the cotton South after the Civil War', *Journal of Economic History*, XXXII (1972), pp. 641–67; 'The impact of the Civil War and of emancipation on Southern agriculture', *Explorations in Economic History*, XII (1975), pp. 1–28; *One Kind of Freedom: The Economic Consequences of Emancipation* (Cambridge, 1977).

11. Atack and Passell, *New Economic View*, p. 497; Wesley C. Mitchell, *Gold, Prices, and Wage under the Greenback Standard* (Berkeley, 1908), pp. 4, 279; Reuben A. Kessel and Armen A. Alchian, 'Real wages in the North during the Civil War: Mitchell's data reinterpreted', *Journal of Law and Economics*, II (1959), pp. 95–113, reprinted in Andreano (ed.), *Economic Impact of Civil War*, pp. 11–30;

Faulkner, *American Economic History*, p. 451; Philip S. Foner, *History of the Labor Movement in the United States*, vol. I (New York, 1947); Clarence D. Long, *Wages and Earnings in the United States, 1860–1890* (Princeton, 1960); Engerman, 'Economic impact', in Andreano (ed.), *Economic Impact of Civil War*, p. 198.

12. For the material in this and the following paragraphs see Lance Davis, 'Capital immobities and finance capitalism: a study of economic evolution in the United States, 1820–1920', *Explorations in Economic History*, I (1963), pp. 88–105; Bray Hammond, *Sovereignty and an Empty Purse: Banks and Politics in the Civil War* (Princeton, 1970); Paul Studenski and Herman Krooss, *A Financial History of the United States* (New York, 1952).

13. Wesley C. Mitchell, *A History of the Greenbacks* (Chicago, 1903), reprinted in Andreano (ed.), *Economic Impact of Civil War*, pp. 85–97.

14. Leonard P. Curry, *Blueprint for Modern America: Nonmilitary Legislation of the First Civil War Congress* (Nashville, 1968), pp. 244–52.

15. E.D. Fite, *Social and Industrial Conditions in the North during the Civil War* (New York, 1910); George W. Smith and Charles Judah (eds), *Life in the North during the Civil War* (Albuquerque, New Mexico, 1966); Barney, *Flawed Victory*, pp. 158–94; J. Mathew Gallman, *The North Fights the Civil War: The Home Front* (Chicago, 1994), pp. 92–108. Some support for the Beard-Hacker thesis is provided in Jeffrey Williamson, 'Watersheds and turning points: conjectures on the long term impact of Civil War financing', *Journal of Economic History*, XXXIV (1974), pp. 631–61. Williamson argues that the tariff allowed retirement of the federal debt and stimulated investment. On Northern agriculture see Wayne D. Rasmussen, 'The Civil War: a catalyst of agricultural revolution', *Agricultural History*, XXXIX (1965), pp. 187–95 reprinted in Andreano (ed.), *Economic Impact of Civil War*, pp. 68–82.

16. Paul H. Giddens, *The Birth of the Oil Industry* (New York, 1938).

17. Beards, *Rise of American Civilization*, vol. 2, pp. 53–4 ; Thomas Cochran, 'Did the Civil War retard industrialization?' in Andreano (ed.), *The Economic Impact of the Civil War*, pp. 167–79.

18. Atack and Passell, *New Economic View*, pp. 363–4, 373.

19. Atack and Passell, *New Economic View*, pp. 363–74; Engerman, 'Economic impact', in Andreano (ed.), *Economic Impact of Civil War*, p. 192.

20. Engerman, 'Economic impact,' in Andreano (ed.), *Economic Impact of Civil War*, pp. 190–1; Ransom, *Conflict and Compromise*, pp. 257–68.

21. Charles Post, 'The American road to capitalism', *New Left Review*, CXXXIII (1982), pp. 30–51, esp. p. 37; Saul Engelbourg, 'The economic impact of the

[304]   Civil War on manufacturing enterprises', *Business History*, XX (1979), pp. 148–62.

22.   This is a tendency prominent within certain strains of Marxist writing and also within many of Beard's writings.

23.   Roy F. Basler (ed.), *The Collected Works of Abraham Lincoln*, 8 vols (New Brunswick, NJ, 1953–5), vol. 4, pp. 426, 438, vol. 3, pp. 478–9; Basler (ed.), *Supplement to the Collected Works of Lincoln* (Westport, Conn., 1974), pp. 43–4. See also *Collected Works of Lincoln*, vol. 2, pp. 240, 364, 438; vol. 3, pp. 24, 459, 462; vol. 4, pp. 240; vol. 7, pp. 512, 528. On Republican ideology see Eric Foner, *Free Soil, Free Labor, Free Men: the Ideology of the Republican Party before the Civil War* (New York, 1970) and John Ashworth, 'Free labor, wage labor, and the slave power: republicanism and the Republican Party in the 1850s', in Melvyn Stokes and Stephen Conway (eds), *The Market Revolution in America: Social, Political, and Religious Expressions, 1800–1880* (Charlottesville, Va, 1996), pp. 128–46.

CHAPTER THIRTEEN

INDIVIDUAL RIGHTS AND CONSTITUTIONAL POWERS: THE IMPACT OF THE CIVIL WAR

PAT LUCIE

'There is quite as much trouble in the reformation of an old constitution as in the establishment of a new one, just as to unlearn is as hard as to learn,' as Aristotle reminds us.[1] To assess the impact of the American Civil War on the Constitution, we have to look backwards to the 1780s when it was framed, and forward to the end of the twentieth century, when it seems alive and well, and outwardly remarkably unchanged from the original.[2] Its longevity suggests a brilliant design. In 1861, however, when the Southern states walked out of the Union in anger, the Constitution came close to failure. To survive, it had to change. Though textual amendments over the last 200 years have been few, those ratified as the result of the Civil War are the most important. Behind the textual changes, however, there was a deeper change in the habits of the Constitution, the understandings and expectations of the people who turned text into life.

Bruce Ackerman has identified three great transformative moments in American constitutional history, when the people sanctioned the making of 'higher law', rules which govern but are beyond ordinary politics.[3] The Philadelphia Convention was the first, when the Constitution was framed and ratified. The second was the Civil War, when the Constitution was repaired and in a sense completed. The New Deal was the third, when the balance of federalism altered decisively in favour of the federal government, not only with respect to the economy, but also the meaning of citizenship. In the wake of the New Deal, the Supreme Court made the Bill of Rights central to constitutional jurisprudence and made individual rights the business of the federal government in ways never contemplated by the Founding Fathers.

There are always risks in selecting and describing transformations. On close inspection they turn out to be complex processes and invariably they invite dispute. In the case of the American Constitution there is another peculiar hazard in describing change. Lawyers, judges and politicians, who write most of the history of the Constitution, have a vested interest in legitimacy. Their investigations of the past are often prompted by the need to find a believable genetic link between their present constitutional agenda and the fundamental law of the Constitution. This means that even as the Constitution is in the process of change, there is a constant 'spin' put on it to explain and reorder the past in such a way as to define an orderly or a true lineage and to oust illegitimate offspring.

The Civil War was fought by two sides claiming legitimacy. Each championed constitutional liberty and self-government and each aspired to achieve it by remaining faithful to the design of the Founding Fathers. The Southern states were the first to make textual changes. The Confederacy was established in 1861 under a new Constitution, which took only two weeks to write and which was closely based on the words and structure of the United States Constitution. It did, however, also contain many significant changes, most of which were designed to redress grievances against the North's supposed malevolent misinterpretations of the Constitution in the antebellum period. The end result, I shall argue, neither preserved the work of 1787, nor improved upon it. Had the Confederacy survived, its leaders would have to have acquired more insight into the science of government as well as the nature of liberty.

The Union side had the advantage of fighting with the ready-made machinery as well as the text of the Constitution, though its adequacy to the task of self-preservation was not a foregone conclusion. Although no changes were made to the text until the Thirteenth Amendment in 1865, the Republicans embarked on a steep learning curve as soon as the first shots were fired at Fort Sumter. Curiously, until then, the Constitution had led a relatively unexamined life. True, it was seldom out of the news in antebellum America. Every purveyor of sectional argument or civic piety wrapped himself in its authority. Serious critical study, however, began with war. President Lincoln and the Congress found within the Constitution the powers and tools of self-preservation without doing serious violence to civil liberty.[4] But in the course of war they also discovered a flaw in the Constitution's design. It was so centred on states rights, so focused on denying powers to the federal government which might deprive citizens of their rights, that it lacked the power to protect and guarantee individuals these rights when they were threatened by the states themselves or by private powers. The vacuum at the heart of federalism was at its most obvious when the government began working out how to protect emancipated slaves in hostile local environments far from Washington. But it also became clear that it was more than a question of what shall be done with 4 million freed slaves. The larger question was about the liberty of all Americans. Did not the Bill of Rights mean that they had rights? What did they amount to if states could take them away and the federal government could do nothing to stop them? What did it mean for the integrity of government if the federal government could not protect its citizens in Massachusetts or South Carolina? These were questions which could not be answered without transforming the Constitution, and altering its text.

In a nutshell, the Republicans made the individual rights of all persons federal business. Between 1865 and 1870, the Constitution was amended three times. The Thirteenth Amendment forbade slavery except as a punishment for crime. The Fourteenth Amendment guaranteed all persons born in the United States the privileges and immunities of citizenship, and all persons the equal protection of the laws and due process. The Fifteenth Amendment denied any government power to deprive United States citizens of the right to vote on account of race. The powers of Congress were enlarged to enforce these guarantees, and Congress passed civil rights laws to do so. The federal courts, as we shall see, became the lynchpins of constitutional change, and to them fell the greatest share in the task of explaining the meaning of the amendments, how far-reaching or otherwise they were intended to be, what was legitimate to build out of them, and how they fitted in to the lineage of the Constitution.

The courts began imposing their own order on history in the immediate aftermath of the war and gradually weaved the meaning of the Civil War and Reconstruction amendments into a fabric compatible with their own times, which by the end of the nineteenth century had no interest in racial justice or the federal protection of individual rights. All that was to change after the New Deal, however, when the Supreme Court's interests moved away from a defence of vested economic rights to take an increasingly active guardianship of the Bill of Rights and the rights of minorities.[5] More specifically, after school desegregation began in the 1950s there was a renewed interest in racial justice and civil rights, often described as the 'Second Reconstruction'. A new generation attempting to make the Constitution serve liberty found itself faced by many of the same questions which had faced Lincoln's generation about the nature of rights, how difficult it was to make and enforce federal norms and how cussed states could be in resisting them. It rediscovered the tools the Civil War had left behind and built a new constitutional jurisprudence upon them.

Even a casual rummage in modern textbooks on constitutional law discloses contemporary reliance on the Civil War's constitutional inheritance. The vitality of the Fourteenth Amendment in the daily lives of Americans is not the only evidence. The 1866 Civil Rights Act enjoyed a revival in 1968 to reach racial discrimination in the private housing market.[6] Acts designed to prevent the Ku Klux Klan depriving black people of their freedom are now in daily use to give all Americans recourse to federal courts against officials who deprive them of any of their fundamental rights.[7] State prisoners today rely on the Habeas Corpus Act of 1867 to challenge violations of their constitutional rights in federal court.[8] Law journals buzz with arguments about potential fresh applications of the Thirteenth Amendment to areas analogous to slavery, including labour law, child abuse and prostitution.[9] A new generation in pursuit of liberty added remarkably little in the way of new tools and text to supplement those left behind from a century earlier.

The continued use of the tools, and the vitality of arguments about them is testimony to the long-term impact of the Civil War on the Constitution. But caution has to be exercised about whether or not the contemporary Constitution has finally realized and brought to fruition a plan which was buried and forgotten for the intervening century. The grass never grows under the Constitution. Since 1937 there has been a transformation of the Constitution just as far-reaching as that of the Civil War. This one has been characterized by judicial creativity rather than the alteration of text. Judges have refought the Civil War to accord with new legitimacies. Liberals have found sustenance if not proof for the view that the Fourteenth Amendment was intended to incorporate the Bill of Rights and make it applicable to the states and also for an expansive interpretation of federal powers to secure an extensive and growing body of rights. Conservatives argue that racism and a belief in states rights limited the vision of the Civil War generation to relatively small changes other than emancipation and basic civil rights for freedmen.[10] The fact that until the mid-1970s the Court was dominated by creative liberals shaped the version of the Civil War which had greatest impact. It was not that liberal judges argued that such things as school desegregation and later affirmative action, gender equality and abortion rights had been on the minds of the Framers, but that these were essentially legitimate contemporary offspring of the language and structure of the Fourteenth Amendment.

A Constitution which, in the latter half of the twentieth century, has become so essentially judge-made, is sensitive to new appointments and liberals are no longer in ascendancy. Indeed the Supreme Court's role as guardian of the Bill of Rights since the end of the New Deal has been a fleeting romance judged in the longer perspective of constitutional history, and it has blown hot and cold at that. Some members of the present Court profess moral scepticism and none is likely to argue for new adventures in individual rights on the strength of the Civil War amendments. Indeed, over the past two decades, conservatives on the Court have argued against adventure on the grounds that the Framers of the Civil War amendments intended relatively little change and would surely turn in their graves if their work was used to achieve gay rights or the right to assisted suicide.[11]

Constitutional discourse in contemporary America is also questioning some long-held assumptions about the culture of individual rights. Some critics question whether creating 'rights-bearing individuals' armed with a lawsuit in a federal court has much to do with liberty. Among the critics are those who regret the impotence of the rights-bearer. Courts and lawyers are expensive and beyond the pockets of many of the poorest and least able to assert rights. Reliance on a battle between individual and the state in a court of law locks rights into a 'perpetrator model' where it is necessary to prove that a state actor has infringed a particular right and that the remedy is tailored to the particular infringement. Even winning an occasional case does not reach the most pervasive aspects of racism and poverty. It is an essentially limited way of looking at rights.[12]

Other critics regret the isolation of the 'rights-bearing individual' rather than his impotence. Communitarian thinkers bring back to constitutional discourse a nostalgic ideal of people with responsibilities as well as rights, working for the good of all in their communities. This is the citizen as participant rather than possessor of rights. Recently there has been a revival of interest in 1787 rather than in the Civil War Constitution as the mainspring of liberty. The 'republican virtues', values drawn from classical Greek republicanism, rather than from the mix of classic liberalism and natural rights philosophies which underpin individual rights, have been much discussed. Civic virtue, whatever that is, is posed as an alternative to rampant individualism.[13] From this perspective, does the Confederate Constitution seem more attractive, and the Republican legacy less so?

The impact of the Civil War on the Constitution is the story of not one impact but many, because its telling is so intricately part of the way each generation connects its own constitutional vision with the past, and the inescapable vision of the Founding Fathers.

Liberty created?
The Philadelphia contribution

For all the preoccupation with individual rights in the recent life of the Constitution, the Framers in 1787 were a great deal more exercised by how to prevent governments infringing them than how to define them as 'entitlements'. Nobody has stated it more succinctly than Leonard Levy when he wrote, 'Americans understood that the individual may be free only if the government is not.'[14] The Constitution is about the arrangements they made to empower the government enough to govern but not enough to imperil the rights which belonged to man by nature. If the body politic was disarmed from the potential for tyranny by a web spun from federalism and separation of powers, then it followed that in the best of all possible worlds, the freedom of the individual was secure. It is a tale too well known to be retold that the Bill of Rights was added to the Constitution only when James Madison and the Federalists bowed to the demands of their political opponents for additional reassurance against federal power. The price of not agreeing could have been failure to ratify the Constitution. Madison, the 'Father of the Bill of Rights', was no admirer of the art of writing lists of rights and regarded the attempts of colonies to do so as rhetorical puff or parchment barriers. Nonetheless he made a passable job of drafting it. He even sounded enthusiastic in his great speech to a bored audience on 8 June 1789 when he presented the resolutions, famously predicting, 'if they are incorporated into the Constitution, independent tribunals of justice will consider themselves in a peculiar manner the guardians of those rights; they will be an impenetrable bulwark against every assumption of power in the legislative or Executive; they will naturally be led to resist every encroachment upon rights stipulated in the Constitution by the declaration of rights.'[15]

This is not the genesis of the rights-bearing individual, however. Indeed the Bill of Rights is what one writer has called a 'mixed ore' of individual rights, rights of 'the people' and rights of states.[16] It is highly selective. Madison had a couple of hundred suggestions for inclusion on his desk. Some of his own proposals failed. The final draft contained 22 rights. It was not that he could not think of more, but that there was no need. The Bill of Rights is as much about structure, and the distribution of powers as is the rest of the Constitution. The enterprise is summed up by the Ninth and Tenth Amendments. The Ninth Amendment makes it clear that rights cannot be diminished by being enumerated, and that the inclusion of certain rights does not protect some at the expense of others retained by the people. Why? Because although rights are not enumerated, powers are. The Tenth Amendment embodies Madison's conviction that the powers of the federal government are so textually limited that they cannot endanger individual rights.

Madison failed to carry the day on two issues which would assume importance later. One was that he originally proposed to slot the amendments into the original Constitution at the place he deemed most relevant, after the section dealing with limitations on the powers of Congress. The reason for this does not seem to have had ideological implications and nobody regarded it as a crucial issue. As it happened the placing of the Bill of Rights as a free-standing 'codicil' to the Framers' will may have made it more plausible for antislavery advocates and some Republicans to argue that it was a source of power to the federal government and a declaration of the rights of all Americans wherever they resided.[17] The other issue on which Madison failed to gain support was one that he regarded as of much greater importance. His fifth resolution for amendment was a limit on the states rather than on the federal government. It prohibited them from violating 'the equal right of conscience, freedom of the press, or trial by jury in criminal cases.' His belief that the states were just as likely to be the source of danger to rights was borne out by history. It could not be fairly argued, however, that the road to civil war begins with the Founding Fathers' failure to adopt this resolution. Madison himself acknowledged that his resolution bound the states only partially, with respect to 'particular rights'. There was never a serious prospect of passing limits on state powers in a Congress whose eyes were firmly focused on potential dangers from the federal government. Madison's proposal to give Congress a veto power over state legislation met the same fate.[18]

As it turned out, the federal government never became a routine transgressor against individual rights. For most of the Constitution's history, indeed up to the New Deal, it was not sufficiently engaged in the everyday lives of its people to make such an impact. There was, for example, very little federal criminal law, and hence not much need to invoke the protections which the Bill of Rights guaranteed to the accused. That is not to say that the fears of the Framers were unjustified. In times of emergency or conflict, the federal government was potentially dangerous. The 1798 Sedition Act, ruthlessly restricting freedom to criticise the government, was an early example. Later the 1850 Fugitive Slave Law purported to protect one man's 'right' to his property at the expense of keeping another in chains and depriving anybody who helped him of his right to due process and jury trial. Later, during the Civil War, stern measures were taken against dissenters, and civilians were tried in military courts where civilian courts and procedures were available. Japanese Americans, Communists and antiwar protesters have been witnesses in twentieth-century America to the legitimacy of the Framers' concerns for limits on government's incursions against individuals. The courts have been sheepish 'bulwarks' of individual rights in these circumstances, however, either upholding government actions or waiting until the crisis was over to make a resounding statement in favour of individual rights. Ex Parte Milligan is one of the most important civil liberties cases to emerge from the Civil War.[19] The Court said that military trial of civilians, with all it entailed for the civilian's loss of procedural guarantees, was impermissible where courts were open. That was in 1866, however, when the war was over and it was politically more safe for the Court to make such declarations. The integrity of the endangered nation drives a hard bargain with rights.

But what of Madison's insight that states were just as likely to endanger the rights of man? No theory of the Constitution allowed that states had such a power. The text of the Constitution, however, was thin on limits to state powers. There were some specific limitations, including a ban on ex post fact laws, bills of attainder and laws impairing the obligation of contracts. There was also federal protection from possible discrimination by states for those who travelled or did business outside their own state. The federal courts were given jurisdiction in cases between citizens of different states. And to the travelling citizen the Constitution guaranteed that, 'The Citizens of each State shall be entitled to all Privileges and Immunities of Citizens in the several States.' The best known judicial interpretation of this clause, in the 1823 case of Corfield v. Coryell, made it clear that strangers could expect to enjoy fundamental rights and be treated equally with respect to the protections of the law. The judge made no attempt to enumerate all the rights the clause guaranteed. It 'may include the franchise'. Enumeration was 'too tedious', he said.[20]

If the visiting citizen had rights out of state, and in some circumstances could call upon the Constitution and a federal court to protect them, it was more than the person who never crossed state lines could count on. If he found his rights in danger from his own state, the Bill of Rights was no help. Chief Justice John Marshall was only expressing an orthodoxy when he held, in the 1833 case of Barron v. Baltimore, that it was a limitation on the federal government and not on the states.[21] The belief persisted, however, that states were adequately limited by their own state constitutions, their courts, and the art of responsive, participatory citizenship. Rascals could be voted out, and justice done. And it worked like that for some. The white, male, conforming, voting citizen probably did enjoy an unparalleled freedom in a spacious, energetic young democracy. Slaves did not. And if freed slaves after the Civil War looked to the legal status of free blacks, women, Chinese or aliens as a model for freedom, they would not have advanced much further than under the infamous Black Codes with which the South greeted their emancipation. Even white, male citizens who did unpopular things, who spoke 'out of turn' against slavery, got caught helping fugitives, or sought state justice against the better judgment of an angry citizenry, might talk to the moon about their

rights. They certainly could not talk to the federal government. Between the
federal government and the individual in the states there was a constitutional
black hole, which in 1861 became of vital interest to the North . . . and of no
interest at all to the Confederacy, to judge from their new Constitution.

Liberty defended?
The Confederate contribution

The Confederacy drafted a Constitution in great haste after secession. Its
Congress unanimously approved the final draft, the fruits of two weeks'
work and forty years of argument, on 11 March 1861. Superficially it bears
close resemblance to the United States Constitution, which is not surprising
given that the Southern states' stated complaint was against the perversion
of the Constitution by Republican politicians rather than against the inadequacy of the Framers' design. Their task was to purify, however, as well as
to imitate, and there was no longer any need for some of the impurities of
compromise which had marked the efforts of a less homogenous society in
1787. The Confederate Constitution looks reassuringly familiar. Most of the
words of the United States Constitution are there. There are quite a lot more
of them, however, and some of the most important are missing or altered.
Although the layout of the document is remarkably similar, it conceals quite
extensive changes to the original 'checks and balances', with considerable
impact on individual rights.

Slavery was nailed into every corner of the Constitution and named
unashamedly. Whatever room for argument there was about the accuracy
of William Garrison's charge that the United States Constitution was a
'covenant with death', this one left no doubt.[22] In the events leading up to
secession, the South's constitutional arguments had been opportunistic
about the role of federal government. As Arthur Bestor observed, the South
demanded the active protection of the government for slaveowners 'property' out of state or in the territories, but made a battering ram of state sovereignty to resist any and all other uses of federal power.[23] The Confederate
Constitution was testimony to the possibility that one can have and eat cake
at the same time. It empowered its government to protect slavery, and trussed
it up like a turkey from impairing it.

The Confederate Constitution actively worked to ensure that there were
no bridgeheads between central government and the individual which could

threaten state sovereignty by giving an individual recourse to anything but the laws and courts of his own state. Take, for example, the relocation of the Bill of Rights. The first eight amendments are there verbatim, but placed in the section limiting the powers of Congress. Although this was no more than what Madison himself had proposed in 1789, the South's relocation of it in 1861 made it very clear indeed that it contained no limits whatsoever on the states, at a time when antislavery groups in the North argued otherwise. Of still greater significance, however, the Ninth and Tenth Amendments were separated from the rest of the Bill of Rights and reworded as well as relocated in Article Six, the supremacy clause. Rights were now retained by 'the people of the several States' rather than by 'the people'. And powers not delegated to the central government or prohibited to the states were now retained by the states or 'the people thereof' rather than by the 'States or the people'. A subtle shift it may seem, but it well and truly locked the central government out of the states for the purpose of protecting as well as infringing rights, and just as clearly locked individuals into the states on both counts. Add to this the omission of the general welfare clause from the Preamble to the Constitution, and the newfound presence of God in it (surely an unconstitutional establishment of religion under the United States Constitution!) and there is not much comfort for those with any reason to fear injustice at the hands of the states.

The Confederacy altered even the fragile pathways the United States Constitution built to prevent discrimination against out-of-state citizens who travelled or did business in another state. The clause which gave federal courts jurisdiction of cases between citizens of different states, to ensure impartial adjudication, was omitted. The comity clause, which entitled the citizens of each state to all privileges and immunities of citizens in the several states, remained, but with an addendum. Citizens were to be entitled to travel to or stay in any state with their slaves without impairment to their property right. What appears to be an afterthought, an extra, is in fact the definition of the clause as far as Southerners were concerned. It is a codification of Dred Scott *v.* Sanford.[24]

The Confederacy had no vision of the 'individual rights-bearer' calling on federal protection from states for any reason other than the protection of slave property. Even then, much of the paranoia of the Confederate Constitution on that point reflects past anxiety rather than perceived dangers after secession. The Confederate faith was still in the local community. Historians have found much to admire in it, and the rediscovery of 'republican' values of civic virtue, community and public service have made alternatives to a culture of individual rights attractive.[25] But is it to be found in the Confederacy?

There were certainly interesting innovations. The president was limited to a six-year term in office and authorized to exercise more budgetary controls over Congress through a line veto. Congress could authorize cabinet ministers to sit and speak to their measures in Congress. Evidence of fiscal frugality and suspicion of party corruption abounds. Peter Parish has written thoughtfully about these and other aspects of 'The Road Not Quite Taken', concluding that whatever merits it had, the Constitution's design was so wedded to serving and perpetuating slavery that the road was ultimately not worth taking. It is hard to argue that civic virtue can be achieved at the price of denying the humanity of 4 million people living in that community.[26] It has something to do with the admissions policies of communities. As Michael Walzer writes, 'The denial of membership is always the first of a long trail of abuses.'[27]

In a sense the Civil War did not shake the Southern belief that their rights were adequately protected by their own states, which obligingly released enlisted men from the clutches of enlistment officers on writs of habeas corpus and otherwise put their own citizens first. Perhaps state citizens did not much miss the lack of a federal presence or bridgehead between them and the states. The Confederate government, however, itself suffered more from this deliberate omission. If there was no great demand to take traffic from the states for adjudication in a federal forum, there nevertheless was a need to take the nation's laws to the states and see that they were obeyed. Unpopular decisions had to be taken by the Davis government, to raise troops, tax, suspend habeas corpus, jail dissenters and confiscate property. Citizens did not always want to obey.[28] Where the North, faced with similar problems, expanded the jurisdiction of the federal courts to see that its writ ran in the states, the Confederate government failed to overcome the states rights culture and harness the potential of courts.

There were Confederate district courts, but their jurisdiction was very limited and they lacked procedural apparatus to assert themselves against state courts which rendered contrary interpretations of the law. The weakness was compounded by the fact that the Confederate Constitution made its federal judges removable by a vote of two-thirds of the state legislature, where the United States Constitution guaranteed independence. The supremacy of Confederate law was thus a matter of state consent. Most interesting of all omissions of federal pathways or arteries in the federal system was that the war ended without the creation of a Supreme Court. The Confederate Constitution provided for one. Several attempts were made to create one, and an extensive debate took place in Congress in the spring of 1863. The furies erupted over

[316] a proposal in the Judiciary Act to give the Court an even more extensive appel-
late jurisdiction over State Supreme Courts than that exercised by the United
States Supreme Court. No agreement could be reached. Although by this point
in the war there was a demonstrated need to resolve issues arising from conflicting interpretations of Confederate laws, past experience raised fears, and
in the case of William Yancey, hysteria.[29] Dred Scott had been a lonely, temporary victory for slaveowners and did nothing to allay the suspicion that
Supreme Courts were dangerous for their inventiveness in expanding implied
power and national authority at the expense of states. However good a friend
Chief Justice Roger B. Taney had been to slavery, he was as good a friend of
the supremacy of national judicial power. It was the North and not the South
which was about to find some of his opinions very useful in building bridges
into the states, turning them to serve freedom instead of slavery.

The Confederacy's generals were better than their lawyers, who created a
federal system with no arteries. Given the chance to rewrite its Constitution,
it is unlikely the Confederacy would have had second thoughts about protecting individual rights in the states. But it might have wanted to do a lot
more to make its laws work effectively upon individuals and governments
in the states. It was when the Union found that there was a link between
individual rights and the integrity of government that it embarked on a
constitutional adventure.

Liberty secured? The Republican contribution

The North had the advantage of working with an established Constitution,
with its pre-existing tools and habits, but was also burdened by the knowledge of their failure to prevent secession. If the Union was to have a future,
something had to be learned. Fortunately the first thoughts of the Republicans were not their last. In March 1861, in a last-ditch attempt to find
grounds for compromise, William H. Seward sponsored this proposed Thirteenth Amendment, startlingly innovative in that it was unamendable by
future generations:

> No amendment shall be made to the Constitution which will authorize or
> give to Congress the power to abolish or interfere, within any State, with the
> domestic institutions thereof, including that of persons held to labor or service
> by the laws of said state.[30]

It passed Congress in March 1861, and Lincoln referred to it in his Inaugural Address.[31] He believed that such a limit on Congressional power was already implied in constitutional law and he had no objection to it being made 'express and irrevocable'. The war came and the proposal became quickly irrelevant. Armies moved. Slaves were at first accidentally freed in the field of their operations and then deliberately. Congress moved in pace with the army, their avowed remit to ensure that freedom was permanent. A very different Thirteenth Amendment was added in 1865 at the war's end. It made all persons free and gave Congress the power to enforce it. The distance between the two proposals for a Thirteenth Amendment was measured by many small steps but in the end they produced changes which fell short of radical change but amounted to considerably more than sticking plaster.[32]

Whereas the Confederacy ruled out any possibility that the Bill of Rights could be relevant to the lives of its citizens within states by allowing them to call on the central government for rescue if they were trampled upon, the Republican Framers of the constitutional amendments and laws crossed state lines with the promise of protection for individual rights. Whereas the Confederacy limited membership of the community who had rights of any kind to whites, the Republicans altered the membership rules. The Declaration of Independence, with its emphasis on birth as a condition of equality of natural rights, was part of the discussion of the meaning of the Constitution in a way that it was not in the South. The Thirteenth Amendment guaranteed freedom. The membership condition was to be human. The Fourteenth Amendment made birth and being subject to the jurisdiction of the United States the only conditions of citizenship of both the nation and the state. As to voting citizens, the Fifteenth Amendment forbade the use of race or previous condition of servitude as a reason for denying the right. The inclusion of women as voting citizens would take longer, despite the hopeful arguments of Elizabeth Cady Stanton and Susan B. Anthony that it was one of their privileges and immunities under the Fourteenth Amendment.[33]

The inclusion of black Americans in the community of free citizens was itself an important change. But what did membership mean in terms of rights? The original Constitution was more about how rights were to be protected than it was about enumerating rights. In practice, it had meant that the states were the unit of government whose laws and customs most affected the lives and liberty of individuals. The task facing the Republicans was to limit the ways in which states could infringe rights. In doing so they did not attempt to make a definitive list of which rights the states could not infringe, although some scholars have mistaken the 1866 Civil Rights Act for just such an

[318] enumeration. These included the right to own and dispose of property, make contracts, and enjoy the process and equal protection of the laws. According to the most conservative appraisals, it was these basic civil rights which formed the backbone of the phrase 'privileges and immunities' of citizens of the United States which the Fourteenth Amendment prohibited states from infringing.[34]

An alternative 'list' is the Bill of Rights. Was that the measure of citizenship, and did the Framers intend to incorporate it within the Fourteenth Amendment and make it a limit on the states as it was on the federal government? It was an argument which some abolitionists had made and there is a good deal of support for it among the speeches of some of the amendment's chief sponsors, especially John Bingham. On the other hand, the case is not self-evident, and it cannot be resolved by an exhaustive war of quotations from the Congressional debates. What made the question matter acutely was that in the 1940s the Supreme Court began to apply more and more of the rights contained in the Bill of Rights to the states and prompted a debate on and off the Court about the historical legitimacy of doing so. In modern constitutional law, the Bill of Rights does now apply almost verbatim to the states, as the result of a gradual process of incorporation. But it would be a mistake to attribute to the Framers an intention to use the Bill of Rights as a definitive 'list' of what it meant to be a citizen.[35]

The Republicans were just as inclined to end a sentence about liberty with 'and so on' as were their forefathers at Philadelphia. The expectations and daily habits of citizenship were too varied to make a federal code of them, even if doing so had been tolerable to the political culture of the day. The Bill of Rights was never intended to enumerate rights. It was about structure and constitutional powers too, and it spoke of rights belonging to the people and the states as well as personal rights. From the Congressional debates on freedom and citizenship during the Civil War, there is plenty of evidence to suggest that Republicans shared a generally broad understanding that these terms straddled natural and common law rights, as well as the personal rights in the Bill of Rights. The Republicans were entirely derivative and frequently sloppy in their thinking about the content of individual rights, and offered no new descriptions. What they did offer was the insight that liberty depended on powers as well as wise restraints.

The Thirteenth Amendment was more than a ceremonial ratification of something already achieved in practice by the war and the Emancipation Proclamation. It was potentially the most radical alteration to the Constitution. It escaped the formula of the Constitution that people were free if their governments were not. Instead it restrained individuals directly from holding anybody to involuntary servitude. For the first time it enlarged national power, the power of Congress, to enforce it. The debates on the amendment make it clear that freedom was not defined as the absence of slavery, but as a positive entitlement to the rights which slavery had denied.[36] Immediate, continued denials to the freed slaves of everyday ingredients of control over their own lives, such as the right to earnings, to own property, enter contracts, give evidence against whites in courts, or rely on the protection of the laws prompted Congress to pass the Civil Rights Act in 1866. It counteracted the Black Codes in the South, but it applied to everyone in the Union. It was the first invocation of Congressional power to reach individuals as well as state officials who denied any citizen of the United States the same protection as white citizens in the having and holding of civil rights. Far from being evidence of a static description of what Republicans meant by freedom, it was the first energizing of a permanent federal power. Only time and experience would identify the impediments to freedom in people's lives. In 1866 the Black Codes were identified as an impediment. Later, Congress identified other things which perpetuated the badges and incidents of slavery, such as exclusion of black people from public accommodations. The Civil Rights Act of 1875 attempted a remedy. The Supreme Court struck it down.[37] By then, judges shied clear of unleashing the full potential of a national power directed to individual conduct and built a defensive wall to protect state rights. The Thirteenth Amendment's impact was dulled by that, but remains to be explored.

The Fourteenth Amendment uses the more familiar formula of securing rights by restraining government. But what matters is that it gives the federal government power to restrain the states. No state, it commanded, shall make or enforce any law which shall abridge the privileges and immunities of citizens of the United States, or deprive any person of life, liberty or property without due process of law, or deny any person the equal protection of the laws. It continued to leave the states to generate the conditions of freedom and the forms of equal citizenship themselves, but although no federal code or fixed meaning was imposed, it did not mean that there were no discoverable federal standards. It was for the federal courts to interpret and articulate them, and to identify state wrongs. Like the Thirteenth Amendment, the Fourteenth invited Congress to enforce it by appropriate legislation. The Fifteenth Amendment contained no federal definition of qualifications for the right of United State citizens to vote, but forbade governments of state or nation to deny the right on grounds of race or former condition of servitude. Once again, it empowered Congress to enforce it.

The constitutional amendments preserved the familiar structures of federalism. But they made it possible for the federal government to exercise potentially radical powers to reach across state lines to secure the rights of individuals from infringements of them both by states, and private powers. Local community was still important, and was expected to be the first, best hope of liberty, but it was not to be blindly trusted. Instead, the Republicans sought a balance between community self-ordering and federal power to ensure that individuals could exercise rights within their communities. How well it worked in practice depended on how communities behaved, how much need there was for federal power to undo state wrongs, how broadly or narrowly Congress and courts identified the rights of United States citizenship, and how they interpreted and acted upon denials of equal protection and due process.

In working out the balance, the federal courts were given the key role. In contrast to the Confederacy's suspicion of courts, the Republicans relied on them. It is a paradox that Chief Justice Taney's inhumane, proslavery opinion in Dred Scott did not make Southerners less suspicious of judicial power, and did not prevent Northern Republicans from greatly expanding it. The impact of the Civil War on the federal judiciary has been of vital and enduring importance.[38]

Throughout the Civil War, the North's efforts to raise an army and implement war policy were hampered by states rights, especially in areas where feeling ran high against conscription, confiscation of land from the disloyal, the arrest of dissenters, and emancipation. State courts were the arena of conflict. Conscripts were released on writs of habeas corpus. Federal officers were prosecuted under state law for trespass, damage to property and countless other offences. Granted that the military must be accountable to civilian authority for unlawful actions, many of the estimated 3,000 suits pending against federal officers in the midwest and border states smacked more of harassment than accountability.[39] Kentucky was the most litigious of places. What was at stake was the integrity of the federal government. If it could not oblige Ohio or Pennsylvania to obey the law, what hope did it have in South Carolina? If it could not protect federal officers from harassment in Tennessee, what hope did it have of protecting freed slaves in Virginia?

The Republicans learned two things. One was that states rights carried to the point of state intransigence was not a Southern phenomenon. The other was that federal courts were vital to federal law. The Habeas Corpus Act of 1863 was one of the most important acts of the war. It allowed federal officers to remove cases against them from state to federal courts. State judges were not always willing to cooperate, and it had to be amended in 1866 to impose sanctions against them. Defending this unaccustomed toughness on state courts, Senator Clark said, 'We have had about enough of this State authority to teach it to yield respect and obedience to the laws of the United States.'[40]

Lessons learned from organizing the war effort were applied to the business of securing freedom and citizenship. Like federal officers, freed slaves needed federal protection in hostile state environments. So did officers of the Freedmen's Bureau who were unpopular for trying to help. Ultimately, so did every citizen in the United States, if he or she could not depend on state authority for the protection of his or her rights, for whatever reason.

Between 1861 and 1875 twelve measures increased the jurisdiction of the federal courts. As early as 1862, in the debates over a confiscation bill, Congressmen discussed the question of how to make the limited emancipation it effected a permanent one. A clause giving the freedman the right to a writ of habeas corpus only narrowly failed to be adopted in the final version.[41] Section twelve of the Wade Davis Reconstruction Bill, pocket-vetoed by Lincoln, used the federal courts to guarantee freedom. One of the strongest regrets of its sponsors was the loss of that judicial remedy. It was a temporary setback, however. All three constitutional amendments made individual rights the business of the federal courts. The Civil Rights Act of 1866 and subsequent enforcement acts borrowed from the machinery of the 1863 Habeas Corpus Act. Although Congress often stumbled towards solutions to particular problems, there is a remarkable unity in the way it fits together. There is much evidence of learning through experience. There could be no rights without remedies, and no remedies without access to federal courts.

And was it enough? Enough for what? It did not achieve equal citizenship or eradicate racial discrimination. It created structures for rescue and remediation, but these were mainly built on the assumption that traffic would be light in the long run and that states would continue to have the primary role in shaping the rights and duties of citizens. Interestingly, in the short run, from the end of the war until about 1873, courts and Congresses, Bureau agents, government officials in the Department of Justice, free black citizens and committed white ones made vigorous use of the tools to hand, interpreting them broadly, and reaching to affect contracts between individuals, and punish violence by private individuals who deprived others of rights.[42] Black citizens did not wait around as passive recipients of rights but acted on their instincts to seek their own liberty as individuals, families and communities.[43] It was never going to be easy. After 1873, the Supreme Court made it more difficult. It interpreted the 'privileges and immunities' clause so narrowly that it effectively killed it, raised high the barriers of the Fourteenth Amendment's 'state action' language to keep federal intervention at bay, misplaced the 1866 Civil Rights Act, and found segregation justified as an equal protection of the law.[44] Meanwhile, white people who had believed that constitutional change included all Americans were disappointed. Women were not to benefit. The Framers intended no change in their legal status or that of Chinese Americans or aliens.[45] Indians and rights were mutually exclusive. Even the rescue strategy for freedmen failed. The Constitution was not a machine which 'would go of itself', even freshly dedicated to freedom and citizenship, and with the expansion of federal jurisdiction.

Of course it was not all down to a Supreme Court 'retreat'.[46] The original design was a riddle. Like the Constitution itself, the Civil War changes were about the distribution of powers and the fixing of restraints as a means to enjoyment of undefined but now equal rights of citizenship. It was not doomed to fail, but it was not destined to succeed either unless enough Americans wanted it to do so. After 1875 or so, they did not. It was a very different society almost 100 years later which produced the 'individual rights-bearer' and the civil rights battles of the 1960s.

Liberty challenged? Equality and community

After the Second World War, America tried again to make the Constitution work for liberty, and gradually for equality too. Nothing concentrated the mind more on what it meant to be Lincoln's 'last best hope of earth' than to be a world power challenged by shortfalls in its own promises at a time when Communist ideologies abroad trumpeted freedom and equality. In the United States, a culture of individualism made room for equal opportunity and racial justice, or so it seemed. President Kennedy's New Frontier and Johnson's Great Society were alive with optimism for change. The Supreme Court not only reflected that under Chief Justice Earl Warren, but was itself a catalyst of change.[47]

The Warren Court effectively applied the Bill of Rights to the states through the due process clause of the Fourteenth Amendment. The states were held to a whole new set of procedural requirements in criminal cases which effected a revolution in standards of state justice. Judicial interpretations of freedom of speech and press reflected a new emphasis on individual self-expression as well as robust, unrestrained political debate. Dissenters to the religious and social values of the majority were beneficiaries of the 'rights-bearing' culture. Although the Burger Court slowed down the pace of criminal procedural change, it maintained and expanded other areas of the Fourteenth Amendment's 'liberty', notably to the unenumerated rights of privacy and abortion.[48] White Americans were as likely as black ones to be the beneficiaries of this expanded protection of individual rights.

The Supreme Court also made race and minority rights an area of special vigilance, and it applied heightened standards of review where discrimination was alleged. The equal protection clause was transformed after Brown *v.* Board of Education in 1954 set it rolling against segregation.[49] Parks, schools, and later housing and employment became battlegrounds to eradicate racial discrimination. Racism has proven deeply resistant to the kind of changes which can be achieved by court battles between lonely individual rights-bearers and the holders of power, private or public. By the 1970s a lively argument was underway that to achieve equality some of the hallowed assumptions about a 'colour blind' Constitution treating individuals alike had to make room for race-conscious remedies which benefited groups rather than individuals. Liberal strategies shifted from equality as a means to equality as an end. A number of state, federal and private affirmative action programmes which did not depend on bringing strict proof of purposeful discrimination to trigger a remedy to a specific victim were upheld by the Court.[50] The Court remained resistant, however, to finding special constitutional protection for people on grounds of poverty. Women, however, finally gained membership of the community of rights-bearers through the equal protection clause. The Burger Court used some of the same strategies against gender discrimination which it had evolved in race cases. Aliens and illegitimate children also won new equal protection rights.[51]

Most, if not all of these developments rested on the amendments and laws passed immediately after the Civil War. The 1964 and 1968 Civil Rights Acts, and the Voting Rights Act of 1965 were the only major additions to the legislative arsenal. The pace and vitality of change came from the courts. The Supreme Court interpreted old Civil War tools creatively, and the lower federal courts worked at the coalface of change to implement it. Almost alone they bore the load of making truculent school boards comply with desegregation orders. Their business expanded exponentially to enforce Civil Rights laws old and new. The Habeas Corpus Act of 1867, reinterpreted by the Warren Court, brought thousands of suits from state to federal courts alleging deprivation of federally protected rights, newly extended to the states through the Bill of Rights. The courts essentially conducted a 'vital national seminar' between states and nation about the meaning of the Constitution.[52]

All this suggested that there was nothing wrong with the design of the Constitution, given the will to make it work, and the commitment of judges to what Dworkin has called 'the moral reading of the Constitution', that its central meaning is about equal respect for individuals.[53] The moral reading is challenged today by a morally sceptical one. In a recent case concerning the right to die, Justice Scalia dissented from the proposition that it was the business of the federal courts to decide at what point life becomes worthless. The answers, he said, were not 'known to nine Justices of this Court any better than they are known to nine people picked at random from the Kansas City telephone directory.'[54] Not all members of the Court pose as such sceptics, but the Court as a whole does shy away from finding any more fundamental rights as part of the liberty of the Fourteenth Amendment unless they are contained in text or tradition. It is a Court which claims to exercise self-restraint, though in reality it has not hesitated to strike down the efforts of the representatives of the people to achieve racial equality through affirmative action.[55] At the same time, it wants less of liberty to be the work of the federal courts and more to be done by the states, by their representatives and in their courts. In theory at least, local communities should have more room to find answers to the modern dilemmas of liberty.

Although communitarians differ in how they define community, the word conveys both the mutuality of neighbourhood and the tyranny of conformity. It is the place where white children walk from suburban homes to schools, but buses carrying black children from the city are not welcome. Although community need not be the same as 'state' within the nation, it is the unit of constitutional community which has caused liberty and equality the greatest problems. Withdrawing from the interventionist role which the federal courts have come to play is not without risks. The desegregation of schools, for example, loses momentum when the courts are not required to remain vigilant and active against resegregation.[56] Abortion remains a constitutional right, but with greater freedom given to states to regulate it from conception to birth.[57] In the matter of criminal process, the Court has shown a willingness to trust state processes in ways which are not warranted. The death penalty is a testimony to what happens when liberty is entrusted to the representatives of the people in the Texas telephone directory, especially when the federal courts stop taking an interest. One of the most important legacies of the Civil War in the modern context, the Habeas Corpus Act of 1867, which played such an important part in reforming state criminal procedures, has been seriously diminished. First the Supreme Court reduced access to the federal courts to state prisoners.[58] Then Congress passed the Effective Death Penalty Act in 1996, codifying these changes and allowing states to proceed more swiftly and less accountably to the gallows.[59]

This is not to say that the only way to secure liberty and equality is through the federalization of individual rights. States have a vital role. Justice William Brennan wrote an article in the *Harvard Law Review* in 1977 at a time when he despaired of the conservative direction the Supreme Court was taking on rights. It was time, he argued, to look to states to regenerate their constitutions and even to craft better and stronger protections than those available from the federal courts.[60] The prominence of some first-rate State Supreme Court judges, and the announcement of a crop of state decisions on criminal justice and gender discrimination which looked promising fuelled his optimism. His message was one of partnership. But it was not to be a green light for states to experiment in ways which could diminish as well as enhance rights. The Bill of Rights and federal decisions on it would be a floor of protection, and not a ceiling. Only above the floor was it safe to consult the Kansas telephone directory! Scholars are divided about how real the new state constitutionalism has turned out to be, and evidence of a flourishing rights discourse in the states has been patchy.[61] Nonetheless Brennan was right in his insight that individual rights cannot flourish when they depend solely on being imported by federal courts to unwilling states.

For all that, there is still much for the federal government to do. The Constitution need not be a charter of negative liberties if more is asked of it. The culture of individual rights-bearing has been to some extent the product of placing the whole weight of social change on courts and litigation. During the Civil War it was Congress that was the schoolhouse of liberty. It made vital use of courts but perhaps did not expect them to be so lonely a century later. There is a latent power in the constitutional amendments still. The Thirteenth is a potential arsenal. Badges and incidents of slavery may be identified under it, and could include the death penalty. Its possible applications to non-racial issues such as prostitution, child abuse and labour law have been the subject of recent literature. Where a person is prevented from exercising control over their lives by the power of others, the amendment may have relevance. All three amendments contain authorizations of power to Congress to enforce them. This is not without difficulty. Important questions have not been answered yet. Does Congress have a broad legislative authority to pass laws on its own interpretation of the amendments, or a narrower, remedial power to correct violations identified by the Court?[62] Can

[326] Congress pass laws to reach private violations of rights under the Fourteenth Amendment?[63] Neither Court nor Congress seems likely right now to use the civil war amendments, or any other constitutional powers to seek brave new worlds, but legislative efforts could tackle issues of poverty, education, racism, housing and the environment, none of which are susceptible to case by case resolution but all of which are necessary to create the collective conditions of liberty within which individual rights and mutual responsibilities take root. Meanwhile, the 'last, best hope of earth' falls short of its own vision in ways in which it need not. Racism and the death penalty are an international embarrassment.[64]

If powers are not used to secure rights, it is a matter of choice.

Notes

1. Quoted in M. Kammen, *A Machine That Would Go Of Itself: The Constitution in American Culture* (New York, 1986), p. 43.

2. The Constitution was amended in 1791, when the first ten amendments, collectively known as the Bill of Rights, were added. Since then, there have been seventeen Amendments. The Thirteenth ended slavery (1865), the Fourteenth guaranteed citizenship rights (1868) and the Fifteenth forbade racial discrimination in the right to vote (1870).

3. B. Ackerman, *We the People. Foundations* (Cambridge, 1991).

4. The best exposition remains H.M. Hyman, *A More Perfect Union: The Impact of the Civil War and Reconstruction on the Constitution* (New York, 1973).

5. A very readable introduction to the changes which began at this time is Henry Abraham, *Freedom and the Court* (Oxford, 1998).

6. Jones *v.* Alfred H. Mayer Co., 392 U.S. 409 (1968). See R. Kohl, 'The Civil Rights Act of 1866, its hour come round at last', 55 *Virginia Law Rev. 272* (1969).

7. 42 U.S.C. S1983 authorizes persons whose constitutional rights are violated by state officials to sue in federal court. It derives from the Ku Klux Klan Act of 20 April 1871. 17 Stat 13. It is today a major source of federal court business.

8. M. Kelman, 'Federal Habeas Corpus as a source of new constitutional requirements for State criminal procedure', 28 *Ohio State Law Journal* (1967).

9. Among them, A.R. Amar, 'Remember the Thirteenth', 10 *Constitutional Commentary* 403 (1993), D. Colbert, 'Liberating the Thirteenth Amendment', 30

Harvard Civil Rights Civil Liberties L. Rev. (1995), L.S. Vandervelde, 'The labor vision of the Thirteenth Amendment', 138 *Univ. of Pennsylvania Law Rev.* 437 (1989).

10. In the 1947 case of Adamson *v.* California, 332 U.S. 46 (1947), Justice Hugo Black argued that the Framers intended to incorporate the entire Bill of Rights through the Fourteenth Amendment, and make them applicable as limits on the states. The Court never accepted the argument, but in practice went on to incorporate most of them, one by one. M. Curtis, *No State Shall Abridge: The Fourteenth Amendment and the Bill of Rights* (Durham, NC, 1986) and A.R. Amar, 'The Bill of Rights and the Fourteenth Amendment', 101 *Yale Law Journal* (1992) are broadly in sympathy with the liberal interpretation of incorporation. C. Fairman, 'Does the Fourteeth Amendment incorporate the Bill of Rights? The original understanding', 2 *Stanford Law Rev.* 5 (1949) is not. Contemporary critics include E. Malz, *Civil Rights, the Constitution and Congress, 1863–69* (Lawrence, Ks, 1990) and L. Gingras, 'Congressional misunderstandings and the ratifiers understanding', *Journal of Legal History* (1996).

11. Chief Justice William Rehnquist is a leading advocate of honouring the original intentions of the Framers. Rehnquist, 'The notion of a living constitution', 54 *Texas Law Rev.* (1976). Also, Justice A. Scalia, 'Originalism, the lesser evil', *University of Cincinnati Law Rev.* (1989).

12. Affirmative action is one attempt to confer benefits on a group rather than as individuals, without proof that they have been discriminated against individually by a specific 'perpetrator'. See O. Fiss, 'Groups and the Equal Protection Clause', 3 *Philosophy and Public Affairs* (1976) for a defence of doing so.

13. M.A. Glendon, *Rights Talk: The Impoverishment of Political Discourse* (New York, 1991); F. Michaelman, 'Law's Republic', 97 *Yale Law Journal* (1988); M. Sandel, *Liberalism and the Limits of Justice* (Cambridge, 1987). For good counterargument, S. Holmes, *The Anatomy of Antiliberalism* (Cambridge, 1986).

14. L. Levy, *Constitutional Opinions: Aspects of the Bill of Rights* (New York, 1986), p. 134.

15. C.F. Hobson and R.A. Rutland (eds), *The Papers of James Madison* (Charlottesville, Va, 1979), vol. 12, pp. 197–210.

16. A.R. Amar, 'The Bill of Rights and the Fourteenth Amendment', 101 *Yale Law Journal* (1992), p. 1265.

17. W.M. Wiecek, *The Sources of Antislavery Constitutionalism in America* (Ithaca, NY, 1977) analyzes the underlying beliefs of abolitionist writers who believed that the Bill of Rights was an entitlement of all Americans and a source of power to the federal government rather than a restraint.

[328]   18. In addition to Madison's speech in the House of Representatives on 8 June 1789, see *Federalist Papers* 10 for evidence of his mistrust of state majorities. On the drafting and adoption of the Bill of Rights, Levy, *Constitutional Opinions* ch. 6, B. Schwarz, *The Great Rights of Mankind* (New York, 1979), and J.H. Hutson, 'The Bill of Rights and the American revolutionary experience', J.N. Rakove, 'Parchment barriers and the politics of rights' in M.J. Lacey and K. Haakonssen (eds), *A Culture of Rights: The Bill of Rights in Philosophy, Politics and Law, 1791 and 1991* (Cambridge, 1991).

19. Ex Parte Milligan, 71 U.S. 2 (1866). But for a balanced view in the context of war and reconstruction see H.M. Hyman and W.M. Wiecek, *Equal Justice Under Law: Constitutional Development, 1835–1875* (New York, 1982).

20. Corfield *v.* Coryell, 4 Wash. C.C. 371 (1823). Historians dispute whether this was intended to be a collection of rights to be enjoyed anywhere or simply a passport to whatever the states offered their own citizens, irrespective of whether it fell below that minimum. Was it a few absolute rights, or a broad one including civil and potentially political rights? P. Lucie, *Freedom and Federalism: Congress and Courts, 1861–1866* (New York, 1986) argues a broad reading, E. Malz, 'Fourteenth Amendment concepts in the antebellum era', 32 *American Journal of Legal History* (1988) a narrow one.

21. Barron *v.* Baltimore, 7 Pet. (32 U.S.) 243 (1833) held that the Bill of Rights was a limit on the federal government but not on the states. Although this was an orthodoxy, it was challenged by the understandings of those in the antislavery movement who argued that Americans were entitled to enjoy rights anywhere in the Union and to call on the protection of the federal government. J. TenBroek, *The Antislavery Origins of the Fourteenth Amendment* (Berkeley, Ca, 1951).

22. The extent to which the United States Constitution was proslavery is disputed by E. Malz, 'The idea of the Proslavery Constitution', 17 *Journal of the Early Republic* (1997). The Confederate Constitution is frankly dedicated to slavery. A Provisional Constitution was adopted on 8 February 1861, at which time seven states had seceded. The text of the final effort is set out and analysed in C.R. Lee, *The Confederate Constitutions* (Westport, Conn.,1973).

23. A. Bestor, 'State sovereignty and slavery: a reinterpretation of proslavery constitutional doctrine, 1846–1860', *Illinois State Historical Society Journal*, LVII (1961).

24. Dred Scott *v.* Sanford, 60 U.S. (19 How.) 1857, holding that residence in a free state did not entitle a slave to sue successfully for freedom on return to a slave state. Whilst denying black Americans citizenship, Taney's opinion appears to interpret the privileges and immunities of white citizens under federal protec-

tion under the comity clause broadly. But see Malz, 'Fourteenth Amendment Concepts' n. 20 above for a narrower interpretation. In practice, slavery was the defining citizenship right for federal protection.

25. One early admirer was W.M. Robinson, 'A new deal in constitutions', *Journal of Southern History* (1938). A more modern view of republican virtues, D. Nieman, 'Republicanism, the Confederate Constitution and the American constitutional tradition' in K. Hall and J.W. Ely (eds), *An Uncertain Tradition: Constitutionalism and the History of the South* (Athens, Ga, 1989). S. Cain, 'The question still lives', *The Freeman* (May, 1993) is less convinced.

26. P.J. Parish, 'The Road Not Quite Taken: the Constitution of the Confederate States of America' in T. Barron, O.D. Edwards and P. Storey (eds), *Constitutional and National Identity* (Edinburgh, 1993).

27. M. Walzer, 'Members and strangers' in S. Avineri and A. De-Shalt, *Communitarianism and Individualism* (Oxford, 1992), p. 84.

28. J.G. de Roulhac Hamilton, 'The state courts and the Confederate Constitution', *JSH* (1938), p. 447 argues against exaggerating conflicts between state courts and the central government, and that by mid 1864 'the states had fully accepted the military power of the Confederacy'. Dissent was a problem, however.

29. W.R. Robinson, *Justices in Grey* (Cambridge, 1941).

30. *Congressional Globe*, 36 Cong., 2 Sess., p. 1403.

31. R.P. Basler (ed.), *The Collected Works of Abraham Lincoln* (New Brunswick, 1953), vol 4, p. 270.

32. H.M. Hyman, *A More Perfect Union: The Impact of the Civil War and Reconstruction on the Constitution* (New York, 1973).

33. See E. DuBois, *Feminism and Suffrage: The Emergence of an Independent Women's Suffrage Movement in America, 1848–1869* (Ithaca, NY, 1978).

34. R. Berger, *Government by Judiciary: The Transformation of the Fourteenth Amendment* (Cambridge, Mass., 1977).

35. Arguments about lists stem in part from the presentmindedness of arguments about the extent to which the Framers' intent binds in particular cases. Originalism is both impossible and undesirable. See P. Brest, 'The misconceived quest for the original understanding', 60 *Boston University Law Rev.* (1980). In this case it diverts attention from the fact that Republicans were more interested in the dynamics of rights than in describing them with precision.

36. Lucie, *Freedom and Federalism,* ch. 5.

[330]   37. In the Civil Rights Cases 109 U.S. 3 (1883), Justice Bradley interpreted the
             scope of rights protected by the Thirteenth Amendment narrowly, and also
             severely restricted the reach of the Fourteenth Amendment to state action.

        38. Hyman, *A More Perfect Union*; S.I. Kutler, *Judicial Power and Reconstruction Politics*
             (Chicago, 1968); W. Wiecek, 'The reconstruction of federal judicial power',
             AJLH (1969); Lucie, *Freedom and Federalism.*

        39. James G. Randall,*Constitutional Problems Under Lincoln* (New York and London),
             pp. 193–4.

        40. *Congressional Globe*, 39 Cong., 1 Sess., p. 2052.

        41. P. Lucie, 'Confiscation: constitutional crossroads', *Civil War History* (1977).
             Both Representatives Morrill and Walton argued for the inclusion of this
             enforcement procedure. *Cong. Globe*, 37 Cong 2 Sess. p. 2362 and p. 2793.

        42. R.J. Kaczorowski, *The Politics of Judicial Interpretation: The Federal Courts, Depart-
             ments of Justice and Civil Rights, 1866–1876* (New York,1985) develops the
             theme. Early interpretation of the Thirteenth Amendment gets interesting cov-
             erage in H.M. Hyman, *The Reconstruction Justice of Salmon P. Chase* (Lawrence,
             Ks,1997).

        43. E. Foner, 'Rights and the Constitution in black life during the Civil War and
             Reconstruction', 74 *J.A.H.* (1987) offers a welcome perspective which gets
             away from courts and into life and politics of black life.

        44. In the Slaughterhouse Cases, 16 Wall. (83 U.S.) 36 (1873), Justice Miller dis-
             tinguished between the privileges and immunities of United States citizenship,
             and state citizenship, interpreting the former very narrowly and the latter
             broadly. In effect it killed the clause. In the Civil Rights Cases, 109 U.S. 3
             (1883), Justice Bradley found that Congress had no power to reach private
             discrimination in access to public facilities under the Fourteenth Amendment
             which reaches state but not private action, and no power under the Thirteenth,
             which does reach private action but only in respect of badges and incidents of
             slavery, of which this was not one. In Plessy *v.* Ferguson, 163 U.S. 537 (1896),
             Justice Brown's opinion held that separate but equal facilities for 'white' and
             'colored' railway passengers was not a violation of equal protection. As the
             'state action' doctrine took hold, the fact that the 1866 Civil Rights Act
             was born of the Thirteenth rather than the Fourteenth Amendment was
             overlooked.

        45. E. Malz, 'The Constitution and nonracial discrimination: alienage, sex and
             the Framers' ideal of equality', 7 *Const. Commentary* (1990), puts this down to
             the restriction of Republican vision to a concept of limited absolute equality all
             round.

46. A thesis ably extended by M. Benedict, 'Preserving federalism: Reconstruction and the Waite Court', *Sup. Crt. Rev.* (1978) to reject the view that the Court was out of line with the Framers.

47. B. Schwartz, *Super Chief: Earl Warren and his Supreme Court – A Judicial Biography* (New York, 1983) is an excellent collective profile of the Court, the times and the key decisions.

48. V. Blasi (ed.), *The Burger Court: The Counter-Revolution That Wasn't* (New Haven, Conn., 1983).

49. Brown *v.* Board of Education of Topeka County, 347 U.S. 483(1954). Best single volume in a vast literature remains R. Kluger, *Simple Justice:The History of Brown* v. *Board of Education and Black America's Struggle for Equality* (New York, 1976).

50. Fullilove *v.* Klutznick, 448 U.S. 448 (1980), Metro Broadcasting, Inc. *v.* FCC, 499 U.S. 547 (1990). Ohers were not upheld, Regents of the University of California *v.* Bakke, 438 U.S. 265 (1978) (though race was not necessarily ruled out as a criterion for admissions), City of Richmond *v.* J.A. Croson Co., 488 U.S. 706 (1989).

51. James *v.* Valtierra, 402 U.S. 137 (1971) on poverty, Craig *v.* Boren, 429 U.S. 190 (1976) on gender, Graham *v.* Richardson, 403 U.S. 365 (1971) and Trimble *v.* Gordon, 430 U.S. 762 (1977) on illegitimacy.

52. In the context of habeas corpus, an excellent analysis of this is R.M. Cover and A. Aleinikoff, 'Dialectical federalism: habeas corpus and the court', 86 *Yale Law Journal* (1977).

53. R. Dworkin, *Freedom's Law: The Moral Reading of the American Constitution* (Oxford, 1996).

54. Cruzan *v.* Director, Missouri Dept. of Health, 497 U.S. 261 (1990).

55. Richmond *v.* J.A. Croson Co., 488 U.S. 469 (1989), striking down a city council plan to remedy racial discrimination in the construction industry and Adarand Constructors, Inc. *v.* Pena, 518 U.S. (1995) striking down a Congressional affirmative action programme.

56. Recent cases signalling a withdrawal of federal court involvement where resegregation occurred were Board of Education of Oklahoma City *v.* Dowell, 498 U.S. 237 (1991) and Freeman *v.* Pitts, 503 U.S. 467 (1992).

57. Planned Parenthood of Southeastern Pennsylvania *v.* Casey 505 U.S. 833 (1992). A woman continues to have a right to decide, but the Court requires state regulations to meet the lesser test that they do not place an 'undue burden' rather than that they amount to a 'compelling state interest'.

[332]   58. For overview, K. Patchel, 'The new habeas', 42 *Hastings Law J.* (1991).

59. Antiterrorism and Effective Death Penalty Act, 28 U.S.C. 2241 *et seq.*

60. W.J. Brennan, 'State constitutions and the protection of individual rights', 90 *Harvard L. Rev.* 489 (1977).

61. E. Malz, 'False prophet – justice Brennan and the theory of state constitutional law', 15 *Hastings Const. Quarterly* (1988), and J.A. Gardner, 'The failed discourse of state constitutionalism', 90 *Michigan Law Rev.* (1992).

62. This question has generated a great deal of interest in recent years. Congress acted on its Section 2 enforcement power to pass the 1866 Civil Rights Act before the Court had an opportunity to interpret the Thirteenth Amendment. The Court upheld broad enforcement power under the Fifteenth Amendment in South Carolina *v.* Katzenbach 383 U.S. 301 (1966) but without specifically addressing the issue of an independent interpretative power of Congress. The most important case in which this was addressed was with respect to the Fourteenth Amendment in Katzenbach *v.* Morgan, 384 U.S. 641 (1966), upholding Section 4(e) of the 1965 Voting Rights Act. It is a difficult case to interpret but could be taken as a broad reading of Congressional power to act on its own interpretation of the amendment. A. Cox, 'Constitutional adjudication and the protection of human rights', 80 *Harvard Law Rev.* (1966) supports a very broad reading of Congressional power. The theory has not been developed by a full Court majority, and one of the problems has been the difficulty posed by the question, that if Congress can interpret the amendment to protect rights, can it also dilute them?

63. One of the great difficulties of modern antidiscrimination law is the barrier which the 'state action' doctrine of the Fourteenth Amendment places in the way of stopping discrimination by private citizens against others. The Thirteenth Amendment poses no such barrier, but is more limited in its substance than the Fourteenth. One solution was to base the Civil Rights Act of 1964 on the interstate commerce clause. Another was to find ways of linking private discrimination to the state. In U.S. *v.* Guest, 383 U.S. 745 (1966), however, six members of the Supreme Court upholding the Force Act of 1870, now codified at 42 U.S.C.A. S241 agreed that Congress had the power to reach private conspiracies against enjoyment of civil rights. It was dictum, however, not part of the main holding and doubts remain unanswered.

64. W. Schabas (ed.), *The International Sourcebook on Capital Punishment* (Boston, 1997).

CHAPTER FOURTEEN

FROM UNION TO NATION? THE CIVIL WAR AND THE DEVELOPMENT OF AMERICAN NATIONALISM

SUSAN-MARY GRANT

It is generally accepted that the American Civil War of 1861–5 and its immediate aftermath – the Reconstruction period of 1865–77 – represents a watershed in American national development. In practical terms, the war that Henry James referred to as the 'great convulsion' certainly provides a definitive turning point in the 'timeline' of American history.[1] In recognition of this, student textbooks frequently divide American history neatly in two, with a first volume covering the period up to the Civil War and Reconstruction, and a second picking up the history of America from Reconstruction onwards. As the years pass this divide will surely have to change, although it is hard to predict what new turning-point the textbook publishers will select once the sheer volume of post-Civil War American history forces an alternative division. More fundamentally, the Civil War is regarded as that event which transformed a 'Union' into a 'Nation'. The Civil War certainly succeeded in holding America together as one nation at a time when it might have come apart. It resolved the question of whether the Union was a voluntary organization from which the separate states had the right to secede – as the South had argued – or whether it was, as Lincoln described it in 1861, perpetual. The Union's perpetuity, according to Lincoln, was assured not only by the Constitution and the law (although he interpreted both in such a way as to deny absolutely the South's right of secession) but by geography. 'Physically speaking, we cannot separate,' he pointed out. 'A husband and wife may be divorced, and go out of the presence, and beyond the reach of each other; but the different parts of our country cannot do this.'[2]

However, the transition from 'Union' to 'Nation' involved much more than the establishment by force of Federal authority over the physical territory of the United States. The military and moral defeat suffered by the Confederacy changed the South dramatically and forever. For the North, too, the change was no less dramatic. The very process of taking up arms against the Southern challenge prompted a transformation in the Northern response both to the idea of Union and to the imperatives of national construction. The specifics of this transformation have yet to be fully explored either by historians of America or nationalism scholars, although the words of Abraham Lincoln provide a tantalizing starting-point for those interested in this process. In his First Inaugural in 1861, Lincoln frequently invoked the 'Union', using the word some twenty times in the course of his address. He did not, however, refer directly to America as a 'nation', relying instead on a vaguer phraseology concerning America's 'national fabric'.[3] By 1863, however, on the occasion of his famous Gettysburg Address, Lincoln's chosen emphasis had changed. In this short but significant speech he did not mention the Union once, but instead referred five times to America as a 'nation'.[4] The question this chapter seeks to address is how and to what extent the American Civil War brought about a perceptible shift in American nationalist ideology. Did Lincoln's reference to the American nation rather than to the Union in 1863 in any sense reflect a change in thinking in America as a whole, and what difference – if any – was there between the idea of the 'Union' and that of the 'nation'?

Union or nation?

Any essential difference between the Union and the nation is obscured by the fact that the two are, clearly, linked in terms of American national development. The nature of the link, however, is not as obvious as it might be. Over thirty years ago, Paul Nagel's study of the Union between the Revolution and the Civil War concluded that the Union 'meant many things to many Americans from 1776 to 1861'. Specifically, he argued, the American response to the Union before the Civil War provides scholars with 'a treasure-trove of the values and images by which Americans sought to comprehend their nature and destiny.' Nagel did not perceive any clear distinction between the idea of the Union and the idea of the nation, as the title of his work, *One Nation Indivisible: The Union in American Thought*, makes clear. Indeed, he saw the Union as an essential component in the construction of a distinctive American national identity that, over time, focused increasingly on the Union as the 'supreme legend'.[5] The year after Nagel's book appeared, however, another American historian was able to devote a full-length study to the

'awakening of American nationalism' without discussing the role of the
Union in this at all.[6]

Over thirty years later, the scholarly approach to the subject of American
nationalism remains diverse. Some argue that in the period before the Civil
War both the Union itself and American nationalism were, in certain fundamental ways, weak, and that it was this weakness which led first to secession
and then to four years of bloody fighting between North and South.[7] This
view has, over the years, come under attack from those who detect the existence of nationalizing forces both in the eighteenth century and in the antebellum period. Those who adhere to this latter view, however, face the task
of explaining why, if nationalist sentiment was strong and the Union stable,
Civil War broke out in 1861.

The recent upsurge in scholarly interest in the subject of nationalism has
extended the boundaries of the debate without really bringing the alternative
approaches to American nationalism into the same orbit. Nationalism scholars
have, in the main, avoided the American example and American historians
continue to approach the subject from a variety of perspectives. Initially, the
colonial and revolutionary periods were seen as crucial in the development of
a distinctive American nationalism. The act of revolution against Great Britain
was regarded as both the outward expression of and the catalyst for a fledgling
but fast-growing sense of national identity.[8] More recent studies, although they
take the Revolution as their starting-point, have examined the early republic,
or what used to be called the 'early national period'. These emphasize the
role played by festivals and celebrations, such as the 4 July festivities, in
nationalism construction in the years before the Missouri Compromise (1820).

Since the focus of the most recent studies is primarily on the emergence
of the American political system, the growth of American nationalism is
examined in the context of the development of party politics and the creation
of a 'national popular political culture' in America during this period.[9] What
they reveal is that it was conflict rather than consensus which encouraged
the growth of national sentiment, 'as contestants tried to claim true American
nationality and the legacy of the Revolution'. The danger is that from this
perspective, American nationalism can be interpreted as little more than 'a
political strategy, developed at different times by specific groups' within
American society.[10] There is no doubt that the different parties, from the
early national period onwards, frequently sought to make political capital
out of national images and ideology. It would be wrong, however, to conclude that the ideology itself was either produced or contained within the
parameters of partisan debate. From the outset, the process of American

national development was entangled with wider sectional impulses which drew on, but at the same time undermined, an overarching national ideology. Indeed, Americans in the eighteenth and nineteenth centuries were no more in agreement about the status and function of the Union and its relationship to the American nation than twentieth-century scholars are. Consequently, whichever period an historian selects from the years before the Civil War is likely to provide evidence of conflict over both the function of the federal Union and the nature of American nationalism.

Conflict, in fact, is the key to understanding the shifting responses both to the idea of Union and that of nation in America: conflict between the fledgling political parties of the early republic but also, and more damaging for the nation as a whole, conflict between North and South. That a coherent sense of 'the nation' should derive from conflict is not as contradictory an argument as it might at first appear. The growth of any nationalist sentiment is normally sustained by opposition to a perceived threat, usually but not exclusively external in nature. In the American case, the threat was first and foremost Great Britain, but that threat was removed by the act of revolution. Having successfully achieved independence, Americans found themselves facing the 'crisis of legitimacy' which all post-revolutionary societies face once the unifying impulse created and sustained by the external enemy has disappeared.[11] For the revolutionary generation the most immediate requirement was the construction of a functioning political Union. This was rendered problematic by the fact that although the separate colonies had acted in concert to some degree in order to achieve independence, in fundamental ways the Revolution had really comprised thirteen separate revolutions. As Daniel Boorstin put it, the American nation was really a 'by-product of the assertion of each colony's right to govern itself' rather than the result of a spontaneous outpouring of national sentiment. The result in political terms was that the period between the Revolution and the Civil War 'was overcast by a federal vagueness'.[12]

Political instability was not the only problem facing the new nation. The experience of revolution had also bequeathed it a divisive legacy. The Revolutionary War itself was a conflict which pitted the colonists against each other as much as one waged solely by the colonists against an imperial power. In the aftermath of the Revolution the Loyalists had, for the most part, fled to Nova Scotia, Canada, New Brunswick or back to Britain, but the revolutionary generation could hardly have forgotten the existence of Loyalist sentiment or its implications. The Union's position was, from any angle, a precarious one. America represented an experiment in a new form of government, and not everyone expected this experiment to succeed. During the early years of the republic the prediction that the Union would not last was so common as to be 'a standard conversational gambit'. Indeed, as Linda Kerber reminds us, 'it was the persistence of union which excited surprise rather than recurring secessionist sentiment.' From the outset, too, it seemed clear that if the Union were to come apart then it would do so because of the essential differences between the North and the plantation South.[13] There was, in effect, little real unity in the early Union. Local and sectional loyalties always threatened to subvert the developing sense of national mission and destiny. In the American case, as has been argued, 'the fears of Montesquieu and older political theorists were not without foundation. If a single great republic was to survive here, it would have to find a way of stemming the secessionist tide.'[14]

One of the ways national consolidation was attempted was through celebratory rites focused on the Revolution, such as the 4 July festivities, but also through the elevation of the war's supporting documents – the Declaration of Independence and the Constitution – and the conflict's military leader and America's first president, George Washington, to the status of national symbols. Over the years additional symbols were added, most notably the Great Seal with its classical allusion '*Incipit Novus Ordo Saeclorum*' (a new order of the ages is born) and the motto '*E Pluribus Unum*' (one out of many). Both were, however, more expressive of future hopes than contemporary realities. The need to downplay the harsh realities of the Revolution led to its outcome being increasingly portrayed not so much as the fruit of military victory over both internal and external foes, but rather as the logical product of an Enlightenment philosophy which found its fullest expression in the new, democratic republic that America represented.[15] This was the beginning of a process whereby Americans sought to justify the Revolution by transforming it into the bedrock of a unifying national mythology. The Revolution soon took its place alongside the foundation myths of the arrival of the Pilgrim Fathers aboard the *Mayflower* and the 'Great Migration' of the Puritans in the seventeenth century in a fast-developing sense of American historical achievement and an as yet 'still inchoate national tradition'.[16] At the centre of this fledgling national mythology stood the Union, the symbol of all that America had achieved by the act of revolution. As 'a divine instrument, as Liberty's harbinger, and as the nation's triumph', the Union encapsulated America's past success and future destiny.[17]

Before the Civil War, however, the Union seemed to be strong only in the face of an external threat. Great Britain played that role once again at the start of the nineteenth century in the so-called 'second war for independence', the

War of 1812. At the conclusion of the conflict the American diplomat and Secretary of the Treasury Albert Gallatin felt enthused enough to observe that the war had 'renewed and reinstated the national feelings which the Revolution had given and which were daily lessened. The people have now more general objects of attachment with which their pride and political opinions are connected. They are more American; they feel and act more like a nation; and I hope that the permanency of the Union is thereby better secured.'[18] Gallatin's recognition of the interconnection between the Union and a sense of the nation is revealing, but his optimism was premature. The upsurge of nationalism induced by the War of 1812 was somewhat soured by the memory of New England Federalist extremists advocating secession from the Union in 1814. In the years following, over-confidence in the American democratic experiment and in the strength of the Union went hand in hand with deep-rooted fears over the national character and the nation's future. The Founding Fathers had been all too conscious that the Union represented at best a 'perilous political experiment'. Succeeding generations, however, held a somewhat different view, or views, rather, since consensus proved difficult to achieve in the years between the Revolution and the Civil War.

Rush Welter has argued that the Americans of this period saw themselves as 'heirs of all the ages', and their nation as the fulfilment of the of 'the progressive dreams of mankind'.[19] Heirs of the ages they might have been, but nineteenth-century Americans could never forget the fact that they were more directly heirs of the revolutionary generation, and that the challenge they faced was to live up to the ideals enunciated in the Declaration of Independence. In effect, they felt – indeed, they welcomed – a sense of responsibility to 'create the excellence which the revolutionaries had demanded'.[20] This was a tall order to live up to and, in a sense, Americans were not equal to the task. Although conscious of an imbalance between their new nation's professed ideals – most notably its devotion to liberty – and the reality of a Union in which slave states coexisted with free, the revolutionaries' progeny failed to grasp the political and moral nettle of slavery and sought compromise rather than closure on this most divisive of issues. In some senses the continuous search for a workable compromise reveals how hard Americans were prepared to strive for the Union. Their efforts were, however, unsuccessful. The Union that they created was built on sand. One did not have to be an abolitionist to realize that there was a fundamental difference in outlook between the North and the South – although of course that helped – and that as time passed the difference was becoming more, not less, pronounced. Americans North and South had much in common: a shared history, however brief, of which migration and the Revolution formed the bedrock; shared heroes, most notably Washington and Jefferson; a shared political system, albeit one prone to change; a shared way of life, in the main; a shared belief in the merits of popular government; and a shared commitment to the ideals of liberty. Alternative interpretations of this last point, however, served only to widen the gulf between the free and slave states. 'We all declare for liberty,' Lincoln observed in the course of the Civil War, 'but in using the same *word* we do not all mean the same *thing*. With some the word liberty may mean for each man to do as he pleases with himself, and the product of his labor; while with others the same word may mean for some men to do as they please with other men, and the product of other men's labor.'[21]

Lincoln was, in this context, referring quite specifically to slavery, but he well knew that the argument over the definition of 'liberty' went beyond the issue of slavery alone. In the midst of the secession crisis in 1861, Lincoln was moved to consider 'what great principle or idea it was that kept this Confederacy so long together'. The answer he arrived at was that the sentiments enunciated in the Declaration of Independence offered 'liberty not alone to the people of this country, but hope to the world for all future time'.[22] For Lincoln, as for many Americans, the Declaration of Independence encapsulated all that the Union represented. It was the American nation's key foundation document. Its ambitious sentiments and inspiring rhetoric not only held out the hope of liberty to the world, but provided the only means to nationhood for a populace as diverse and varied as Americans were in the nineteenth century. In the course of the famous Lincoln–Douglas debates in 1858, Lincoln had addressed the question of American nationality and the role of the Revolution and the Declaration of Independence in this. Aware that many Americans could not 'carry themselves back into that glorious epoch' on the grounds of ancestry, Lincoln argued that the Declaration of Independence enabled them to establish their American nationality since they had the 'right to claim it as though they were blood of the blood, and flesh of the flesh' of those who penned it. The moral sentiment of the Declaration of Independence, Lincoln averred, constituted an 'electric cord' which linked the nation together.[23]

Union and nation?

The Declaration of Independence, as Lincoln interpreted it, provided a basis both for ideological unity and, by extrapolation, for political Union, but not everyone saw it that way. Indeed, its precepts were a major bone of

[340] contention for Lincoln's generation. The North came increasingly to interpret the Declaration of Independence as their nation's 'mission statement', and used it to justify an expansive and outward-looking philosophy which drew on America's revolutionary heritage both to define and encourage a growing sense of what would, in the 1840s, be termed 'Manifest Destiny'. Building on the eighteenth-century belief that America represented the New Israel and its populace God's new chosen people, many Americans regarded it as their divinely-inspired right to expand across the continent. When Lincoln argued in his First Inaugural that the North and South could not physically separate, he was expressing a belief in geographical predestination that informed America's expansionist aims.[24] This was not solely a Northern perspective. The South was equally, if not more, keen on expansion in the years prior to the Civil War. However, the fact that it saw this as a means to consolidate the 'peculiar institution' of slavery rather than as an opportunity to spread the benefits of liberty placed it at odds with the sense of national mission that Lincoln had invoked both in 1858 and 1861. From a European perspective, of course, Lincoln's argument was hardly watertight. It may have been undesirable, but it was certainly not inconceivable that the United States should have split into two separate countries, as many in the South came to argue in 1861. For the South, the Declaration of Independence came to represent less a mission statement than an insurance policy against the encroachments of centralized power. The argument that a people had the right to 'alter or abolish' a government which no longer guaranteed their 'safety and happiness' became more important to Southerners than the 'life, liberty, and the pursuit of happiness' philosophy that, Lincoln argued, informed America's national doctrine.

In the decade immediately prior to the Civil War, opinion on the meaning, and the future, of the American democratic experiment was mixed. In 1853 the Massachusetts senator Caleb Cushing exuberantly described his country as 'that colossus of power, that colossus of liberty, that colossus of the spirit of nations.'[25] In the following year, however, the famous New York lawyer and diarist, George Templeton Strong, sounded a more cautious note when he confided to his diary that Americans 'are so young a people that we feel the want of nationality, and delight in whatever asserts our national "American" existence. We have not, like England and France, centuries of achievements and calamities to look back on; we have no record of Americanism and we feel its want.'[26] In the absence of any strong sense of nationality, all Americans really had was the Union, but in the antebellum period it was becoming clear that without a strong sense of nationality the existence of the Union was in serious jeopardy. The link between the Union and the nation was evident, too, in that none of the potentially unifying, nationalizing, features of American life made sense without the Union. By the antebellum period, Americans had constructed a basis for national definition predicated on a number of factors: the 'Great Migration' of the Puritans to New England in the seventeenth century, and the eventual establishment of a Godly Commonwealth in the New World; success in the Revolution, a success that was later validated by France's adoption of America's revolutionary principles; and, above all, the construction of a functioning Federal Union which represented a new, democratic, popular form of government. The outbreak of Civil War placed all this in jeopardy. If the Union failed, the American experiment failed, and both the physical struggle across the Atlantic and the military upheaval of the Revolution would have, in a sense, been in vain.

As far as national construction was concerned, initially it seemed as if the Confederacy, at least, had been successful. In the second year of the Civil War, the British Chancellor of the Exchequer, William E. Gladstone, speaking at a dinner in Newcastle-upon-Tyne, expressed the view that of the two sides involved in the war it was the South which deserved the appellation 'nation'. The North, he argued, ought to accept the dissolution of the Union, since 'Jefferson Davis and other leaders of the South have made an army; they are making, it appears, a navy; and they have made what is more than either, they have made a nation.'[27]

Whether the Confederacy did constitute a separate 'nation' has been a matter of debate among historians for many years. Part of the confusion stems from a lack of consensus on what, exactly, is meant by nationalism: is it the construction of a strong central state; does it refer to that now over-used phrase of Benedict Anderson's, the 'imagined community'; or is it a combination of the two? Another part of the debate derives from the perceived differences between nationalist sentiment in the antebellum South and that which developed during the Civil War. Scholars frequently acknowledge the growth, in the antebellum period, of a distinct sense of 'The South', and some go so far as to argue that this constituted a fledgling 'southern nationalism'. The Confederacy's failure in the Civil War, however, is offered up as evidence that Southern nationalism as an ideology was insufficient to sustain Southerners in their attempt at national construction and that it was, therefore, not a true nationalist ideology at all. Whilst it is recognized that 'Confederate nationalists surely existed', Confederate nationalism is dismissed as 'more a dream than anything else'.[28]

The argument that military defeat revealed a fatal flaw in Confederate nationalist sentiment relies, however, on hindsight. The Civil War's outcome validated Northern nationalist claims, and placed the Confederacy firmly and forever in the 'Lost Cause' camp. The nationalism of the Union triumphed, and so historians too frequently reason that the Northern variant of American nationalism had always been the stronger and more valid. From the perspective of the time, however, the war's outcome was by no means certain, and in any case the failure of the South to break away from the Union does not in itself prove that Confederate nationalism was fundamentally weak – only that it was, ultimately, unsuccessful. Neither does it prove that American nationalism as promulgated by the North was, by comparison, strong.

More recent research has succeeded in showing that Confederate nationalism was rather more than a pipe dream and that the ideology that sustained the South's attempt at secession had both form and substance. Yet, crucially, these studies continue to examine the Confederacy almost in isolation. Lacking the wider context of the Union's search for national meaning, they continue to present the Confederacy very much as a world, and a nation, apart.[29] Certainly this is what the Confederacy very much hoped to be, but despite its best efforts the battle for Confederate nationalism was conducted both in the context of and in ironic parallel with a similar process in the North. The Confederate struggle toward national definition was tightly bound up with the Union's defence of the Civil War and its reformulation of American nationalism during the war years. Each relied, in fundamental ways, on the other. Conflict – ideological as well as military – between the Union and the Confederacy helped each side to construct and then defend its relative position. The Union victory ensured that its particular interpretation of American nationalism would dominate, but this new nationalism was both forged and, to a degree, tainted by the challenge offered to the Union by the South. In short, the experience of the Civil War operated on the construction and refinement of both Union/American and Confederate nationalism in much the same way.

Studies of the contemporary response to the war have concluded, for example, that 'a substantial portion of the Confederate people identified strongly with their southern republic.' Using the letters and diaries of Southerners written during the conflict, Gary Gallagher has shown how Southerners frequently employed terms such as 'our nation' and 'my country', which clearly 'reflected national identification and purpose'. Yet Union troops were equally prone to such sentiments, and similarly cited love of their 'country' as their motivation to fight.[30] In referring to their 'country', of course, Johnny Reb and Billy Yank meant rather different things, but their devotion to their respective 'nations' was equally strong. Similarly, troops in both the Federal and the Confederate armies as well as the civilians on the home front found that military service encouraged the development of a broader, more national outlook than had prevailed before the war began. Gallagher has argued that this was particularly the case for Southern civilians, whose links with loved ones fighting far from home 'broadened their horizon and led them to think nationally as well as locally'.[31] However, the same was true for Northerners, many of whose relatives were fighting on battlefields even further away from their homes. For the troops themselves, as the war progressed and casualties mounted, they often found themselves fighting alongside men from different units and other states. This experience intensified and made solid a national-ist perspective that many of them had in theory but which, up until the war, few had experienced in practice. Indeed, as Peter Parish has argued, the Union army itself 'was one of the most potent agencies of American national-ism'. Not only did it introduce its troops to 'places and people hitherto remote, but now fixed in their minds as part of the same American nation to which they belonged,' but the involvement of non-combatants in supporting and maintaining the army inculcated a far stronger sense of 'commitment and loyalty' to the nation than had ever existed prior to 1861.[32]

In a very real sense, too, both North and South drew on exactly the same ideas and symbols of nationhood in their defence of the Union and the Confederacy respectively. Both sides were completely immersed in the ideology and symbolism of the Revolution, with the result that it was held up as defence and justification for both the act of secession and the military response against this. As Reid Mitchell notes, indeed, the Civil War 'proved curiously filled with echoes of the American Revolution.'[33] Keeping the example of the Revolution continuously before them, troops, non-combatant spokesmen and politicians on both sides saw themselves as defenders of the nation's glorious past, and frequently compared themselves to the revolu-tionaries of the previous century. A captain in the 5th Alabama Infantry, there-fore, felt prompted to consider how 'trifling were the wrongs complained of by our Revolutionary forefathers, in comparison with ours', while an officer in the 101st Ohio recalled how 'our fathers in coldest winter, half clad marked the road they trod with crimson streams from their bleeding feet that we might enjoy the blessings of free government.'[34] Both sides argued, too, that they were upholding the ambitions of the revolutionary generation and sticking to the letter, and the sentiment, of both the Constitution and the Declaration of Independence.

The point is often made that, in constructing a separate Confederate Con-stitution, Southerners did little more than imitate the Constitution of 1787, and in their declarations of the causes of secession the various states similarly

[344] drew on the Declaration of Independence. There were, of course, telling differences between the original documents and the revised Confederate versions.
Most obviously, the idealistic desire 'to form a more perfect union' contained
in the Preamble to the original Constitution became, in the Confederate
version, a rather prosaic intention 'to form a permanent federal government'.
Nevertheless, this reliance on America's founding documents as support for a
nation which was attempting to secede from the Union revealed not only that
the South was, and remained, very much in two minds about its actions, but
also demonstrated that Southerners regarded themselves as 'the authentic heirs
of the Founding Fathers, the true defenders of the ark of the covenant'.[35]

In many ways, it was a much more straightforward matter for Southerners
to find historical precedents for their attempt at separate nationhood than
it was for Northerners to defend their opposition to secession. Southerners
could far more easily align themselves with the revolutionary generation, and
declare

> *Rebels* before
> Our fathers of yore,
> *Rebel's* the righteous name
> *Washington* bore.
> Why, then, ours be the same.[36]

Put so starkly, the South's assertions brooked little argument. The invocation
of George Washington was a particularly powerful symbol. As a Southerner
himself, and as Father of his Country, the Confederacy could not have found
a more impressive figure to appropriate for their cause in the America of
the nineteenth century. Washington was the ultimate national figure, and if
Southerners perceived any irony in using the man who had warned his countrymen to beware of sectional rivalries and to 'properly estimate the immense
value of your national Union to your collective and individual happiness' to
support their destruction of that Union they did not show it.[37] As Jefferson
Davis patiently explained, in 'order to guard against any misconstruction of
their compact, the several States made explicit declaration in a distinct article
– that *each* State *retains its* sovereignty, freedom, and independence, and every
power, jurisdiction, and right which is not by this Confederation *expressly
delegated* to the United States in Congress assembled.'[38] Faced with this deadly
combination of emotive and legalistic argument in favour of secession,
Northerners struggled to offer not just an alternative, but an overwhelmingly
persuasive argument in support of their assertion that America was constructed as, and ought to remain, one nation.

Initially, those who supported the Union set out a variety of relatively straightforward arguments in its favour. In an article written for the London *Times* and published just over a month after the start of the war, John Lothrop Motley praised the Northern response to Lincoln's initial call for troops, noting that 'the loyalty of the Free States has proved more intense and passionate than it had ever been supposed to be before. It is recognized throughout their whole people that the Constitution of 1787 had made us a *nation*.' Motley set out the case for Union succinctly, arguing that the 'Union alone is clothed with imperial attributes; the Union alone is known and recognized in the family of nations; the Union alone holds the purse and the sword, regulates foreign intercourse, imposes taxes on foreign commerce, makes war and concludes peace.' The Revolution, he reminded his readers, had made America 'a nation, with a flag respected abroad and almost idolized at home as the symbol of union and coming greatness.' Yet in recalling the Revolution, Motley had hit on an important and troubling point, although it is doubtful if he recognized the fact. Secession, he argued, was nothing more than a case of 'rebellion'. However, if it proved successful, then it became 'revolution'.[39] This was much more than a distinction without a difference. The difference between 'rebellion' and 'revolution', in an American context, was vast. The American nation, and the Union that the North was fighting to save, was the product of a revolution, a fact that the South had not been slow to pick up on and use in defence of its actions in 1861. Although equally keen to align themselves with the ideals of the revolutionary generation, Northerners found it difficult to break through this particular part of the South's defences. As it was understood at the start of the war, the Revolution seemed better suited as justification for the Confederacy than as prop for the Union. To acknowledge that the South was engaged in an act of revolution was, in a very real sense, to validate secession and to recognize that the South had the right to attempt to establish a Confederate nation.

One possible response, and the one favoured by Lincoln himself, was to argue that the act of secession was less an attempt to construct a separate nation than an attack on an established Union which had to be met with force. Lincoln regarded secession as rebellion, pure and simple. Further, he saw it as rebellion not of but in the South. This was a theme he developed throughout the first year of the war. Some months before the fall of Fort Sumter he had questioned 'what principle of original right is it that one-fiftieth or one-ninetieth of a great nation, by calling themselves a state, have the right to break up and ruin that nation as a matter of original principle?' Once war had broken out, he encouraged support for the Union by reflecting that 'this issue

[346]   embraces more than the fate of these United States. It presents to the whole family of man the question, whether a constitutional republic, or a democracy – a government of the people, by the same people – can, or cannot, maintain its territorial integrity against its own domestic foes.' By the end of the year he was still reiterating his firm belief that secession constituted nothing more or less than 'a war upon the first principle of popular government – the rights of the people'.[40] Lincoln would continue to develop and refine his arguments in defence of the Union throughout the war – putting them most succinctly and powerfully in his Gettysburg Address of 1863 – but his position, however persuasive it seems with hindsight, was by no means impregnable. Throughout the conflict, Lincoln, and those who concurred with his viewpoint, had to work hard to defend themselves against attack not just from the South but from opposition forces within the Union.

Union to nation?

As the war progressed, the initial enthusiasm which Motley had described had began to wane. The dreary and dangerous reality of fighting, combined with military setbacks for the Federal forces in 1861 and 1862, resulted in an overall decline in morale on both the military and the home fronts. The Emancipation Proclamation of 1 January 1863 was not especially well-received at first, and this, too, led to a crumbling of support for the Union cause. Increasingly, Lincoln and his government came under attack from Democratic opponents of the war like Clement L. Vallandigham, who was critical of the impact that the war was having on civil liberties. Under Lincoln, he declared, '[c]onstitutional limitation was broken down; *habeus corpus* fell; liberty of the press, of speech, of the person, of mails, of travel, of one's own house, and of religion; the right to bear arms, due process of law, judicial trial, trial by jury, trial at all; every badge and muniment of freedom in republican government or kingly government – all went down at a blow.'[41]

Peace Democrats like Vallandigham walked – and frequently overstepped – a very fine line between loyal opposition to the Republican government and actual disloyalty to the Union, a fact that caused the epithet 'Copperhead' (a venomous pit viper) to be applied to them. Nevertheless, the accusations they made had to be countered if support for the Union was not to suffer further. Lincoln defended the particular point about habeus corpus in a famous letter to his Democratic critics in 1863, when he repeated his belief that secession was nothing more than 'a clear, flagrant, and gigantic case of rebellion; and the provision of the Constitution that "The privilege of the writ of habeus corpus shall not be suspended, unless when in cases of rebellion or invasion, the public safety may require it" is *the* provision which specifically applies to our present case.'[42] No matter how accurate, however, a constitutional defence of the Federal government's actions was never going to be enough to silence all criticism, nor persuade the Northern public to continue supporting a war that many in 1861 had believed would be but a brief affair but which was, by 1863, showing little sign of ending.

Increasingly, the Federal government found itself under attack on issues far beyond the constitutional. John O'Sullivan, the editor of the *Democratic Review* and the man credited with coining the phrase 'Manifest Destiny', argued, for example, that the North's attempt to force the South back into the Union served 'to stultify our revolution; to blaspheme our very Declaration of Independence; to repudiate all our history.' This was a serious allegation, and one that had to be answered.[43] The Northern response could not help but be informed by the South's swift appropriation of America's national symbols and its use of the Revolution that had created the Union for its own secessionist ends. Northerners had, in a sense, to return to first principles, not so much to reconstruct but rather to reinterpret the ideology of the American Revolution and the actions of the Founding Fathers in order to defend themselves against the criticism that in seeking to suppress secession, they were acting against the basic tenets of 'Americanism'. As George Fredrickson has shown, Northerners soon found themselves 'led into far-reaching speculations on the deeper meaning of such current bywords as loyalty, patriotism, and nationality.'[44] In effect, Northern politicians, soldiers and intellectuals found themselves forced to look far longer and harder at the basis of American national construction than they would otherwise have done. Although one of the most widely-published propagandist pamphlets of the Civil War argued that 'the true solution of our whole difficulty, the only force which can give vitality or permanence to any theory of settlement' was military success, in fact the problem that the Union faced stretched far beyond the battlefield.[45]

The outbreak of the Civil War had highlighted the fault lines in America's national fabric. Ultimately, North and South could not agree on either the form or the function of their federal union. As a result, their nation *qua* nation, between 1861 and 1865, ceased to exist. The issue was complicated by the fact that the threat to American national survival came not from an external foe but from within. The problem that the North faced between 1861 and

1865, therefore, was twofold: the defence of the political Union went hand in hand with the defence of the ideological nationalism which supported that Union. Forcing the South back into the Federal fold required military success; justifying the attempt to do so required a different approach entirely. In the face of the South's desire to wreck the republican experiment, to dissolve the Union handed down to Americans by the revolutionary generation, those who supported the Union felt rightly indignant. Barely a month after the fall of Fort Sumter, a Boston *Post* editorial argued that it was 'the age of nationalities. Fired by our example, the oppressed of the world would have aspired to the dignity of nationalities. Shall the first to set the example, and the grandest in the procession of the nations,' the paper asked, 'suffer its nationality to depart, at the bidding not of a foreign foe, but of rebel traitors of the soil?'[46] There was no easy or immediate answer to this question. As events were to show, the Federal forces were able to save the Union on the battlefield, but military victory was only one part – admittedly the major part – of the process of American national construction.

The ideological issues accompanying the war forced the North to move toward a redefinition of nationalism that both justified its actions in the face of the challenge offered by the Confederacy and offered a basis for post-war reconstruction of the American nation. The centrality of the Revolution, to American as well as Confederate and Union nationalism, meant that the Union had to find some way of showing that the original Revolution had been the result of 'a legitimate nationalistic impulse' which bore no relation whatsoever to the act of secession that had prompted the Civil War. Northerners had, in short, to show that 'the American Revolution was over and that revolutionary ideology had no further application to American society.'[47] In the process of addressing this problem, intellectuals like the German political exile Francis Lieber and New England minister Horace Bushnell gradually shifted the ground on which American nationalism was constructed. In arguing against the South's right of secession and in favour of loyalty to the Union, these conservative intellectuals sought to bring American nationality down to earth, as it were. The Union, they asserted, merited support not because it represented the hope of liberty for the world but because it provided the rather more tangible and traditional basis of American national power. Further, since their arguments in support of loyalty to the Union were directly linked to their support of the Federal war effort, the logical conclusion of their deliberations was to show that 'the ultimate America to which allegiance was due was not some vague and improbable democratic utopia but the organized and disciplined North that was going to war before their eyes.'[48]

The intellectual debate over American nationalism, however, although undoubtedly persuasive both in terms of defining and defending the North's position, offered little that would help North and South come together again once the fighting was over. Although informed by the experience of war, the debates of intellectuals took place in a world far removed from the harsh reality of the battlefield. Northern thinkers and writers such as James Russell Lowell might well have believed that the Civil War had 'increased the power and confidence of the nation and certified "to earth a new imperial race"', but their view of the war was, as Richard Marius somewhat harshly concludes, 'humidly sentimental . . . like war imagined in a greenhouse'.[49] Equally sentimental is the description, frequently employed, of the Civil War as a 'brother's war'. This glib phrase, so redolent of childhood arguments, disguises the brutal reality of a conflict in which Americans killed Americans in appallingly large numbers and in fairly gruesome ways. There was little brotherly sentiment in the reaction of one Southern officer who, after the Battle of Fredericksburg described how he 'enjoyed the sight of hundreds of dead Yankees. Saw much of the work I had done in the way of severed limbs, decapitated bodies, and mutilated remains of all kinds. Doing my soul good. Would that the whole Northern Army were as such & I had my hand in it.'[50] Finding some basis for national reconciliation in the light of such deep-rooted hatred was hardly going to be a straightforward matter.

In the end, sentimentality too frequently acts as a hindrance to an understanding of the American Civil War, both of the issues involved and the outcome. Frequently, the relative positions of the North and South during the war are over-simplified. In particular, the cause for which the South was fighting is too readily romanticised. In recalling the 'Lost Cause' of the Confederacy, Americans think of Robert E. Lee, 'Stonewall' Jackson, and *Gone With the Wind*. Of course, the South also stood for slavery, a brutal system of coerced labour which denied the most fundamental human rights to the slave and bequeathed to the South a racist outlook which was extreme even by the standards of the nineteenth century. There was, therefore, a certain moral justice in the South's defeat in the Civil War. Yet the tragic overtones of that defeat, the *hubris* that afflicted the South, is too often seen to reside in its aspirations to separate nationhood, not in its essential racism, and so the romance of the 'Lost Cause' prevails. The North, by contrast, represents the pragmatic element in the uneasy equation that comprised the antebellum American Union. More firmly wedded to the practicalities of Union, less overtly racist although hardly enlightened in that regard, the North is seen as being more in tune with and ahead of the sweeping changes that were transforming

[350] nineteenth-century America. If Confederate nationalism was a dream, Northern nationalism was the reality. There was no romance in the Northern soul, scholars conclude, and so during the Civil War, the 'issue for the Northern states, clearly, was one of the territorial and political extent of the American nation, rather than its ideals.'[51] Certainly this was the logical conclusion of much of the Northern intellectual debate that took place during the Civil War. Similarly, Lincoln's famous declaration to Horace Greeley, editor of the New York *Tribune*, that his 'paramount object in this struggle *is* to save the Union, and is *not* either to save or to destroy slavery' can be taken at face value to support this interpretation of Northern war aims.[52]

However, if the Confederacy was, in reality, rather less romantic than history has chosen to portray it, then the North was certainly more idealistic than it sometimes appeared. His deceptively straightforward answer to Greeley notwithstanding, Lincoln knew very well that there was more involved, and much more at stake, in the Federal war effort than the maintenance of the Union. American national ideals represented the heart of the Union's position. The North continued to hanker after that 'more perfect Union' of the nation's Founding Fathers, and saw the Civil War as the means to achieve this. This was the essence of Lincoln's 'Gettysburg Address', and the reason that Lincoln chose that occasion to emphasize the nation over the Union. In the 'Gettysburg Address' it was the nation's ideals that concerned him, and he reminded his audience not only that the Founding Fathers had brought forth 'a new nation, conceived in Liberty, and dedicated to the proposition that all men are created equal', but that men had given their lives to consecrate that nation and that proposition. Obviously enough, when Lincoln spoke on the battlefield at Gettysburg he was not addressing a truly national audience, but he was certainly reaching out to one with his carefully-chosen words. It was not the first nor the last time that he did so. 'We are not enemies, but friends. We must not be enemies,' Lincoln urged in the emotive conclusion to his First Inaugural and, as at Gettysburg, he invoked the revolutionary generation and the 'mystic chords of memory, stretching from every battlefield, and patriot grave' which bound the American nation together.[53] In these statements, and in others made throughout the war, Lincoln set out his belief in the inspirational side to the American Union, his reverence for the nation's ideals, and the importance of the struggle to live up to them.

Lincoln was not alone in seeing the Civil War as an opportunity not just to save but to improve on the federal Union. The African-American writer and activist Frances Harper argued for a radical transformation of the American nation:

This grand and glorious revolution which has commenced, will fail to reach its climax of success, until throughout the length and breadth of the American Republic, the nation shall be so color-blind, as to know no man by the color of his skin or the curl of his hair. It will then have no privileged class, trampling upon and outraging the unprivileged classes, but will be then one great privileged nation, whose privilege will be to produce the loftiest manhood and womanhood that humanity can attain.[54]

Harriet Beecher Stowe, similarly, expressed the hope that the Civil War would bring America 'forth to a higher national life'.[55] The North's victory in the Civil War gave impetus to such aims, and hope for the future. The war was seen to have settled, once and for all, the lingering questions over slavery and states rights which had undermined the Union. The Massachusetts Senator Charles Sumner certainly saw the outcome of the war as an unqualified victory for the nation, asserting that if 'among us in the earlier day there was no occasion for the word Nation, there is now. A Nation is born.'[56] As a result of the Civil War, the 'federal vagueness' of the antebellum Union was replaced by an integrated state with both territorial and political sovereignty. Yet the enmity between North and South, both a cause and a consequence of the Civil War, was not so easily dispelled. American nationalism was, therefore, left in an extremely fragile position in the years immediately following Appomattox.

Ultimately, North and South used the war that had driven them apart as one means of bringing them back together again. For the troops who had fought, battlefield commemoration ceremonies provided some ground – both literally and figuratively – on which the opposing sides could meet. For Confederate veterans, particularly, such ceremonies offered a way back into the American nation. This was not, however, a quick process, but one which took several decades and which involved a certain amount of compromise, to the detriment of those ideals which Lincoln held to be so important to the American nation. It would be going too far to say that the outcome of the Civil War was a pyrrhic victory for the North, but it was certainly not all that Lincoln himself might have hoped for.

The revolutionary generation had passed on a divided legacy to the nation, and the Civil War generation did the same. As the Civil War took its place alongside the Revolution in the civic religion of the American nation it came to be seen less as a brutal and bloody conflict, and more as a process of redemption, as the war that had preserved the nation and made it both better and stronger than it had been before. Certainly the nation that emerged from the conflict was very different from the Union that had entered it. The emancipation of the slaves had not only been effected, but consolidated in important amendments to the Constitution. The validity of the American experiment in democratic government had been established. As Lincoln had hoped, the federal government had proved to the world 'that those who can fairly carry an election, can also suppress a rebellion – that ballots are the rightful, and peaceful, successors of bullets; and that when ballots have fairly, and constitutionally, decided, there can be no successful appeal back to bullets.'[57] The antebellum Union had been open to interpretation, but after the Civil War the nation was built on firmer ground. Yet the transition from Union to nation was not without cost, and not just in lives. By resorting to warfare to compel a national identity that was clearly not going to be established by voluntary means, the North found itself in the paradoxical position of breaking the original contract of the Declaration of Independence in the process of defending it. Further, the emancipation of the slaves, and the passage of the Thirteenth and Fourteenth Amendments, was not accompanied by any obvious lessening of racism, and it was not too many years before the South had managed to establish the racial *status quo ante bellum* in all but the strictly legal sense. Ultimately, although the North's victory in the Civil War succeeded in welding North and South together more firmly than before, the transition from Union to nation left a legacy of racial and sectional bitterness that to this day continues to divide America's national landscape.

Notes

1. Henry James, *Hawthorne* (London, 1879), p. 144, quoted in George M. Fredrickson, *The Inner Civil War: Northern Intellectuals and the Crisis of the Union* (1965; paperback reprint, New York, 1968), p. 1.

2. Abraham Lincoln, *First Inaugural Address*, 4 March 1861, in Peter J. Parish (ed.), *Abraham Lincoln: Speeches and Letters* (London, 1993), pp. 161–9; quotations at pp. 163 and 167.

3. Lincoln, *First Inaugural*, in Parish (ed.), *Abraham Lincoln: Speeches and Letters*, p. 165 and passim.

4. Abraham Lincoln, *Address at Gettysburg*, Pennsylvania, 19 November 1863, in Parish (ed.), *Abraham Lincoln: Speeches and Letters*, pp. 266–7.

5. Paul C. Nagel, *One Nation Indivisible: The Union in American Thought, 1776–1861* (New York and Oxford, 1964), pp. 3 and 177. See also Nagel, *This Sacred Trust: American Nationality, 1798–1898* (New York and Oxford, 1971).

6. George Dangerfield, *The Awakening of American Nationalism, 1815–1828* (New York, 1965).

7. The Union's relative weakness prior to the Civil War, and the role of the war in establishing both the Union and American nationalism, is discussed in, among others, Liah Greenfeld, *Nationalism: Five Roads to Modernity* (Cambridge, Mass. and London, 1992) and Richard Franklin Bensel, *Yankee Leviathan: The Origins of Central State Authority in America, 1859–1877* (New York and Cambridge, 1990).

8. One of the earliest studies of American nationalism is to be found in Hans Kohn, *The Idea of Nationalism: A Study in its Origins and Background* (New York, 1945), followed by his *American Nationalism: An Interpretative Essay* (New York, 1957). More recent studies which assess the colonial and revolutionary eras include Greenfeld, *Nationalism* and Anthony D. Smith, 'Origin of nation', *Times Higher Education Supplement*, 8 January 1993, pp. 15–16. For additional commentary on this, see Susan-Mary Grant, 'When is a nation not a nation? The crisis of American nationality in the mid-nineteenth century', *Nations and Nationalism*, 2, 1 (1996), pp. 105–29.

9. Simon P. Newman, *Parades and the Politics of the Street: Festive Culture in the Early American Republic* (Philadelphia, Pa, 1997), p. 6. See also David Waldstreicher, *In the Midst of Perpetual Fetes: The Making of American Nationalism, 1776–1820* (Chapel Hill, NC, and London, 1997).

10. Waldstreicher, *In the Midst of Perpetual Fetes*, pp. 6 and 9. On this subject see also Newman, *Parades and the Politics of the Street*, pp. 112–13, and Grant, 'When is a nation not a nation?' p. 113.

11. Seymour Martin Lipset, *The First New Nation: The United States in Historical and Comparative Perspective* (1963; reprint New York and London, 1979), p. 16.

12. Daniel J. Boorstin, *The Americans: The National Experience* (1965; reprint New York and London, 1988), pp. 400–1. The same point is made by John M. Murrin in 'A roof without walls: the dilemma of American national identity', in Richard Beeman *et al.* (eds), *Beyond Confederation: Origins of the Constitution and American National Identity* (Chapel Hill, NC, and London, 1987), pp. 333–48, 339.

13. Linda Kerber, *Federalists in Dissent: Imagery and Ideology in Jeffersonian America* (1970; reprint Ithaca, New York and London, 1983), pp. 1–35, quotation at p. 34. On the Federalists and the South, see also Waldstreicher, *In the Midst of Perpetual Fetes*, pp. 251–62.

14. Boorstin, *The Americans: The National Experience*, p. 418.

[354]   15.   This point is explored further in Susan-Mary Grant, 'Making history: myth and
the construction of American nationhood', in Geoffrey Hosking and George
Schöpflin (eds), *Myths and Nationhood* (London, 1997), pp. 88–106, and see
also John Shy, *A People Numerous and Armed: Reflections on the Military Struggle for
American Independence*, revised edn (Ann Arbor, Mi., 1990), pp. 25–6.

16.   Boorstin, *The Americans: The National Experience*, p. 368. On the role of the
Revolution in American historical development see Reid Mitchell, *Civil War
Soldiers: Their Expectations and their Experiences* (1988; reprint New York, 1989),
pp. 1–2 and especially Michael Kammen, *A Season of Youth: The American Revolu-
tion and the Historical Imagination* (New York, 1978). On the impact of the 'Great
Migration' to national myth, see Virginia deJohn Anderson, *New England's Gen-
eration: The Great Migration and the Formation of Society and Culture in the Seventeenth
Century* (New York and Cambridge, 1991). For a fuller assessment of this process see Susan-Mary Grant, ' "The Charter of its Birthright": the Civil War and
American nationalism', *Nations and Nationalism*, 4, 2 (1998) pp. 163–85.

17.   Nagel, *One Nation Indivisible*, p. 147.

18.   Albert Gallatin to Matthew Lyon, 7 May 1816, quoted in Dangerfield, *The
Awakening of American Nationalism*, pp. 3–4.

19.   Rush Welter, *The Mind of America, 1820–1860* (New York and London, 1975),
pp. 23 and 3–5.

20.   Kerber, *Federalists in Dissent*, pp. 1–2. On this point, see also Jean H. Baker, 'The
ceremonies of politics: nineteenth-century rituals of national affirmation', in
William J. Cooper *et al.* (eds), *A Master's Due: Essays in Honor of David Herbert
Donald* (Baton Rouge, La and London, 1985), pp. 161–78.

21.   Abraham Lincoln, *Address at Sanitary Fair, Baltimore, Maryland*, 18 April 1864, in
Parish (ed.), *Abraham Lincoln: Speeches and Letters*, pp. 276–8, quotation at p. 277.

22.   Abraham Lincoln, *Speech in Independence Hall, Philadelphia*, 22 February 1861, in
Parish (ed.), *Abraham Lincoln: Speeches and Letters*, pp. 158–9, quotation at p. 158.

23.   Abraham Lincoln, *Speech at Chicago, Illinois*, 10 July 1858, in Parish (ed.),
Abraham Lincoln: Speeches and Letters, pp. 88–95, quotation at p. 93.

24.   On this point, see Albert K. Weinberg, *Manifest Destiny: A Study of Nationalist
Expansion in American History* (1935; reprint Gloucester, Mass., 1958), pp. 38ff.

25.   Cushing quoted in Weinberg, *Manifest Destiny*, p. 203.

26.   Diary entry for 8 November 1854, in Allan Nevins and Milton Halsey Thomas
(eds), *The Diary of George Templeton Strong*, 4 vols (New York, 1952) vol. 3, *The
Turbulent Fifties, 1850–1859*, p. 197.

27. Gladstone quoted in Peter J. Parish, *The American Civil War* (New York, 1975), p. 448.

28. Richard E. Beringer *et al.*, *Why the South Lost the Civil War* (Athens, Ga and London, 1986), p. 77. This work contains an extremely useful summary of the historiography of southern nationalism (up to 1986, obviously) on pp. 64–81.

29. See Drew Gilpin Faust, *Confederate Nationalism: Ideology and Identity in the Civil War South* (Baton Rouge, La and London, 1988) and Gary Gallagher, *The Confederate War* (Cambridge, Mass. and London, 1997).

30. Gary Gallagher, *The Confederate War*, pp. 7 and 63; James M. McPherson, *What They Fought For, 1861–1865* (Baton Rouge, La and London, 1994), pp. 11, 33 and passim.

31. Gallagher, *The Confederate War*, p. 73.

32. Parish, *American Civil War*, p. 637.

33. Reid Mitchell, *Civil War Soldiers: Their Expectations and Their Experiences* (New York and London, 1988), p. 1.

34. McPherson, *What They Fought For*, pp. 9 and 28.

35. Peter J. Parish, 'The Road Not Quite Taken: the Constitution of the Confederate States of America', in Thomas J. Barron, Owen Dudley Edwards and Patricia J. Storey (eds), *Constitutions and National Identity* (Edinburgh, 1993), pp. 111–25, quotation at p. 113.

36. Quoted in Faust, *The Creation of Confederate Nationalism*, p. 14.

37. Quotation from Washington's *Farewell Address*, 1796, in Robert Birley (ed.), *Speeches and Documents in American History*, vol. 1, *1776–1815*, p. 223.

38. Jefferson Davis, *Message to the Confederate Congress*, 29 April 1861, in Birley (ed.), *Speeches and Documents*, vol. 2, *1818–1865*, p. 261. Davis was here referring to Article X of the Bill of Rights.

39. John Lothrop Motley, 'The causes of the American Civil War: a paper contributed to the *London Times*' (New York, 1861) in Frank Freidel (ed.), *Union Pamphlets of the Civil War, 1861–1865*, 2 vols (Cambridge, Mass., 1967), vol. 1, pp. 29–54; quotations at pp. 31, 42, 48 and 51. Motley's article first appeared in the paper on 23 and 24 May 1861.

40. Abraham Lincoln, *Speech at Indianapolis*, 11 February 1861; *Message to Congress in Special Session*, 4 July 1861; and *Annual Message to Congress*, 3 December 1861, all in Parish, *Abraham Lincoln: Speeches and Letters*, pp. 154–6, quotation at p. 156; 173–86, quotation at p. 177; and 189–93, quotation at p. 191.

[356]   41. Clement L. Vallandigham, 'The Great Civil War in America. (Speech in the House of Representatives, January 14, 1863)', in Freidel (ed.), *Union Pamphlets*, vol. 2, pp. 697–738, quotation at p. 700.

42. Lincoln to Erastus Corning *et al.*, 12 June 1863, in Parish (ed.), *Abraham Lincoln: Speeches and Letters*, pp. 244–51, quotation at p. 247.

43. John O'Sullivan quoted in George M. Fredrickson, *The Inner Civil War: Northern Intellectuals and the Crisis of the Union* (1965; reprint New York, 1968), pp. 132 and 144.

44. Fredrickson, *The Inner Civil War*, p. 132.

45. Charles Janeway Stillé, 'How a free people conduct a long war: a chapter from English history' (Philadelphia, Pa, 1862), reproduced in Freidel (ed.), *Union Pamphlets*, vol. 1, pp. 381–403, quotation at p. 397.

46. *Boston Post*, 16 May 1861.

47. Fredrickson, *The Inner Civil War*, pp. 133 and 135.

48. Fredrickson, *The Inner Civil War*, p. 150. For an extended and detailed discussion of the intellectual response to the war, see especially pp. 130–50, and passim.

49. Fredrickson, *The Inner Civil War*, p. 185. The poem under discussion is James Russell Lowell's 'Commemoration Ode' (1865), which can be found, together with his comments on it, in Richard Marius (ed.), *The Columbia Book of Civil War Poetry: From Whitman to Walcott* (New York and Chichester, 1994), p. 372.

50. McPherson, *What They Fought For*, p. 23.

51. Greenfeld, *Nationalism*, p. 473.

52. Abraham Lincoln, letter to Horace Greeley, 22 August 1862, in Parish (ed.), *Abraham Lincoln: Speeches and Letters*, pp. 214–15, quotation at p. 215.

53. Both the 'Gettysburg Address' and the First Inaugural can be found in Parish (ed.), *Abraham Lincoln: Speeches and Letters*, pp. 266–7 and 161–9 respectively. Quotations at pp. 266 and 169.

54. Frances E.W. Harper, 'We Are All Bound Up Together', from *Proceedings of the Eleventh Women's Rights Convention* (1866), in Karen L. Kilcup (ed.), *Nineteenth-Century American Women Writers: An Anthology* (Cambridge, Mass. and Oxford, 1997), p. 157.

55. Harriet Beecher Stowe, 'The Chimney-Corner', *Atlantic Monthly*, 15 January 1865; Louis P. Masur, *The Real War Will Never Get in the Books: Selections from*

Writers During the Civil War (1993; reprint New York and Oxford, 1995), [357]
p. 251.

56. Charles Sumner, 'Are we a nation?' (1867), quoted in Greenfeld, *Nationalism*,
p. 480.

57. Abraham Lincoln, 'Message to Congress in special session', 4 July 1861, in
Parish (ed.), *Abraham Lincoln: Speeches and Writings*, pp. 173–86, quotation at
p. 185.

INDEX